International Law and the History of Resource Extraction in Africa

This book investigates the historical economic and legal regimes that legitimated the resource extraction and exploitation of Africa between the 15th and 19th centuries and led to the continent's trajectory of underdevelopment in the world system.

The book interrogates the economic and legal structures that supported European intervention in Africa. It explores the trade and private property rights which were to shape the economic future of the continent, most notably the trade in human beings as legitimate private property by European powers. The book then looks at the techniques used to submerge African sovereignty under European sovereignty during the scramble for territorial control in the 19th century, concluding with the validation of occupation in international law following the 1884–1885 Berlin Conference. The book argues that the doctrines of trade and property rights sanctioned by international law led to a trend of African dispossession that set the continent on a path to underdevelopment, with long-reaching consequences.

This book will be of interest to researchers and students across law, history, economics, international relations, and African studies.

George Forji Amin (Dr. of Law—Public International Law) is Teaching Fellow at the School of Law, University of Manchester, and Affiliated Research Fellow at the Manchester International Law Centre (MILC), UK.

Routledge Studies in African Development

Engendering Democracy in Africa
Women, Politics and Development
Niamh Gaynor

Social Protection, Pastoralism and Resilience in Ethiopia
Lessons for Sub-Saharan Africa
Edited by Zeremariam Fre, Bereket Tsegay, Araya M. Teka, John Livingstone and Nicole Kenton

Sustainable Development in Post-Pandemic Africa
Effective Strategies for Resource Mobilization
Edited by Fred Olayele and Yiagadeesen Samy

Socioeconomic Shocks and Africa's Development Agenda
Lessons and Policy Directions in a Post-COVID-19 Era
Edited by Evans Osabuohien, Gbadebo Odularu, Daniel E. Ufua and Romanus A. Osabohien

Africa's Economic Partnership with China
An Holistic Analysis
Mussie Delelegn Arega

Microfinance, Livelihoods and Poverty Reduction in Ghana
Aaron Alesane

International Law and the History of Resource Extraction in Africa
Capital Accumulation and Underdevelopment, 1450–1918
George Forji Amin

For more information about this series, please visit: www.routledge.com/Routledge-Studies-in-African-Development/book-series/RSAD

International Law and the History of Resource Extraction in Africa

Capital Accumulation and Underdevelopment, 1450–1918

George Forji Amin

Routledge
Taylor & Francis Group
LONDON AND NEW YORK

First published 2024
by Routledge
4 Park Square, Milton Park, Abingdon, Oxon OX14 4RN

and by Routledge
605 Third Avenue, New York, NY 10158

Routledge is an imprint of the Taylor & Francis Group, an informa business

British Library Cataloguing-in-Publication Data
A catalogue record for this book is available from the British Library

ISBN: 978-1-032-20890-9 (hbk)
ISBN: 978-1-032-20893-0 (pbk)
ISBN: 978-1-003-26574-0 (ebk)

DOI: 10.4324/9781003265740

Typeset in Galliard
by SPi Technologies India Pvt Ltd (Straive)

To the Children of Africa caught up in the tragedies of World History

Contents

1 The Third World and Nature of World Order

1.1 Introduction

International law is a double-edged sword. At the core of its essence is the universal promise for emancipation of peoples and nations. Notwithstanding international law's expressive commitments to international peace, security, justice and fairness,[1] a barrage of legal scholarship has historically—and even more so in contemporary times—perceived the discipline as an instrument of the powerful for the domination of the weak. Between the 16th and the 20th centuries, the legality of European domination over non-Europeans was directly expressed through conceptions of private property (*dominium*) and territorial sovereignty (*imperium*).[2] The application of the two conceptions enabled European states to annex non-European territories, whereupon they extended their vision of sovereignty and exigencies of commercial capitalism.[3] Thanks to the differentiation between property and sovereignty, colonialism over the ages effectively shaped the development and evolution of international law. In *Imperialism, Sovereignty and the Making of International Law* (2005), Anthony Anghie succinctly observed that the edifice of international law's core doctrines, such as territorial acquisition, sovereignty, state succession, state responsibility, and freedom of the seas, stemmed from the exigencies of colonialism.[4]

Although colonialism is now commonly scorned in academic circles, the trend is rather recent. In fact, in the decade preceding Anghie's magnum opus, Anthony Carty regrettably noted that in international law, "no systematic undertaking is usually offered of the influence of colonialism in the development of the basic conceptual framework of the subject."[5] Between the 16th and 20th centuries, international law projected Europe and Europeans in material terms as a superior continent and peoples, respectively. European colonial annexations of non-European territories as a result was seen as necessary duty in order to organise and enlighten backward peoples, as well as for instituting law and order—all conditions that were expected to bring wealth and prosperity to these nations.[6] At the core of the international society is the idea of law—the idea that law, order, and progress are indispensable, while chaos, disorder, and backwardness by contrast are inimical to a just and stable

DOI: 10.4324/9781003265740-1

world.[7] In *An Introduction to the History of the Law of Nations in the East Indies* (1967), C. H. Alexandrowicz observed that international law frequently gave the impression of Europeans as endowed with an implicit duty to civilise the behaviours and societies of non-Europeans, and to lead the latter towards progress and advancement.[8] European imperialism—habitually expressed through the vocabularies of humanitarianism and universality—was accordingly projected as a fulfilment of the global common good.

A new critical intellectual movement that saw the day in the aftermath of the 1955 Bandung conference[9] (but that really garnered steam only in the 1990s), and that came to be known as Third World Approaches to International Law (TWAIL), has forcefully challenged the celebratory accounts of classical international law. Led by B. S. Chimni, Anthony Anghie, Upendra Baxi, Balakrishnan Rajagopal, James Thuo Gathii, Makau Wa Mutua, and Obiora Chinedu Okafor,[10] the movement has adopted the viewpoint that international law's pursuit of perceived "global common good" goals, not only exploited the third world economically, politically, culturally, and socially, but moreover confined them within a subordination relationship to the west. While early TWAILers (R.P. Anand, Keba M'baye, Upendra Baxi, Mohammed Bedjaoui, and Christopher Weeramantry)[11] were deeply associated with the New International Economic Order (NIEO) struggle that rocked the international society in the 1960s and 1970s, the second generation of TWAILers (authors writing after the close of the cold war in 1991) have been far from monolithic thinking—expanding their scholarship to varying areas such as "feminism," "Critical Legal Studies (CLS)," "New Approaches to International Law (NAIL)," "Marxism," "poststructuralism," "critical race approaches to international law," "global politics,"[12] etc.

According to B. S. Chimni, the nexus between "capitalism, imperialism and international law" accounts for the fact that "third world peoples, especially its subaltern groups" have always been disadvantaged in world order structure.[13] It is observed that in spite of the political decolonisation of the third world from colonisation in the 1960s, their economic sovereignty has nonetheless ever since been assigned by international law to international institutions that regulate production and exchange processes in an imperial fashion.[14] The collective agencies of the new Transnational Capitalist Class (TCC),[15] together with hegemony of international institutions, embody the distinctive trend of imperialism in the 21st century. In *The Accumulation of Capital* (1913), the German Marxist theorist Rosa Luxemburg observed that the records of the 16th to 19th centuries showed imperialism was inevitable for the survival of capitalism.[16] Her observation that "imperialism is the political expression of the accumulation of capital in its competitive struggle for what remains still open of the non-capitalist environment,"[17] foreshadowed the era of neo-colonialism, which some contemporary scholars have spotted as the modern nature of imperialism. While the term was first coined in 1956 by the French philosopher Jean-Paul Sartre[18] to indict French policies in Algeria, it is Kwame Nkrumah, the pioneer president of Ghana, who nevertheless popularised the concept, in his well-acclaimed book *Neo-Colonialism: The Last Stage of Imperialism* (1965). More elaborate and expansive than Sartre's usage, Nkrumah's depiction of "neo-colonialism" symbolised indirect forms of control over newly sovereign states (imbalanced trade, capitalism, international financial institutions, cultural imperialism, etc.), by former colonial powers and international bodies.[19]

Nkrumah's thesis fitted squarely with concerns of African states and their third world counterparts in the immediate aftermath of decolonisation in the 1960s. It sought to uncover the causes of stagnant economic growth in the third world in general and independent African states in particular. Prior to attaining independence, these countries previously depended on the laws of the colonial powers. Upon becoming full actors of international law, the newly independent states envisaged exercising full sovereignty over their territorial jurisdictions and natural resources. Before long, however, they collectively perceived prevailing international law as fundamentally limiting their ability to exercise absolute sovereign rights over their natural resources. The act of political independence was perceived as having failed to translate into economic sovereignty.[20] According to one observer, many African, Asian, and Latin American states were in particular sensitive not just to their recent colonial mishaps, but more so scared about the potential of sacrificing their right to self-determination through "economic dependence on industrialized states or multinational corporations."[21] They perceived international economic law as putting much emphasis on the protection of foreign investments against expropriation, yet as indifferent to the protection of their national economic interests.[22] Faced with these stakes, third world countries collectively advocated for a New International Economic Order (NIEO), in order to alleviate noticeable gaps in the world order.

Overall, colonial discourse and TWAIL scholarship together with Marxist analysis have been instrumental in showing the international society as interwoven, and countries of the world not as existing in isolation, but as structurally linked together through economic, social, and political ties that in many ways define every nation's development or underdevelopment pattern. The nature of the linkages constitutes the essence of world (global) order, defined by Richard Falk as "the distribution of power and authority among the political actors on the global stage."[23] These schools of thought contend that European powers' aggressive quest for extraterritorial trade in the 16th century resulted in defining encounters with non-Europeans, and the harmonisation of doctrines that justified the former's dominion of the latter. While projecting the dominating actors of the system as heavily benefiting from emanating encounters at the expense of dominated subjects, poverty and underdevelopment are explained as the natural consequence of global structural inequality. International law is conceived by these analyses as invariably inseparable from economic modes of social relations.

In spite of its historical mishaps, international law has nevertheless frequently provided ample openings for challenge, contestation, and reshaping of the discipline's normative structure.[24] Third-world nations derived legitimation during their quest for self-determination in the immediate aftermath of the Second World War (WWII) by reviving international law's universal guarantees for justice and equity amongst nations and peoples. The attainment of independence by extension implied that the key stumbling block which had long prevented third-world states from contesting international law (that is, the privilege of sovereign equality), was finally removed.[25] As full actors of international law that could at long last intercede in their own names and right, third-world countries sought to eradicate remnants of imperialism and to reform international law rules by voting as a united bloc at the United Nations General Assembly, where they constituted an overwhelming majority. A number of resolutions sponsored by these countries successfully passed in the 1960s, such as Resolution 1514 "on the Granting of Independence to Colonial Countries and Peoples," Resolution 1541 (XV) affirming the right of self-determination, and Resolution 1803 on "Permanent Sovereignty over Natural Resources (PSNRs)."[26] The hallmark of their activism and normative achievement saw the day in 1974 when the assembly enacted the resolution on the NIEO, otherwise dubbed as the Charter of Economic Rights and Duties of States (CERDS), over vigorous objections from industrialised countries.[27] The CERDS charter notwithstanding, neo-colonisation continued unabated as the proliferation of Bilateral Investment Treaties (BITs) effectively rendered the charter as a dead letter.

In spite of its historical and present shortcomings in addressing questions of poverty and underdevelopment, especially in sub-Saharan Africa, this study nonetheless observes that by accommodating more critical voices—most notably from Marxism and TWAIL—contemporary international law has shown both the will and readiness for constructive remedies and reform. The fact that many publicists are now drawn to Marxism is self-evident of the strength of the counter-hegemony project in international law. As Tony Judt eloquently puts it, "from first to last, Marxism's strongest suit was … the moral seriousness of [the] conviction that the destiny of our world as a whole is tied up with the condition of its poorest and most disadvantaged members."[28]

1.2 On the Causes of Underdevelopment

What causes poverty and underdevelopment especially in the third world—where the scourge has persisted since independence? Academics have grappled with this question since the end of the Second World War (WWII)—following the attainment of independence by the majority of third world countries from colonial rule. From the vast barrage of writings on development studies, three mutually exclusive schools of thought emerged, to wit: modernisation, dependency, and the world systems theory. All three paradigms sought to comprehend the causes of underdevelopment, and to formulate efficient solutions through which nations could simultaneously improve the living conditions of their populace and transition from impoverishment unto modern societies. The modernisation school—derived from Keynesian economics—was dominant in the 1950s and 1960s and adhered to western structural functionalism.[29] Dependency scholarship arose in the 1960s through the 1990s while the world systems theory commenced in the 1970s, both positing as critical responses to the modernisation school. Positioning themselves as neo-Marxists, both variants of *dependency* (the dependency school, and world systems theory) generally perceived the causes of underdevelopment to be rooted in the historical process of the expansion of capitalism.[30] Europe's relationship with non-European worlds was based on exploitation of natural resources, labour, and accumulation of capital from the colonies unto the metropoles.[31]

Championed by Walt Whitman Rostow, Neil Smelser, and Dean C. Tipps,[32] the Modernisation school perceived economic development as a catch-up project.[33] Rostow's five step analysis in *Stages of Economic Growth* (1960)[34] portrayed economic development as unavoidably evolutionary. The economic disparity between industrialised countries and third world countries was seen by the school as a function of the failure of the latter states to conform to the natural process of capitalism. Third world societies were admonished to dismantle their traditional institutions and embrace western modern values as the sole modality for transformative change. In "Social Patterns (Structures) and Problems of Modernization" (1967), Marion Levy observed that "as time goes on, they [third world countries] and we will increasingly resemble one another because the patterns of modernization are such that the more highly modernized societies become, the more they resemble one another."[35]

Unlike the modernisation school, both variants of *dependency* were revolutionary rather than evolutionary.[36] They perceived development and underdevelopment as originating from the same historical process of capitalist expansion—whereupon developed societies attained their growth by annexing, exploiting, and appropriating non-European societies, thereby impoverishing them. In *Critique and Anti-Critique* (1984), Andre Gunder Frank inquired about the best and most efficient scientific approach to comprehend the contradictions in global development and underdevelopment, to which he asserted thus:

> For development and underdevelopment, the causal determinant is without a doubt the world capitalist system, since it was capitalist development throughout the last five centuries that promoted economic development in some parts of the world at the cost of simultaneously generating, as an integral part of the same process, the development of underdevelopment in Asia, Africa, Latin America, and some other areas.[37]

In *The Political Economy of Growth* (1957), Paul Baran traced the origins of development and underdevelopment to the 16th century, when European colonisation of non-European territories sparked a process of capitalist primitive accumulation.[38] While European powers flourished economically by accumulating and shipping the surplus of the colonies to Western Europe, the colonies by fulfilling the exigencies of the metropoles resultantly witnessed stagnant growth.[39] Baran's work revealed that in spite of political independence, the newly sovereign nations were "comprador" governments that lacked autonomous development of their own, as not only did their productive forces retain the same colonial structures that benefited advanced economies, but their national surpluses were moreover still being siphoned through foreign investments and capitalist relations.[40] The process of underdevelopment as a result continued unabated.

In "The Development of Underdevelopment" (1966), Andre Gunder Frank concurred with Baran's thesis, observing that the contemporary state of third world underdevelopment was a result of their participation in the historical process of world capitalist development.[41] Although the study focused largely on Latin America, it nonetheless had implications that were relevant to the third world in general. In the course of analysing the scope of development in Brazil and other Latin American countries during the colonial period, Frank observed that what appeared as economic development during this period was in reality "satellite development which was neither self-generating nor self-perpetuating."[42] According to him, the resulting structure of international trade occasioned a process of underdevelopment in Latin America.[43] Gunder Frank's analysis became one of the leading studies in the unmasking of the nexus between metropolitan states and economic colonies—a structure which over the centuries defined the development of the world capitalist system.[44]

Inspired by the work of Gunder Frank in Latin America, the Egyptian Marxian economist Samir Amin, upon identifying two global distinct patterns of growth—one pertaining to development at the "centre" and the other to "dependent development in the periphery"—observed that Africa and Asia, like their Latin American counterparts, were incorporated into the global order through a parallel historical process and were exploited by the same capitalist process.[45] Qualifying this process as "accumulation on a global scale," Amin showed that while developed countries generated wealth by extracting the surplus of the third world, the latter were confined within a state of dependency and stagnant growth.[46] In line with Baran, Gunder Frank and Samir Amin both settled on the 16th century as the moment when Latin America and Africa became capitalist societies. While Gunder Frank found the European colonisation of the Americas as being the event that occasioned their integration into the world economy, Amin on his part observed that the same process incorporated sub-Saharan Africa through a commercial scheme that involved Africans being transported into the Americas as slaves to erect plantations and generate wealth for their owners.[47]

Given the nature of capital and labour relations between colonising powers and the colonies, a structural *international division of labour* soon emerged between the two worlds, which, despite variations over the centuries and post-colonial times, is believed by dependency scholars as continuing to define economic exchanges and international trade between the two worlds. In a relationship characterised by uneven development, most of the former colonies constitute the periphery of the world system, while the former colonial powers constitute what Immanuel Wallerstein has dubbed as the "core," as he examined the nature of international division of labour.[48] The world systems theory, which he developed, in effect shows the inescapable interdependence between a three-tier hierarchical nexus ("periphery"-"semi-periphery"-"Core"), that makes it so hard for poor countries to break free from the underdevelopment trap. Conceiving the world economy as a single world market, dependency scholars underscore the nature of international trade arising from the expansion of capitalism as confining various geographical markets was to specific economic roles. Following the encounter between Europeans and non-Europeans, a peculiar "internationalization of production processes"[49] slowly but surely saw former colonies specialising in labour-intensive and semi-skilled sectors which tended to yield meagre profits. Meanwhile, the former metropoles specialised in skilled, industrial, and capital-intensive sectors that typically fetch huge profits.

1.3 Might Makes Right: Sub-Saharan Africa, Property Rights, and the Resource Curse Thesis (RCT)

As already observed, the majority of poverty and underdevelopment studies reveal that the nature of expansion of the world economy since the 16th century successively converted the third world into export economies, based on a structured international division of labour modality. The focus of this study is on sub-Saharan Africa—currently assessed by global economic matrixes as the least developed and poorest region of the world. It is deduced from the vast body of literature on underdevelopment studies that not only was sub-Saharan Africa historically incorporated into the global order in a very coercive and extractive manner, but its current linkage to the global order is still based on structures of exploitation. Particular emphasis is placed on the way in which international law, beginning in the 16th century, introduced two economic institutions that have shape the economic future of Africa for centuries, namely: *trade* and *private property*.

According to the 2016 UNICEF-World Bank Poverty Report, nearly half of all children in sub-Saharan Africa's 48 states (49%) live below the international poverty line of $1.90 per day.[50] This dire situation is ironic, given that quite a number of countries in the sub-region (for instance, Democratic Republic of Congo, Nigeria, Sierra Leone, Gabon, Angola, Mozambique, Equatorial Guinea, Niger, etc.) are heavily endowed with valuable natural resources, yet are not only the least developed but amongst the most contentious parts of the world, marred by low economic growth, abject poverty, stagnant development, misappropriation of natural resources, civil wars, low life expectancy, bad governance, and other adversities.[51] Beginning in the 1990s, a new neoliberal school dubbed as the Resource Curse Thesis

(RCT)—and led by Richard Auty, Jeffrey Sachs, Andrew Warner, and Michael Klare, advanced the concept of *resource curse*, or *paradox of plenty*, to elucidate this irony.[52] Natural resources by nature are high concentrations of wealth and value. As Michael Klare observed in his book *Resource Wars*,

> theoretically the development of resources could produce great wealth for these nations, but historically it leads to the concentration of wealth in the hands of a few—those who monopolize the collection of rents from the mining or the drilling for oil—and the exclusion of the majority from any benefit.[53]

Although a stumbling block to the prosperity of many sub-Saharan African countries, natural resources have incidentally served as the foundation for growth and propelled some other resource-rich countries into relative success stories—not just in the industrialised countries but in the third world as well. As one commentator has observed,

> thirty years ago, Indonesia and Nigeria—both dependent on oil—had comparable per capita incomes. Today, Indonesia's per capita income is four times that of Nigeria. A similar pattern holds true in Sierra Leone and Botswana. Both are rich in diamonds. While Botswana averaged 8.7% annual economic growth over the past thirty years, Sierra Leone plunged into civil strife.[54]

It is apparent from the dichotomy that there is a disturbing trend of unaccountability, unjust exploitation, and violation and denial of human rights in the resource-rich countries, facing the "curse." Faced with this enigma, it is imperative to examine a number of corollary questions, to wit: Who owns the resources of a state? Who is empowered to exploit them? And, for what purposes should a country's natural resources be exploited?

In two seminal works, *Blood Oil* (2015) and "Property Rights and Resource Curse" (2008), Leif Wenar argued that the injustice of the resource curse is a symptom of the violation of property rights inherent in the nature of international trade.[55] To him, the regime of international trade fundamentally violates property rights, as it not only disregards violence deployed in the extraction of natural resources but legitimises the purchase of all "stolen goods" emanating from natural resources.[56] Furthermore, he explained, the curse is not imbedded in the resources, but rather "results from a defect in the rules that allocate control over these resources. The fault is not in nature, but in human institutions, here specifically, markets."[57] As to who owns the resources of a country, Warner, reading from Article 1 of the International Covenant on Civil and Political Rights (ICCPR) and Article 21 of the African Charter on Human and Peoples' Rights, has affirmed that the resources clearly belong to the people of a country, rather than personal property of leaders. Article 1 of the ICCPR provides thus:

1. All peoples have the right of self-determination. By virtue of that right they freely determine their political status and freely pursue their economic, social and cultural development.
2. All peoples may, for their own ends, freely dispose of their natural wealth and resources without prejudice to any obligations arising out of international economic co-operation, based upon the principle of mutual benefit, and international law. In no case may a people be deprived of its own means of subsistence.[58]

Article 21 of the African Charter on Human and Peoples' Rights on its part stipulates that "all peoples shall freely dispose of their wealth and natural resources. This right shall be exercised in the exclusive interest of the people. In no case shall a people be deprived of it."[59]

In spite of the contemporary established principles affirming ownership of natural resources of a country to its citizens, the blessings of the resources have frequently turned into a curse "when tyrants and insurgents are allowed to sell off the country's resources while crushing popular resistance, and to use the proceeds in ways that make the people worse off."[60] It is at this juncture that he found an upsetting inconsistency in the practice of international law. What the discipline gives citizens of a country with one hand, it appears to take it away with another hand, through rules of international commerce that legitimise theft.

In the current international customary practice, Wenar observes,

> all that is necessary for a group to acquire the legal right to sell off a country's resources is the power to inflict violence on the territory's people. Whoever can maintain coercive control over a country's population (or in the case of civil warriors, over part of a population) is recognised internationally as legally authorised to sell off a country's resources.[61]

Wenar qualifies this customary rule as "Might makes right," whereupon the capacity for violence is equated with the right to own and sell a country's resources.[62] Wenar's theory is very synonymous with the "Resource" and "Borrowing" privileges argument, advanced by Thomas Pogge in *World Poverty and Human Rights* (2002),[63] a volume which vigorously argues that authoritarian regimes not only harm citizens of their countries by stealing and selling their resources, but, moreover, exacerbate poverty by borrowing and misappropriating funds in their names.

1.4 Application of the Doctrine of Property Rights in Africa

How do things get owned? What are the legal modalities for appropriating things in foreign lands? Against these questions stand another: what constitutes property and/or commodity? When Europeans travelled to non-European territories in the 16th to 19th centuries, they invoked European doctrines on private property rights to regulate their relations with newly encountered peoples. The application of these principles on non-Europeans led to the legitimation of crucial benchmarks—and the failure of the latter to meet these benchmarks led to the dispossession and transfer of their property rights unto Europeans.

Theories of private property date back to ancient and medieval times. They became commonplace in the 17th and 18th centuries as an essential vocabulary for the conception of liberty and the justification of European extraterritorial trade and imperialism. In *Commentaries on the Laws of England* (1765), William Blackstone observed that there was nothing "which so generally strikes the imagination and engages the affections of mankind, as the right of property."[64] Property for him symbolised the "sole and despotic dominion which one man claims and exercises over the external things of the world, in total exclusion of the right of any other individual in the universe."[65] Kenneth Vandevelde has interpreted Blackstone's definition as embodying two related elements, to wit: (a) the necessity of an "external thing to serve as the object of property rights," and (b) exclusive and absolute power of dominion by the owner over the thing.[66] For classical political economists and international lawyers, ownership, property, and labour were facts of life that promptly needed to be accounted for.[67]

Property rights doctrines have since the 16th century paved the way for the legitimation of European imperialism in non-European territories. Following European extraterritorial expansions to foreign lands, political economists and international lawyers not only routinely contended that European private property rights doctrines were extendable to non-Europeans, but moreover articulated new standards that justified the hegemony of the former over the latter. In the aftermath of the conquest of the Americas, Francisco de Vitoria (1483–1546) recognised the classical Roman doctrine of occupation—*law ferae bestiae* (literally translated as law of the wild beasts) as an established rule of the Law of Nations. Based on the understanding that man had dominion over all wild beasts in the forests, Vitoria showing preference for the term in lieu of the commonly used synonym of *res nullius*, observed that "in the law of nations (*ius gentium*) a thing which does not belong to anyone (*res nullius*) becomes the property of the first taker, according to the *law ferae bestiae*."[68] For Vitoria, the doctrine was both just and imperative, as it was an efficient modality to divide the world which God had bequeathed unto man in common, thereby ensuring that all unused lands were placed into productive use.

Following the advent of industrial revolution in Europe in the 19th century, European corporations were increasingly drawn into conflicts as they competed for territory and raw materials in Africa. As the rivalries intensified, the German chancellor Otto von Bismarck, in an attempt to avert the possibility of a full-blown war, convened an international conference in the winter of 1884–5—whereupon he invited all recognised members of the family of nations to his palace in Berlin. Strikingly, no African sovereign was invited to the gathering. The main objective of the conference was for the delegates to set up uniform international law principles through which European powers could annex and extend sovereignty unto African territories.[69] As a modality against fictitious occupations—which had become rampant in the build-up to the meeting, the "General Act of the Berlin Conference" in its Articles 34 and 35 inaugurated the concept of "Effective Occupation," which obliged all annexing powers to have effective administration on the ground, before any occupation could be deemed legitimate.[70] It was in the aftermath of the conference that the newly formed *Institut de Droit international*, a professional association of international lawyers, responded affirmatively to the General Act by articulating a new concept dubbed *territorium nullius*, which enabled the legitimate appropriation of Africa's lands and European settler colonisation.[71]

While *res nullius* was a strictly private law principle of property and occupation, the European colonial push into non-European territories established a nexus with a corresponding *ius gentium* concept of sovereignty. With regard to Africa, international lawyers following the Berlin conference grappled with the legality of colonising the continent, given that the continent was effectively occupied by indigenous populations and leaders on the continent unanimously recognised to be exercising effective administration over their territories. Having acknowledged that most African lands were not *res nullius*, the lawyers at the *Institut de Droit International* in 1885 commissioned the German jurist, Ferdinand von Martitz, with the task of "developing and completing" the practical legality of the provisions contained in Articles 34 and 35 of the General Act of the Berlin Conference.[72] In 1887, Martitz presented a draft document intended to be guiding legal reference for European colonisation in Africa to the *Institut*, in which he formulated a distinction between property and sovereignty which correspondingly enabled the framing of lands which Africans had owned for centuries as *territorium nullius*. He defined the concept of *territorium nullius* in the draft document thus:

> It is considered *territorium nullius* [therefore suitable to be occupied] each region that is not actually under the sovereignty or the protectorate of any of the states forming the community of the law of nations, it does not matter that this region is or is not inhabited.[73]

The doctrine of *territorium nullius* thus enabled European jurists to detect a huge deficient gap in the level of modernity and civility between Africa and Europe.[74]

Although 80% of the continent at the time was still under the full control of local African rulers and European influence was limited to the coastal areas—in what was a re-enactment of doctrines of *dominium* and *imperium*—a legal rationale was sanctioned according to which the first civilised entity to annex lands was legally mandated with the duty to set up protectorates and lead its occupants towards civilisation.[75] Although most European jurists observed that Africans could not be legally dispossessed of proprietary rights over their lands, there was nonetheless a near consensus that acts of European powers who had the ability to set up protectorates were legitimate. The new principle of *territorium nullius* was thus a legal instrument of occupation that enabled European sovereigns to exercise authority over African colonies.[76] Being a regime of exception, the European colonial powers were effectively empowered to treat appropriated colonies as leaderless—as a result, the sovereignty of African states became dependent on the authority of the European metropoles.

1.5 John Locke's Classical Conception of Property Rights and Dispossession

The English philosopher John Locke (1632–1704) is indispensable to intellectual discourse on government, property rights, and imperialism, considering the immense influence his works had on academics, politicians, and political revolutions. In 1689, he anonymously published the *Two Treatises of Government* in an incomplete form, and he reportedly never owned copyright of the material during his lifetime.[77] Generally considered as a seminal text on the foundations of government because of the defence of individual liberty and delimitation of the contours of sovereignty, the *Two Treatises* earned Locke the moniker of "Father of Liberalism."[78] While individual liberty was front and centre of his thesis, his postulations nevertheless metamorphosed and became the framework for legitimately dispossessing non-Europeans of their property rights. Elsewhere in this study, I will show that Locke's direct participation in the transatlantic slave trade, whereupon Africans were exploited and confined in bondage, severely contradicted his postulations on human dignity and freedom from oppression.

As previously noted, Locke's *œuvre* evolved to become one of the most impactful political theses of the 17th and 18th centuries. The work has two parallel arms, to wit: a political theory outlining grounds for political revolution and the limits of government on the one hand, and the conception of property—especially the circumstances when private property is deemed to have arisen—either as a private right or in exclusivity, on the other hand.[79] Locke's *First Treatise* was a critique of absolute rights of kings as propounded by Robert Filmer, and the devastating implications of the latter's doctrines on civil liberties. Filmer (1588–1653) was an English political theorist. His classical work: *Patriarcha, or The Natural Power of Kings* (1680), cogently defended the divine right of kings, and further observed that the citizenry had a duty to loyally obey the commands of the sovereign.[80] For Locke, any observance of Filmer's doctrines was inevitably going to enable an unjust government—reminiscent of the Stuart monarchy that was notorious for its arbitrariness, excesses, and rampant abuse of civil liberties.[81] The *Second Treatise* was more impactful because of the compelling assessment of liberal democracy—not just because the subject was front and centre of the political discourses of Locke's time—but more so because of his radical solutions to the problems posed.

In line with other social contract theorists of his time, like Thomas Hobbes, Locke situated the *Second Treatise* around the state of nature and the modalities of transition from that state into a civil society. While people were necessarily free in a state of nature, justice could be served only if liberties were regulated in accordance with peoples' necessities and needs. The *Second Treatise* in fact enunciates the modalities according to which the right to property arises. Consistent with other social contract theorists, Locke's main contention was to the effect that it was legitimate to overthrow an unjust government. But through what barometer can people determine unjust governments? In what was a clear attempt at addressing this concern, Locke advanced the concept of legitimate property ownership and through it effectively tied justice to property rights. The denial of property rights by any government, he observed, inevitably amounted to an act of injustice.[82] A government rooted on such abuses according to Locke was by default unjust.

What is property? To Locke, property symbolised three crucial necessities: "Lives, Liberty and Estates."[83] Given that each of these attributes encapsulated invaluable things which any man owns, the necessities as a totality embodied the essence of life itself. This naturally triggers the question of why individuals submitted themselves to a government in the first place, especially considering the risk that it could eventually become tyrannical and unjust. Locke observed that people subjected themselves to a government in order to safeguard and protect their property.[84] People owed allegiance to the government as long it safeguarded property rights. It went without saying that they consented to a civil government to be better off than they would have been, had there been no government.[85] This determination enabled Locke to establish a limit which a legitimate government could not cross—namely, ruling only to the extent that people could tolerate.[86] Any political authority that negates on its fundamental duty of protection and systematically violates peoples' property rights loses its legitimacy, and people as a consequence are within their legitimate right to wage a war to overthrow it.

As to why property rights were so sacrosanct, Locke provided that they were natural rights and predated all other social arrangements.[87] Locke not only equated natural law with God's will (moral law), but moreover contended that it was imperative for the observance of "peace and preservation of all mankind."[88] The pre-civil government era, he observed, was one of equality and freedom, and given that there was no overriding authority, everyone necessarily needed to control their individual possessions. While everyone could do as they pleased with their property, they were nevertheless vulnerable without any protection and regulation.[89] Upon surrendering authority to the civil government, all actions it took, both for the preservation of possessions and to foster peace, became legitimate because they conformed to natural law, hence they were a fulfilment of God's will.[90]

There seemed to be a mismatch between Locke's observation of equality, freedom, and the imperativeness of a civil government to regulate property rights. As a quick fix, Locke conceptualised the modality through which people came to legitimately own private property. Re-enacting an earlier postulation by Robert Filmer, Locke observed that God bequeathed the earth to Adam and his posterity including "the Fruits it naturally produces, and Beasts it feeds," to all mankind in common.[91] No one in principle thus had an exclusive right to property. How, then, did private property arise when the earth was bequeathed to all humans in common? To Locke, men acquired exclusive right over property by mixing labour with things.[92] He expatiated on this by laying forth an agricultural argument, namely that God bequeathed the earth to man strictly to cultivate and turn it into productive yield. That is, when God gave the earth to men in common, he also gave them:

> reason to make use of it to the best advantage of life and convenience. The earth, and all that is therein, is given to men for the support and comfort of their being ... no body has originality in private dominion, exclusive of the rest of mankind, in any of them, as they are thus in their natural state: yet being given for the use of men, there must of necessity be a means to appropriate them in one way or another before they can be of any use, or at all beneficial to any particular man.[93]

In order to convert land into productive use, one needed first of all to have ownership over it. Anyone who puts land to productive use fulfils the exigencies of both natural law and God's will, namely, peace and preservation.[94] Understanding how susceptible his theory was to abuse, Locke, in a bit to ensure that natural law was not violated, pre-emptively set some limits on the right of private property. His first limit was in relation to spoilage. Man could own or exploit only such volume of the earth as was necessarily needed. Any remaining surplus ought to be shared away, else it could be forcefully taken away.[95] Despite its apparent noble intentions, the downside of the argument was the slippery slope tendency by which it could be invoked to justify imperialism, when foreign lands were annexed. The argument also presupposed that there could be no limit to ownership as long as there was no spoilage. Locke concurred, contending that natural law was not violated by the quantity of possession but instead by waste.[96] He further observed that spoilage could be overcome through the use of money: "as different degrees of Industry were apt to give Men Possessions in different Proportions, so the Invention of Money gave them the opportunity to continue and enlarge them."[97]

Considering the largess and elasticity of his theory of property rights, Locke, in a bit to avoid ambiguity, laid forth a second limitation, to the effect that whoever took possession was bound to be considerate, leaving a reasonable portion for others to exploit as well.[98] The main problematic with this provision was that its respect inevitably depended on the goodwill of the first taker. Be it as it may, it becomes apparent that the second limitation does more to fulfil the first condition than stand on its own. It is also apparent from both limitations that, just as man acquires property rights through appropriation, he can by the same modality lose all or some of it by waste, destruction, or neglect. A juxtaposition of these considerations in the 19th century showed African lands as having not been put into productive use. European protectorates were thus expected to teach African inhabitants ways of modernity.

1.6 Trade, Africa, and International Law

In *Perpetual Peace: A Philosophical Sketch* (1775), Immanuel Kant revisited the ancient Greek notion of *Kosmos*, which framed all humans as having a shared community and shared morality. While envisaging a common world federation for all humanity, Kant observed that *ius cosmopoliticum* naturally endowed every human with two contingent rights of visit and hospitality. This in essence implied that anyone who visited foreign soil was entitled to the right to visit and hospitable treatment: "he [the visitor] must not be treated with hostility, so long as he behaves in a peaceable manner in the place he happens to be in."[99] While Kantian cosmopolitanism facilitated trade across territorial borders and hypothetically evidenced what seemed to be conventional ethics for human encounters, it nonetheless also opened a slippery slope for colonial conquest and domination. Who was empowered to ascertain the fulfilment of protections of the two contingent rights of visit and hospitality? And what was to be the fate of societies that were deemed as falling short of the standard? From the Dominican jurist-theologians to Grotius, one of the frequently invoked rationales justifying the colonisation of non-Europeans by Europeans is situated on the former's interference with the latter's alleged right to trade.

European colonial expansions in the 16th century were propelled by trade rivalries amongst European powers, and the search for lucrative trade routes. While Locke perceived private ownership of lands as the best modality for improvement and profits, 18th-century political economists on their part, most notably Adam Smith and David Ricardo, envisaged specialisation and division of labour as the productivity principle for gainful free trade—hence, increment in the "wealth of nations."[100] Their theoretical disparities notwithstanding, they all perceived colonisation as beneficial only in so far as it fulfilled the exigencies of agriculture and commerce. To that effect, arguments advanced for the legitimate occupation of territories were routinely tied to trade routes and failure of local inhabitants to use land productively. The agricultural argument of exploitation presupposed that while all peoples had a common right of exploitation over earth's resources, Europeans had nevertheless "gained superior and particular rights through their acts of exploitation or occupation."[101]

Classical free trade doctrines had tremendous implications for sub-Saharan Africa. Having annexed the Americas, European powers found many opportunities for capital accumulation through plantation agriculture. Following the high mortality rate amongst American indigenous populations, sub-Saharan Africa was engaged through the transatlantic slave trade to supply the American colonies with badly needed labour. African labour and agricultural output steadily became the defining footholds for the colonial society in the New

World—with international law legitimating the global system—characterised by bondage of the labourers to the capitalists.

1.7 Aim and Scope of the Study

International law has a long history of operating as a hegemonic instrument, primarily exploited by stronger actors of the international society in order to dominate and subjugate weaker actors. Its adversities notwithstanding, the discipline's promise of emancipation of all peoples the world over has been vital in uniting both proponents and detractors, who collectively uphold the discipline as the best modality for the articulation and redress of universal rights and wrongs. This convergence has habitually been useful not only in shaping the relationship between the west and non-west worlds, but moreover in configuring and legitimating the world order as we know it today.

On the foregoing premise, this study has two broad goals. The first main objective is to explore specific progressive initiatives which international law historically legitimated for sub-Saharan Africa (between the 16th and 19th centuries), and in what ways that they shaped the continent economically. Particular emphasis is placed on grandiose schemes which at inception were billed as intended for uplifting the welfare of the African populace from a supposed state of backwardness to one of modernity.

The second objective is to explore the set of economic resources from sub-Saharan Africa that influenced the evolution of international law during the epochs under examination, but more importantly, how they impacted economic development within the subcontinent. Particular emphasis is placed on the way in which international law introduced two economic institutions that have shaped the economic future of Africa for centuries, namely: *trade* and *private property*. Did any or both of these mechanisms enable international law to fulfil its heralded promise of economic progress and the liberation of Africa from the burden of backwardness?

1.8 Methods

This work embraces two interdisciplinary methodologies which are primarily historical, but also critical and philosophical: Marxism, and Third World Approaches to International Law (TWAIL). Whereas the former emphasizes the exploitative nature of the international legal order and its historiography, the latter conceives international law from the standpoint of the third world, denouncing its current oppressive nature while at the same time underlying its liberating potential. One advantage of digging into legal history rests on the fact that the approach affords an unrivalled possibility to examine the less discussed but crucial nexus of international law and its "others." Generally speaking, the history of international law has traditionally been the least explored area of the discipline. Nevertheless, the study of the discipline's past has recently experienced an upsurge with the publication of a range of significant works dealing with international legal history. The latest of these publications—the *Oxford Handbook of the History of International Law*, edited by Bardo Fassbender, Anne Peters, Simone Peter, and Daniel Högger—is a monumental work that includes 44 articles, in addition to 21 biographical portraits covering a variety of topics related to the discipline's past.[102]

1.8.1 Historical Materialism and Uniqueness of Marx

One of the strengths of Marxism lies in the ability of the analysis to account for underlining social relations governing capitalism.[103] Contrary to classic enlightenment scholars, Karl Marx observed that capitalist societies created their wealth through "an immense accumulation of commodities."[104] He took history very seriously. Through the discipline, he was able to look backward, see the present and predict the future, or, better still, reshape the future. Finding himself at the crossroads of history, Marx perceived a necessity to probe deeper into unanswered questions on social relations pertaining to class struggle, social inequality, economic disparity, and structural exploitation. His primary contempt stemmed from the advent of industrial capitalism in Europe, and the perceived normalisation of exploitation of wage labour by factory owners. He made a forceful case for history to be understood in materialist terms (historical materialism). Social relations, he pointed out, were structured around material development and powered by a specific mode of production: "legal relations as well as the forms of the state are to be grasped neither from themselves nor from the so-called general development of the human mind, but rather have their roots in the material conditions of life."[105]

Historical materialism is thus a method grounded on the idea that "history is, fundamentally, the growth of human productive power, and that forms of society rise and fall accordingly as they enable and promote, or prevent and discourage that growth."[106] Using the dialectics of historical materialism, Marx examined capitalism, shedding light on the hidden value of commodities in social relations and the impact of capitalism's core premise, namely, that everything had a price and could be bought and sold.[107] His ideas on the hidden essence largely overlap across different works. While in *The German Ideology*, Marx and Friedrich Engels conceived history as setting pre-eminence on material progress: "relations of different nations amongst themselves depend upon the extent to which each has developed its productive forces, the division of labour and internal intercourse."[108] In *Grundrisse* and *Capital*, on the other hand, Marx portrayed history as being set on the pedestal of class struggles. Material history, Marx illustrated, is a by-product of class division and class struggles. In order to understand the basis of class division, it is incumbent to first understand the factors that determine relations of production.[109] Capitalism to Marx was by design a class system, characterised by an unequal class division between the propertied capitalists who own the means of production versus the working class who work for the capitalists as they lack the means of production.

As a method, historical materialism is uniquely important because it deconstructs the sources of societal problems, vividly illustrates how capitalist relations have evolved to dominate life and social well-being, and, by so doing, bringing clarity to the impact of social arrangements in peoples' material conditions. With this understanding, it becomes easier to articulate initiatives for creative change in society. Although Marx is widely acknowledged as the founder of historical materialism, it was Engels who coined both the terminology and the concept of dialectical materialism in two separate works: *Anti-Dühring* (1885) and *The Dialectics of Nature* (1883).[110] Engels certainly coined the terminologies not to take any credit but rather on behalf of Marx—to depict his analysis on social relations.

1.8.2 Marxist International Law and Questions of Imperialism

While only international lawyers in the Soviet Union and socialist states typically engaged Marxism in their scholarships throughout the cold war period (1947–1991), the trend gradually began to change in the 1990s, first with B. S. Chimni's book: *International Law and World Order: A Critique of Contemporary Approaches* (1993).[111] In the volume, Chimni dedicated one full chapter to Marxism under the title: "Towards an Integrated Marxist Approach to International Law (IMAIL)"[112] wherein he examined the role of imperialism in the development of international law. Having criticised the realism and liberalism of four international law theorists—Hans Morgenthau, Myres McDougal, Richard Falk, and Grigory Tunkin—in the preceding chapters, Chimni provided that these treatises did not adequately conform with socio-economic conditions of third world countries in the international society. To that effect, he developed a class-based account of international law whereupon he embraced Marxist-Leninist doctrines as appropriately encapsulating the unequal and unjust conditions of third world states in the world order structure. *International Law and World Order* launched Chimni not just as a prominent legal Marxist, but moreover as one of the pioneers of the Third World Approaches to International Law (TWAIL) movement.

Apart from Chimni, not much Marxist legal scholarship saw the day in the 1990s. It took a decade before a new wave of Marxist international law theses resurfaced. This revival was pioneered in part by Eric Bowring—who in 1996 had already prescribed a return to Marxism—as a critical legal theory by which international law could address questions of law and injustice in the postmodern era.[113] His book *Degradation of the International Legal Order* (2008)[114] set its theoretical foundations around Susan Marks's *Riddle of All Constitutions* (2000), which on its part perceived the discourse of international law as grounded on a firm harmony between exploitation and domination.[115] Upholding a similar line of argument, Bowring observed that the world order was marred by structural injustice, as a result of capitalism being ingrained by imperialism in its very essence. Capitalism, he observed, was characterised by an "unceasing urge to valorise itself, in which every social relationship, every intellectual creation, and every human appropriation of the material world is reducible to money."[116] Structuring his arguments on notions of self-determination and human rights, Bowring contended that although contemporary international law emerged in the post–Second World War era from anti-imperial struggles—with decolonised states gaining sovereign recognition in international law—the triumph did not mark the end of imperialism but rather paved the way for the transformation of its nature to more subtle forms of intervention in the third world.[117]

Another robust Marxist lens to international law stemmed from China Miéville's rediscovery of Evgeny Pashukanis's writings on the commodity and legal form. In *Between Equal Rights* (2005), Miéville engaged Pashukanis's thesis as an explanation of the indeterminacy of international law in social relations.[118] While Chimni and Bowring envisaged avenues by which international law could be reformed to fulfil its promise of universal justice, Miéville for his part, upon locating the hegemony of the discipline from structural relations of international capitalism, disagrees with the mainstream consensus that international law has the capacity to accomplish two contrary schemes (imperialism and emancipation through human rights) at one and the same time. For him, not only is international law exclusively imperialistic, but coercion and violence are deeply imbedded in its core form—hence capitalist imperialism. As a result, "the chaotic and bloody world around us is the rule of law."[119]

Meanwhile, a 2004 symposium on Marxism and international law resulted in a special issue of the *Leiden Journal of International Law*, followed by an edited volume a few years later titled: *International Law on the Left* (2008).[120] Two of the contributors (Martti Koskenniemi, A. Claire Cutler) are critical legal theorists who do not typically identify themselves as Marxists but rather perceive Marxism as informative to some of their legal arguments. Of the remaining seven contributors, four (B. S. Chimni, China Miéville, Bill Bowring, and Anthony Carty) are generally considered to be core legal Marxists, while the other three (Brad R. Roth, Susan Marks, and Obiora Chinedu Okafor), although passive Marxists, are core TWAIL theorists in actuality.

This study shows to some degree that the criticalness of Marxist international law postulations is not limited to deconstructing modes of imperialism in the world order, but more importantly for affording modalities for subjects affected by structural injustice to emancipate themselves from exploitation and injustice.

1.8.3 Third World Approaches to International Law (TWAIL)

International lawyers are currently locked down in a debate whether imperialism is a relic of the past or has transitioned to the present; and if so—what is its nature and impact on international relations moving forward? For TWAILers, imperialism of the West on third world economies is not only constant but a continuing reality. While observing that the nature of imperial formations habitually "corresponds to the stage and character of global capitalism," B. S. Chimni has contended that its continuing trend if anything is bound to worsen, unless there is a radical reversal in the structure of world order.[121]

Conceiving the global order and character of the international law as "unequal, unfair and unjust," the purport of TWAIL movement is both "oppositional" and "reconstructive."[122] The oppositional goal of TWAIL involves revealing how international law legitimated the colonialism over non-Europeans. It most especially deconstructs the nature of the colonial encounter, continuities of the structural relations, as well as emanating impacts which have been very detrimental to most third world countries.

The reconstructive goal of TWAIL is twofold. First, it involves articulating narratives for resistances to different forms of colonialism. It moreover involves clamouring for a reformation of the world order into one that is fair, equitable, and void of exploitation for third world countries—the attendant consequence being that sovereign equality represents not just a legal slogan, but factual reality.

The premise of TWAILERS is rooted on the assumption that it is through the colonial encounter that powerful countries subdued non-European societies within exploitative economic structures and politico-legal regimes. To that effect, a historical revisit is imperative not just to understand "the nature of the current international legal regime," but moreover to expose and reform global patterns of exploitation, inequality, injustice, and unfair treatment.[123]

For TWAIL scholars, an understanding of the nexus between capitalism and imperialism is primordial for an understanding of the development and evolution of international law.[124] Anthony Anghie has observed that colonisation was central, rather than peripheral, to the project and evolution of international law.[125] In harmony with Gerrit Gong, who observed that the 19th-century international law allowed Europeans to colonise non-Europeans using the standard of civilisation, Anghie concurred that a "dynamic of difference" which demarcated the international society between the civilised and the non-civilised effectively resulted to a space of inclusion version exclusion, respectively.[126]

1.9 Outline and Structure

For structural purposes, this study is spaced out into six key chapters. This chapter has furnished the background to the inquiry by highlighting the nature of world order as we know it today and its historical nexus with development and underdevelopment. It has shown that the edifice of these processes saw the day through the workings of political economy and legitimation by international law. While sub-Saharan Africa was shown as heavily endowed with a set of resources badly needed by the international society, its populace, rather than benefiting from these endowments, experienced a resource curse effect as a result of various systematic schemes orchestrated by both external and domestic exploiters.

Chapter 2 revisits Marxist explanations of the origins of the capitalist system and identifies primitive accumulation on a global scale, as the modality through which the Americas and sub-Saharan Africa were both incorporated into the nascent world order. International law in the age of primitive accumulation is shown to be very agrarian in character, frequently legitimating the exploitative interests of European powers over the Americas and Africans imported into the New World. Capitalism garners steam on a global scale through accumulation by dispossession, and continuity through violence and further accumulation techniques.

Chapter 3 examines the transatlantic slave trade and highlights the modality according to which international law legitimated a commodification process that accorded European powers with the right to own and trade sub-Saharan Africans as chattel property, for the production of goods and services in the Americas. With the engagement of sub-Saharan Africa into the world order geared at realising the labour needs of plantation capitalism, it is observed that both the rise and fall of the transatlantic slave trade was directly linked to profit margins. The contradictory shift of international law from legitimating the Atlantic slave trade to championing the abolition of the trade at the clock of the 19th century is explained as provoked by the rise of industrial capitalism as a more profitable mode of production thanks to machines, compared to the cumbersome plantation capitalism which, relying solely on slave labour, quantitatively produced less output.

Chapter 4 examines industrial capitalism in the 19th century, and concepts of improvement and the civilising mission in Africa, as legitimated by international law. It is shown that a binary differentiation of the civilised versus the uncivilised by 19th-century international lawyers enabled European powers to justify both the scramble and colonisation of Africa. According to the standard of civilisation, the international society was restricted to civilised nations, while colonised territories lacked sovereignty and were submerged into their metropolis as administrative provinces.

Chapter 5 examines the practical scramble for Africa and the various manoeuvres of non-state actors, that is, private law arrangements that foreshadowed a realm of cession treaties between European powers and African tribal leaders. These treaties were later invoked by rival European states to justify their sovereign rights of over "ceded" territories.

Chapter 6 evaluates the public law arrangements that crystallised the private law acts through the colonisation of the continent. The colonisation of Africa and the establishment of protectorates by European powers are explained as the pursuit for an international free trade regime to fulfil the exigencies of industrialised countries. The study further makes a comparative overview of different colonial systems using classical examples from four different protectorates (French Assimilation policy in Senegal, British Indirect rule in Nigeria, Leopold's Company Rule in the Congo Free State and the German Indirect Rule in Cameroon). Chapter 7 offers concluding remarks.

Notes

1 Article 1 of the UN Charter stipulates thus:

The Purposes of the United Nations are:

1. To maintain international peace and security, ...
2. To develop friendly relations among nations based on respect for the principle of equal rights and self-determination of peoples, ... and
3. To be a center for harmonizing the actions of nations in the attainment of these common ends."

(See: *Charter of the United Nations and Statute of the International Court of Justice* (United Nations Publications, San Francisco: 1945) at 1–2)

2 Colonialism and Imperialism are thus technically different. While *dominium* denotes economic sovereignty over a territory (the right of ownership and control), *imperium* on the other hand signifies political sovereignty—the power to impose, regulate, and making of rules. While this study exceptionally uses the terms Colonialism and Imperialism interchangeably, care is taken to place either concept in its proper context, whenever that is needed.

3 James Thuo Gathii, 54 *Buffalo Law Review* (2006–2007) at 1013–1014.

4 Anthony Anghie, (Cambridge University Press, 2005) at 108–110, 202, 209–210, 213.

5 Anthony Carty, (Pluto Press, 1996) at 5.

6 Mieke van der Linden, (Wolf Legal Publishers, 2014) at 2.

7 Malcolm N. Shaw, (Cambridge University Press, 1997) at 1.

8 C H Alexandrowicz, (Clarendon Press, 1967) at 10–13.

9 Taking place from 18 to 24 April 1955, the Bandung Conference was a maiden large-scale gathering of newly independent African and Asian states. The main goal of the conference was to oppose colonialism in all its forms. The conference paved the groundwork for the Non-Aligned Movement (NAM), which was founded in Yugoslavia in 1956.

10 Bhupinder S. Chimni, (Sage, 1993); Anghie, (Cambridge University Press, 2005); Upendra Baxi, (N.M. Tripathi, 1993); Gathii, 'Imperialism, Colonialism, and International Law' 1013–1066; Obiora Chinedu Okafor, *43 Osgoode Hall Law Journal* (2005) 171–192.

11 R.P. Anand, *56 AJIL* (1962) 383–406; Ram Prakash Anand, (Martinus Nijhoff Publishers, 1987); Christopher Weeramantry, (Lake House, 1984).

12 Okafor, 'Newness, Imperialism, and International Legal Reform' at 178.

13 B. S. Chimni, *14 Oregon Review of International Law* (2012) at 17. M. Sornarajah has also observed that "international law that was shaped in the colonial era was not a neutral discipline but an instrument of naked power, skillfully dressed up so as to hide its objective of controlling the colonized world for the benefit of the colonial powers. Doctrines were made by the founders who were described as universalists but whose mercenary purposes in shaping the content of international law are increasingly coming to be questioned." See: M. Sornarajah, *5 Singapore Journal of International & Comparative Law* (2001) at 285.

14 Chimni, 'Capitalism, Imperialism, and International Law' at 20.

15 The TCC according to Chimni comprises "segments of the capitalist class in advanced capitalist countries and emerging economies that gain from the globalization process at the expense of the subaltern classes in both the first and third worlds, or what may be termed the transnational oppressed classes." *See*: Chimni, 'Capitalism, Imperialism, and International Law' at 19.

16 Joan Robinson, "Introduction" (Routledge & Kegan Paul, 1951) at 28. Cf: Chimni, 'Capitalism, Imperialism, and International Law' at 24.
17 Robinson, "Introduction". Cf: Chimni, 'Capitalism, Imperialism, and International Law' at 24.
18 Jean-Paul Sartre, *123 Les Temps Modernes* (March–April 1956) 1371–1386.
19 Kwame Nkrumah, (International Publishers, 1965).
20 Norbert Horn, *16 Journal of World Trade Law* (1982) at 339.
21 Horn, 'Normative Problems of a New International Economic Order' at 340.
22 Phillippe Cullet, *10 European Journal of International Law* (1999) at 566, 567.
23 Richard Falk, *98 Current History* (1999) at 29.
24 Sundhya Pahuja, (Cambridge University Press, 2011) at 2–3.
25 Ibid at 3–4.
26 United Nations General Assembly Resolution 1514; United Nations General Assembly Resolution 1803 (XVII); United Nations General Assembly Resolution 1541 (XV).
27 United Nations General Assembly Resolution 3281 (XXIX). See also Charles N. Brower, & John B. Tepe, *9 International Lawyer* (1975) at 295.
28 Tony Judt, *14 New York Review of Books* (2006) at 89. *Emphasis mildly added. See also*: Tony Judt, (Vintage Books, 2008) at 139.
29 Keynesian economics is derivative analysis of John Maynard Keynes in the aftermath of the 1933 Great Depression, on modalities that the United States needed to take to overcome economic crisis, restore full employment, and sustain growth. *See*: John Maynard Keynes, (Atlantic Publishers, 2016).
30 The conception of capitalism especially amongst dependency scholars is purely Marxian—in terms of relations of exchange—where production is tailored satisfying global market exigencies rather than personal (domestic) needs.
31 Andre Gunder Frank, (Monthly Review Press, 1969) at 9–13.
32 Walt Whitman Rostow, (Cambridge University Press, 1960); Neil Smelser, (Basic Books, 1964); Dean C. Tipps, *15 Comparative Studies in Society and History* (1973) 199–226.
33 Wai, *32 Africa Development* (2007) at 76.
34 Rostow, *The Stages of Economic Growth.*
35 Marion J. Levy, "Social Patterns (Structures) and Problems of Modernization" in Wilbert Moore & Robert M. Cook (eds.), (Englewood Cliffs, 1967) at 207.
36 Walter Rodney opened his seminal book *How Europe Underdeveloped Africa* (1973) with the following quote from Che Guevara: "The unquestionable fact that underdeveloped countries are in total stagnation and the rate of economic growth is lower than that of population increase. These characteristics are not fortuitous; they correspond strictly to the nature of the capitalist system in full expansion, which transfers to the dependent countries the most abusive and barefaced forms of exploitation. It must be clearly understood that the only way to solve the questions now besetting mankind is to eliminate completely the exploitation of dependent countries by developed capitalist countries, with all the consequences that this implies." Che Guevara, 1964. Cf: Walter Rodney, (Revised edition, Pambazuka Press, 2012) at 3.
37 Andre Gunder Frank, (Praeger, 1984) at 4
38 Paul Baran, (Penguin, 1973) at 268.
39 Ibid at 268.
40 Ibid at 236–238.
41 Andre Gunder Frank, (Monthly Review Press, 1969) at 8.
42 Frank, "The Development of Underdevelopment" at 8.
43 Andre Gunder Frank, (Penguin, 1971) at 2–5.
44 Frank, "The Development of Underdevelopment" at 4.

45 Samir Amin, *1 Review of African Political Economy* (1974) at 9.
46 Samir Amin, 'L'Accumulation à L'Echelle Mondiale' *Editions Anthropos* (1970); Now translated into English as 'Accumulation on a World Scale' *2 Monthly Review Press* (1974).
47 Frank, *Capitalism and Underdevelopment* at 10–12, 273; Samir Amin, *10 The Journal of Modern African Studies* (1972) 503–524.
48 Immanual Wallerstein, (Academic Press, 1974) at chapter 5.
49 Richard Higgott, (Palgrave Macmillan, London: 1986) at 286.
50 2016 UNICEF-World Bank
51 In a recent article, Leonard Wantchekon surveyed the performance of 141 countries over a period of four decades and found the presence of natural resources as having a direct correlation with an increase in the incidence of bad governance and national misery. Leonard Wantchekon, *2 Journal of African Finance and Economic Development* (2002) 57–77.
52 Richard M. Auty, (Routledge, 1993); Jeffrey D. Sachs & Andrew M. Warner, (Working Paper No. 5398, National Bureau of Economic Research: 1995); Jeffrey D. Sachs & Andrew M. Warner. *59 Journal of Development Economics* (1999) 43–76.
53 Michael Klare, (Macmillan, London/New York: 2001) at 196. [*Emphasis mildly added*].
54 Joseph Stiglitz, "We Can Now Cure Dutch Disease" *The Guardian*, of 18 August 2004.
55 Leif Wenar, (Oxford University Press, 2015); Leif Wenar, *36 Philosophy & Public Affairs* (2008).
56 Wenar, 'Property Rights and the Resource Curse' at 2.
57 Ibid at 8.
58 Article 1, International Covenant on Civil and Political Rights, *See*: Wenar, 'Property Rights and the Resource Curse' at 9.
59 Article 21 of the African Charter on Human and Peoples' Rights. *See*: Wenar, 'Property Rights and the Resource Curse' at 9.
60 Wenar, 'Property Rights and the Resource Curse' at 9.
61 Wenar, 'Property Rights and the Resource Curse' at 9.
62 Ibid at 12–13.
63 Thomas W. Pogge, (Polity Press, 2008); Thomas W. Pogge. *19 Ethics & International Affairs* (2005) 1–7.
64 William Blackstone, (University of Chicago Press, 1979) at 2. Cf: Kenneth J. Vandevelde, *29 Buffalo Law Review* (1980) at 325.
65 Vandevelde, 'The New Property of the Nineteenth Century' at 331.
66 Vandevelde, 'The New Property of the Nineteenth Century' at 331.
67 Paul Thomas, *84 Representations* (2003) at 31.
68 Francisco de Vitoria, (Cambridge University Press, 1991) at 280. Cf: Andrew Fitzmaurice, (Cambridge University Press, 2014) at 57.
69 Fitzmaurice, *Sovereignty, Property and Empire* at 365–366.
70 Articles 34 & 35 of the General Act of the Berlin Conference.
71 Fitzmaurice, 'Liberalism and Empire in Nineteenth-Century International Law' at 124.
72 Luigi Nuzzo, "Territory, Sovereignty, and the Construction of the Colonial Space", In: Martti Koskenniemi, Walter Rech, & Manuel Jiménez Fonseca (eds.), (Oxford University Press, 2017) at 278.
73 Fitzmaurice, *Sovereignty, Property and Empire* at 279.
74 Ibid at chapter 10.
75 Jörg Fisch, "Africa as Terra Nullius" at 356.
76 Fitzmaurice, *Sovereignty, Property and Empire* at 331.

77 John Gingell, Adrian Little, & Christopher Winch, (Routledge, 2003) at 65.
78 Urmila Sharma & S.K. Sharma, (Atlantic Publishers, 2006) at 440.
79 All references to both the First and Second Treatises are culled from: John Locke, *Two Treatises of Government: A Critical Edition*, Peter Laslett (ed.); (Cambridge University Press, 1960).
80 Robert Filmer, (Cambridge University Press, 1991).
81 Gingell, Little & Winch, *Modern Political Thought* at 66.
82 John Locke, (Cambridge University Press, 1960) at 120–128.
83 According to Locke, "An individual seeks out and is willing to join in society with others, who are already united, or have a mind to unite, for the mutual preservation of their lives, liberties, and estates, which I call by the general name, property." (Locke, *Second Treatise of Government* at 46).
84 Locke, *Second Treatise of Government* at 127.
85 Ibid at 168.
86 Ibid at 169–170.
87 Ibid at 26–29.
88 Ibid at 6–8.
89 Ibid at 4–5.
90 Ibid at 3, 6.
91 Ibid at 26.
92 Ibid at 27–28.
93 Ibid at 26.
94 Ibid at 32.
95 Ibid at 36.
96 Ibid at 45–46.
97 Ibid at 300.
98 Ibid at 33–34.
99 Immanuel Kant, (Cambridge University Press, 1991) at 106.
100 Adam Smith, (Liberty Classics, 1981) at chapter 1; David Ricardo, (John Murray, 1817) at chapter 7.
101 Fitzmaurice, *Sovereignty, Property and Empire* at 4.
102 Forji, 'Book Review: The Oxford Handbook' at 90; Bardo Fassbender & Anne Peters & Daniel Högger (eds.), (Oxford University Press, 2012).
103 Phil Gasper, *49 International Socialist Review* (2006) at 3.
A Marxist is any scholar who subscribes to the usage of *dialectical materialism* in examining social relations in the international society. *See*: Harry C. Meserve, *1 Ufahamu: A Journal of African Studies* (1970) at 52.
104 Marx, *Capital: Critique of Political Economy* at 35.
105 David Mclellan (ed.), (Oxford University Press, 2000) at 424–425. Cf: Marks, "Introduction" in *International Law on the Left* at 2.
106 Gerald A Cohen, (Oxford University Press, 1988) at 3.
107 Barbara Stark, *42 George Washington International Law Review* (2011) at 197.
108 Karl Marx & Friedrich Engels, (Progress Publishers, 1976) at 38.
109 Gerald A. Cohen, (Oxford University Press, 1988) at 14.
110 Andrew Vincent, *20 Journal of Law and Society* (1993) at 373.
111 B.S. Chimni, *International Law and World Order*.
112 Chimni, *International Law and World Order*, chapter 7, at 440–550.
113 Bill Bowring, *2 Soundings* (1996) 213–224.
114 Bill Bowring, (Routledge-Cavendish, 2008).
115 Susan Marks, (Oxford University Press, 2000).
116 Bowring, *Degradation of the International Legal Order* at 3.
117 Ibid at 38–42.
118 China Miéville, (Brill, 2005).

119 Ibid at 319.
120 Susan Marks, (Cambridge University Press, 2008); Miéville, *Between Equal Rights* at 62.
121 Chimni, 'Capitalism, Imperialism, and International Law' at 18.
122 Okafor, 'Newness, Imperialism, and International Legal Reform' at 176.
123 Ibid at 177.
124 Chimni, *International Law and World Order* at 27.
125 Anghie, *Imperialism, Sovereignty and the Making of International Law* at 3, 197.
126 Antony Anghie, *27 Third World Quarterly* (2006) at 742.

References

African Charter on Human and Peoples' Rights, of 27 June 1981 (Adopted 27 June 1981, OAU Doc. CAB/LEG/67/3 rev. 5, 21 I.L.M. 58 (1982), entered into force 21 October 1986).
Alexandrowicz, Charles H.: *An Introduction to the History of the Law of Nations in the East Indies:16th, 17th and 18th Centuries* (Clarendon Press, Oxford: 1967).
Amin, Samir: 'Accumulation and Development: A Theoretical Model' *1 Review of African Political Economy* (1974) 9–26.
———: 'L'Accumulation à L'Echelle Mondiale' *Editions Anthropos* (1970).
———: 'Underdevelopment and Dependence in Black Africa—Origins and Contemporary Forms' *10 The Journal of Modern African Studies* (1972) 503–524. (Republished in: *9 Journal of Peace Research* (1972) 105–120).
Anand, Ram Prakash: *International Law and the Developing Countries: Confrontation or Cooperation?* (Martinus Nijhoff Publishers, Dordrecht: 1987).
———: 'Role of the "New" Asian-African Countries in the Present International Legal Order' *56 American Journal of International Law* (1962) 383–406.
Anghie, Anthony: *Imperialism, Sovereignty and the Making of International Law* (Cambridge University Press, Cambridge: 2005).
———: 'The Evolution of International Law: Colonial and Postcolonial Realities' *27 Third World Quarterly* (2006) 739–753.
Auty, M.: *Richard: Sustaining Development in Resource Economies: The Resource Curse Thesis* (Routledge, London/New York: 1993).
Baran, Paul: *The Political Economy of Growth* (Penguin, Harmondsworth: 1973).
Baxi, Upendra: *Marx, Law, and Justice* (N.M. Tripathi, New Delhi: 1993).
Blackstone, William: *Commentaries on the Laws of England* (University of Chicago Press, Chicago: 1979).
Bowring, Bill: *Degradation of the International Legal Order: The Rehabilitation of Law and the Possibility of Politics* (Routledge-Cavendish, Oxford: 2008).
———: 'Law and Injustice: Is There An Exist from the Post-Modern Maze?' *2 Soundings* (1996) 213–224.
Brower, Charles N. & Tepe, John B.: 'The Charter of Economic Rights and Duties of States: A Reflection or Rejection of International Law?' *9 International Lawyer* (1975) 295–318.
Carty, Anthony: *Charter of the United Nations and Statute of the International Court of Justice* (United Nations Publications, San Francisco: 1945) at 1–2.
———: *Was Ireland Conquered? International Law and the Irish Question* (Pluto Press, London/Chicago: 1996).

Chimni, Bhupinder S.: 'Capitalism, Imperialism, and International Law in the Twenty-First Century' *14 Oregon Review of International Law* (2012) 17–46 at 17.

———: *International Law and World Order: A Critique of Contemporary Approaches* (Sage, New Delhi: 1993).

Cohen, Gerald A.: *History, Labour and Freedom: Themes from Marx* (Oxford University Press, Oxford: 1988).

Covenant on Civil and Political Rights, of 16 December 1966 (General Assembly resolution 2200A (XXI)). (n.d.).

Cullet, Phillippe: 'Differential Treatment in International Law: Towards a New Paradigm of Inter-State Relations' *10 European Journal of International Law* (1999) 549–582.

Falk, Richard: 'World Orders, Old and New' *98 Current History* (1999) 29–34.

Filmer, Robert: *Patriarcha and Other Writings*, Johann P. Sommerville (ed.) (Cambridge University Press, Cambridge: 1991).

Fisch, Jörg: 'Africa as *Terra Nullius*: The Berlin Conference and International Law' in Stig Forster, Wolfgang Mommsen & Ronald Robinson (eds.), *Bismark, Europe and Africa: The Berlin Africa Conference 1884–1885 and the Onset of the Partition* (Oxford University Press, Oxford: 1988) at 356.

Fitzmaurice, Andrew: *Sovereignty, Property and Empire 1500–2000* (Cambridge University Press, Cambridge: 2014).

Forji, Amin George: 'Book Review: *The Oxford Handbook of the History of International Law*, Bardo Fassbender, Anne Peters, Simone Peter & Daniel Högger (Editors)' *16 Journal of the History of International Law* (2014) 90–95.

Frank, Andre Gunder: *Critique and Anti-Critique: Essays on Dependence and Reformism* (Praeger, New York: 1984).

———: "The Development of Underdevelopment" in Andre Gunder Frank (ed.), *Latin America: Underdevelopment or Revolution* (Monthly Review Press, New York/London: 1969) 3–17.

Gasper, Phil: 'Classics of Marxism' *49 International Socialist Review* (2006) 1–10.

Gathii, James Thuo: 'Imperialism, Colonisation and International Law' *54 Buffalo Law Review* (2007) 1013–1066.

General Act of the Berlin Conference, of 26 February 1885, in Edward Hertslet, *The Map of Africa by Treaty* (HMSO, London: 1909).

Gingell, John, Little, Adrian & Winch, Christopher: *Modern Political Thought: A Reader* (Routledge, London/New York: 2003).

Higgott, Richard: "Africa and the New International Division of Labour" in John Ravenhill (ed.), *Africa in Economic Crisis* (Palgrave Macmillan, London: 1986) 286–306.

Horn, Norbert: 'Normative Problems of a New International Economic Order' 16 *Journal of World Trade Law* (1982) 338–351.

Judt, Tony: Goodbye to All That? *14 New York Review of Books* (2006) 88–92.

———: *Reappraisals: Reflections on the Forgotten Twentieth Century* (Vintage Books, London: 2008).

Kant, Immanuel: "Perpetual Peace: A Philosophical Sketch" in H. S. Reiss (ed.), *Kant: Political Writings* (Cambridge University Press, Cambridge: 1991).

Keynes, John Maynard: *The General Theory of Employment, Interest and Money*, first published 1936 (Atlantic Publishers, New Delhi: 2016).

Klare, Michael: *Resource Wars: The New Landscape of Global Conflict* (Macmillan, London/New York: 2001).

Koskenniemi, Martti, Rech, Walter & Fonseca, Manuel Jiménez: *International Law and Empire: Historical Explorations* (Oxford University Press, Oxford: 2017).
Levy, Marion J.: "Social Patterns (Structures) and Problems of Modernization" in Wilbert Moore & Robert M. Cook (eds.), *Readings on Social Change* (Prentice-Hall, Englewood Cliffs, New Jersey: 1967).
Locke, John: *Two Treatises of Government*, P. Laslett (ed.), (Cambridge University Press, Cambridge: 1998).
Marks, Susan: "Introduction" in Susan Marks (ed.), *International Law on the Left: Re-examining Marxist Legacies* (Cambridge University Press, Cambridge: 2008) 1–29.
———: *The Riddle of All Constitutions: International Law, Democracy, and the Critique of Ideology* (Oxford University Press, Oxford: 2000).
Marx, Karl & Engels, Friedrich: *The German Ideology* (Progress Publishers, Moscow: 1976).
McLellan, David: *Karl Marx: Selected Writings* (Oxford University Press, Oxford: 2000).
Meserve, Harry C.: 'The Teaching of African History: A Marxist View' *1 Ufahamu: A Journal of African Studies* (1970) 52–63.
Miéville, China: *Between Equal Rights: A Marxist Theory of International Law* (Brill, Leiden/Boston: 2005).
Nkrumah, Kwame: *Neo-Colonialism: The Last Stage of Imperialism* (Thomas Nelson & Sons, London: 1965).
Okafor, Obiora Chinedu: 'Newness, Imperialism, and International Legal Reform in Our Time: A TWAIL Perspective' *43 Osgoode Hall Law Journal* (2005) 171–192.
Pahuja, Sundhya: 'Decolonizing International Law: Development, Economic Growth and the Politics of Universality' *University of Melbourne Legal Studies Research Paper* (2011) 1–417.
Pogge, Thomas: 'World Poverty and Human Rights' *19 Ethics & International Affairs* (2005) 1–7.
———: *World Poverty and Human Rights: Cosmopolitan Responsibilities and Reforms* (Polity Press, Cambridge: 2002).
Ricardo, David: *On the Principles of Political Economy and Taxation* (John Murray, London: 1817).
Robinson, Joan: *"Introduction" to Rosa Luxemburg, The Accumulation of Capital* (Routledge & Kegan Paul, London: 1951).
Rodney, Walter: *How Europe Underveloped Africa*, Revised edition (Pambazuka Press, Cape Town/Dakar/Nairobi/Oxford: 2012).
Rostow, Walt Whitman: *Economic Progress* (Institut de Recherches Economiques et Sociales, Louvain: 1955).
———: *The Process of Economic Growth* (Oxford University Press, London: 1953).
———: *The Stages of Economic Growth: A Non-Communist Manifesto* (Cambridge University Press, Cambridge: 1960).
———: 'The Take-Off into Self Sustained Growth' *66 The Economic Journal* (1956) 25–48.
Sachs, Jeffrey D.: 'The Big Rush, Natural Resource Booms and Growth' *59 Journal of Development Economics* (1999) 43–76.
Sachs, Jeffrey D. & Warner, Andrew M.: *Natural Resource Abundance and Economic Growth* (Working Paper No. 5398, National Bureau of Economic Research: 1995).

Sartre, Jean-Paul: "La Mystification Néo-colonialiste" in 'le colonialisme est un système' *123 Les Temps Modernes* (March–April 1956) 1371–1386.
Sharma, Urmila & Sharma, S. K.: *Western Political Thought* (Atlantic Publishers, Washington: 2006).
Shaw, N. Malcolm: *International Law*, 4th edition (Cambridge University Press, Cambridge: 1997).
Smelser, Neil: *Toward a Theory of Modernization* (Basic Books, New York: 1964).
Smith, Adam: *An Inquiry into the Nature and Causes of the Wealth of Nations* (Liberty Classics, Indianapolis: 1981).
Sornarajah, M.: 'The Asian Perspective to International Law in the Age of Globalization' *5 Singapore Journal of International & Comparative Law* (2001) 284–313.
Stark, Barbara: 'What's Left?' *42 George Washington International Law Review* (2011) 191–215.
Stiglitz, Joseph: "We Can Now Cure Dutch Disease" *The Guardian*, of 18 August 2004. Available online: https://www8.gsb.columbia.edu/faculty/jstiglitz/sites/jstiglitz/files/We_Can_Now_Cure_Dutch_Disease.pdf. Last Accessed 10 November 2017.
Tipps, Dean C.: 'Modernization Theory and the Comparative Study of Societies: A Critical Perspective' *15 Comparative Studies in Society and History* (1973) 199–226.
Thomas, Paul: 'Property's Properties: From Hegel to Locke' *84 Representations* (2003) 30–43.
UNICEF-World Bank "Ending Extreme Poverty: A Focus on Children" Report. 2016. Available online: https://www.unicef.org/publications/index_92826.html?CID=POV_TT_Poverty_EN_EXT. Last Accessed 9 November 2017.
United Nations General Assembly Resolution 1514 (XV). 14 December 1960, *Declaration on the Granting of Independence to Colonial Countries and Peoples*, U.N. Doc. A/4684. (n.d.).
United Nations General Assembly Resolution 1541 (XV). 15 December 1960, *Principles Which Should Guide Members in Determining Whether or Not an Obligation Exists to Transmit the Information Called for under Article 73e of the Charter*, U.N. Doc. A/4684.
United Nations General Assembly Resolution 1803 (XVII). 14 December 1962, *Permanent Sovereignty Over natural Resources*, UNDoc A/Res/1803 (XVII).
United Nations General Assembly Resolution 3281 (XXIX). 12 December 1974, *Charter of Economic Rights and Duties of States*, UN. Doc. A/9631 (1974).
van der Linden, Mieke: *The Acquisition of Africa: The Nature of Nineteenth-Century International Law* (Wolf Legal Publishers, Oisterwijk: 2014).
Vandevelde, Kenneth J.: 'The New Property of the Nineteenth Century: The Development of the Modern Concept of Property' *29 Buffalo Law Review* (1980) 325–368.
Vincent, Andrew: 'Marx and Law' *20 Journal of Law and Society* (1993) 371–397.
Vitoria, Francisco de: "On the American Indians" in A. Pagden & J. Lawrance (eds.), *Vitoria: Political Writings* (Cambridge University Press, Cambridge: 1991) 231–292.
Wai, Zubairu: 'Wither African Development? A Preparatory for an African Alternative Reformulation of the Concept of Development' *32 Africa Development* (2007) 71–98.
Wallerstein, Immanuel: *The Modern World-System I: Capitalist Agriculture and the Origins of the European World-Economy in the Sixteenth Century, with a New Prologue* (University of California Press, California: 2011).

Wantchekon, Leonard: 'Why Do Resource Dependent Countries Have Authoritarian Governments?' *2 Journal of African Finance and Economic Development* (2002) 57–77.
Weeramantry, Christopher: *Law: The Threatened Peripheries* (Lake House, Colombo: 1984).
Wenar, Leif: *Blood Oil: Tyrants, Violence, and the Rules That Run the World* (Oxford University Press, Oxford: 2015).
———: 'Property Rights and the Resource Curse' *36 Philosophy & Public Affairs* (2008) 2–32.

2 From Latin America to Africa

Primitive Accumulation, the Modality of Sub-Saharan Africa's Incorporation into the World Order

2.1 Introduction

Beginning in the late 15th century, European powers, in an effort to enhance domestic growth and prosperity, steadily embarked on aggressive extraterritorial trade campaigns in non-European territories, setting the contours of their international relations during every century around specific capitalist modes of production. Driven by the necessity to dominate and appropriate natural resources from non-European territories, European colonisers frequently legitimated and justified their actions using various coercive manoeuvres. Inspired by Walter Benjamin's thesis on "law-making and law-preserving violence" (*rechtsetzende und rechtserhaltende Gewalt*) on the contradictory nature of legal violence,[1] one scholar has qualified the process by which European countries arrogated sovereignty over non-European societies during colonial times as having been driven by "capital-positing and capital-preserving violence."[2]

Informed by the vast body of literature on underdevelopment studies, this study notes that three major momentous schemes—borne out of European–non-European encounters—have since the 16th century propelled capital accumulation from infancy to maturity, culminating into a uniform world order. During watershed moments of capitalist expansion drives, international law frequently legitimated the privatisation and commodification of capitalist accumulation schemes by offering "authoritative vocabularies of private economic rights—namely private property rights, the right to trade, and the right to occupy," supposedly applicable to all nations.[3] International law tied this necessity to the idea of progress—the notion that backward societies just like regressive behaviours could be transformed by applying a set of superior progressive values—thus benefiting all of humankind.[4]

The imperativeness of a profitable mode of production and trade resulted to European powers devising three pivotal capitalist accumulation schemes: plantation capitalism (16th–18th centuries), industrial capitalism (19th century), and development capitalism (20th century and beyond),[5] coupled with a strong desire for a uniform body of law to govern international trade and labour relations. Perceived as the ultimate arbiter of the international society, this new discipline—termed at its genesis as the Law of Nations—steadily

DOI: 10.4324/9781003265740-2

legitimated European notions of trade and property rights as universal givens. Cutting across several centuries, the three pivotal schemes were respectively expressed and enforced through the evangelising, the civilising, and the modernisation missions. Although these missions clearly showed either explicit or implicit imperial undertakings, international law nonetheless habitually admonished each of them as humanitarian ventures—geared towards the improvement of human well-being as well as the uniting of all societies unto the family of nations.

2.2 From the Americas to Africa: Original Accumulation, Political Economy, and the Gentle Development of the Law of Nations

2.2.1 European–Latin American Encounter and Articulation of Rights over Natural Resources

This study, as afore-noted, perceives the resource curse phenomenon to be five centuries old. Not only has "might makes right" existed as a doctrine of international society ever since the conquest of the Americas, European and western imperialism over non-Europeans has long been the driving force behind property rights and international law doctrines. The "discovery" (so to speak) of the "new World" attracted imperialism to the American continents, principally because of the regions' immense richness in resources seen as vital for commerce, population resettlement, and burgeoning economic development. The 15th and 16th centuries were in fact decisive moments in the history of international relations for two crucial reasons: It inaugurated western colonialism, and it gave birth to the international society as we know today. The encounters between Europeans and American indigenous inhabitants subsequently sparked a genesis of legal rules for the regulation of interactions in the nascent global order. In direct contrast to the preceding epochs when the world was geographically fragmented along regional communities—living independent of each other for the most part—these two centuries on the other hand witnessed rigorous intensification of global trade routes as well as complex political and economic interactions, culminating into what has now evolved into a veritable intertwined international community.

The global champions of exploration—Portugal, Spain, England, Holland, and the Catholic Church, starting from the 15th century—habitually framed their voyages as discovery expeditions, based on the "doctrine of discovery."[6] The doctrine of discovery was more importantly invoked by international lawyers in order to facilitate the exploitation of non-Europeans' natural resources by European conquerors. Up until the 16th century, belligerence was common currency, and nations worldwide were almost exclusively constituted not by dialogue but rather through brute force—the strong ruling the weak, and victors annexing defeated lands after each war as a means of compensating their triumphs. In the absence of a definite international standard rule, such occupations generally lacked any concrete legitimacy even when occupied peoples swore allegiance to occupiers given that their relationship was grounded on duress. This study further illustrates in Chapter 3 how Iberian nations in order to accord their actions legality, profoundly relied on papal authority to validate their various claims to territory—the so-called "Papal donations". The pope as Christ's vicar was believed by Europeans in medieval times to be legally vested with universal dominion over the souls of all humankind. He could thus freely donate or transfer ownership of rights over land anywhere in the world as he found fit. This was an era when Europe was ruled by absolute monarchs, each professing to be exercising a divine mandate, thus accountable to no one else except God or his representative.

In *Imperialism, Sovereignty and the Making of International Law* (2004), Anthony Anghie deviated from two conventional absolutes often pinpointed to as the starting point of international law, namely: the conception of the Peace of Westphalia (1648), which ended the thirty years' war in Europe,[7] as signalling the origin of the nation state, the sovereignty doctrine, and the legitimation of interstate relations, on the one hand; and the general acknowledgement of Hugo Grotius as the father of international law on the other hand. To Anghie, it was the Spanish colonisation of the Americas and religious-legal teachings of jurist-theologian-Dominican scholars that legitimated relations of domination across societies belonging to different cultural systems (moulds), and inaugurated the discipline of international law.[8] Both in the volume and elsewhere, Anghie argued that Grotius's thesis owed an indebtedness to Francisco de Vitoria's two classic lectures, "*De Indis Noviter Inventis*"[9] and "*De Jure Bellis Hispanorum in Barbaros*,"[10]

> and to Vitoria's identification of certain fundamental theoretical issues confronting the discipline. Scholars still refer to the enduring significance of Vitoria's thinking on the law of war (Franck, 1995: 248) and on the rights of dependent peoples.[11]
>
> (Wright, 1930; Weeramantry, 1992: 78)

The international legal system that we have today has in fact been traced by contemporary publicists to the much-heralded voyage of the Italian (Genoese) explorer Christopher Columbus to the Americas in 1492. Working under the auspices of the Spanish Catholic monarchs, Columbus and his crew, inspired by the earlier exploits and successes of the explorer Marco Polo[12] and seeking to re-enact a similar journey to the East Indies by sailing westward (rather than eastward, as was the trend)—instead found themselves in the Americas. Right from the outset, the mission which the Spanish Crown assigned to Columbus and his fleet— *La Pinta, La Niña y La Santa María*—was economic in orientation: to locate new tradable commodities overseas that could yield surpluses to the kingdom, thereby guaranteeing growth and advancement.[13] It was a drive aimed at expanding domestic production and exchange—at unravelling the direct source of highly priced foreign resources as well as grabbing the fabulous fortunes of the East on behalf of the Spanish monarchy. These economic treasures were in return expected to trigger colossal personal and national political grandeur.[14]

Determined to give his assignment the most seriousness that it deserved, Columbus did not miss any opportunity to construct his presence on the American continent strictly in terms of modalities of exploitation of the newly found natural resources, and the immense benefit that their exploitation could bring to the Spanish Crown. Erroneously believing that he had sailed to the East Indies as intended, Columbus on 4 March 1493, in "Letter to the Sovereigns Announcing the Discovery," happily reported back to the Spanish Catholic monarchs proclaiming mission accomplished—that he had as planned captured, in their name, several rich islands overflowing with abundant natural resources. His description of the people of these islands was even more sarcastic. Most of the places he visited, he proclaimed, were densely populated; the tribes were wild, and many practiced cannibalism; hamlets of one tribe known as Faba were all born with a tail; and inhabitants of all the various islands were heathens who had no government, and he seriously doubted whether or not they had private property rights. Columbus, one observer has noted, had hoped "he might acquire riches, fame and honour becoming a Viceroy and Governor-General, taking rank amongst the mightiest of the earth."[15]

As one scholar has noted, "once Columbus landed in the New World ... he praised God and inquired urgently after gold."[16] Upon noticing that the land was overly rich in untold natural resources, the mission swiftly delved into the necessity to exploit and extract the newly found wealth. From the sighting of the new vast land, abundant gold minerals, and myriad natural resources, the Spanish conquerors (*conquistadores*) wasted no time in picturing the Spanish Crown instantly transitioning into a giant amongst global powers, most especially through the extraterritorial extension of the kingdom's political sphere of influence into the Americas, new lands for population resettlement, a new vast market, new opportunity to spread Christianity, etc.[17] For this vision to materialise, the *conquistadores* imperatively needed to establish the grounds according to which they could possibly have a better legal entitlement over the local inhabitants to the lands and its natural resources. Interested European academics addressed this problematic by variously articulating doctrines of trade and private property that construed rights based on levels of advancement and capacity to exploit natural surroundings for productive or positive purposes—so to speak.

For the jurist-theologian Francisco de Vitoria, the encounter between Spaniards and Amerindians presented an opportunity for bilateral trade—a commercial exchange whereupon both parties could be beneficiaries—with Europeans trading their textiles, fabrics, and other goods for Latin American gold and silver.[18] Although Vitoria—informed by his theologian calling, was opposed to unequal exchanges, he nevertheless favoured profits derived from commerce. To him, profits in addition to serving as appropriate compensation for commercial exchanges were also the best incentive for trade expansion and growth.[19] Having based his canon on commercial reciprocity, Vitoria then perceived the sanctity of the right to trade as a fulfilment of natural law—an imperative for progress—whereupon different societies could share knowledge and collectively grow accordingly. As he put it, "the barbarians can no more prohibit Spaniards from carrying on trade with them, than Christians can prohibit other Christians from doing the same."[20]

In spite of Vitoria's abstract defence of trade reciprocity, an asymmetric gap between the Spaniards and the Amerindians was in practical terms constant between the two groups. While the Spaniards had the luxury of trading across the Atlantic amongst fellow European, Asian, and African communities—and had concrete knowledge of the immense value of gold and silver—Amerindians, on their part, were not predisposed with this *a priori* knowledge. The fierce resistance that Amerindians staged in the face of European incursion also testifies to their unwillingness to trade away commodities in their subsoils. While gold, silver, and other rich minerals in Latin America were highly valued amongst indigenous populations, they were for utterly different purposes and not destined for commerce as desired by Europeans. Gold was used in Aztec, Chocó, Incan, and Mayan societies, for instance, as an indispensable element when they performed ritual worships and made offerings to their gods.[21] This practice was variously interpreted by the *conquistadores* as a misuse of crucial precious natural resources and evidence of the inhabitants' inability to use the land's riches for productive purposes.

In the face of the Spaniard-Amerindian encounter, Spanish scholars and theologians articulated legal doctrines borrowed from *ius publicum Europaeum* antecedents that they projected as the Law of Nations based on their universal framings. Upon perceiving Latin American societies as backward entities that faced countless shortcomings, the Law of Nations sought to redeem the latter from impoverishment and stagnation by articulating canons of trade and property rights said to be the universal harbinger for advancement and progress. The said canons habitually assumed the character of coercion and steadily empowered the Spaniards to enforce hegemonic "just-war" doctrines across newly occupied lands. This right was not limited to Spain but further extended to other Europeans powers such as the Dutch, the English, the French, and the Portuguese, who followed in Spain's wane and carved out colonies for themselves across the Americas. From the standpoint of 16th-century publicists, theologians, and political economists, given that Europeans were perceived as having attained a satisfactory level of advancement, they imperatively owed the international society a natural duty to uplift backward peoples and guide them on the ways of progress. Juan Ginés de Sepúlveda (1490–1573), a Spanish philosopher, theologian, and early avid proponent of colonial slavery, constructed an intellectual imagery of Amerindians that showed them as animal-like and inferior to Europeans—lacking both rationality, Christian belief, and capability for self-rule. To him, they were "as inferior to the Spaniards as children are to adults, women are to men … and finally, I shall say, almost as monkeys are to men."[22] He further stated that in spite of their backwardness, Amerindians if properly guided were nevertheless capable of evolving into rational beings. To him, it was incumbent on Amerindians for their own benefits to submit themselves to Spanish authority and the Christian faith, and to dutifully mimic European values and standards:

> What could be more convenient to the barbarians than being subjugated to the imperium of those whose prudence, virtue and religion would transform them from barbarous, so that they barely deserved to be called human beings, to civilized men as far as they can be; from inept and libidinous, into truthful and honest, from impious and servants of the devil, into Christians and worshipers of the true God.[23]

In the face of such enormous backward deficiencies, Sepúlveda provided that any voluntary submission of indigenous populations to Spanish authority guaranteed their protection by the latter. By the same logic, he interpreted any potential resistance by Amerindians as tantamount to a defiant rejection of Christianity and human progress—synonymous to a declaration of war. Since the imperativeness of progress, improvement, and Christianity to Sepúlveda were sacrosanct, he provided that Spaniards were legally justified to wage a just war on resisting Amerindians—whereupon they were to assume the duty of evangelising to them and also teaching them higher values that could lead to their evolution.[24] In his chef-d'œuvre, *De Jure Belli ac Pacis* (*On the Law of War and Peace*), Hugo Grotius (1583–1645) concurred with Sepúlveda, noting that "the most just war is against savage beasts, the next against men who are like beasts."[25] While the stated aim of these pretentions was to improve the welfare and progress of Amerindians, in practical terms, the Spanish colonial administration enforced an *encomienda* system that supposedly extended the humanitarian benefits of protection and administration in exchange for compulsory labour for the Crown.[26]

In Chapter 3, this study expatiates on the manner in which the Spaniards in their pursuit for increased exports and profit maximisation overworked the Amerindians culminating to a drastic shrink in population. Not only were Amerindians dispossessed of their lands, they were legally also converted into servants and labourers for the extraction of natural resources on behalf of their colonisers. This technique became the defining method for engaging other non-European peoples into the international society. This was the case most especially with sub-Saharan Africa that was soon engaged through a uniquely transatlantic slave trade scheme, whose primary purpose was the supply of cheap labour—badly needed for mass extraction of natural resources and the development of the newly conquered colonies in the Americas.

2.2.2 Towards Primitive Accumulation: Intersection of Political Economy and the Law of Nations

Starting in the 16th century, capitalism—a peculiar economic system designed for the means of production to be privately owned and primarily geared at generating profits[27]—was heralded by Europeans as the best catalyst for the improvement of all societies. In fact, European political economists throughout the 16th, 17th, and 18th centuries assumed the role of framing what they perceived as the best doctrines for wealth creation and economic development for their motherlands, and by extension, supposedly, for the broader international society as well. Classical economists—the likes of the 16th- and 17th-century physiocrats such as François Quesnay (1694–1774) and Anne-Robert-Jacques Turgot (1727–1781)—were preoccupied with framing the best possible mode of production to improve the human condition and realise social evolution. Perceiving land and nature as the invaluable source of economic value, they highlighted the imperativeness of productive work as the inescapable modality for wealth creation and national growth.[28] Adam Smith and David Ricardo sturdily subscribed to the specialisation and division of labour as the essential driving force for increased productivity, gainful free trade and thus increment in the "wealth of nations."[29]

Inspired by Locke, Smith and Ricardo framed the capitalist mode of production not just as a free market economy but as the finest guarantor for liberty, growth, and progress in the international society. To Smith,

> the more improved any society is and the greater length the several means of supporting the inhabitants are carried, the greater will be the number of their laws and regulations necessary to maintain justice, and prevent infringements of the right to property.[30]

Locke's *Two Treatise on Government*—which had a pivotal bearing on both Smith and Ricardo, as afore-noted—was in effect a two-edged sword. In spite of its reputation as a foundational document on the doctrine of liberty, it was nevertheless ironically also a foundational instrument in defence of global dispossession. The volume's forceful justification of the sanctity of private property afforded later political economists a solid springboard for the articulation of doctrines of capital accumulation.

While classical political economists historicised private property in terms of personal property which ultimately led to growth, Karl Marx on his part turned the argument on its head by showing that the process of capital accumulation was marred by structural inclusion of few versus exclusion of the majority. The concept of private property to him accordingly encompassed all productive possessions that rendered a profit to its owner, such as slave ownership.[31] With this understanding, Marx thoroughly outlined the dual contradictions in the nature of capitalism, and the nature of class struggles in social relations. In the first volume of *Das Kapital* (1867), subtitled "Critique of Political Economy," Marx—while exploring the origins of uneven development in the international society—refused to buy into the political economists' conception of capitalist order as an equitable and just system. He found capitalism at its essence to be marred with a dual contradiction, namely: on one pole, he perceived it as generating mass profits for the capitalists; yet on the opposite pole, generating rampant untold poverty for the exploited class. By strongly deriding conventional ideals of political economy on liberty and growth, Marx was essentially unlocking what academics habitually term as the *Lockean Provisio*.[32] The *provisio*, so to speak, denotes the classical contention that formed the basis of Locke's *Two Treatises of Government*, namely, that everyone is entitled to the products and fruits of their labour. While the *provisio* at a quick glance seemed quite benevolent and just, Marx's analysis revealed that considering the manner in which the dynamics of capitalism were structured, the *provisio* was in a practical sense malevolent. Instead of the fruits of their labour, what the vast majority of peoples—the exploited class of the international society—typically reaped and experienced in social relations of production was exploitation and unfairness.

The question then becomes: how did benevolent global promises of everyone enjoying the by-products and fruits of their labour end up with extensive injustice and exploitation? A reading of *Das Kapital* suggests that it results from the structure of the dominant mode of production and accompanying legal system legitimating it. As Marx insinuated, although nominally entitled to the products and fruits of their labour, the global proletariats, deprived of private property, were routinely left with no other choice except to trade the only one thing they have left—their labour—to the capitalist for survival. As Marx put it:

> In times long gone by there were two sorts of people; one, the diligent, intelligent, and, above all, frugal elite; the other, lazy rascals, spending their substance, and more, in riotous living. The legend of theological original sin tells us certainly how man came to be condemned to eat his bread in the sweat of his brow; but the history of economic original sin reveals to us that there are people to whom this is by no means essential. Never mind! Thus it came to pass that the former sort accumulated wealth, and the latter sort had at last nothing to sell except their own skins. And from this original sin dates the poverty of the great majority that, despite all its labour, has up to now nothing to sell but itself, and the wealth of the few that increases constantly although they have long ceased to work. Such insipid childishness is every day preached to us in the defence of property.[33]

With the economic order structured to benefit the capitalist/bourgeois class, Marx introduced the concept of bloody legislation—according to which he explained that rampant injustice and unfairness were as a result of the laws being squarely implemented, and not because of the failure to enforce the laws.[34] The imbalances in the international system, he observed, unavoidably created uneven growth. Marx further observed that the disparity between the benefitting and exploited classes was bound to endure in perpetuity, as long as the capitalist mode of production was the defining commercial process.

In spite of their vast ideological disparities, both Smith and Marx nevertheless each constructed their arguments by adopting the same rational thinking, namely, revisiting the original scheme that brought about the initial global mode of production (*die sogennante ursprüngliche Akkumulation*), and by extension the international society, as we know it today. While Smith in his seminal book *The Wealth of Nations* (1776) briefly referred to this beginning process as original (or previous) accumulation,[35] Marx—referring to Smith—adopted the term "*ursprünglich*" (primitive accumulation), which for him was merely a literal German translation of Smith's concept. Although Smith's concept of "previous accumulation" and Marx's supposedly refined coinage "primitive accumulation" at face value seemed as two distinct notions, they in fact alluded to the same historical question, namely the source and causes of profits and income disparities in societies, on a micro level, and development versus underdevelopment amongst nations, on a macro level. Upon borrowing Smith's terminology, Marx's translation of "previous" into German as "*ursprünglich*"[36] in *Das Kapital* was subsequently erroneously reworded into English by academics as "primitive"—causing the two framings to endure as two separate notions.[37] Be that as it may, both thinkers perceived this original accumulation process as being the onset of division of labour and profits in trade relations. Their normative understanding notwithstanding, they nonetheless disagreed extensively on more fundamental questions, namely, the nature, impact and even purposes of the process.

Capital I dwelled on the process of capitalist production—the manner in which it evolved into the global dominant mode of production, as well as the relationship between labour and capital. Marx showed the nexus as paving the way for global uneven development, with the enrichment of a tiny bourgeois class to the detriment of the vast majority that inadvertently constituted the proletariats of the international society—with that gap expanding over the centuries. True to the spirit of the volume as a critique of political economy, Marx sarcastically framed the book's last chapter as "On So-Called primitive accumulation"—which was most probably his own unique way of alerting readers of his readiness to attack the rationale of the concept as spelt out by political economy. Put differently, he was not driven by a need to introduce a new concept as such, but was rather compelled by the need to challenge existing myths on the subject—thereby, in the process, establishing what he perceived as tangible truths about political economy (capitalism). The cynical framing in tandem served as a useful catalyst to categorically dismiss Smith's characterisation of liberty (distinct from true freedom from his perspective), the causes of profits, inequality, and global uneven development.

To Smith, the rift in the division of labour first occurred through a peaceful process whereupon workers who were more diligent accumulated an immense amount of wealth from their hard-earned efforts, thus leaving the lazy and less diligent workers to settle for minimum wages for their labour.[38] The "accumulation of stock," Smith contended, was the essential precondition for the division of labour, and by analogy the driving force for increase in productivity.[39]

To Smith, the entire process was driven by the free will, cooperation, and mutual consent of concerned participants—the so-called *laissez-faire*. Although Marx concurred with Smith on the claim of original accumulation as being the source of uneven growth and development, he nonetheless totally disagreed on the contention of the process having been borne out of peoples' free will. He observed that capitalist relations, and by analogy the body of laws regulating them at their core, were marred by violence, coercion, and by analogy—injustice: "capital comes dripping from head to toe, from every pore, with blood and dirt. ... [workers are] tortured by grotesquely terroristic laws in accepting the discipline necessary for the system of wage labour."[40]

2.2.3 Sub-Saharan Africa's Involvement: Primitive Accumulation as Original Driver of Resource Curse

While Smith's conception of original accumulation was quite uncritical of political economy as a system, Marx's deconstruction and analysis of a peculiar historical form of the concept—namely, how it manifested on a global scale—triggered an imperativeness for his contemporaries and beyond to relook at the overriding claim. While primitive accumulation on a world scale first saw the day in the Americas in the 16th century, and was then promptly extended unto sub-Saharan Africa through the Atlantic slave trade, it had nonetheless been prevalent across Europe since the Middle Ages thanks to a customary practice commonly referred to as *feudalism*.[41] Feudalism was characterised by theocratic aristocracy (monarchs who conquered and dominated nations and professed to have a sovereign divine mandate), the caste system (hereditary classes were commonplace, determined by one's birth) and the advent of the nation state (different peoples began clustering themselves under political entities).[42] Property relations were purely for profit motives. Marx in essence provided that primitive accumulation on a domestic and regional scale first originated from feudal exploitation in Europe, where a proletariat class was created; but it was then exported to the Americas, where it blossomed on a world scale. In an 1877 note to the editors of *Otechestvennlye Zapiskl* explaining his analysis of primitive accumulation, Marx provided that:

> The chapter on primitive accumulation does not pretend to do more than trace the path by which, in Western Europe, the capitalist order of economy emerged from the womb of the feudal order of economy. It therefore describes the historical movements which by divorcing the producers from their means of production converts them into wage-workers ... while it converts those who possess the means of production into capitalists ... Now what application to Russia could my critic make of this historical sketch? Only this: if Russia is tending to become a capitalist nation after the example of the West European countries ... she will not succeed without having first transformed a good part of her peasants into proletarians.[43]

For Marx, the concept of primitive accumulation represented both an economic, legal, and political system. With serfs tied to the lands under conditions of indentured servitude to landed owners and prevented from becoming property owners—thus preventing economic development—this stage began facing immense resistance at the close of the 15th century, after progressive forces staged political revolutions in different nation states, paving the way for European powers to begin looking extraterritorially for an alternative mode of production. With the conquest of the Americas in the 16th century, capitalism was borne as the preferred economic means of production, steadily spreading to the rest of the world.

Even as Marx variously termed Smith's conception of original accumulation as "childishness" and a reflection of a "mythical past" rather than reality, he nevertheless still did not completely shy away from the latter's account, but instead borrowed his terminology, and turned it over its head by assigning it with a contrasting theoretical meaning. Distinct from Smith's analysis that projected capital as stock, Marx emphasised that primitive accumulation from the onset was solidly grounded on capital as class relations.[44] Primitive accumulation was for Marx not just the initial process of global capitalist expansion, but more importantly, the roots of class separation, legal differentiation, and global uneven development.

Marxists generally take a cue from Marx by conceiving the starting point of unevenness in global development as stemming from the violent seizure and exploitation of other peoples' means of production and survival around the world and converting affected populations into peculiar labour roles—with the output mainly benefiting the privileged capitalist classes, the drivers of the mode of production. While the forcible seizure of lands from others has been recurrent throughout history and was certainly not unique to the 16th century, the structural dispossession of peoples' lands for commercial gain, which characterised the process of primitive accumulation, was nonetheless a notable historical novelty. Contrary to Smith's claim of a peaceful entente in the primitive accumulation process as well as beneficial gains in the international division of labour scheme, Marx—approaching the subject through the lenses of social division of labour inherent in the accumulation process—found that not only did the scheme necessitate the forcible redistribution of labour, but a conflict-free development of capitalism was moreover virtually impossible. Given that the process of primitive accumulation on a world scale was marred by "conquest, enslavement, robbery, murder, in short, force played the greatest part"[45]—that is, conditions that triggered the separation of the labouring populations from their long-standing means of existence—it accordingly also marked the highest stage of European imperialism and natural resource exploitation.

Having sparked the wheels of global exploitation of commodities and labour, primitive accumulation by so-doing effectively triggered the first manifestation of the resource curse phenomenon on a world scale. Immediately following the triggering of the process, regions of the globe which

Europeans perceived to be endowed with crucial resources and commodities necessary for economic development and progress[46] suddenly became the object of political economy treatises and legal doctrines, valorising discovery, conquest, trade (including the trade in humans), and property rights. The articulation of these doctrines engendered two specific resource curses that devastatingly afflicted non-European societies on either side of the Atlantic that had the most commercial contacts with Europeans during that epoch, namely: the Americas and sub-Saharan Africa. The said curses were based on two corollary set of extractive merchandises which European powers—heavily reliant on them for labour needs and economic advancement—suddenly perceived as constituting legitimate commodities in international trading, to wit: (a) inanimate natural resources; and (b) human capital, which basically signified human beings traded as chattel slaves. Between the 16th and 18th centuries, core debates in political economy and the Law of Nations centred on these elements, especially with regard to linking them to trade and property regimes.

The Law of Nations in the age of primitive accumulation (16th through the 18th centuries) was very agrarian in character—given that academics recurrently placed undue emphasis on the sanctity of trade and property—two complimentary engines of growth whose relevance depended on the need and ability to harness labour and exploit natural resources in distant lands. Seen as sacrosanct necessities, European extraterritorial colonial quests resulted in property law—hence international law, witnessing its most potent codification, perfection, and internationalisation.[47] In his epic geopolitical book *The Nomos of the Earth in the International Law of Jus Publicum Europaeum* (1950), Carl Schmitt, the German legal and political theorist, noted while digging into the origins of the Eurocentric global order that "the history of colonialism in its entirety is a spatially determined process of settlement in which order and orientation are combined. At this origin of land-appropriation law and order are one; where order and orientation coincide."[48]

The European colonial infrastructure in the New World and beyond was in fact an agricultural arrangement whereupon Amerindian lands became the object of discovery and exploitation, whereas imported Africans into their colonies were legally reduced into owned property (slaves) and cheap labour, indispensable for plantation (agricultural) production. Blackstone, just like Locke, conceived property as signifying advancement and improvement. To him, the best modality for the realisation of this vital goal was to "enclose" lands (plantation agriculture), in order to avoid wastage.[49] Plantation agriculture was a potent guarantee for mass production and huge profits, hence an effective way for a country to augment its gross domestic production and upset foreign balance of payments.

Blackstone strongly contended that all lands were *res nullius* when men first trod the earth.[50] While a picture of the world as *res nullius* clearly lacked any historical context, it nonetheless proved useful for appreciating property rights, and further for articulating a moral theory of occupation (wastage, enclosures, right to sojourn, trade, evangelise). The peoples to champion these noble causes were advanced peoples of Europe who were already schooled, enlightened, and nurtured in the ideas of progress.

Given that millions of Amerindians perished in their initial contacts with Europeans, as a result of the combination of the former's lack of immunity to European germs as well as violence inflicted on them by European conquerors, most Amerindian tribes were going extinct as a result; Europeans promptly ended all endeavours at further enslaving the remaining local populations. The measure was taken as a safeguard modality for preserving the survivals, who had shrunken into just a tiny fraction of the previously populated continents.[51] Still bent on the pursuit for wealth through the exploitation and extraction of the Americas' untold riches, the conquerors suddenly turned to sub-Saharan Africa for labour needs. Unlike Latin America, sub-Saharan Africa did not inhibit the factors that had resulted to Amerindian deaths. Trade between European merchants and sub-Saharan African societies especially along the coasts, though limited in scale, nonetheless dated as far back as Ancient times and continued unabated over the centuries. The sustained contacts enabled both peoples to develop natural immunity to one another's germs.[52] The tropical climate in Africa was moreover similar to that of Latin America and most North America environments. It was thus assumed that African labourers imported into the Americas were going to easily acclimatise and adapt to their new surroundings.

The transatlantic trade that European powers engineered in their pursuit for profits, and which lasted between the 16th and 19th centuries, has been projected as the largest historical scheme of forced migration across continents, accompanied by untold sufferings.[53] What began as a singular encounter between Europeans and Amerindians steadily led to global trade implications that were very devastating to the pattern and trajectory of not just the Americas, but Africa's economic development as well. While the massive extraction of sub-Saharan African labour in the Americas brought about transformative growth on behalf of the European colonisers, it severely altered production patterns amongst affected African societies—as the sub-region traded its most resourceful human capital for European articles of paltry values. Given that relations between European and societies on the opposite sides of the Atlantic were respectively based on the forceful appropriation of lands and the structural extraction of natural resources (in the cases of both South and North America) and export of human capital out of their habitats (in the case of Africa), ingredients which prior to the encounter were the bedrock of well-being and transformative growth, suddenly transitioned from obvious blessings into a curse for affected societies. The doctrinal justifications vindicating these acts were expressed through the agricultural argument (Section 2.3.3) and doctrines legitimating the imperativeness of the right of Europeans to enslave native Americans and sub-Saharan Africans most especially (Chapter 3).

2.2.4 Structural Violence: Accumulation by Dispossession, Continuity by Renewed Accumulation

Central to Marx's critique of political economy was his frustration with the discipline's blind grandstanding of *laissez-faire* claims and its supposed assumption of mutual benefits in capitalists' international relations. The supposed benefits of capitalism were expressed at the backdrop of complete failure in political economy discourse to account for the violence, expropriation, and forcible dispossession that characterised the creation and functioning of the capitalist global order.[54] Violence was the key enabling catalyst in

> the colonization of the Americas, along with the establishment of colonial enclaves and coastal trading posts in Africa and Asia, the mass extermination of non-European populations on several continents, the expropriation of peasants and the repression of the poor in the old world, the deportation of millions of Africans and their reduction to slavery, the bloody mercantile wars of the 17th and 18th centuries among Spain, Holland, England and France.[55]

Although Marx never articulated any normative theory of law, he nevertheless offered thorough comprehensive insights on the concept of justice and law, especially through his contentious critique of political economy. Having deconstructed the nature of alienation faced by exploited peoples in the framework of primitive accumulation, Marx concluded that both the political economists' canons of liberty, justice, and mutual benefits said to be derivatives of capitalism on one hand, and the global legal system as a whole on the other, collectively were false universals.[56] While jurists and political economists had long settled on the consensus that the institution of law was in place to safeguard the interests of all constituent members of the international society, Marx chose to differ with this overriding characterisation. He rather perceived the function of law as geared towards the representation, protection, and promotion of the interests of the colonising/dominating class to the detriment of colonised/dominated, exploited peoples. In his epic work *Between Equal Rights*, the Marxist legal scholar China Miéville contended that whereas contractual parties to capitalist labour in principle generally enter into social relations as two equals, in practice commodity exchanges between the juridical subjects stringently derive their basis from coercion.[57]

In the essay *On the Jewish Question* (1844),[58] Marx articulated a peculiar materialist conception of history. While criticising two earlier studies by the young Hegelian, Bruno Bauer, on the "*Rights of Man*," Marx confronted and addressed the question of what it means for a person to be free as a human—distinct from the illusory freedom advanced by political economy. In response, he distinguished between political emancipation and human emancipation. While political emancipation to Marx implied freedom as per the law or legal system, human emancipation meant being truly free as a human being. While political freedom offered humans essential guarantees (rights of man) such as provisions that all men are free and equal before the law, these guarantees were in a practical sense just formal, and political economists focused on these. Real freedom to him was human emancipation—the kind of freedom that the exploited of the world were deprived of; that is, freedom from alienation.[59] By framing law as a purely formal system, Marx was laying the claim that political emancipation is not true liberation but rather a stumbling block to real human emancipation. Despite claims of political freedoms, the concrete reality of social relations of labour in primitive accumulation for the vast majority of peoples necessitated not an enjoyment of human emancipation, but their bondage to the economic system.

While Marx borrowed the concept of *alienation* (*Entfremdung*) from Georg Wilhelm Friedrich Hegel (a term previously limited to religion), he proceeded to reframe it as a more objective modality for social justice in a human society.[60] He importantly retailored the concept to address the everyday experiences of workers in the age of colonisation. Having applied the concept of alienation to historical processes, Marx was able to reveal the plight of the working class in colonial encounters.[61] Marx, dismissive of the outlined benefits of division of labour in manufacturing and specialisation, qualified the conditions described by Smith and Ricardo as a form of alienation and un-freedom rather than redemption for the workers employed in capitalist peripheral productions. Having established a linear correlation between European colonisation in the 16th century and imperial quests in the 19th century (sparked by the nascent industrial revolution), he employed the theory of alienation[62] to exemplify the adversarial ways by which workers and affected societies were degraded and even dehumanised as soon as the division of labour was stimulated. For Marx, one could not talk of human progress except in terms of human dignity. Whereas the classical Roman term *dignitas hominis* historically signified inherent natural rights that all persons were logically entitled to just by virtue of being humans, Marx observed that this consideration was frequently waved aside wherever it conflicted with imperial quest for natural resources and growth. The dignity of the worker, he contended, could only be appreciated if economic processes allowed "autonomy, responsibility, and self-fulfillment"[63]—that is, conditions necessary for workers to truly realise the fruits of their labour.

Sixteenth-century capitalist relations were perceived by Marx as being driven by coercion and peculiar structural violence rather than liberty (human freedom), as evidenced by the "complete separation between the workers and the ownership of the conditions for the realisation of their labour."[64] In the words of one contemporary scholar, Marxian primitive accumulation model depicted the "historical process that gave birth to the preconditions of a capitalist mode of production."[65] The preconditions involved three crucial dimensions: (a) the creation of a dual class structure (the beneficiary class versus the exploited class), (b) rules of commodity trading, and (c) the accumulation of profits by the capitalists. Stretching over several centuries, various capitalist accumulation schemes and processes inevitably steadily resulted in class separation, dispossession, and social disintegration.

While the resource endowments of the Americas attracted European imperialism into the "New World," the professed necessity to exploit, improve, and develop acquired lands compelled European powers to conceptualise doctrines that sought to spell out conditions whereupon private property could be derived, as well as delimit the contours of what could be deemed as constituting legitimate commodities in international trading. In the first instance, Amerindians were brutally dislodged from their lands, which was their principal means of economic production and subsistence, in order to pave the way for European-inspired enclosures (plantations). This scheme necessitated extensive land grabs. In the second instance, the drive for profits necessitated not just the exploitation of land but an imperativeness to extract their labour. While European powers eventually resolved against the enslavement of Amerindians, they promptly imported sub-Saharan African peoples, turned them into slaves, and brutally exploited them for all their labour needs. Not only were natural resources extracted and traded for profits, but African labourers, having been converted into merchandised chattel (property), were subjected to the same rules reserved for market exchange of goods. In fact, both labour relations and productivity in the "New World" were stringently organised around norms of exploitation and brute violence, regardless of whether the peoples enslaved were Amerindians or Africans.

Unlike political economists who framed the origins of private property in *laissez-faire* doctrines as spontaneous, Marx on his part countered and conceived it to be marred by sustained violence. Capital, he argued, engulfed the world "dripping from head to toe, from every pore, with blood and dirt."[66] He elaborated on the global application of original capital's structural violence thus:

> The discovery of gold and silver in America, the extirpation, enslavement and entombment in mines of the indigenous population of that continent, the beginnings of the conquest and plunder of India, and the conversion of Africa into a preserve for the commercial hunting of black skins, are all things which characterize the dawn of the era of capitalist production. These idyllic proceedings are the chief moments of primitive accumulation. Hard on their heels follows the commercial war of the European nations, which has the globe as its battlefield ... These different moments are systematically combined together at the end of the seventeenth century in England; the combination embraces the colonies, national debt, the modern tax system, and the system of protection. These methods depend in part on brute force, for instance the colonial system. But they all employ the power of the state, the concentrated and organized force of society, to hasten, as in a hothouse, the process of transformation of the feudal mode of production into the capitalist

> mode, and to shorten the transition. Violence is the midwife of every old society which is pregnant with a new one. It is itself an economic power.[67]

The contention of various dependency writers—that the colonisation of the Americas sparked the process of binary separation of the world into core and periphery—not only constitutes the centrepiece of Marxism, but has in fact now witnessed a heightened approval in other academic circles. Although the usage of the word "primitive" in describing original accumulation typically points to a distant past, the Marxian conception of the concept on a global scale not only presents readers with a historical argument but a continuity one as well. In critiquing political economy, Marx, unlike Smith, limited his conception of original accumulation not to a static moment, but rather to the structural manifestation of the concept. While primitive accumulation depicted a peculiar origin, the manifestation of the process revealed that it was an incessant process that recurrently reproduced itself in different epochs through different economic exigencies in vogue and drives for profit maximisation. While highlighting the nexus between historical colonial jurisprudence and structural violence, Patrick Wolfe forcefully noted that "invasion is a structure, not an event."[68] The structural process that sparked off the initial accumulation process was indeed not only continuous since inception but steadily blossomed into the world order as we know it today, albeit through different defining schemes, which frequently necessitated the perpetual subornation of South (periphery) to the North (core) of the world economy.[69] The world order stemmed from "one single and continuous process of capital accumulation" which has existed for over five centuries.[70] Having resulted from a binary uneven world and sustained through structural violence, epic capitalist accumulation schemes have during varying epochs been manifestly tied to the causes of global poverty and deprivation.

Having dismissed Smith's fable of the origins of division of labour, Marx followed with his own allegory, whereupon he observed that primitive accumulation's role in political economy was as immense as that played by the classical primitive sin in theology.

> Adam bit the apple, and thereupon sin fell on the human race. Its origin is supposed to be explained when it is told as an anecdote about the past. Long, long ago there were two sorts of people: one, the diligent, intelligent and above all frugal elite; the other, lazy rascals, spending their substance, and more, in riotous living ... Thus it came to pass that the former sort accumulated wealth, and the latter sort finally had nothing to sell but their own skins. And from this primitive sin dates the poverty of the great majority who, despite all their labour, have up to now nothing to sell but themselves.[71]

Although shown to be the original form of imperialism, primitive accumulation was nevertheless most relevant to Marx in terms of its domino effect—that is, the nature of its reproduction and expansion—in different places and over different eras. Placed at opposite poles of capitalism, the periphery, unlike the core, endured a sustained period of stagnant growth, as its labour duties were tailored at satisfying the exigencies of the core rather than their own economies. Colonisation and capitalism were for Marx two birds of the same feather—whereupon categories of imperialism were profoundly embedded in capital—and capitalism in return was in essence the most classical form of colonisation. For legal Marxists such as Neocleous, Balibar,[72] and Miéville, the nexus was cemented through processes of categories of international law through law making and law reforms.

The aforementioned imperativeness of profit-making has historically conditioned the conceptual west[73] to devise three momentous capitalist modes of production schemes: plantation capitalism (16th–18th centuries), industrial capitalism (19th century), and development capitalism (20th century and beyond). Each of the schemes were conditioned by an abundance of specific natural resources in the peripheries of the world, and the imperativeness for their extraction in order to benefit the core. In two connecting works,: "Accumulation by Dispossession" (2003) and *A Brief History of Neoliberalism* (2005), the Marxist political scientist David Harvey introduced the term "accumulation by dispossession" as a modality for linking contemporary neoliberal capitalist policies with classical exploitative practices which Marx hitherto termed as primitive accumulation.

As primitive accumulation "entailed taking land, say, enclosing it, and expelling a resident population to create a landless proletariat, and then releasing the land into the privatized mainstream of capital accumulation," this ultimately resulted in the creation of a binary world order, with the peripheries of the world either fine-tuned or inadvertently disintegrating into various global schemes of accumulation by dispossession.[74] While primitive accumulation of the past was attained through common core evils: war, violence, enslavement, and colonialism, the western contemporary practices and doctrines on "privatization, financialization, management and manipulation of crises, and state redistributions" to Harvey were the contemporary techniques of "accumulation by dispossession" of the global peripheries by the core.[75] Harvey conceived all forms of capitalism as primitive accumulation. While Harvey by the claim was certainly trying to show a linear connection throughout the history of capitalism, it nevertheless is a stretch to conceptualise capitalism as unalterable, given that capitalism—just like international law—has metamorphosed enormously since its origins—from mercantilist system, through industrial capitalism, unto development capitalism. Harvey is nevertheless correct in his contention that the wheels of accumulation that were sparked off by primitive accumulation are a permanent fixture of capitalism—namely, the subjugation of the peripheries of the world into an international division of labour, whereupon they are structurally confined into fulfilling the economic exigencies of the core countries.

Sub-Saharan Africa has been implicated in each of the aforementioned three watershed schemes. Collectively, the schemes are imperative in understanding global uneven development in historical terms. The human capital of the sub-region was abusively and coercively extracted through slave trade in the first scheme to fulfil Europeans' labour needs in the Americas, while correspondingly hampering the continents' growth trajectory. The second commercial scheme saw the day in the 19th century in the aftermath of the industrial revolution, when rivalries amongst European corporations degenerated into the proliferation of capitulation treaties between Europeans and African leaders, culminating to Europeans establishing sovereignty over Africans—when international law legitimated the process of protectorates[76] through a newly formed doctrine of "effective occupation." Informed by the stadial theory that was developed by the Scottish Enlightenment on transitional stages and steps that primitive and backward societies needed to take in order to reach an advanced commercial stage, 19th-century international lawyers cogently embarked on language of civilisation as a philanthropic duty which advanced countries needed to assume towards non-Europeans.

The third major scheme falls outside the scope of this study but deserves mentioning. It was inaugurated in the aftermath of the Second World War through the logic of development—which, in spite of its promises of economic redemption, nevertheless rather fortified the integration of sub-Saharan Africa into the global order in a very subordinate manner. The beginning of the era of development is traced to Harry Truman's inaugural address of 20 January 1949—whereupon he divided the world between developed and developing countries.[77] Having acknowledged the poverty and hardships of the underdeveloped parts of the world, Truman proposed a "fair deal" based on western science and technology as a remedy for helping the underdeveloped out of their predicament.[78] The third world's willing self-identification with the identity of "backwardness" permitted international law to introduce conditions of economic inequality through the framework of international institutions (Bretton Woods institutions, or BWI) over their sovereignty. The international society as a result became a "system of hierarchy without exclusion."[79]

While this present chapter is tailored on unmasking the general foundations of primitive accumulation on a global scale—hence the process of uneven development by analogy, Chapters 3 to 6 narrow down the discourse to the practical application of emanating capitalist accumulation schemes in sub-Saharan Africa and the historical implication for its economic development trajectory. The study, for the sake of specificity, is generally limited to the first two schemes—that is, the process of incorporation of sub-Saharan African into the Atlantic slave trade scheme, as well as the rationale for the colonisation of Africa following the industrial revolution in Europe. Collectively, the chapters underscore the manner in which sub-Saharan Africa unswervingly furnished vital sets of commodities necessary for European capitalist accumulation during eventful periods of international law—with the attendant consequence being its progression towards underdevelopment. With regard to the historical reproduction of primitive accumulation, the study observes that the aforementioned three watershed schemes inform us in at least two crucial ways of how to comprehend the process of underdevelopment in sub-Saharan Africa. First, they show that the curse of having resources is part and parcel of African history. The schemes moreover succinctly reveal that sub-Saharan African was incorporated and sustained into the global order as we know it today, in a very coercive and extractive manner.

2.3 On the Question of Old European Imperialism, International Law, and Capital Accumulation

2.3.1 The Making of Unequal Rights: Primitive Accumulation as International Law's Secret

Until the early 1990s, international law textbooks variously conceived the Peace of Westphalia (1648) as the beginnings of the nation state, the sovereignty doctrine, and the legitimation of interstate relations, as well as the general acknowledgement of Hugo Grotius as the father of international law. While placing strong emphasis on abstract legal and political relations—with focus on interstate acts, the Westphalian account of international law accordingly largely disregarded other subjects of the international society. Colonies, colonial relations, and colonised peoples were in fact largely missing from the equation, since colonies were conceived as legitimate provinces of European colonisers. Given that colonies from conception were not considered autonomous entities, the metropoles' administrative laws accordingly generally governed them. Noting that "Grotius transferred the notion of liberty-as-property to the state in international affairs, viewing the character of state boundaries as that of a private estate," China Miéville has insinuated that sovereign states, just like individual private property owners, generally interact amongst one another in the international society as property owners of their territories—having consolidated their power "in a context of increasing international interaction and conflict."[80] Colonies according to this frame were perceived and treated as legitimate proprietary domains of the colonisers. The sovereigns accordingly treated one another as commodity owners when they conducted international trade.[81]

Thanks to a steady stream of new critical scholarships in international law (TWAIL especially), the questions of colonialism from previously being perceived as a marginal exception, has during the past three decades witnessed spectacular acceptance within mainstream international law. TWAIL's underlining conception of the origins and development of the Law of Nations as a by-product of colonialism's undercurrents coincides with Marxism's projection of colonialism as the defining global regulatory system. In *The Permanent Revolution* (1906), Leon Trotsky conceived of Marxism as taking its point of departure from world economy, "not as a sum of national parts but as a mighty and independent reality which has been created by the international division of labour and the world market, and which in our epoch imperiously."[82] This observation mirrors the similar contention by prominent TWAILers. Bent on the fervent commitment to the study of critical pasts, most especially on the origins of international relations and international legal doctrines, TWAIL and Marxist discourses coincide in direction and purpose. Advocates of both philosophies adhere to the supposition that imbedded within the genesis of political economy lies the crucial smoking gun to a better understanding of not just the character of the international society but the global order and international law as well. These analyses have become vital especially in the past three decades, in underscoring the quest for natural resources as the natural driver for the making, reforming, and deforming rules and regulations in international society.

While the overriding consensus amongst TWAILers and Marxists is fixated on the 16th century as the starting point of the global order as we know it today, the two schools of thought arrive at that juncture from opposite pathways. In spite of the fact that primitive accumulation was central to Marx's critique of political economy, its examination or even mention has ironically been almost non-existent in legal writings, including those championed by TWAILers. The impassiveness of international lawyers on the subject, or accumulation of any sort, is somewhat surprising, given that Marxists typically invoke the concept of primitive accumulation to highlight such questions as the sanctity of legitimate violence or the legality of the use of force, property rights doctrines, the politics of dispossession, gross human rights violations, etc.—all of which are core issues naturally front and centre in mainstream international legal discourse. In the footsteps of Marx, Marxists habitually perceive the history of all forms of capital accumulation as variously marred by the prevalence of the use of coercion and violence in separating peoples from their means of subsistence (natural resources), whereupon they are compelled into schemes of international division of labour. This framing accordingly presupposes capital accumulation at the epicentre of the logic of colonisation. Having identified the colonial encounter as the pivotal starting point of international law, one would have expected this recognition to naturally trigger TWAIlers to correspondingly delve into a closer examination of the historical processes of capital accumulation.

The lack of attention by international lawyers on the question of primitive accumulation has been explained as due to the prevalent but erroneous assumption amongst most jurists, to the effect that Marx was not overly concerned with the question of colonialism. In the article "International Law as Primitive Accumulation; Or the Secret of Systematic Colonization" (2012), Mark Neocleous stood out as a leading voice clamouring for international lawyers to incorporate the language of primitive accumulation into the corpus of international law. While lamenting on the disinterest of international law on the subject, he nevertheless perceived the misapprehension of jurists variously as an honest mistake, and as somewhat of a misreading of *Das Kapital*.[83] To that effect, he deduced that misapprehension as largely stemming from Marx's general unconventional style of writing, most especially in *Das Kapital*, rather than deliberate omission. Neocleous's allusion certainly pertains to the prevailing consensus amongst both proponents and critics of Marx who contend that although Marx was evidently one of the most prolific thinkers of his time, he nonetheless was far from being an organised writer. It is common knowledge that he needed the collaboration and thorough editorial touch of Friedrich Engels (1820–1895), a German philosopher, journalist, and activist who became his self-made confidante, in order to put most of his manuscripts together.[84] Even so, Marx's magnum opus, *Das Kapital*, in spite of its monumental significance, is in fact neither easily readable nor a conventional text whose core elements can be straightforwardly decoded. Neocleous has noted that jurists as a consequence frequently either eluded one key underlining argument in the text—namely, the centrality of primitive accumulation in social relations of capital and law-making—or interpret the concept rather as an appendix.

The indifference of publicists notwithstanding, Neocleous conceives the entire first volume of *Das Kapital* as principally triggered by the question of primitive accumulation, and colonialism by analogy. He further observes that Marx, true to his character as a disorganised writer, completely failed to explicitly emphasise this fact, right until the very last chapter of *Das Kapital*. Even then, the central claim was not explicitly expressed until the very last paragraph of the chapter—where he highlighted the concept of primitive accumulation as capitalism's true secret. Naturally, many readers tend to have built a strong opinion on a book before the last chapter—with the end of the book, for that matter, frequently seen by many as a resume or an appendix to the arguments already raised. The last paragraph in question reads thus:

> However, we are not concerned here with the condition of the colonies. The only thing that interests us is the secret discovered in the New World by the political economy of the Old World, and loudly proclaimed by it: that the capitalist mode of production and accumulation, and therefore capitalist private property as well, have for their fundamental condition the annihilation of that private property which rests on the labour of the individual himself; in other words, the expropriation of the worker.[85]

For Marx, primitive accumulation was the defining yet hidden secret behind systematic colonialism and dispossessions around the globe. For the process of primitive accumulation to replicate itself on a global scale, colonisers necessarily needed to articulate a mode of production.[86] Different from previous systems, Europeans found out that mammoth wealth and profits could be generated through a system of "capitalist mode of production and accumulation, and therefore capitalist private property as well."[87] The system was characterised by the annihilation of private property which rested on the labour of individuals—in other words, "the expropriation of the workers."[88] It is within processes of capital accumulation that the core and peripheries of the world system were created. The management of labour on a world scale reveals the manipulative nature of the international division of labour, whereupon peripheries of the world system are exploited through various capitalist accumulation schemes in order to benefit the core countries.

Neocleous read Marx's analysis approvingly and on his part contended that since primitive accumulation (and processes of capital accumulation in general) is the key vector for the fulfilment of global hegemonic ambitions—domination, exploration, and exploitation—it goes without saying that it is evidently part and parcel of international law.[89] Put differently, the secret of primitive accumulation embodies not only the core secret of capital, but also the hidden secret of international law. To Neocleous, *Das Kapital* is a classical book of secrets, with several minor secrets throughout the volume such as

> the "secret history" of the Roman Republic, the "secret purpose" of the Chinese assignats, the "secret foundations of Holland's wealth in capital," the "secret dungeons" on Celebes. The volume also emphasizes "the secret of the flourishing state of industry in Spain and Sicily under the rule of the Arabs," the "secret" of Henry VII's lack of success, the "secret of [bourgeois] 'sympathy' for widows, poor families and so on," [and] "the secret of the capitalists complaints about the laziness of the working people."[90]

While each of these secrets has ample historical and even legal relevance, it is the secret of capital accumulation which Neocleous, following the footsteps of Marx, perceives as most impactful to the plight of exploited peoples around the world. For Neocleous, in the absence of a vivid portrayal of social relations that enabled the accumulation of capital and international division of labour, international law is not only bound to be abstract and incomplete, but moreover set to miss the vital smoking gun and the missing link with realism. This is because it is through the lenses of primitive accumulation that Marx was able to reveal the systematic nature of imperialism and structural violence inherent in capitalism, and in so doing reveal the character of the international legal framework, by analogy.[91] Neocleous perceives Marx's usage of the term primitive accumulation as geared towards illustrating the original form of imperialism—which to him underlies the hidden secret of global capitalism, and by analogy, the concealed character of international law.[92] While the conditions in the colonies are depicted throughout *Das Kapital* as heinous, Marx is nonetheless less concerned with these, and instead invites readers to look at an even bigger picture—namely, the enabling framework—in other words, capital's secret. Capital's secret to Marx is hidden in its modality of making profits in the midst of alienation and exploitation of the masses—or, as he succinctly postulated, it is hidden under the interaction of commodities and how capital manages labour.[93]

Unlike other approaches, the examination of primitive accumulation is perceived as best suited for unveiling the class-based account of international law. Whereas mainstream international law scholarship focuses almost exclusively on the nation state, a class focus enables jurists to treat international law in connection with social relations, peoples, and their well-being.[94] Marx posited that social relations of capital were not only central to the legal form but also synonymous of the fiercest conflict in human relations, namely: class war. The history of capital accumulation schemes uncovers international division of labour as a class-based frame by design, whereupon peripheral countries of the international society are tailored to specialise in disadvantaged primary production processes, whereas core countries focus on industrial manufacturing and thereby reap most of the emanating surplus from international trade. By being so oblivious to the question of capital accumulation, international law is seen by some as having failed by analogy to adequately consider the problematic of economic violence in its analytical framework. Neocleous has in fact found a fervent proponent in China Miéville with regard to the logic of coercion being the driving force behind international law. Unlike Neocleous, the basis of the coercion argument for Miéville does not rest on international law habitually obscuring its connection with colonisation/imperialism. Fixated on the character of the discipline, he perceives the entire body polity of international law as colonial by nature (legal form as inherently imperial).[95] Deviating from Neocleous's approach, Miéville observed that the overprojection of the nexus between international law and colonisation as a relic of the past not only obscures contemporary forms of imperialism, but moreover undermines the fact that colonialism is inherently imbedded in the very nature of the discipline. To that effect, he has formulated the commodity form theory of law.

2.3.2 International Law as Bloody Legislation

Legal Marxists generally perceive the prevailing world order as Capitalist victor's justice.[96] While Marx generally shied away from directly discussing law, he nevertheless made a notable exception in Chapter 28 of *Capital I*, titled: "Bloody Legislation Against the Expropriated, from the End of the 15th Century. Forcing Down of Wages by Acts of Parliament"—wherein he perceived the instrument of law as the modality by which Europeans beginning in the late 15th century relied on in order not only to dispose lands and natural resources from the populace, but moreover to discipline subjugated peoples into both free (slavery) and wage (industrial) labour. These actions were for the attendant purpose of individually expanding capital accumulation exigencies. To Marx, dispossession of peoples of their lands and natural resources on their own was not enough to create the proletariat, given that many disposed persons would have naturally preferred crime and vagabondage rather than submit themselves to the misery of exploitative wage labour. Capitalists imperatively needed the backing of the state apparatus and legal infrastructure in order to legitimate actions of their appropriations, compel the populace into labour relations, as well as to protect acquisitions against all threats.[97] Marx variously qualified these legal tactics as "police methods" and "bloody legislations." Bloody legislation to him symbolised the threefold functions that law was perceived to play in social relations both for the facilitation and regulation of unjust appropriations. It was Acts that outlawed vagabondage, wandering. and general offences.[98] Moreover, it involved Acts regulating enclosures whereupon laws were enacted for the sole purpose of separating peoples from their means of production (land, natural resources, etc).[99] Finally, the ultimate goal of instituting bloody legislation was to free the peasantry into either slavery or wage labour.[100]

Upholding the proposition that there could be no capital accumulation without separation[101] of peoples from means of production, Marx accordingly projected capitalist social relations not only to be inherently unjust and exploitative, but moreover as historically marred by three complimentary forms of theft, to wit: the theft of land, the theft of labour, and the theft of profits—all these processes being backed by legal force.[102] As a direct consequence, the act of forcible separation prompted a detachment between producers and their means of production as well as existence. Laws regulating capital accumulation were steadily perfected over the centuries for the sole purpose of capitalist development, and for inclusion versus exclusion into the surplus generated out of labour processes. In Chapter 27, titled "Expropriation of the Agricultural Population from the Land," Marx outlined the historical process that first created the proletariat in Europe. The process was driven by a series of parliamentary Acts and executive decrees that robbed the masses of the common lands, plunging many as a result into vagabondage, while at the same time converting and bestowing confiscated domains solely unto landowners as private property.[103] Given the violence involved in dispossessing the indigenous populations of their lands as well as the asymmetric imbalance in power relations vis-à-vis the European colonisers, international law as a consequence naturally took the form of bourgeois ideology.[104]

These confiscations of subjugated peoples' natural resources, coupled with the accompanying legal Acts, resulted to the worsening of social "circumstances of the lower ranks of men [being] altered in almost every respect for the worse," such as reducing them first into serfs and later into hired labourers, thereby necessitating a condition whereupon peoples freed into the proletariat imperatively needed to work as labourers for the landowners for basic subsistence.[105] Contrary to the classical political economists' routine observation of the process variously as peaceful and a free-will act, most affected peoples nevertheless did not enthusiastically engage in capitalist wage labour—at least, so long as they had an alternative.[106] For those peasants hesitant or unwilling to submit themselves to capitalist labour, various "terroristic laws" (bloody legislation) were passed in order to outlaw and punish all alternative means of support which they could rely on, such as: vagabondage, wandering, begging, and idleness: "agricultural people [were] first forcibly expropriated from the soil, driven from their homes, turned into vagabonds, and then whipped, branded, tortured by laws grotesquely terrible, into the discipline necessary for the wage system."[107]

While Marx used the English enclosures Acts as a classic case to illustrate the manifestation of bloody legislations in regulating property rights, he was nonetheless quick to note that the trend quickly spread throughout Europe in the first instance, and moreover on a more devastating scale across the colonies. In his 1853 newspaper column "The Future Results of British Rule in India," Marx observed that capitalism, despite its European origins, has always acted as a global system amongst nations: "the profound hypocrisy and inherent barbarism of bourgeois civilization lies unveiled before our eyes, moving from its home, where it assumes respectable form, to the colonies, where it goes naked."[108] Upon annexing the Americas, a replica system of universal primitive accumulation as already observed, was not only started but perfected between the 16th and 19th centuries through doctrines of private property, which were by analogy crystallised into norms of international law. As a global system, rules regulating capital accumulation quickly shaped international relations and assumed the guise of universal doctrines. Meanwhile, the politics of enclosures were strictly formulated in defence of, and out of categories of, bourgeois ideology; the Law of Nations nonetheless approvingly embraced it, for it was perceived as exemplifying the idea of progress, namely, the imperativeness for improving all acquired lands whether at home or abroad, and by analogy for advancing the general welfare of peoples and humanity in general.

The imperativeness of avoiding wastage and improving uncultivated lands occupied a central place in the discourse of not just political economists but jurists as well. Prominent thinkers such as Locke and Blackstone perceived all uncultivated lands that were not enclosed as wasted. The ownership and control of natural resources by backward peoples was accordingly perceived to be in contravention of the law of nature. It was incumbent, they argued, on advanced peoples of Europe who had the know-how to enclosed as much wasted lands in discoverable places as possible.[109] Having observed that the right to property symbolised the "sole and despotic dominion which one man claims and exercises over the external things of the world, in total exclusion of the right of any other individual in the universe," William Blackstone forged a nexus between imperialism and enclosures as corollaries of advancement and improvement, noting that "the lord of the manor may enclose so much of the waste as he pleases."[110] For classical international lawyers, enclosures indisputably represented on one hand a salient remedy against waste and non-productivity, and on the other hand, the most effective modality for engaging all humankind in trade and labour relations, hence progress for all.[111] The enclosures movement was re-enacted across the Americas through expansive plantation agriculture, whereupon property law doctrines were strictly tilted into legitimating the appropriation of lands and natural resources from indigenous populations, and the enslavement and extraction of free labour from millions of Africans that were imported into the Americas. Geared at a common direction and purpose, the pursuit of progress united the three categories of property regime, colonisation, and the Law of Nations into one common framework. In the following section, I illustrate that the debates on the subject—heavily reliant on the imperativeness of avoiding wastage and improving welfare—were expressed through what became known as the agricultural argument.

2.3.3 The Agricultural Argument, International Law and Triangular Trade

While articulating doctrines of private property, classical thinkers formulated concepts that justified the imperial acquisition of lands from so-called backward peoples, by peoples of advanced creed. While Vitoria defended the rights of local sovereigns over their lands, he nevertheless also afforded caveats. Based on his application of the *law ferae bestiae*, Spanish settlers could appropriate riches from those lands if they were left vacant. It is unclear from Vitoria's postulation whether he included lands of local sovereigns within the scope of the doctrine.[112] Several doctrines of agricultural arguments were advanced in defence of appropriation of American lands between the 16th and 18th centuries, Locke and Emer de Vattel offering some of the most poignant propositions.

The Lockean conception of property had several implications not just for general land usage and appropriation of lands in North America but also on narratives of labour, consumption, and economic growth. Despite his strong advocacy for individual ownership, Locke nevertheless favoured enclosures as a modality for fulfilling natural justice and for civil societies to attain greater advances. Observing that Amerindians, unlike Europeans, had no system of physical enclosures, Locke concluded that they were in effect still holding land as common property: "the wild Indian, who knows no enclosure, and is still a tenant in common."[113] This state of affairs, to him, posed two problems. Firstly, without clear-cut land demarcations and boundaries, Amerindians—although living in a state of nature—did not afford an enabling environment for private property and a civil government.[114] Secondly, as a result of common ownership of lands, and without the possibility to exercise private property claims, lands were not put into optimal productive use as there was no competitive zeal.[115] An enabling environment for private property was imperative for humans to transition from a state of nature into a civil society, where they could be creative with their labour and pursue the path of progress.[116]

In his defence of English colonisation in the New World, Locke provided that the best modality for productive land usage—hence economic growth—was the mode of production based on agriculture.[117] Agriculture—the practice of tilling, planting, harvesting, and increasing yields over lands—could sustain the livelihood and living expenses of the vast majority of the population than any other primitive activity.[118] Reproving the approaches of the Dutch and Spaniards who focused extensively on trade, Locke reportedly endorsed the English approach of balancing trade with plantation agriculture as more salient, given that England through that technique clearly outwitted its rivals:

"the English … have cleared and improved fifty plantations for one, and built as many houses for one the Spaniards have built."[119]

Locke, as afore-noted, also famously traced the origin of legitimate ownership of property to whoever mixes his labour with things.[120] The doctrine was very inspiring for Europeans who appropriated lands in the Americas and erected plantations, hence bringing development unto the lands. By setting up plantations or mining on the land, they were mixing their creativity and labour with the land. By the same consideration, Europeans who travelled long distances to the African continent with their brandy, powder, firearms, and other manufactured products (capital) could count on their effort as the labour that they mixed together in order to get Africans in the form of property. But Locke's concept is astutely problematic for its open-endedness, and for simplifying possession as equivalent to ownership (while seemingly overlooking how the possession was acquired in the first place). Since it can be acceptable to own people, what then becomes the limit to other things that one can own? Can one own the earth, sea, moon, sun, stars, other planets, etc?

The agricultural argument remained influential for over a century amongst academics, including scholars writing on the Law of Nations. In *The Law of Nations or the Principles of Natural Law*, originally published in French as *Le Droit des Gens* (1758), Vattel, having established that the American Indians failed in their natural duty to convert their lands into productive use, rejuvenated and expanded on Locke's contention, making the case as to why the appropriation of the Indian lands for the purpose of agriculture was justified. Considering that the human population was on constant growth, the Indian hunter-gathering practices were a disservice to progress.[121] In other words, failing to engage in agriculture, it was going to be impossible for humans to meet the exigencies of the growing human population.

Although Vattel recognised the sovereignty of American Indians over their lands, he nevertheless observed that their right was exclusive only if they exercised their right of use over the lands. Although land "is destined to furnish sustenance for its inhabitants, it cannot do this unless it be cultivated. Every Nation is therefore bound by the natural law to cultivate the land which has fallen to its share."[122] Given that nations had an inherent obligation to cultivate the earth, Vattel provided that where savage tribes took more land than they reasonably needed or were unwilling to cultivate, European nations that came to these "lands which the savages have no special need of and are making no present or continuous use of, they may lawfully take possession of them and establish colonies in them."[123]

Upon uncovering the massive agricultural potentials of the Americas, and having ascertained on the legitimacy of appropriating lands, Europeans found it imperative to employ all necessary means to meet necessary economic exigencies.[124] In a distant land where all alternative forms of labour were scarce or expensive, slavery emerged as the cheapest and most attractive modality to exploit the land, accumulate capital, enhance growth, and compete with rivals. To that effect, European powers steadily embarked on plantation agriculture not just as the modality for rendering their respective colonies economically profitable, but moreover for fulfilling God's purpose of progress for the earth.[125]

It was in the drive of fulfilling the imperativeness that host countries embarked on the transatlantic slave trade as a necessary scheme to supply the necessary labour for economic growth. This fact has been thoroughly examined by A. G. Hopkins, who in *An Economic History of West Africa* (1973) located the driving force of the transatlantic trade in the quest for cheap labour, given that all other alternative sources of labour were expensive at the time.[126] In the following sections, I show that following a disastrous trial with indigenous populations and their high mortality rates, European powers decided to concentrate on black Africans as their source of labour. Contrary to Hopkins's observation, Claude Meillassoux has countered and noted that delimiting the motives of the transatlantic trade to the quest for cheap labour undermines the corollary framework on which the slave trade was construed, sustained, and registered—namely, the power to construct ideology, frame notions of private property, and drive the ideology.[127]

Although the immediate impact of European annexations in the New World, based on the agricultural argument, was felt by the Amerindians, its consequences were nonetheless global and steadily culminated into the creation of a peculiar world economic order. Being the progenitors, most of the profits from the system would during the next four centuries be principally reaped by Europe, thanks to the latter's ability, as observed by Meillassoux, to set the rules of engagement. Besides the Americas, the continent most directly affected by the twist of events was sub-Saharan Africa, as Europe upon capturing the New World immediately engaged the former in slave trade; thus guaranteeing that it constantly supplied their colonies in the Americas with slave labour. Spain at the onset relied on American indigenous populations for slave labour. The imperativeness of African labour to capital accumulation and growth in the New World was apparent to merchants and policy makers. Having assessed all European commerce across the New World, especially in Mexico, Peru, South and Central Americas, William Fowler, a notable English merchant, concluded that "the best trade in those places is of negroes"[128]

During the next three centuries, the slave trade became the principal means of engagement between the four corners of the Atlantic (Africa, Europe, South America, and North America). With one continent assuming the role of a provider of labour and two others its principal recipient (some slaves were shipped to Europe, though in much smaller proportion compared with the New World), the transatlantic slave trade effectively set the pace for the emergence, fortification, and consolidation of contrasting paths of economic growth for different parts of the world, and by analogy creating global conditions of capital accumulation and underdevelopment. This is a phenomenon that Immanuel Wallerstein describes as development and underdevelopment.[129] The transatlantic slave trade over time became a major factor in stimulating increase in agricultural productivity, leading to agrarian revolution across Europe. African economy during the same period drastically slumped even as sub-Saharan Africa continued to play the role of the source of labour for the flourishing European and American economies. Europe's benefit from its control of international commerce was striking.

2.4 Concluding Remarks

The successful launch of primitive accumulation on a global scale by European powers, as previously noted, was characterised by their extraction of labour and the compelling of labour from colonised/enslaved non-Europeans. Professing to be filled with fervent desire to uplift humanity towards growth and improvement, European jurists and political economists promptly justified the emanating capitalist mode of production (which was marred by violence and exploitations of non-Europeans) as a fulfilment of natural law.

Except for the gold and silver found by the Spaniards in Latin America, the New World without Africa would have been much less valuable. It has been observed that prior to the importation of Africans into the New World as slaves, the lands were far less valuable in terms of capital returns.[130] In the aftermath of importing African slave labour, the New World not only instantly became commercially profitable, a vibrant economy and trading regime was begun which steadily expanded to link all the four corners of the Atlantic and beyond.[131] In spite of the intensity of the trade, classics of international law were nonetheless silent for the most part on its corrosive exploitation, atrocities, and human degradation. When they did express opinion, it was not directly on the Atlantic trade but frequently in relation to slavery (distinct from slave trade), natural law, and the fate of prisoners of war within Christendom.[132]

Chapter 3 confronts such questions as: Why did so many European publicists side with their motherlands in legitimating the violence and inhumanity of the transatlantic slave trade? Could it be that they considered the legality of the trade to be settled law based on the edicts of *Justinian's Institutes*, and ancient and medieval scholars such as Aristotle and Saint Thomas Aquinas? Was it a tacit recognition of the trade as illegal because of the trade's glaring cases of human atrocities, or were they simply conflicted to speak against it since it constituted a vital source of capital and growth for their respective fatherlands? How did they reconcile the contradictions of enslavement versus liberty and rights which formed the bulk of their intellectual pronouncements?

Notes

1 Walter Benjamin, (Harcourt Brace, 1978) at 283. To Benjamin, given that legal violence naturally perceives the ends as justifying the means, it correspondingly guarantees the state wielding it, both power and property rights.
2 Onur Ulas Ince, *46 Political Theory* (2018) 885–914.
3 Manuel Jiménez Fonseca, (Unigrafia, 2017) at 4–5.
4 See for instance, Emer de Vattel, (T & J. W. Johnson, 1844).

5 The pivotal epochs in question were shaped by epic economic revolutions, most notably in the 16th century following the European colonisation of the Americas, the industrial revolution in the 19th century and the international development project that dominated international relations in the post–World War II period. The revolutions in turn were sustained with renewed forms of capital accumulation. Anibal Quijano, Immanuel Wallerstein, and Antonio Barrera-Osorio, are amongst some of the many authors that have provided that Christopher Columbus's voyage to the Americas in 1492 launched the advent of the capitalist world economy and it quickly devolved into a uniform global process of economic development and international relations.
(Anibal Quijano and Immanuel Wallerstein, *134 International Journal of Social Science* (1992) 549–554; Antonio Barrera-Osorio, (University of Texas Press, 2006).
6 Friedrich August Freiherr von der Heydte, *29 AJIL* (1935) 448–471.
7 The thirty years' war was characterised by the struggle for "self-determination" in identity and government against the hegemonic power of the Holy Roman Empire, with the Westphalian peace (actually two separate treaties, Münster and Osnabrück) resolving the conflict by validating the state system and affirming the full juridical autonomy of every state in managing its own affairs. *See*: Stephen Lee, *27 California Western International Law Journal* (1997) at 241.
8 Anghie, *Imperialism, Sovereignty and the Making of International Law.*
9 On the Newly Discovered Indies.
10 Concerning the Law in Spain's Barbarian Wars.
11 Antony Anghie, (1996) at 321; Anghie, *Imperialism, Sovereignty and the Making of International Law* at 13.
12 Antonio Truyol y Serra, *3 University of Toledo Law Review* (1977) at 307–308.
13 *See generally*, John Cummins, (Weidenfeld and Nicolson, 1992).
14 Earl J. Hamilton, *27 Economica* (1929) at 345.
15 Margarita Zamara, (University of California Press, 1993) at 7–9; Cecile Jane (Ed.), (Dover Publications, 1988) at 17.
16 Angus Mackay, *Spain in the Middle Ages: From Frontier towards Empire 1350–1500* (McMillan, Hong Kong: 1977) at 173.
17 Tzvetan Todorov, (University of Oklahoma Press, 1999) at 8–10.
18 Francisco de Vitoria, (Cambridge University Press, 1991) at 282; Anghie, *Imperialism, Sovereignty and the Making of International Law* at 13–23.
19 Ileana Porras, *27 Leiden Journal of International Law* (2014) at 649.
20 Vitoria, "On the American Indians" at 280.
21 Mackay, *Spain in the* Middles Ages at 173; Caroline A. Williams, (Liverpool University Press, 2005) at 205–206.
22 Juan Ginés de Sepúlveda, (Fondo de Cultura Económica, México: 1941). Cf: Fonseca, *Civilizing Nature* at 113.
23 Ibid at 135.
24 Ibid at 135.
25 Hugo Grotius, (Clarendon Press, 1925) at 60.
26 Timothy J. Yeager, *55 The Journal of Economic History* (1995) at 843–844.
27 "In capitalist economies, land and produced means of production (the capital stock) are owned by private individuals or groups of private individuals organized as firms." Mariana V. Rosser & J. Barkley Rosser, (MIT Press, 2003) at 7.
28 Ronald L. Meek, (Cambridge University Press, 1976) at 174.
29 Smith, *An Inquiry into the Nature* at chapter 1; Ricardo, *On the Principles of Political Economy* at chapter 7.
30 Adam Smith, (Liberty Classics, 1978) at 35.
31 "From the standpoint of a higher economic form of society, private ownership of the globe by single individuals will appear quite as absurd (*abgeschmacht*) as private ownership of one man by another. Even a whole society, a nation, or even all

simultaneously existing societies taken together, are not the owners of the globe. They are only its possessors, its usufructuaries, and, like *boni patres familias*, they must hand it down in an improved condition." Karl Marx, (Progress Publishers, 1966) at 776.

32 Karl Marx, (International Publishers, 1967); A. John Simmons, (Princeton University Press, 1994) at 293.
33 Marx, *Capital: Critique of Political Economy* at 713–714.
34 Ibid at chapter 28.
35 According to Adam Smith, "the accumulation of stock must, in the nature of things, be previous to the division of labour." Adam Smith, (Liberty Classics, 1976) at 277.
36 Karl Marx & Friedrich Engels, (Progress Publishers, 1969–1973) at 740.
37 Michael Perelman, (Duke University Press, 2000) at 25.
38 Smith, *An Inquiry into the Nature* at 277–280.
39 Ibid at 277.
40 Marx, *Capital: Critique of Political Economy* at 899.
41 Immanuel Wallerstein, (University of California Press, 2011).
42 Hal Draper & Ernest Haberkern, (New York University Press, 2005) at 44.
43 Cf: Jairus Banaji, *3 Journal of Contemporary Asia* (1973) at 395.
44 Massimo De Angelis, *2 The Commoner* (2001) at 5. Adam Smith's construction that it was accumulation of stock that originally paved the way for division of labour is certainly at odds with the natural sequence of things in society. There has always been some degree of division of labour amongst most living species (for instance. humans, animals, birds, ants, and insects) whenever they settle in a fixed community. It is in the fulfilment of such assigned labour tasks that each organisms or every member assumes a specific purpose in the particular community.
45 Marx, *Capital: Critique of Political Economy* at 874.
46 In Chapter 3, this study notes that even prior to the Spanish encounter with Latin America in the 16th century, beginning in 1441, Portugal had made notable inroads into sub-Saharan Africa—where they captured some of the continent's inhabitants through raids and took them to Portugal as slaves. Perceiving the Portuguese aggression as a modality of bringing new souls unto Christianity, the Papacy, which at the time frowned heavily at paganism, blessed and vindicated the Portuguese actions through papal bull decrees, as fulfilments of both divine and natural law. The chapter further notes that rights which Portugal accrued as a consequence of the papal bulls paved the doctrinal base upon which Europeans could frame more refined trade and property rights regimes across Latin-America, in the 16th century and beyond. By and large, papal bulls steadily became a mechanism which its European beneficiaries (Portugal and Spain) exploited for the enslavement of non-European pagans in Africa and Latin America, and further for the supposedly "lawful" appropriation of their lands and other property rights. *See*: James Muldoon, (University of Pennsylvania Press, 1977) at chapter 1.
47 Neocleous, 'International Law as Primitive Accumulation' at 951.
48 Carl Schmitt, (Telos Press, 2003) at 81.
49 Blackstone, *Commentaries on the Laws of England* at 74.
50 Ibid at 251.
51 George Raudzens, (Brill, Leiden: 2001) at 31–39.
52 Alfred W. Crosby, (Praeger, 2003) at 96–106.
53 B. W. Higman, (Cambridge University Press, 2011) at 98–99; Martin A. Klein & Jan Hogendorn, (Duke University Press, 1992).
54 *See*: Michael Ignatieff, (Routledge & Kegan Paul, 1981) at 130–131.
55 Jean Batou, *79 Science & Society* (2015) at 16.
56 Marx essentially saw law as part of the problem, and not the solution to the injustice and exploitation faced by the global exploited class.

57 China Miéville, (Brill, 2005) at 8.
58 Karl Marx, (Norton & Company, 1978) at 26–46.
59 Mclellan (ed.), *Karl Marx: Selected Writings* at 88, 91–95, 110.
60 Karl Marx & Joseph O'Malley. (Cambridge University Press, 1977).
61 Marx & O'Malley. *Critique of Hegel's' Philosophy of Right*, chapters 1–4.
62 In *Economic and Philosophic Manuscripts of 1844*, Marx outlined four kinds of alienations that workers suffered from as a result of industrial production: alienation from their products, alienation from acts of production, alienation from their essence as human species, and alienation from fellow workers. See: Oliver Christ, *11 European Scientific Journal* (2015) at 551, 555–557.
63 E. G. West, *21 Oxford Economic Papers* (1969) at 1.
64 Marx, *Capital: Critique of Political Economy* at 874. [*Emphasis mildly added*].
65 Massimo De Angelis, *2 The Commoner* (2001) at 1.
66 Marx, *Capital: Critique of Political Economy* at 916.
67 Ibid at 915–916.
68 Patrick Wolfe, *8 Journal of Genocide Research*h (2006) at 388.
69 De Angelis, 'Marx and Primitive Accumulation' at 1.
70 Andre Gunder Frank, *2 Dialectical Anthropology* (1977) at 87.
71 Marx, *Capital: A Critique of Political Economy* at 873.
72 Étienne Balibar, *17 Historical Materialism* (2009) 99, at 109.
73 I use the term "conceptual west" to denote countries considered as Western which are not geographically located in the western world (such as Australia and Japan).
74 David Harvey, (Oxford University Press, 2003) at 146–150.
75 David Harvey, (Oxford University Press, 2005) at 145–146, 149. See Chapter 4 in general.
76 Oliver J. Lissitzyn, (Carnegie Endowment for International Peace, 1963) at 4–7.
77 Pahuja, *Decolonising International Law* at 3–4.
President Harry S. Truman, "Inaugural Address" (20 January 1949).
78 Natsu Taylor Saito, *6 Florida A & M University Law Review* (2010) at 7.
79 Onur Ulas Ince, (Edward Elgar, 2015) at 16.
80 Miéville, *Between Equal Rights* at 191; Miéville, "The Commodity Form Theory of International Law" at 96, 109,.
81 Miéville, *Between Equal Rights* at 191
82 Leon Trotsky, (Red Letter Press, 2010) at 160.
83 Mark Neocleous, *23 European Journal of International Law* (2012) 941–962.
84 Even though analysis of political economy became Marx's core conviction, he nevertheless got to it by chance, after an encounter with Friedrich Engels (1820–1895) in 1843, following the article "Outline of a Critique of Political Economy," which the latter submitted to *Deutsch-Französische Jahrbücher*—a Paris-based journal where Marx served as an editor. Bent on speaking realism to the world as it was, Marx soon borrowed the irresistible title as subtitle for his monumental work: *Das Kapital*. The two men not only became best friends, but increasingly relied on one another in their pursuit of justice for the global working classes. Engels not only supported Marx, who was unemployed during much of his later life, but moreover assumed the role of his confidante and unpaid editor.
See: Vincent, 'Marx and Law' at 393.
85 Marx, *Capital: A Critique of Political Economy* at 940.
86 Eugene Preobrazhensky, (Oxford University Press, 1965) at 1–6.
87 Marx, *Capital: A Critique of Political Economy* at 940.
88 Ibid
89 International law is an integral part of legitimating not just commodity relations but capitalism as a whole.
90 Neocleous, 'International Law as Primitive Accumulation' at 947.
91 Ibid at 946.

92 *See in general*: Neocleous, 'International Law as Primitive Accumulation' at 941–962.
93 Marx, *Capital: A Critique of Political Economy* at 280, 745–760, 940.
94 B. S. Chimni, *21 The European Journal of International Law* (2010) at 57–58.
95 Miéville, *Between Equal Rights*, at 169, 226.
96 *See*: Grietje Baars, (Oxford University Press, 2013) at 163–192.
97 Marx first outlined these concerns in *Debates on the Law of Thefts of Wood* (1842)—an essay which Marx published in five separate segments in *Rheinische Zeitung*—where he served as editor-in-chief. It was in this essay that Marx first articulated his first critique on the conception of private property. The essay explored the injustice faced by ordinary peoples in Germany during his time from the hands of land owners. Even though woods were privately owned, there was nonetheless a longstanding tradition over the centuries of ordinary peoples walking freely in the bushes and picking fallen logs for firewood and other basic needs. Irritated by these free riders, wood owners increasingly petitioned the state to stop this practice. The state responded by instituting laws protecting private property and barring ordinary peoples from further collecting fallen woods. While the state justified the law on theft of woods on grounds of safeguarding universal interest, Marx observed its enforcement of "universal" interest unfairly tilting in a particular manner. The law on theft of woods is in effect just an instance of how the bourgeois monopolise state apparatus in order to protect self-interests. What is dubbed as universal interest stems from the privatisation of the state by the bourgeois. In his words, "The wood thief has robbed the forest owner of the wood but the forest owner has made use of wood thief to purloin the state itself." While laws protecting private property formally seemed neutral, they had, practically speaking, been usurped by property owners to defend their self-interests. See: Karl Marx, (Lawrence and Wishart, 1975) at 262–263. From the foregoing, the populace are exploited at both ends by the capitalists. Not only are they not slowed to pick fallen woods in the lands of landowners, their own lands sooner or later are also subject to confiscations backed by law, thus compelling them to sacrifice their labour to the capitalists for survival.
98 Marx, *Capital: Critique of Political Economy* at 874–896.
99 Marx, *Grundrisse* (Penguin Books, 1993) at 87–88.
100 Marx, *Capital: Critique of Political Economy* at 874–896.
101 The German "*die Trennung*," translated into English as "Separation," is understood to generally imply exploitation of peoples.
102 Marx, *Capital: Critique of Political Economy* at chapter 28.
103 Ibid at chapter 27.
104 Neocleous, 'International Law as Primitive Accumulation' at 952.
105 Marx, *Capital: A Critique of Political Economy* at 885.
106 Perelman, *The Invention of Capitalism* at 2.
107 Marx, *Capital: A Critique of Political Economy* at 896–898.
108 Karl Marx, *The New York Daily Tribune* of 8 August 1853.
109 Blackstone, *Commentaries on the Laws of England* at 12, 27–28, 74; Cf: Vandevelde, *29 Buffalo Law Review* (1980) at 331.
110 Blackstone, *Commentaries on the Laws of England* at 2; Cf: Vandevelde, 'The New Property of the Nineteenth Century' at 331.
111 Mark Neocleous, *75 Science and Society* (2011) 506–528.
112 Manuel Jiménez Fonseca, (Unigrafia, Helsinki: 2017) at 92–94.
113 Locke, *Second Treatise of Government* at 26.
114 Locke was by this contention trying to show that individual property rights inevitably precede the formation of a civil government. *See*: Locke, *Second Treatise of Government* at 25–26, 49–50.

115 Locke, *Second Treatise of Government* at 26–29.
116 As Locke framed it: "in governments, the laws regulate the right of property, and the possession of land is determined by positive constitutions" (Locke, *Second Treatise of Government* at 29).
117 Locke, *Second Treatise of Government* at 25.
118 Ibid at 25.
119 *See*: Josiah Child, (Oxford University Press, 1804) at 185–186. Cf: Barbara Arneil, *55 Journal of the History of Ideas* (1994) at 599. The English emphasis on agriculture was in direct contrast to the Dutch, for "what they do in the East Indies being only by war, trade, and building of fortified towns and castles upon the seacoasts, to secure the sole commerce of the places and with the people whom they conquer, not by clearing, breaking up of ground, and planting, as the English have done." (Arneil, 'Trade, Plantations, and Property' at 599).
120 Locke, *Second Treatise of Government* at 26.
121 To Vattel,

> those who occupy this idle mode of life occupy more land than they would have need of under a system of honest labour, and they may not complain if other industrious Nations, too confined at home, should come and occupy part of their lands. Thus, while the conquest of the civilized Empires of Peru and Mexico was a notorious usurpation, the establishment of various colonies upon the continent of North America might, if done within just limits, have been entirely lawful. The peoples of those vast tracts rather roamed over them than inhabited them.
>
> *See*: Emer de Vattel, (Oceana, 1964) at 38

122 Vattel, *The Law of Nations* at 37.
123 Vattel, *The Law of Nations* at 85.
124 In spite of the prominence of the agricultural argument especially during the first stages of European settlement, English colonial authorities in North America eventually tended to recognise indigenous inhabitants as true owners, and resorted to the practice of legitimate purchase of lands. *See*: Stuart Banner, (Harvard University Press, 2007).
125 Kees Van der Pijl, (Pluto Press, 2007) at 62.
126 A. G. Hopkins, (Longman, 1973) at 22–24.
127 Claude Meillassoux, (Maspéro, 1975) at 14–16.
128 See: Rawley, *The Transatlantic Slave Trade* at 3.
129 Immanuel Wallerstein, (University of California Press, 2011) at 66–69.
130 Barbara L. Solow, *17 Journal of Development Economics* (1985) at 103.
131 Solow, 'Caribbean Slavery and British Growth' at 103.
132 Allain, *Slavery in International Law* at 10–11.

References

Allain, Jean: *Slavery in International Law: Of Human Exploitation and Trafficking* (Martinus Nijhoff, Leiden/Boston: 2013).

Angelis, De Massimo: 'Marx and Primitive Accumulation: The Continuous Character of Capital's Enclosures' *2 The Commoner* (2001) 1–22.

Anghie, Anthony: 'Francisco De Vitoria and the Colonial Origins of International Law' *5 Social Legal Studies* (1996) 321–336.

———: *Imperialism, Sovereignty and the Making of International Law* (Cambridge University Press: Cambridge, 2005).

Arneil, Barbara: 'Trade, Plantations, and Property: John Locke and the Economic Defense of Colonialism' *55 Journal of the History of Ideas* (1994) 591–609.
Baars, Grietje: "Capitalism's victor's Justice? The Hidden Story of the Prosecution of Industrialists Post-WWII" in K. Heller & G. Simpson (eds.), *The Hidden Histories of War Crimes Trials* (Oxford University Press, Oxford: 2013).
Balibar, Étienne: 'Reflections on Gewalt' *17 Historical Materialism* (2009) 99–125.
Banaji, Jairus: 'Backward Capitalism, Primitive Accumulation and Modes of Production' *3 Journal of Contemporary Asia* (1973) 393–413.
Banner, Stuart: *How the Indians Lost Their Lands: Law and Power on the Frontier* (Harvard University Press, Cambridge: 2007).
Barrera-Osorio, Antonio: *Experiencing Nature: The Spanish American Empire and the Early Scientific Revolution* (University of Texas Press, Austin: 2006).
Batou, Jean: 'Accumulation by Dispossession and Anti-Capitalist Struggles: A Long Historical Perspective' *79 Science & Society* (2015) 11–37.
Benjamin, Walter: "Critique of Violence" in Peter Demetz (ed.), *Reflections: Essays, Aphorisms, Autobiographical Writings* (Harcourt Brace, New York: 1978) 62–70.
Blackstone, William: *Commentaries on the Laws of England* (University of Chicago Press, Chicago: 1979).
Child, Josiah: *A New Discourse on Trade* (Oxford University Press, Oxford/London: 1804).
Chimni, Bhupinder S.: 'Prolegomena to a Class Approach to International Law' *21 The European Journal of International Law* (2010) 57–82.
Crosby, Alfred W.: *The Columbian Exchange: Biological and Cultural Consequences of 1492* (Praeger, London: 2003).
Cummins, John: *The Voyage of Christopher Columbus: Columbus Own Journal of Discovery Newly Restored and Translated* (Weidenfeld and Nicolson, London: 1992).
Draper, Hal & Haberkern, Ernest: *Karl Marx's Theory of Revolution* (New York University Press, New York: 2005).
Frank, Andre Gunder: 'On So-Called Primitive Accumulation' *2 Dialectical Anthropology* (1977) 87–106.
Fonseca, Manuel Jiménez: *Civilizing Nature: Revisiting the Imperialist History of International Law (1511–1972)* (PhD Dissertation: Unigrafia, Helsinki: 2017).
Hamilton, Earl J.: 'American Treasure and the Rise of Capitalism (1500–1700)' *27 Economica* (1929) 338–357.
Harvey, David: *A Brief History of Neoliberalism* (Oxford University Press, Oxford: 2005).
———: "Accumulation by Dispossession" in David Harvey (ed.), *The New Imperialism* (Oxford University Press, Oxford: 2003) at 146–150.
Higman, B. W.: *A Concise History of the Caribbean* (Cambridge University Press, Cambridge: 2011).
Hopkins, Antony Gerald: *An Economic History of West Africa* (Longman, London: 1973).
Ignatieff, Michael: "Primitive Accumulation Revisited" in Raphael Samuel (ed.), *People's History and Socialist Theory* (Routledge & Kegan Paul, London/Boston/Henley: 1981) 133–134.
Ince, Onur Ulas: 'Between Equal Rights: Primitive Accumulation and Capital's Violence' *46 Political Theory* (2018) 885–914.

———: "Development" in Jean d'Aspremont & Sahib Singh (eds.), *Fundamental Concepts in International Law: The Construction of a Discipline* (Edward Elgar, London: 2015) 179–200.
Jane, Cecile: *The Four Voyages of Columbus: A History in Eight Documents, Including Five by Christopher Columbus, in the Original Spanish* (Dover Publications, New York: 1988).
Klein, Martin A. & Hogendorn, Jan: *The Atlantic Slave Trade: Effects on Economies, Societies and Peoples in Africa, the Americas, and Europe* (Duke University Press, Durham, North Carolina: 1992).
Lee, Stephen: 'A Puzzle of Sovereignty' *27 California Western International Law Journal* (1997) 241–264.
Lissitzyn, Oliver J.: *International Law in a Divided World* (Carnegie Endowment for International Peace, New York: 1963).
Locke, John & Laslett, Peter: *Second Treatise of Government: A Critical Edition with an Introduction and Apparatus Criticus by Peter Laslett* (Cambridge University Press, Cambridge: 1960).
Mackay, Angus: *Spain in the Middles Ages: From Frontier towards Empire 1350–1500* (McMillan, Hong Kong: 1977).
Marx, Karl: *Capital: Critique of Political Economy*, Frederick Engels (ed.) (Charles H. Kerr & Co., New York/Toronto: 1906).
———: *Capital, Vol. 3: The Process of Capitalist Production* (Progress Publishers, Moscow: 1966).
———: "Debates on the Law on Thefts of Wood" in Karl Marx and Frederick Engels (eds.), *Collected Works, Vol. 1* (Lawrence and Wishart, London: 1975) 224–248.
———: *Grundrisse*, Martin Nicolaus, trans. (Penguin Books, London: 1993).
———: "On the Jewish Question" (1843), in Robert Tucker (ed.), *The Marx-Engels Reader* (Norton & Company, New York: 1978) at 26–46.
———: "The Future Results of British Rule in India" in *The New York Daily Tribune* of 8 August 1853.
Marx, Karl & Engels, Friedrich: "Feuerbach: Opposition of Materialist and Idealist Outlook" in *Selected Works in Three Volumes* (Progress Publishers, Moscow: 1969–1973) 57–73.
Marx, Karl & O'Malley, Joseph: *Critique of Hegel's' Philosophy of Right* (Cambridge University Press, Cambridge: 1977).
McLellan, David: *Karl Marx: Selected Writings* (Oxford University Press, Oxford: 2000).
Meek, Ronald L.: *Social Science and the Ignoble Savage* (Cambridge University Press, Cambridge: 1976).
Meillassoux, Claude: *L'Esclavage en Afrique Précoloniale* (Maspéro, Paris: 1975).
Miéville, China: *Between Equal Rights: A Marxist Theory of International Law* (Brill, Leiden/Boston: 2005).
Muldoon, James: *The Expansion of Europe: The First Phase* (University of Pennsylvania Press, Philadelphia: 1977).
Neocleous, Mark: 'International Law as Primitive Accumulation; or, the Secret of Systematic Colonisation' *23 European Journal of International Law* (2012) 941–962.
———: 'War on Waste: Law, Original Accumulation, and the Violence of Capital' *75 Science and Society* (2011) 506–528.

Pahuja, Sundhya: 'Decolonizing International Law: Development, Economic Growth and the Politics of Universality' *University of Melbourne Legal Studies Research Paper* (2011) 1–417.
Perelman, Michael: *The Invention of Capitalism* (Duke University Press, Durham, North Carolina/London: 2000).
Porras, Ileana: 'Appropriating Nature: Commerce, Property, and the Commodification of Nature in the Law of Nations' *27 Leiden Journal of International Law* (2014) 641–660.
Preobrazhensky, Eugene, Pearce, Brian & Nove, Alec: *The New Economics* (Oxford University Press, Oxford: 1965).
Raudzens, George: "Outfighting or Outpopulating? Main Reasons for Early Colonial Conquest, 1493–1788" in George Raudzens (ed.), *Technology, Disease and Colonial Conquest, Sixteenth to Eighteenth Centuries: Essays Reappraising the Guns and Germs Theories* (Brill, Leiden: 2001) 31–57.
Rawley, James A.: *The Transatlantic Slave Trade: A History* (University of Nebraska Press, Lincoln/ London: 2005).
Rosser, Mariana V. & Rosser, J. Barkley: *Comparative Economics in a Transforming World Economy* (MIT Press, Cambridge, Massachusetts/London: 2003).
Saito, Natsu Taylor: 'Decolonization, Development, and Denial' *6 Florida A & M University Law Review* (2010) 1–47.
Schmitt, Carl: *The Nomos of the Earth in the International Law of Jus Publicum Europaeum* (Telos Press, New York: 2003).
Sepúlveda, Juan de Ginés: *Tratado sobre las Justas Causas de la Guerra contra los Indios, con una advertencia de Marcelino Menendez y Pelayo y un estudio por Manuel García-Pelayo* (Fondo de Cultura Económica, México: 1941).
Simmons, A. John: *The Lockean Theory of Rights* (Princeton University Press, Princeton, New Jersey: 1994).
Smith, Adam: *An Inquiry into the Nature and Causes of the Wealth of Nations* (Liberty Classics, Indianapolis: 1981).
———: *Lectures on Jurisprudence*, R. L. Meek, D. D. Raphael & P. G. Stein (eds.) (Liberty Classics, Indianapolis: 1978); (*Republished by*: Liberty Fund, Indianapolis: 1982).
Solow, Barbara L.: 'Caribbean Slavery and British Growth' *17 Journal of Development Economics* (1985) 99–115.
Trotsky, Leon: *The Permanent Revolution & Results and Prospects* (Red Letter Press, Seattle: 2010).
Truman, Harry S.: *Inaugural Speech: Public Papers of the President* (US Government Printing Office, Washington, DC: 1949b).
———: Second Inaugural Address, 20 January 1949, Delivered before the US Congress, Full speech in *Department of State Bulletin*, 30 January 1949a.
Todorov, Tzvetan: *The Conquest of America: The Question of the Other* (University of Oklahoma Press, New York: 1999).
Truyol y Serra, Antonio: 'The Discovery of the New World and International Law' *3 University of Toledo Law Review* (1977) 305–321.
Vandevelde, Kenneth J.: 'The New Property of the Nineteenth Century: The Development of the Modern Concept of Property' *29 Buffalo Law Review* (1980) 325–368.
van der Pijl, Kees: *Nomads, Empires, States: Modes of Foreign Relations and Political Economy* (Pluto Press, London: 2007).

Vattel, Emer de: *The Law of Nations; or Principles of the Law of Nature Applied to the Conduct and Affairs of Nations and Sovereigns* (T & J. W. Johnson, Philadelphia: 1844).

Vincent, Andrew: 'Marx and Law' *20 Journal of Law and Society* (1993) 371–397.

Vitoria, Francisco de: *On The American Indians* in Francesco de Vitoria, *Political Writings*, A. Pagden & J. Lawrance (eds.) (Cambridge University Press, Cambridge: 1991).

Von Der Heydte, Friedrich August Freiherr: 'Discovery, Symbolic Annexation and Virtual Effectiveness in International Law' *29 American Journal of International Law* (1935) 448–471.

Wallerstein, Immanuel: *The Modern World-System I: Capitalist Agriculture and the Origins of the European World-Economy in the Sixteenth Century, with a New Prologue* (University of California Press, Berkeley, California: 2011).

West, E. G.: 'The Political Economy of Alienation: Karl Marx and Adam Smith' *21 Oxford Economic Papers* (1969) 1–23.

Williams, Caroline A.: *Between Resistance and Adaptation: Indigenous Peoples and the Colonisation of the Chocó, 1510–1753* (Liverpool University Press, Liverpool: 2005).

Zamara, Margarita: *Christopher Columbus' "Letters to the Sovereigns" Announcing the Discovery: New World Encounter*, Stephen Greenblatt (ed.) (University of California Press, Los Angeles: 1993).

3 People as Property

The Transatlantic Slave Trade, International Law, and the Making of the New World

3.1 Introduction

Freedom and bondage have both co-existed and haunted humankind throughout recorded history. Driven by the quest for wealth creation, profits, and economic growth, the conquest of Americas in the 16th century prompted European policy makers and academics to contemplate improved modalities for organising labour and trade, as well as devising ways whereupon the motherlands could benefit from arising relations with the colonies. While framing doctrines of private property as vectors of liberty, classical political economists frequently tied their narratives of justice with the exigencies of entrepreneurship and economic growth.[1] They specifically highlighted the wage-labour aspect of the capitalist system in order to justify the capitalist mode of production as one of *laissez-faire* and benefits—thereupon correspondingly distinguishing the system from all other alternative systems, which, to them, were perceived as marred by backwardness and bondage. For Classical political economists, the capitalist system inevitably allowed for individual liberty and mobility, given its professed inclination of enabling peoples with the flexibility to choose what economic sectors best suited their labour talents.

In *Das Kapital*, Marx examined the *laissez-faire* claims of political economy and roundly debunked the long-standing celebratory accounts of capitalism that it personified. Grounding his critical analysis on the concept of primitive accumulation whereupon he conceived the capitalist system in terms of social relations, Marx ultimately reached an opposite conclusion from that of his contemporaries. The foundation of the capitalist mode of production, to him, was sturdily erected on a nuance contradiction of freedom and well-being on one pole, and poverty and un-freedom on another pole. It was, in other words, marred by a sharp contrast between the [European] capitalists' drive for profits and exploited labour of colonised and enslaved non-Europeans.

Amongst other things, Marxian primitive accumulation distinguished from Smithian on the emphasis it placed on the essential prerequisite that global capitalism imperatively needed to fulfil for it to take off, namely, the

DOI: 10.4324/9781003265740-3

establishment of a sustainable labour force (through primitive accumulation). As he framed it,

> The accumulation of capital pre-supposes surplus-value; surplus-value pre-supposes capitalistic production; capitalistic production pre-supposes the pre-existence of considerable masses of capital and of labour-power ... The whole movement, therefore, seems to turn in a vicious circle, out of which we can only get by supposing a primitive accumulation ... an accumulation not the result of the capitalist mode of production, but its starting point.[2]

From the foregoing, he thus not only perceived the enslaved humans exploited by the conquering Europeans across the New World as the foundational essence of the commodity form, but moreover as constituting the original capital that gave birth to the global capitalist mode of production.

Per Marxian primitive accumulation, the colonial encounter and looting of non-European worlds and peoples by European capitalists was thus the veritable stimulant for European growth since the 16th century. Central to this claim was his underlining of imbalanced Atlantic relations between Europe, the Americas, and Africa. Restlessly relying on the labour power of non-Europeans in order to generate surplus and profits, Europeans not only led the triangular relations between these distant continents but also framed the rules of engagement.[3] When the Spaniards enslaved the Amerindians following their annexation of South America, and the latter died in alarming numbers—in part because of colonial brutality—but mostly because of their lack of immunity to European diseases,[4] the Spanish Crown, in its desperate drive to extract natural resources from the Americas, promptly turned to sub-Saharan Africa for labour needs. Having proven to be exceedingly profitable, the Atlantic slave trade attracted the interest of most European maritime nations (Portugal, Holland, France, England), who, in the footsteps of Spain, all ventured into the New World and steadily rooted their pathway to capital accumulation, hence economic and political grandeur, on the forceful enslavement of imported sub-Saharan African peoples.[5]

Dubbed as the Atlantic slave trade, the scheme denotes a historical modality whereby economic exploitation and racial constructs merged together to produce a distinctive mode of production that was very profitable for its progenitors, but very damaging to the trajectory of sub-Saharan Africa's economic growth. It was marked by over 400 years of arguably the most systematic sustained, vicious violence, brutality, and un-freedom ever registered in the annals of humankind. As Marx observed, slavery single-handedly gave value to the colonies and set the trajectory in motion for revolution in growth amongst the capitalists: "Slavery [gave] value to the colonies. The colonies created world trade; world trade [was] the necessary condition of large-scale machine industry."[6] The contemporary Marxist Eric Williams concurred, noting that plantation owners "would have gone to the moon, if necessary, for labour.

Africa was nearer than the moon, nearer too than the most populous countries of India and China."[7]

In practical terms, European's exclusive reliance on slave labour as a mode of production in the New World marked the advent of foundational theories of early international commodification and the capitalist system, as we know it today. The harmony in doctrines for progress amongst political economists and jurists permitted for the legitimation of slavery and slave trade between the 16th and 19th centuries. The transatlantic slave trade not only became the principal driver for lawful private contracts in the New World[8] (*asientos*, for instance) and the doctrinal basis for concepts of war and peace, but was moreover used by involved countries to shape national policies—based on profit expectations.[9] As European conceptions of property rights justified slavery and legitimately empowered some to own and exploit others, this to Marx defeated the whole purport of *laissez-faire* pretentions, given that peoples confined to bondage were denied not just fundamental rights of individualism, freedom, and mobility but the fruits of their labour as well—as per the *Lockean provisio*.[10]

This chapter illustrates how the transatlantic trade founded a peculiar rigid concept of bondage based on race, for the purposes of value-making. It is observed that while its origins were purely economical, the trade nonetheless steadily became grounded on the racial construct of black inferiority and white superiority—with the former compelled to serve the latter. As a result, racism became a recurrent toxic by-product of capital accumulation process throughout the New World. The rigidity of the racial construct was so systemic and severe to the extent that neither the conversion of the enslaved "to the religion of the master nor marriage with the master could prevent [black] persons and their descendants from inheriting the status of a slave."[11] Not only were laws articulated setting up modalities for slaves' exploitation, but they were moreover degraded to a perpetual status of inferior proletariats. The chapter further shows how the toleration of the institution of slavery prompted and codified many doctrines on trade and property rights hence merging the drive of political economy with the vision of international law between the 16th and 19th centuries. I further highlight the different frameworks according to which classical publicists—reading from ancient statutes and literature—justified both the trade and institution of slavery.[12] Naturally, the very basis of this history begs the question: how could the Law of Nations—a discipline positing as the harbinger of universal rights—defend slavery—the gravest form of human exploitation and subjugation?

Although this study acknowledges two other foreign slave trades (the trans-Saharan and the Arab slave trades) that prevailed in Africa prior to the European scheme, the primary focus nevertheless is on the transatlantic slave trade, which kicked off in the aftermath of the conquest of the Americas and lasted between the 16th and 19th centuries. The study reasons with earlier findings of economic determinist scholars—the likes of Eric Williams, C. L. R. James, Walter Rodney, Samir Amin, Robin Blackburn, and

Paul Finkelman—who observed that both the rise and fall of the transatlantic slave trade was influenced by a renewed quest for profit margins, propelled by mutations in economic modes of production.[13]

The study further revisits the politics of the abolition of the slave trade—observing that the movement's social justice altruism revealed how capitalism by nature is predisposed with two contradictory ideologies, viz. profit-making versus humanitarianism. It is obvious from the foregoing that capitalism is not just an economic arrangement of societies but is moreover a set of ideas laden with economic, political, and legal implications.

3.2 Slavery and Slave Trade as Constructs: From Ancient to Capitalist Doctrines

The word "slave" denotes a number of misgivings, top amongst which are coercion, mistreatment, alienation, and denial of rights. While slavery naturally is the antithesis of liberty, it has nonetheless existed in most human societies at some point in history. Indeed, it is amongst the oldest known human institutions (beside the family).[14] For the better half of human existence, slavery has been legally protected and regulated in both public and private law disciplines.[15]

Central to the definition of slavery is the element of exploitation, whether it is obtained by force or compulsory labour. Ordinarily, to be a slave is to be completely subordinated to the will of another person as his property—who legally enjoys the right of ownership over the enslaved person. *Dominium* is the legal notion of ownership. Orlando Patterson has traced the origin of the legal concept of *dominium* as derivative from attempts by Roman law to address the question of slavery and the basis of absolute right of slave owners over slaves.[16] He defined slavery as the "permanent, violent domination of naturally alienated and generally dishonoured persons."[17] The uniqueness of slavery from other forms of commodities is not just on the right of ownership, but moreover on the power that accompanies the right to title—namely, the right of exploitation.[18] The centrality of the definition of both slavery and slave trade rests in the structural reduction of a human being from an inherent status of personhood into a merchandise chattel—a thing or property that can be owned and controlled at will by another person asserting a right of ownership.

3.2.1 Ancient and Medieval Doctrines on Slavery

3.2.1.1 Aristotle's Conception of Natural Slave and Born Rulers

Writing on diverse subjects ranging from ethics, logic, metaphysics, and biology to government, society, and politics, Aristotle (384–322 BC) was certainly the greatest philosopher of his time. A prolific writer, his influence transcended beyond his native Greece both during and after his lifetime. While classics of international law over the ages were often conflicted on the slave trade and human freedom—typically justifying enslavement whenever they did only as an exception, Aristotle before them found no such aberration with the institution of slavery. To him, it was a function of nature and natural law. He conceived slaves as persons whose identities were stringently imbedded into that of their masters. A slave, he noted, is anyone

> who is by nature not his own but another's man, is by nature a slave; and he may be said to be another's man who, being a slave, is also a possession—and a possession may be defined as an instrument of action, separable from the possessor.[19]

By emphasising absolute right of possession of slaves by slave owners, Aristotle's conception encapsulated the gross magnitude of exploitation inherent in the institution of slavery. In his book *Politics*, he addressed the looming question of whether it was natural or against the law of nature for some people to be held in slavery. Reaching the conclusion that the institution of slavery was in conformity with the law of nature, Aristotle observed some people from birth were conditioned to be superior, and the rest inferior. To him, "for, that some should rule and others be ruled is a thing not only necessary, but expedient, from the hour of their birth, some are marked out for subjection, others for rule."[20]

Natural slaves for Aristotle were non-Greeks. He perceived them as lacking autonomous rationality and *eudaimonia* (highest human good).[21] Although he conceded that natural slaves were "human and have a share in reason," he nevertheless proceeded with a rationale justifying their status as objects of servitude on grounds that they lacked the part of the soul which makes "moral virtue complete" and as a result also lacked the capacity for independent human existence.[22] Aristotle's position on slavery and natural law provoked but failed to address the question of what was to be the status of children procreated from marriages or unions between born rulers and natural slaves.

Aristotle extended the scope of natural slaves beyond born-slaves to include prisoners of war, but was unclear whether Greek captives could also be converted to slaves. To him, victors of conflicts were entitled to the spoils of war: "the convention by which whatever is taken in war is supposed to belong to the victors."[23] In spite of the rigidity of his doctrine, Aristotle nonetheless provided that natural law allowed slavery only where there was an affectionate co-existence between the masters and the slaves: "where the relation of master and slave between them is natural, they are friends and have a common interest, but where it rests merely on convention and force the reverse is true."[24] In spite of Aristotle's considerate concern, the disproportionate imbalance of power inherent in the master-slave relationship severely put to question the basis on which his affirmation rested.

Conceiving the so-called natural slaves as having impaired rationality, Aristotle ultimately perceived their fate as objects of servitude to be a permanent one. Considering slavery as necessary, expedient, and beneficial to both the slavers and the enslaved, Aristotle observed that society attained progress when the backward natural slaves were placed under the permanent supervision of those born to an advanced creed.[25] How could slaves benefit from their enslavement in the hands of the so-called advanced peoples? Aristotle addressed this nuance by framing a rationale around the idea of progress. To him, by graciously performing their natural roles, slaves facilitated the fulfilment of the law of nature, which apportioned labour tasks to everyone according to their ability—and most especially freed their owners from the burden of wasting time on subservient labour, giving them ample time to concentrate on worthwhile activities and intricate chores that could move society forward.[26] Aristotle's postulation can be read as an early though unrefined formulation of the doctrine of division of labour.

Despite the fact that natural slaves had an impaired rationality and lacked an autonomous reasoning, they nevertheless still enjoyed better well-being thanks to the accomplishments and great advancements realised by their masters—especially given that masters generally saw themselves and slaves as one person—and as having a common stake, even as their bodies were physically separated.[27] All things considered, while Aristotle's reasoning effectively paid great dividends to the aristocratic class to which he belonged, material benefits and rights failed to trickle down to those held in bondage.

3.2.1.2 Jus Gentium *Doctrines on Slavery*

Following the Aristotelian conception of enslavement, the idea that slavery was determined by one's condition of birth became central not just to ancient thinking, but prolonged right unto the beginning of medieval times. One of Aristotle's fervent admirers—Saint Thomas Aquinas (1225–1274)—an influential Italian Dominican friar, jurist, and philosopher, while examining the same problematic but from a Christian perspective, nevertheless digressed and differed significantly from him especially on the narrative of the natural slaves and born rulers. To Aquinas, the institution of slavery was first and foremost an abnormality from God's design for the earth. Slavery, he observed, came about as a result of the fall of man through sin, rather than biological or cultural inferiority.[28] To Aquinas, life was utopia under natural law. Man had, however, transitioned from natural law to *jus gentium*. While common societal evils (war, slavery, greed, exploitation, etc.) were absent in the state of natural law, these ills were nonetheless prevalent in a state of *jus gentium*.[29]

The *Justinian's Institutes* that set out to codify Roman law in the 6th century was more in line with Aquinas's conception than Aristotle's postulation when it defined slavery as "an institution of *jus gentium* by which, contrary to nature, a person is subjected to the domination of another."[30] Following the *Justinian's Institutes*, it became established law in Rome that "slavery is [was] *iuris gentium*, but *contra naturam*."[31] The uniqueness of *jus gentium*'s conception of slavery was the official legitimation of the institution of slavery with respect to property rights but distinct from natural law. Under Roman law, slaves in effect constituted a *res*—that is, a thing or merchandised chattel, and were as a result regulated according to laws of personal property. At the core of *Justinian's Institutes* supposition was a binary classification of peoples into two opposite classes, with membership in a given class becoming the determining barometer of whether one was to be free or become a slave: "the principal distinction in the law of persons is that all men are either free or slaves—there is no third, intermediate, category in Roman law."[32]

Following the *Justinian's Institutes*, Roman law delimited the scope of slavery under *jus gentium* (which necessarily involved foreigners) to cases of war and conquest, distinct from *jus civili*, where the scope of legitimate enslavement was confined to such cases as sale and purchase of slaves, domestic criminals, and voluntary submission into slavery by persons afflicted by poverty, etc.[33] Being an abnormality according to natural law, the point of entry of slaves as legitimate private property according to Roman law was the moment of their capture in warfare by their conquerors. As Jean Allain has explained, they at that point lost their rights and liberties as humans and became "*captis deminutio maxima*"—that is, suffered their greatest fall in status[34] from rights-bearing humans to non-rights-bearing property. Their fall in status translated in practical terms to loss of "freedom, citizenship and family."[35] Given that the primary source of slaves under *jus gentium* was from prisoners of war, the same author has assumed that the rigidity of *captis deminutio maxima* provision was most likely intended to compel Roman soldiers to fight to the death at each battle and avoid being captured, since capture ultimately meant enslavement and loss of rights, citizenship, and natural privileges.[36]

Although the *Justinian's Institutes* made attempts to set limits on slave owners especially with the mistreatment of slaves, it nonetheless shied away from explicitly spelling out any enforceable rights unto slaves. It is deduced that it was incumbent on the goodwill of slave masters to treat their slaves humanely, and not to starve them to hunger or mistreat them. This notwithstanding, Alan Watson has observed that the subject of slavery is the only occasion in Roman law, where there is any explicit acknowledgement of conflict between natural law and *jus gentium*.[37] He further observed that since slavery was considered as an abnormality even by *jus gentium* standards, the institution nevertheless found moral backing[38] as a result on the grounds that the alternative was worse, namely death. The rationale was to the effect that although slaves were confined to enslavement, they nonetheless not only had their lives spared but moreover became nurtured towards civility and progress by their owners.[39]

3.2.2 The Transatlantic Slave Trade, Legality, and Capitalist Relations of Production (15th to 19th Centuries)

Africa experienced three different international slave trades between 1400 and 1900. The transatlantic slave trade, otherwise known as the triangular trade

(1493–1880), by far overshadowed the others with unprecedented volume, magnitude, economic exploitation, duration, and brutality. The other two slave trades, namely, the trans-Saharan slave trade (8th–16th centuries) and the Indian Ocean slave trade or Arab slave trade, also known as the Oriental slave trade (650–1900) pre-dated the transatlantic trade.[40] While these latter two slave trades were equally devastating to the trajectory of sub-Saharan African economic development and growth, they do not fall under the scope of this study.

Its chequered origins notwithstanding, the transatlantic trade portrayed a major irony in scholarly theories. Begun in the late 15th century, during an age when Europe had just transitioned from the Middle Ages into a state of Renaissance, the slave trade as evidenced by postulations of Aquinas, *Justinian's Institutes*, and some Dominican theologian's flirtation with Aristotle's conception of slavery, became one discourse whereupon intellectual thinking still loosely anchored unto and mirrored medieval doctrines. Paradoxically, the trade also became the vehicle for Europe's remaking and transition into the modern era. Begun by Iberian powers (first Portugal and later Spain), other powerful European monarchies soon joined—notably France, England, and Holland (although not a power at the time, it nevertheless heavily invested in the commercial revolution).[41] The Mediterranean world was generally perceived during the Age of Renaissance as the economic centre of Europe.[42] It has been observed, however, that following the transatlantic slave trade, the economic centre was transferred from the Mediterranean to the New World.[43]

Marxian primitive accumulation, as afore-noted, underscores the incessant drive of political economists in the aftermath of European conquest of the Americas, to invent a new improved mode of production that could guarantee economic growth for their motherlands. To this effect, foundational theories of international commodification and capital accumulation were conceived and institutionalised throughout the American colonies. The capital accumulation scheme according to this framing was distinctive in two specific ways, namely the historical conjecture and the exclusive reliance on coerced labour (marked by the mobilisation of slave labour), to fulfil wide-ranging exigencies of economic growth.[44] In the words of one scholar, the scheme "occurred at the dawn of capitalism, and was characterized by the forcible separation of the direct producer from his/her means of production, a process of dispossession which—as Marx made clear—could only be achieved by considerable violence."[45]

Marxist scholars led by Edward E. Baptist, Walter Johnson, and Adam Rothman have highlighted four key modalities whereupon the Atlantic slave trade triggered the capitalist world system as we know it today.[46] These features are: the profit motive of the slave trade scheme, class differentiation by the use of race as a barometer for rights, the commodification process (especially the commodification of persons), and the world system structure of core, periphery, and semi-periphery.[47] All these features paved the way for a steady progression from primitive to mature capitalism. The commodification of peoples enabled them to be "bought, sorted, moved, and sold wherever they would be most valued" in the same light as other markable commodities.[48] Patrick Manning has observed that the Atlantic slave trade was generally speaking a manifestation of high-level corruption, as "it involved theft, bribery, the exercise of brute force as well as ruses. Slavery thus may be seen as one source of pre-colonial origins for modern corruption."[49]

Classed as chattel property rather than persons, the slaves in the New World did not receive any wages but rather a portion of their labour power, necessary for their subsistence, and at the behest of their masters. In fact, in spite of firmly anchoring itself on Atlantic slavery for the provision of labour force necessary for the production of goods and services, the nascent international capitalist system ironically restricted the exploited slaves outside of the commodity system, having stripped and reduced them from the status of personhood to mere commodities, hence not deserving of rights and privileges. Placed outside the confines of the commodity system which came into being through their labour-power, plantation slaves were moreover denied the right to directly access systems of justice or the right to generate internal demands. Perceived as merchandised chattel or commodities (resources), they could not claim rights.[50]

More than previous forms of slave trades, both the rise and fall of the trans-atlantic slave trade was directly linked to market forces, trade monopolies, capital accumulation, and profit margins. Owing to its intensity and geographical outreach, the transatlantic trade not only emerged as the most intense form of capitalist accumulation in terms of its appropriation of commodities but accordingly occasioned a complex system of credit and exchange thereby elevating the trade in slaves into a global capitalist mode of production.[51] It functioned according to a specific economic vicious cycle: goods and commodities (firearms, powder, brandies, etc.) were shipped from Europe into Africa to buy slaves, who were in turn transported to the tropical Americas to work on European plantations. The crops produced from the farms were in turn shipped to Europe, where they were processed into manufactured goods for re-export to Africa to buy more slaves—hence the name, triangular trade.[52]

It was more convenient for the Iberian states (Spain and Portugal) in the aftermath of the conquest of the Americas to justify the sanctity of slavery than other European powers, given that unlike their rivals, they not only had a slave culture but strongly subscribed to Roman and Canon laws. Both legal regimes approved the institution of slavery in a number of instances. The major preoccupation of Iberian states in the New World was not so much in relation to the legality of slavery and the slave trade, but rather about establishing whether the enslavement of non-Europeans in the Americas was in harmony with or in violation of Roman and Canon codes.

Although most European colonial powers in the New World (Holland, Denmark, Sweden) had no institutional slaves in their various metropolises, they nonetheless quickly adapted to reliance on Atlantic slave labour thanks to their firm attachment to Roman law, wherefrom—just like Iberian states—they derived foundational legal justifications. While French judges and legal practitioners occasionally referred to Roman law, they nonetheless stringently relied on French civil law in their legal practice. Although slavery existed in France prior to the conquest of Americas, it was not inscribed in the country's civil law. While French jurists were well aware of Roman and Canon doctrines on slavery, France was nonetheless well noted for habitually freeing people held in slavery as well as foreigners brought into the country as slaves.[53] As Iberian states steadily reaped immense wealth from the transatlantic slave trade, France felt compelled to join the commerce as a safeguard for competitiveness with rival states. The French king Louis XIV issued the *Code Noir* decree in 1685, which amongst other things officially legalised the enslavement of black peoples in French colonies, as well as defined the conditions of the exercise of the trade in French colonies.[54] The *Code Noir* proved decisive in enabling France to fit in the Atlantic slave trade trend. In spite of its solid feudal history, England on its part nevertheless had neither a systematic culture of slavery nor institutional laws on slavery. Although many English merchants were avid in joining the booming trade, jurists and policy makers across England, right up to 1607, frequently insinuated that the trade was at odds with Common Law.

The conception of slavery during the transatlantic trade era was generally narrower in scope, in comparison to the ancient and medieval doctrines on the subject. In all European colonies across the New World, the conception of persons eligible to be slaves slowly but surely came to be limited to persons of sub-Saharan African descent. In *Black Marxism: The Making of the Black Radical Tradition* (1983),[55] Cedric J. Robinson used the term "racial capitalism" to illustrate how the incessant exploitation and commodification of Africans and peoples of African descent formed the bedrock of the world capitalist system, to the detriment of the exploited class. Given the imbalanced class configuration of Atlantic slavery and slave trade whereupon Africans enslaved in the New World were abused and conditioned to produce needed goods and services, and European enslavers reaping all the surplus and profits, social relations between the two classes inevitably became marred by conflict, tension, anger, and resentment.

In *The Transatlantic Slave Trade: A History* (2005), James A. Rawley contends that Atlantic slave trade marked the highest hallmark in European commercial revolution.[56] The conquest of the New World triggered a steady commercial revolution amongst involved countries appropriating the lands, as they each began heavily investing in highly priced commodities of the age: cotton, tobacco, sugar, indigo, etc.[57] Having engaged Africa to furnish the labour necessary to power the new commercial revolution, as well as the supply of staple and luxurious agricultural produce, European nations began realising the capital necessary to build new vibrant cities across the New World, and economic centres on the European continent—the likes of Lisbon, Liverpool, Bristol, Bordeaux, and Nantes.[58] Key economic areas such as shipbuilding and insurance, as well as banking and finance, were highly stimulated, thus placing the economies involved on the trajectory of sustained growth. The commercial revolution owed its form and successes in part to "the growth of national states that replaced feudalism and lent their support to the trade, to the rise of towns, the broadening of commerce, the development of merchant classes, and to new outlooks upon competition, profits, and capital formation."[59] While participating in the slave trade and sacrificing their invaluable manpower to Europeans for them to meet their Atlantic labour exigencies, African political collectivities steadily crumbled, while the subcontinent's economic trajectory degraded by the same proportion of their manpower deficiency.

3.3 Historical Background and Manifestation of the Atlantic Slave Trade

3.3.1 Background

Using African middlemen, European slavers continually intensified their raids on villages as profits from the trade skyrocketed. The west and central coasts of Africa from the Gulf of Guinea through the Congo Basin right down to Angola and Mozambique were so thoroughly infested by slavers that entire populations escaped inlands for safety; but the slavers, propelled by huge profits, followed them right into the interiors.[60] It has been observed that there were two different transatlantic (north and south) slave trades, demarcated geographically around the equator. While the Portuguese dominated the trade south of the equator, stretching from Angola all the way down to Mozambique, the other European powers focused their ventures in the north of the equator.[61] While Portugal shipped most of its lot to Brazil, the other Europeans (France, Holland, Spain, and England) shipped theirs to their respective colonies in the Americas.

Approximately 15 million people were exported from Africa as slaves during the transatlantic trade, excluding an estimated 7 million others who died in the course of the trade either during raids, journey to the coasts, or at high seas—thus marking one of the largest and most vile forced migration of persons in human history.[62] Some other 5–6 million Africans were exported through the two earlier slave trades. It has been estimated that "for every 300 slaves that survived in The Americas, 700 had died—500 during the raids and the tortuous march to the coast, 125 in the slave ships and 75 after landing in the New World."[63] In one study, Patrick Manning estimated that the population of Africa in 1850 was barely half of what would have been had the slave trade not taken place.[64] Persons who were most wanted as slaves were strong youths in their prime—their twenties, the continent's most productive labour force.

Resistances and Conformity

Kingdoms that were once powerful and famous slowly but surely began to succumb to the mundane economic order of the day, re-orientating their economies to meet the labour demands of the New World, as huge proceeds from the triangular slave trade steadily suppressed other traditional forms of economic activity.[65] One other factor that favoured slave raids was the imbalance between the strength of kingdoms. African leaders engaged themselves in the slave trade at a high prize both for their authority and the rupture of socio-political relationships. The trade "negated political, economic cultural and social development; it stultified the growth of civilization and destroyed whatever civilization there was … [the] relationship between powerful and weaker neighbours, e.g. the Bugandans and the environs were exacerbated by the trade."[66] In fact, the collectivities were severely debased and destroyed by the slave trade with little or no respect now attached to the political institutions.

Since villages and families could legitimately raid one another, the villages and collectivities were severely weakened, and where the villages had previously developed into larger-scale village federations, relations between the villages grew increasingly hostile. Faced with insecurity, people were "confined within ethnic boundaries constructing spheres of interaction."[67] The end result was a high level of ethnic fragmentation that has lasted until the present time, and this had a robust negative impact on economic development considering the correlation between "ethnic fractionalization and long term economic growth"[68] One of the major consequences of the demise of African kingdoms and collectivities was the question of authority. Most of the economic scars from the slave trade originated from the loss of respect and honour for traditional socio-political institutions and norms. According to one scholar,

> [A] fundamental transformation in a political system [occurs] when support has shifted from one set of authorities to a different set, in which the organization, solidarity symbols (that is, symbols validating and defining limits of power), and central characteristics with regard to the way in which power is used have all undergone change. Once support begins to shift away from these aspects of authority, which I shall call collectively the structure of authority, the systems will be said to be in a process of change.[69]

It is commonly understood that slavery was rampant throughout African societies and kingdoms prior to the 16th century. It is common knowledge that Europeans did not introduce the slave trade on the continent. They simply fitted themselves into existing trading patterns along the African coasts and gradually came to dominate it, as the trade became crucial for capitalist development. Even though the transatlantic slave trade became the new basis of trade between the European states and Africa, the trade had already been around for quite some time, albeit in varying degrees. Until the commodification of Africans during the transatlantic slave trade, however, Africa had not been a slave economy, nor was slavery a main mode of production.[70] It has been observed that in spite of domestic slavery across sub-Saharan Africa prior to the transatlantic slave trade, there was nonetheless "no reservoir of slaves in Africa ready for export at the time of European contact".[71]

As to the status and nature of slaves in sub-Saharan Africa prior to the transatlantic trade, Rawley observes that while the African slavery institution shared similarities with European conception and forms of servitude—mainly as captured prisoners of war, it nevertheless also digressed significantly in terms of denial of rights. While many European thinkers favoured slavery as a permanent status, the main rights that slaves lost in Africa was the "institutionalization of marginality"—as acquired slaves were never allowed to fully become leaders, but remained marginal.[72] He further contended that in African societies, the slavery that existed

> was not the chattel slavery that flourished in the Americas. Nor was it plantation slavery, whose keen harshness took so many lives in tropical America. It was not characterized by caste or class and it was not the antithesis of the Western concept of freedom. It was an integral part of complex social structures.[73]

Slaves in sub-Saharan Africa in fact were integrated into families and were an integral part of societies.[74] African domestic slavery was in effect a social institution rather than an economic one. People acquired slaves mostly "to increase the size of one's group, more often for prestige than the sake of wealth ... men and women alike were assimilated into the master's social group."[75] That is probably one reason why it could so easily be traded off to foreigners, as African societies were not wholly dependent on it.

It was almost impossible for the sub-Saharan African economy to thrive economically from the triangular trade, not just because the continent's manpower was continually shipped into the Americas for centuries, but moreover because slaves were exchanged for overpriced articles of little or insignificant value, such as guns, trinkets, perfume, powder, and brandy, items which could never transform a society towards growth.[76] Samir Amin has contended that rewards from participation in the triangular trade were not unevenly distributed, as it did not enable Africans to accumulate capital in the same way that Europeans were doing.[77] The attendant effect of this imbalance in relations, another scholar has concurred, was a general growing sense of inferiority amongst Africans, with many people suddenly seeing themselves as instruments to serve the ends of the white men.[78] Accordingly, sub-Saharan Africa, like the Americas, from the very beginning joined the world system not as an equal trading partner but rather as a dependent element, and that dependence would become almost perpetual.

The mass exodus of slave labour into the New World marked the sowing of seeds of underdevelopment, given that it triggered a colossal decline in productive forces throughout the continent, thus slowing down the natural development of the African economy. Reduced to the sole function of supplying slave labour for the American plantations, "Africa lost its autonomy. It began to be shaped according to foreign requirements, those of mercantilism."[79]

Gradually shaped towards satisfying foreign needs, the African economy steadily became subordinated to the interest of Europe, especially as the slave trading system recurrently substituted European manufactured products for those which would have normally been produced locally.[80]

3.3.2 *Africa Prior to the Transatlantic Slave Trade and State of Economic Development: Historical Overview*

The pan-Africanist scholar Samir Amin has demarcated sub-Saharan African history into four key epochs, thereby identifying the key events and factors that shaped key transformations in the subcontinent's economic development, to wit: the pre-mercantilist period, the mercantilist period, the industrial/colonial period, and the era of third world dependence.[81] He observes that Africa during the pre-mercantilist period forged relations with the outside world more or less on an egalitarian basis, and this was vital in the strengthening of political institutions and economic development.[82] The continent's level of development during this time was pretty similar to that of the rest of the world. In the mercantilist period, Africa traded its populace as slaves for European plantations in the New World—the outcome being the first retrograde signs of underdevelopment compared to the rest of the world.[83] The industrial period was characterised by the European attempt to expand control across the African continent via colonisation, evidently to bolster European economies as well as to serve the personal interests of individual empire builders. The resulting systems were alternative forms of slavery to a good extent. During the last pivotal period (postcolonial state), Africa has effectively descended into a veritable periphery of the world capitalist system.[84]

Samir Amin's conception of African history dispels the long-standing myth by some Eurocentric authors that Africa had no history of its own prior to its encounter with Europeans, and even if there was any—they contend—it was either redundant, of little relevance to the modern world, or nothing to take home—a strong supposition that nothing happened there in its "prehistory."[85] Such an assumption presupposes that Europeans in effect brought history to Africa. Besides oral testimonies, they assume, historical accounts of life in Africa before the arrival of the Europeans was at best scanty. Not only were most Eurocentric historians uninterested in African accounts, but many who wrote about the continent more often than not perpetuated the sense that the history of Africa was the history of white activity on the continent. To them, African customs and traditions were little more than a mere curiosity. The English historian Hugh Trevor-Roper summed the erstwhile Eurocentric sentiments of Africa thus:

> perhaps in the future, there would be some African history to teach. But at present there is none, or very little: there is only the history of the Europeans in Africa. The rest is darkness … and darkness is not a subject for history.[86]

Many enlightenment thinkers fashioned their conception of the world in terms of binary opposites: modern versus pre-modern, rational versus irrational, western versus oriental, and so on—the attendant consequence being that they ended up validating an asymmetric system of global power relationship.[87] In 1930 the British ethnologist Charles Gabriel Seligman published *Races of Africa*, purportedly explaining the cultural and historical reasons for Africa's underdevelopment. Having divided the continent into four major distinct races—Bushmanoids (Bushmen), Negroids, Pygmies, and Caucasoids (Hamites)—the author concluded that everything of economic value in Africa originated outside the continent, almost exclusively from Caucasoid origins.[88]

Contrary to popular myths, Africa's history and its engagement with the outside world did not begin with the arrival of Europeans. Prior to transatlantic trade relations, Africa was well economically integrated with the rest of the world and had been an active participant in international relations, not as an object but mostly as an active subject of the system. Contacts and relations between the various continents were for the most part maintained by traders and also occasionally by missionaries, rather than by state officials. Contrary to conventional myths, economic development worldwide has historically not always been uneven. Every society has at different times experienced both watershed moments and great mutations. Just like Europe, African history and economic development unfolded in an unbroken line-up until the dawn of the triangular trade—whose effects on the continent were tremendous and traumatic, as its traditional and socio-political institutions were heavily disrupted in favour of foreign capital exchange, thus compelling Africans to adapt to much harsher realities.

It is understood that there was no substantial technological or industrial progress in any part of the world prior to the 15th century. China and India were relatively more materially advanced than all other civilisations, though.[89] It is "not by superiority in production but by superiority in commerce and conquest" that Europe began to dominate Africa and the rest of the world in the aftermath of mercantilism.[90] Although each region developed autonomously, Africa during the pre-triangular trade period by some accounts was relatively at par in economic and political development with the progressive regions of the world—including the Mediterranean and the European continent—and in no way appeared inferior or vulnerable.[91] The French historian Fernand Braudel has pointed out that Mediterranean Europe in the 16th century

> was overwhelmingly a world of peasants and of the tenant farmers and landowners; crops and harvests were the vital matters of this world and anything else was superstructure, the result of accumulation and of natural diversion towards the towns. Peasants and crops, in other words food supplies, and the size of the population silently determined the destiny of the age.[92]

Comparing the economic performance of Africa and medieval Europe, the British anthropologist Jack Goody, found their patterns of trade to be strikingly similar, even as he observed vast differences in their agricultural technologies, with that of Europe relatively more advanced.[93] This slight differentiation notwithstanding, Africa's position in the world system at the time remained very similar to that of Europe. In fact, the continent developed evenly until the advent of the transatlantic slave trade. Obviously, if placed side by side nowadays, Europe and Africa would strikingly reveal the practicalities of uneven development of societies.

Unlike the state system as understood in European context, Africa was mainly composed of nations, kingdoms, and kingships. The nations—traditionally formed along ethnic lineages—typically paid allegiance to the powerful kingdoms. Arabs were the continent's principal trading partners, although there was also a very strong presence of European and Asian traders along the coasts, whose presence increased in the region beginning in the late 14th century. The question then becomes whether or not the presence and influence of these foreign traders was beneficial to African economic development. The Arabs termed all of Africa south of the Sahara as *Bilad as-Sudan*, meaning land of the Blacks.[94] This explains why African empires were often referred to as Sudanic empires. The most powerful of these prior to the 16th century included: to the west, Benin (1440–1897), Ghana (800 BC–1600), Songhai (1462 -about 1593), and Mali (1230–1600); the Great Lakes and North-East, Ethiopia (1137–1975), Buganda (1300–present), Kitara (2000 BC–1600), and Sultanate (1504–1821); Kongo: Kingdom of the *kongo* (1400–1888), Kanem-Bornu (1380–1893), and Luba (1585–1885); and in southern Africa, Mutapa (1450–1629) and Merina (1540–1897).[95] These kingdoms were notable not just for their military prowess but also for their economic might and socio-political institutions. They were the distinct cradles of physical development.

One good way of assessing the level of African economic development in pre-transatlantic trade times is by evaluating the quality of its economic products. Prior to mercantilism, Africa had already found its own path for a sustainable society and affluent livelihood.[96] Sub-Saharan Africa as a whole exhibited great skills and ingenuity in areas such as music, design, arts, crafts, traditional medicine, and food preservation. In fact, the ever-increasing Arab, European, and Asian traders along the African coasts were heavily aroused by the material advancement and quality of African art, manufactured goods, minerals, and exotic agricultural products.[97] The Ife and Benin bronzes that have been discovered in recent decades and traced by archaeologists to date as far back as the 14th century must not be construed as unusual; they are testimony of Africa's pinnacle of achievement at least in fine arts by that age. A Dutch sailor who sailed along the African coasts, ending up in the ancient city of Benin in 1602, not only attested that African economic development was similar to that of Europe at the time, but moreover gave a very romantic picture of city. He wrote the following account in his diary:

> The town seems to be very great. When you enter into it, you go into a broad street, not paved, which seems to be seven or eight times broader than the Warmoes street in Amsterdam …

> The King's palace is a collection of buildings which occupy as much space as the town of Harlem, and which is enclosed with walls. There are numerous apartments for the prince's ministers and fine galleries, most of which are as big as those on the Exchange at Armsterdam. They are supported by wooden pillars encased with cooper, where their victories are depicted, and which are carefully kept very clean.
>
> The town is composed of thirty main streets, very straight and 120 feet wide, apart from an infinity of small intersecting streets. The houses are close to one another, arranged in good order. These people are in no way inferior to the Dutch as regards their cleanliness, they wash and scrub their houses so well that they are polished and shinning like a looking glass.[98]

Benin and Holland were certainly not exactly equal. The passage from the Dutch sailor nevertheless depicts a self-reliant and orderly society standing on its own feet. It evidences the smooth working of its socio-political institutions. It also indicates that at least the economically vibrant parts of the continent were most likely on a parallel with European economic development. Walter Rodney, for instance, has observed that the exceptional high quality of African leather products—tanned and dyed in the Mali kingdom by Hausa and Madinga specialists—quickly came to the notice of the outside world, especially in Europe. The same goes for superb local clothes and tissues made from cotton, bark, and palm fibre in the *Kongo* kingdom.[99] African potters made a wide range of utensils using clay such as pots, pans, and bowls, and these were widely used around the world. Ghana and Timbuktu were reputable amongst other things for their blacksmiths, jewelleries, tailoring guilds, and local brass and bronze industries.[100]

Until the conquest of the Americas, the trans-Saharan trade linking Africa, the Mediterranean, and Europe afforded one of the most vibrant and important trade routes anywhere in the world, enabling Africans to exchange items such as gold, fabric, minerals, and tropical crops with salt, clothes, drugs, weapons, iron bars, and perfumes marketed by Arabs and European traders.[101] The trade empowered and strengthened many African kingdoms, as they taxed the trade and ploughed back the proceeds to finance their political institutions. The states actively promoted the trade because the accruing revenues not only strengthened state centralisation but also stimulated growth and progress amongst the populace. Each of the trading parties not only highly valued the goods of the other parties; they saw themselves as equal autonomous partners engaged in profitable trades—a win-win engagement. Because of the egalitarian nature and autonomy of the partnership, ideas which accompanied this trade were easily accepted.[102] For instance, Islam was widely entrenched throughout Central and West Africa, dating as far back as the 10th century, and its spread by Arab traders was by free will, not Jihad.[103] By contrast, despite the increase in trade relations during the transatlantic trade era, there was hardly any fusion in ideas between Europeans and Africans, since both functioned more on necessity rather than on egalitarian terms.

In effect, two external influences affected indigenous African customs during the pre-transatlantic trade epoch, both of which were wilfully embraced to wit: Islamic influences mostly affecting the interiors, and European influences mostly centred on the coastal areas.[104] Islam in particular hugely contributed to literacy amongst the elites. The important significance of this is that most of the kings' wise men (interpreters, aides, advisers, etc.) were often schooled in Islam, in order to better serve the Kingdom.[105] What was the nature of economic development—the mode of production in Africa—prior to the transatlantic slave trade, and how was it regulated? How did it correspond to or differ from the rest of the world in general and Europe in particular? Prior to the transatlantic slave trade epoch, the economic system of Africa was sound and worked well for its society. Despite the fragmented nature of African collectivities, they all observed communalism as a societal mode of production, partly because of the reverence given to eldest members of the society.[106] Whether blindly or spontaneously, African societies typically bestowed power on a specific family or clan—based on the belief that certain families or clans were destined to rule for the benefit of the entire community. Thus, family and blood relations were vital in the constitution of early social settings.[107] Communalism thus was ultimately a family mode of production. It favoured kings overseeing all lands (the major means of production) and subsequently partitioning them between families (not individuals) for agricultural produce and construction. Depending on whether a society was patrilineal or matrilineal, every member of the society had his or her position defined in terms of his father's or mother's relations.[108] One advantage of communalism is that it attributed a series of rights and obligations to all members of the society, with seniority often playing a decisive role. For instance, beside the ruling elite, there were no classes; there was equal access to land through kinship and equality in distribution. Because of the kinship nature of communalism, work on farms was mostly communal, with a whole family or community typically forming a "work bee" to make work more efficient and lively.[109]

One scholar concluded in one study that the slave trade was high-level corruption, given that "it involved theft, bribery and the exercise of brute force as well as ruses. Slavery thus may be seen as one source of pre-colonial origins for modern corruption."[110] Unlike the preceding trades, Africans during the transatlantic slave trade enslaved individuals of the same or similar ethnicities—and this had particularly detrimental effects on the continent's socio-economic and geo-political performance, to wit: "social and ethnic fragmentation, political instability and the weakening of states, and the corruption of judicial institutions."[111]

While some postcolonial Afrocentric scholars—the likes of Taslim Olawale Elias, R. P. Anand, and James Thuo Gathii[112]—have forcefully countered the myths of Africa as a continent without a history, Onuma Yasuaki has nevertheless cautioned that by taking this position, these authors also ended up inadvertently projecting European categories as universal, given that their overall conclusions without thoroughly scrutinising the Eurocentric civilisational image of the discipline tended to take the contemporary concept of international law as granted. They have unwittingly stayed within the western paradigm in order to criticise the west.[113]

Although international law as a European construct was hardly present in pre-transatlantic Africa, this in no way presupposes an absence or deficiency of the rule of law. African kingdoms and nations had conventional kingdom (state) apparatus and entertained normal interstate relations, and this was possible only because of their institutional set-ups as well as societal bonds to longstanding customary norms. Customary traditions formed part and parcel of societal law, and although laws were generally unwritten, there remains abundant evidence pointing to both formal and informal relations between the different collectivities, peoples, and kingdoms.[114] Although there was a multiplicity of customary laws, it would still be germane to qualify them together as African customary law, for the rules were collectively very similar both in letter and in spirit. Strong societal respect of traditional values were permitted for the sealing and administering of contracts by oath-taking. Given that African customary laws afforded a platform for interstate relations and moreover a bonding mechanism between the different collectivities, kingdoms, and peoples of Africa (a form of unity in diversity); they can thus be collectively qualified as African law or *droit public de l'Afrique* in much the same way as European public law. Islam was introduced in the African interiors beginning around the 10th century, accompanied by adaptation of Islamic laws amongst the new converts. In most places, Islamic law and African laws were infused into one legal regime, especially in areas such as warfare, arbitration, and the treatment of prisoners of war.[115] However, Islamic law, like any other external influences, generally remained subordinate to African customary laws.

As per European categories, pre-transatlantic African state relations indeed fitted squarely with conventional international relations, as the various collectivities sufficiently addressed pertinent questions of peace, war, treaties, trade, and frontiers. A sound economic system naturally presupposes the ability to regulate both internal and external relations. Both internally and internationally, African kingdoms developed extensive trading systems and satisfactorily formulated and administered law and order in their collectivities, including the regulation of trade and wars. Arabs and other Muslim states typically exchanged emissaries with various collectivities. All the prominent African kingdoms had emissaries—the equivalence nowadays of ambassadors (variously termed then as messengers), both in other African states and around the world, especially in the Arab world and Europe. For instance, the Kingdom of Benin and Portugal had resident emissaries in each other's territory until 1539, when Portuguese missionaries in Benin protested to King John III of Portugal about the Oba (king) of Benin's poor habit of ill-treating foreign dignitaries in his kingdom. Moreover, the first Congolese (*Kongo*) embassy in Rome has been traced to 1514.[116]

3.4 Varying Slave Trade Practices: The Cases of Portugal, Spain, and England

3.4.1 The Portuguese Actions in Africa and Origins of Transatlantic Trade

The 15th century marked the beginning of what generally became known as the Age of Discovery, considering the unprecedented frequency with which Iberian states penetrated non-European societies in Africa, the Americas, and Asia—claiming "discovery" and establishing trading relationships.[117] Portugal was led by their ambitious prince, Henry the Navigator (1394–1460). Third third son of King John I of Portugal and the Algarve and a strong advocate of maritime and commercial expansion, the prince personified the spirit of Portugal's economic nationalism. Bent on exploring the coastal areas south of Morocco, his crew sought out to establish trade relations with the great West African kingdoms while searching for the sea route to India. During the next half century (1434–1481), more Portuguese expeditions followed, sailing their trading ships to the Gulf of Guinea including Cape Verde in 1460, Kongo in 1483, and the Cape of Good Hope in 1488. These expeditions culminated to Portuguese trading posts all across West Africa and the Canary Islands, as well as a foothold in some uninhabited islands, namely Azores, Cape Verde, and Madeira.[118]

In the course of their expeditions, the Portuguese met with stiff resistance along the West African coast and the Canary Islands. In spite of the resistance,[119] Portugal became the first European country to enslave Africans. While most of the early missions focused on barter trade such as exchange of European articles with African gold, gum, ivory, hides, and nuts, one of the notorious expeditions led by Captain Antam Gonçalvez severely deviated from the orthodox tradition in 1441 when his team ventured inland and looted and apprehended ten African captives in raids on Mauritania.[120] A follow-up raid that same year attacked Cape Bojador on the West African coast, capturing 240 more Africans, and on the merchants' return to Portugal, some of the captives were handed over as gifts to the Portuguese Crown, while the vast majority were sold as slaves. Upon converting the captives on their return to Portugal as chattel slaves, the merchants promptly recognised the immense benefit of slave trafficking as an economic enterprise.[121]

Europeans reportedly inhibited a superstitious belief on Africa prior to 1434 that the sea below Cape Bojador "boiled and the sun turned [white] men's skin black."[122] Following the successful Portuguese expedition, this myth was broken, thus paving the way for more adventurous explorations and the erection of the first slave forts on Arguim Island.[123] Although delighted by the Portuguese loot, Prince Henry was very disturbed by the atrocities that were reportedly committed in the process on the African West Coast. In a bit to clear his conscience and redeem the Portuguese state, the prince—despite writing the pope (Eugenius IV) seeking spiritual indulgence while also detailing plans for future raids, nevertheless also represented the nature and purpose of Portuguese commerce that formed the object of his letter as a "warlike crusade." The pope responded with some praise for the Portuguese deeds, blessing any further raids thus: "to all those who shall be engaged in the said war, complete forgiveness of all your sins."[124]

Pertaining to the question of slavery and slave trade, the Catholic Church perceived the institution in the 15th and 16th centuries as an appropriate punishment for the enemies of Christendom.[125] The role of the Catholic Church was paramount to European juridical thinking process—the influence dating many centuries back. As far back as AD 380, Christianity was decreed by Theodosius I (Roman emperor from AD 379 to 395) to become the legal religion of the Roman Empire.[126] By the 16th century, Iberian Crowns (Portugal, Castilla, and Aragon), like much of Western Europe, frequently based the foundations of their legal traditions on Christian doctrines. They all subscribed to the belief that the papacy had the absolute authority to grant definitive rights of possession to Christian powers over infidel states, especially when there were conflicting claims to title.[127] Human social order and political life was governed by *lex naturalis*, which was mostly derived from theological doctrines and widely viewed by publicists at the time as universal in application. Accordingly, the church was conceived as the primary source for the dissemination of knowledge, interpretation of ethical behaviour, and enactment of sound laws. One of the reasons why Columbus and his crew chose to sail westwards to the Indies, for instance, was principally to avoid any outright interference with the papal grant of African monopoly to Portugal.[128]

Begun since the 6th century but commonplace only from the 15th century on, papal bulls were in essence decrees issued by popes, awarding donations of sovereignty and monopoly in foreign lands to European Christian sovereigns.[129] To the papacy, the tradition of awarding bulls was perceived as a modality of maintaining extraterritorial certainty, hence law and order amongst European sovereigns both within and withal Europe.[130] Upon reviewing the conventional features of contemporary international tribunals (jurisdictions arbitrating disputes between sovereign states, and arbitration chambers whereby parties in litigation must consent to the primacy of the court), one scholar has observed that the papacy court clearly functioned in the medieval period as an international tribunal.[131] By papacy court, Ullmann was referring not just to ecclesiastical courts which administered canon law, but to papal pronouncements and decrees as well, which, as has been documented, not only had strong legal appeal but were fervently recognised and enforced by nation states. Pope Innocent IV said as much in his annotation on *Liber Extra V.XXXIX*, wherein he pronounced the papacy as court of universal jurisdiction.[132] In spite of the unparalleled international legal authority exercised by popes during the underlined epochs, it seems to me that the contentions of Ullmann and Pope Innocent IV are at best a stretch, given that the papacy as an institution at no point in time effectively functioned as a traditional tribunal.

King Afonso V of Portugal (1432–1481) lent his support to Portuguese slave trafficking by making an all-encompassing compelling case for invasion to the papacy wherein he solicited for the church's blessings and authorisation for future African raids and occupation of those lands.[133] A series of correspondence between Afonso V and the pope as well as a number of papal bulls issued by the papacy culminated into a doctrine of *evangelising mission* that legally justified the enslavement of Africans and peoples of the Canary Islands, while linking the doctrine with the idea of progress.[134] The inhabitants of the Canary Islands and similar peoples, Afonso V claimed in his correspondence, were overly primitive and constantly violated the law of nature. He then rhetorically asked the pope the question whether subjecting them to servitude was a befitting punishment for such violations and gross transgressions.[135] The insinuation was that the peoples to be raided were a lost people, and it was for their own benefit to come under the supervision of advanced peoples, as they were accordingly going to be drilled according to norms of Christendom and civility. Having overcome their backward predicament, they could then pursue the imperative path of progress.[136] Pope Eugenius IV having consulted with his top lawyers responded in the affirmative, approving but also spelling out a set of principles which Portugal had to abound to, in the papal bull *Illius Qui*.[137] The Portuguese missions were in fact authorised only as long as they were missionary undertakings geared at converting heathen populations into the Christian faith. Whereupon peaceful missionaries were attacked, Portugal was within its legitimate right to use troops to protect missionaries in invaded territories, and all inhabitants who attacked the missionaries could be defeated and enslaved as punishment.[138]

With the papal authorisation, what begun as Portuguese trade diplomacy with African societies was beginning to give way to a right of just war—or, as one scholar has observed, central to Portuguese ideology and strategy was the conception of trade as war.[139] Acting on this mindset and with the blessing of the papacy, Portugal established a strong foothold along the West African coast and the Canary Islands. Basil Davidson has noted that

> by 1506, Duarte Pacheco Pereira is writing that goods exchanged at Arguim and elsewhere consisted of gold, black slaves, oryx leather for shields, and other items, against Portuguese red and blue stuffs and various textiles, both poor and good quality, as well as horses.[140]

The validity of Portuguese monopolistic acquisitions were re-confirmed in 1455 by Pope Nicolas V through a papal bull dubbed *Romanus Pontifex* to Afonso V, wherein the pope decreed that Portugal was authorised to subdue and convert all pagan societies in all the regions south of Morocco.[141]

Far more unambiguous than previous papal letters, *Romanus Pontifex* explicitly accorded the king of Portugal the right to enslave and exploit Africans and the peoples of the Canary Islands. As for the sanctity of slavery, Nicolas V, like the pontiffs before him, perceived it as an appropriate deterrence against barbaric behaviour prominent amongst heathens. For all lands that Portugal had "subdued and peacefully possessed," Afonso V was accordingly accorded "general and indefinite powers to search out and conquer all pagans, enslave them and appropriate their lands and goods."[142] As to what constituted "subdued and peacefully possessed," the bull insinuated that slavery was legitimate if slaves were acquired from a just war or a barter purchase. As one scholar has pondered, buying slaves from barter trade presupposed that the people dubbed slaves were legitimately owned in the first place.[143] While slave merchants reverted to regulated commercial exchange and bargaining in slaves during the epoch of transatlantic trade, Portugal, following its initial raid on Mauritania and for over three decades, nevertheless mostly acquired its slaves through similar pillaging operations. Portugal's slave imports in the Americas rose from 142,300 by 1518 to 241,400 by 1600, 560,000 by 1700, 1,909,730 by 1810, and 1,445,400 by 1866—totalling 4,298,830 people shipped out of Africa into slavery.[144]

The Portuguese hegemony inspired new commercial interests and anxieties amongst other European powers who sought to replicate Portugal's economic successes. The trade that resulted from these countries engaging with sub-Saharan Africa linked Europe with Africa and the New World, and economic processes steadily relied on African slave labour for sustenance and profitability. While *Romanus Pontifex* granted exclusive right of enslavement of Africans and peoples of the Canary Islands to Portugal, profits from the trade soon attracted other Europeans (Holland, England, France, Spain, etc.), and Pope Alexander VI was compelled to issue a new bull of demarcation dubbed *Inter caetera* in two parts, one in 1493 and a second in 1494, wherein he figuratively divided the non-European world across the Atlantic between two competing Iberian states: Portugal and Spain.[145] While Spain by this new bull was accorded all lands of non-Christians in the west and south coasts of the Americas and around the Cape Verde Islands in Africa, Portugal received all lands 300 miles to the east.[146]

Following *Inter Caetera*, a peace treaty (treaty of Tordesillas) was signed between Spain and Portugal to delimit their spheres of influence across the Atlantic Ocean.[147] As a result of *Inter Caetera* and the Treaty of Tordesillas, Portugal enjoyed an exclusive monopoly over African lands and the area surrounding the Amazon—which later became Brazil—while Spain's monopoly covered all of South America and parts of Central and North America. This demarcation and delimitation became the turning point for Spain's policy on the slave trade during the first half century of their conquest of the New World. Although *Inter Caetera* did not explicitly mention slavery or the slave trade, it nevertheless set the blueprint for extraterritorial sovereignty by delimiting spheres of influence and right of possession to the first settler or occupier who undertook the duty to preach the gospel and convert pagan populations into Christianity.[148] Once in possession, subjects from any other Christian nation needed to take permission from the monarch in control before entering or preaching in those lands.

Overall, the expansion of Europe to the New World beginning in 1492 came to depend on the economic foundations engineered by the Portuguese in Africa, in the previous decades. The fervent adherence by European Christian powers to papal jurisdiction had the effect of propelling mercantilist practices. That is, papal bulls were sought for the dual goal of recognising colonial claims over conquered territories, and moreover for excluding rival Christian nations from trading in already-claimed territories, except they sought permission from the duly authorised sovereign. As a result, Christian sovereigns who were empowered by papal bulls enjoyed absolute right to institute monopolies in annexed lands. The papal bulls collectively had the effect of crystallising the doctrine of discovery.[149] The doctrine would later justify every European colonial act around the globe, with publicists of rival powers generally recognising rival claims as legitimate. The doctrine steadily evolved to mean that Christian nations could freely and lawfully invade (discover) non-Christian lands, with the "discovering" country automatically entitled to claim both sovereign and property rights over these new territories.[150] Although Vitoria was a dissenting voice on the subject—noting that "discovery" could not be a legal ground for Spanish dominion in America, European Christian nations nevertheless used variants of the doctrine as a useful shorthand to legitimate their extraterritorial actions and domination in non-Christian nations, and moreover to resolve potential conflicts with rivals over explorations and trade.[151]

3.4.2 Spain, Encomienda, Asiento, *and African Slavery*

Following *Inter Caetera* and the Treaty of Tordesillas, Portugal exercised its territorial privilege by importing scores of Africans to work as slaves in its American plantations, while Spain, delimited by the two acts, exclusively relied on Amerindians for slave labour during the first half century of their conquest.[152] After Columbus returned to Spain in 1494 from his second voyage in the Americas with Amerindian slaves as special tribute to the Spanish crown, the question as to whether the Crown or the *conquistadors* (explorers of the Spanish Empire) could legitimately exploit the labour of the local inhabitants became a key consideration for both the sovereign and Spanish legal practitioners.[153] Upon consideration, the Spanish Crown empowered its conquerors to extract labour from local inhabitants all over Hispaniola, and compel them to pay taxes to the Crown. The basis of enslaving Amerindians was framed on their lack of political organisation and their perceived incapability of ruling themselves. Their enslavement was thus conceived in terms of servitude rather than slavery. Astutely framed by Spain as the minimal indebtedness that local inhabitants needed to pay the Crown for protecting them, improving their welfare, drilling them towards progress, and training them in the Spanish language, Amerindian enslavement essentially fulfilled the requirement of taxation to the state.[154]

To give procurements a sense of legality, Spain for instance self-abided to a special proclamation known as the *Requerimiento* as a necessary prerequisite prior to annexing various American communities. The *Requerimiento* was a declaration of dominion and war. Written by Juan López de Palacios Rubios—a professor of law at Salamanca who doubled as Council of Castile jurist in 1510, the *Requerimiento* provided the theoretical basis and doctrinal foundation of Spanish acquisitions in the Americas.[155] As a prerequisite, the reading of the *Requerimiento* was to be duly witnessed by a notary; informing indigenous peoples in Spanish what would happen to them if they failed to submit voluntarily to European authority and convert to Christianity. A typical *requerimiento* read thus:

> We shall forcibly enter your country and shall make war against you in all ways and manners that we can … we shall take your wives and your children, and shall make slaves of them … and we shall take away your goods and do all the harm and danger that we can … and we protest that all the deaths and losses which shall accrue from this are your fault, and not of their Highnesses, or ours, or of the gentlemen who come with us.[156]

Spain enforced the collection of "taxes" and tributes from Amerindians by applying an *encomienda* system on local inhabitants—a mercantilist-like labour system according to which the Crown granted monopoly over the local population to assigned individuals with the duties of, amongst other things, extracting labour, instructing them in Christianity and Spanish culture, and suppressing any subversion against the Crown.[157] Bent on staying economically competitive with other European powers, beneficiaries of *encomiendas* overworked the Amerindians, which led to a steady drastic shrink in populations. Although the Spanish Crown acknowledged this fact and declared the death of one in every ten Amerindians, in actuality, the mortality was nine in ten.[158] Bartolomé de Las Casas, a prominent 16th-century Dominican friar, lamented the gravity of the atrocities, stating that

> the reason why the death toll was so high was because, in a bit to maximize profits, the *conquistadors* who financed slave-fleets arranged for the vessels to carry nothing in the way of victuals except a basic minimum for the crew and so there is hardly any food or water for the poor prisoners who, as a consequence, perish from thirst and hunger and are consigned to a watery grave.[159]

Like Las Casas, the enslavement of Amerindians became a contentious subject of debate amongst other Dominican friars. Despite Las Casas's humanitarian position, there was not so much debate amongst Dominican friars on the legitimacy of slavery as an institution, but rather on standards of just war. Whereas for Francisco de Vitoria (1483–1546) and Francisco Suarez (1548–1617), slaves were spoils of war, Las Casas limited the principle only to Africans, excluding Amerindians, although he in later years recanted from endorsing any form of slavery. Vitoria first approached the question of slavery by reassessing

Aristotle's contention of the natural slave and the natural rulers. Despite expressing serious doubts on Aristotle's narrative of obligation of servitude versus dominance as derivative from physical weakness and physical strength, Vitoria nevertheless insinuated that Aristotle's thesis ought not to be read from the letter but rather from the spirit of what he perceived as constituting legal slavery. To him, Aristotle's characterisation was plainly speaking a case for paternalism. That is, according to Vitoria, by natural slaves, what Aristotle

> means is that by defects of the nature that they need to be ruled and governed by others and that it is good for them to be subject to others, just as sons need to be subject to their parents until full age, and a wife to her husband.[160]

Vitoria obviously read Aristotle not as conventionally interpreted, but as derivative from the standpoint of a supposed lack of political institution and capacity of certain persons to rule themselves. On the rationality of the enslaved, Vitoria argued that "brutes, who do not move by their own will but are moved by some other, as Aquinas says cannot have any dominion."[161] Independently, Vitoria conceived any legitimate institution of slavery only as a temporal modality to nurture societies or peoples with defects into maturity, upon which time they could gain their manumission. Contrary to Aristotle, however, Vitoria conceived a window of political liberation for the enslaved. Even so, while Aristotle conceived slavery as a function of law of nature, Vitoria in harmony with many of his contemporaries observed that Amerindians could not be annexed or enslaved per natural law, but rather through *jus gentium* as spoils of war.[162] It was a given of *jus gentium* that the Spaniard, just like all persons, were endowed with the right to travel in the New World, sojourn there and lawfully trade with the local inhabitants.[163] As a result, the Spaniards were within their right to declare war on native populations if the latter resisted or infringed on the legitimate right of the Spaniards to trade. Contending that "it is the universal rule of law of nations that whatever is captured in war becomes the property of the conqueror," Vitoria in effect opened the legal possibility for Amerindians to be legitimately enslaved.[164]

Vitoria's contemporary Francisco Suarez concurred with him that slavery was only legitimate as per just war caveats of *jus gentium*. Although Suarez in his construction conceived the institution of slavery as an unnatural act, he nonetheless provided that it constituted a legitimate exception in *jus gentium*, for the purpose of enabling progress and safeguarding law and order:

> For peoples and nations, in their relations with one another, put into practice the law regarding slavery, although that institution was not necessary for the standpoint of natural reason; for, as I have said, another mode of punishment could have been introduced, to wit: death. Under present conditions however, the law in question exists in such form that the guilty are bound to submit to the punishment of slavery in accordance with the

manner in which that custom has been introduced, while the victors, on their side, may not justly punish their conquered enemies more severely at the close of the war unless there exists some other special ground for punishment which would justify such a course of action.[165]

Unlike Vitoria and Suarez, Las Casas adopted a totally contrary view against the enslavement of Amerindians, arguing that just war doctrines did not apply to them, for as he saw it, they were not rebels against the Spanish Crown, but rather mere pagans. Perceiving their offence of paganism as failing to meet the threshold warranting legitimate enslavement, Las Casas recommended that the *conquistadors* instead make it a duty to convert the locals into Christianity.[166] While Las Casas was an arduous critique of slavery in America, which earned him the monikers of "humanist" and "protector of Indians" amongst contemporary commentators, he nevertheless, paradoxically, expressed total support of the enslavement of Africans.[167] This implies that he may have been either more concerned with the pace of extinction of the American population which Spain envisaged to convert to Christianity, or the fate of the Tainos that he knew so well.

In spite of his critique of the exploitation of Amerindians, the timing of the irony in Las Casas's stance in defence of the enslavement of Africans was evidently economically driven, considering Spain's helplessness in generating effective labour in the New World. For an estimated population of 50 million Amerindians in Spanish-controlled territories in the New World at the time of conquest, just barely 8 million survived three decades later.[168] In order to mitigate the alarming mortality amongst the Amerindian population, Spain badly needed to revert to the African slave trade by 1516, in order to maintain its economic competitiveness with European rivals.

While Spaniard harsh labour extraction practices certainly led to many deaths, the vast majority of Amerindian mortality nevertheless was as a result of the population's exposure to European diseases and their weak immunity thereto.[169] Africans, on the other hand, not only had strong immunity against malaria and yellow fever, but were also perceived as suitable for tropical labour.[170] One study has found that the Amerindian population drastically shrunk from 54 million in 1492 to only 6 million by 1650, with local populations virtually extinguished in many areas.[171] In 1545, Spain completely abolished its *encomienda* policy in the New World, categorically stating that:

> neither by war nor any other means, even if it be under the guise of rebellion, nor by barter, nor in any other way, shall any Indian whatsoever be made a slave, and we wish them to be treated as vassals of the Crown of Castille, for such they are.[172]

Although pockets of African slaves were present in Spanish colonies across the New World as far back as 1502—mostly as servants of the *conquistadors*—it took at least two more decades before Spain considered African slavery as the main source of labour. In 1510, King Ferdinand of Spain ordered the *Casa de Contratacion* to send 250 Africans to the Spanish colonies to substitute the Amerindian labour shortage.[173] Las Casas's backing of the sanctity of African enslavement was based on the consideration that since slaves who were brought from Africa into the New World were far removed from their native lands, they could easily adapt in their new environment even better than the Spaniards. As he observed, "when put to hard tasks, Africans carried them out more effectively."[174] The British historian Vincent T. Harlow audaciously noted that "for the money that procured a White man's services for ten years could buy a negro for life."[175] In line with Las Casas's thinking, Africans were conceived as a perfect fit for slavery given that they were less vulnerable to European diseases than Amerindians, and being strangers in the New World, they were also seen as less likely to attempt to escape. The Spaniards reportedly claimed that "one negro was worth four Indians"[176] In the aftermath of Spain's enslavement of Africans and rampant spread of their exploitation in plantations across the New World, Las Casas later regretted and repented from his earlier perspective, noting that

> This suggestion to issue a license to bring Negro slaves to the Indies was made first by the cleric Casas [referring himself in the third person], not seeing how unjust the Portuguese were in taking slaves [on the coast of Africa]. Later on he realized how unjustly and tyrannically Africans were taken slaves, in the same fashion as Indians.[177]

The Spanish resolve to revert to African slavery faced two legal stumbling blocks, to wit: the papal bulls to Portugal, and the Treaty of Tordesillas that delimited territorial monopolies between the two Iberian states. Having been delimited by these two regimes, Spain devised a new policy of *asiento de negros*, as a modality of supplying its New World colonies with African slave labour. An *asiento* symbolised "a treaty between the Spanish crown and a legal person, that is, a private person or a company, by which the crown rented to the contracting party for a defined period the monopolistic right to merchandise a certain commodity."[178] Without their own slave forts and trading posts in Africa, *asiento* licences emerged as a convenient approach of generating profits for the colonies, since it is the beneficiaries who ultimately bore the risks of trade but also had to pay taxes to the Spanish Crown and operate under Spanish law.[179]

With the institution of *asiento de negros*, there was an exponential rise in the number of slaves shipped into Spanish colonies in the New World from Africa between the close of the 16th century and the 19th century. But the increase was also due in part to the birth of Reformation in European thinking, which began when Martin Luther published his legendary 95 theses against the Roman Catholic Church, thereby giving birth to Protestantism against erstwhile conventional Christian dogmas.[180] Lasting until the Peace of Westphalia in 1648, the Reformation age sprouted a whole new awakening in European thinking. For the first time in many centuries, the hegemony of the papacy as the harbinger of universal justice was directly questioned, challenged, and defied by a significant number of the European metropolitan public. Spain was always Catholic and was the master of counter-reformation, but was nonetheless no longer stringently bound by the Reformation. This relaxing in policy weakened the rigidity of papal bulls to Portugal and the Treaty of Tordesillas, which delineated the Spanish Crown from the African slave trade.

In the spirit of the Reformation, the Italian jurist Alberico Gentili (1552–1608), Regius professor of civil law at the University of Oxford, in his 1598 book *De Iure Belli Libri Tres*, questioned the basis of the laws of war, captured prisoners, and the legal rationale for slavery. He observed that the laws of war on captured prisoners which allowed them to be enslaved were not only harsh and unfair but moreover disproportionately affected subordinate soldiers.[181] As he observed, while the lives of top military commanders were spared or exchanged for ransom, it was common practice to kill or enslave ordinary soldiers. Observing that the perpetual imprisonment of soldiers—or their enslavement—could only be an act of injustice, Gentili put forward a narrative of justice that envisaged all captives, irrespective of their military ranks, to be spared.[182] While Gentili's legal precursors largely validated just war doctrines for enslavement of prisoners of war as a substitute for death, Gentili on his part broke away from the conventional thinking, arguing that slavery inevitably depicted bondage—a state of man when all hopes of freedom are lost, and the individual is reduced to conditions of subhuman.[183] Conceiving the natural (original) state of man as one of freedom, Gentili observed that considering that the institution of slavery stripped humans of all natural liberties, it ought to be qualified as beast-like rather than progress—it was as good as death.[184]

Despite strongly decrying the injustices of slavery, Gentili lamentedly concluded that the "slavery belongs to the law of nations and today is common to Christians with all infidels ... our laws restrain the cruelty of masters, as well as the shamelessness and ill-treatment of their slaves."[185] As to why slavery in spite of its perceived injustice could be in harmony with the law of nature, Gentili invoked Aquinas's rationale that this was because it allowed prisoners to be punished.[186]

3.4.3 *Virginia, African Enslavement, and Shifts in English Colonial Jurisprudence*

3.4.3.1 England's First Enslaved Africans

Following the initiation of the transatlantic slave trade by Iberian states, English merchants and investors continually appealed to the English Crown for permission to participate in the triangular trade. In spite of the pressure, the Crown for almost a century unwaveringly resisted countless appeals petitioning the country to reform the common law and recognise the ownership of peoples as slaves or legitimate property. At the dawn of the 17th century however, England—fearful of being surpassed by fellow European rivals that were amassing untold riches in the New World and expanding by leaps and bounds—made a swift turn in orientation and decisively joined the transatlantic slave trade, thereby becoming the last European power to do so.

In its capacity as the first English colony in the New World, Virginia was a trendsetter for British colonial jurisprudence, especially on questions of slavery and the slave trade. The neighbouring colonies of North Carolina and Maryland as well as the southern colonies of South Carolina and Georgia (which collectively later became part of the United States) were not only borne out of the plough back profits from the enslavement of Africans in Virginia but moreover wholly followed Virginia's lead by co-opting the territory's legal codes, especially on slavery and the slave trade. While the supply of indentured servants from England to Virginia was for several decades initially adequate in meeting English planters' needs, the scheme was nonetheless perceived not only as expensive but moreover as preventing the territorial expansion of English colonies especially in comparison to rival colonial powers.[187] Beginning in 1619, the English administration in Virginia embarked on developing a legal system that not only accommodated slavery and slave trade, but moreover formed the bedrock of its swelling plantation agricultural scheme.

In August 1619, John Rolfe, an English tobacco cultivator in the colony of Virginia—most famous for his marriage to Pocahontas[188]—wrote a letter to Edwin Sandys, one of the founders of the Virginia Company of London, wherein he reported that "20 and odd Negroes" had just been offloaded at Point Comfort, Virginia, from an English vessel.[189] The "odd Negroes," Rolfe attested, were reportedly sold to them by "Dutch man of warre."[190] Rolfe's account was corroborated by John Pory, the Colony's Secretary of state, in a correspondence to the English envoy to The Hague, Sir Dudley Carleton.[191] The "Dutch man of warre" was a slaving ship, aptly named for its monopolising of a peculiar kind of violence, namely, the transatlantic slave trade that had now received universal acceptance amongst all European powers as a modality of capital accumulation and growth. As it turned out, the "20 and odd Negroes" had been violently kidnapped and chained by an intruding slaving Portuguese crew that stormed a village in what is present-day Angola, whereupon they forced their captives unto their ship named *San Juan Bautista* with the intent of taking them to the Spanish colonies in Veracruz as slaves.[192] The ship was subsequently attacked by two English Warwick-based pirates' vessels, one of which sailed under the flag of the Duke of Savoy, while the other (Dutch man of warre) was flying a Dutch flag.[193]

In view of the historical conjecture, Rolfe's metaphorical account was not a casual comment but rather laden with some noteworthy significance. It signalled England's decisive entry into the Atlantic slave trade. While his specification of "20 and odd Negroes" was a methodical way of conceptualising the kidnapped Africans as subhuman, his valorisation of the "Dutch man of warre," true to the spirit of primitive accumulation, was a vivid signal of the imperativeness of violence and oppression as a corollary for extracting labour from slaves, in the colony's drive of growth and profits. Frequent acts of violence on enslaved Africans in due course ranged from sexual rape, corporal punishment, and various forms of physical brutality, to outright killing. While the report of "20 and odd Negroes" marked the first official acknowledgement of slaves in Virginia, they were nonetheless not the first enslaved Africans in the colony. The Virginia census of March 1619 noted the presence of "32 Negroes ... 17 men and 15 women" working "in the service of seu[er]all planters, since the begininge of March 1619."[194]

Although the triangular trade became central to the English economy only in 1650, English merchants had nevertheless been very involved in the African slave trade both before and afterwards. One notorious English slaver, John Hawkins—well noted for his brute methods—made three expeditions to Africa between 1562 and 1567. Following his first voyage whereupon he captured 300 Africans as slaves, he famously stated that he obtained them "partly by the sworde, and partly by other meanes."[195] Queen Elizabeth I was so impressed with him for his successes that she re-assigned him in a ship named *Jesus* to replicate the mission on her behalf. Hawkins's crew had six vessels altogether during the fateful 1567 voyage. Reportedly fighting alongside an African local ruler in Sierra Leone in a war with a neighbouring African kingdom, Hawkins succeeded in kidnapping over 500 Africans as bounty. On his return to England, Elizabeth I made him a knight "with a demi-moor in his proper colour bound with a chord as his crest." Hawkins celebrated his coronation by choosing an African bound in chains as his coat of arms.[196]

In spite of England's late entry, it nonetheless steadily came to dominate the trade in African slaves throughout the 17th and 18th centuries.[197] Its dominance over fellow European slaving nations was due to two key favouring circumstances. Firstly, English trading stations of Gambia and Ghana in Africa coupled with its expansive Caribbean colonies proved to be of enormous strategic importance. While the African stations were central for assembling captured slaves in Africa, the Caribbean colonies were exceptionally fertile and conducive for plantation agriculture.[198] England seized on this and heavily invested in sugarcane and cotton in its American colonies—crops which before long became the dominant agricultural commodities of the era. While North American was configured to specialise in the production of cotton and tobacco as dominant crops, the Caribbean specialised in sugar production. Barbados in particular, by reason of being the leading sugar producer amongst the English colonies, was variously dubbed "the mother of West Indian sugar islands" and "the brightest Jewel in His majesty's Crown."[199] In order to keep up with the heightened demand for both sugar and cotton, England was compelled to disproportionately traffic more in the slave trade than competing European slaving nations. Being the dominant exploiter of African slave labour, England, which steadily invested heavily in cotton and sugar—dubbed by several academics as the most valuable dominant commodities in international trade at the time—reaped the most benefits as well from the colonisation of the

Americas. Not only did the hegemony in these commodities sparked English geographic expansion and growth beyond Virginia into the rest of North America and the Caribbean, it also effectively curbed the entire European reliance on Asian textile and fabrics.[200] On becoming the leading global supplier of textile and sugar, England steadily revamped virtually every sector of its economy.

England was moreover favoured by its huge advances in shipbuilding and maritime prowess. On entering the triangular trade, England was better equipped to handle recurrent difficulties faced by merchant slaving ships, which frequently resulted in loss of lives and cargo.[201] Coupled with this advantage, England enacted a number of protectionist acts that guaranteed monopolistic trade throughout its colonies. While the English Navigation Act of 1651 required all goods transported into England (and its colonies) to be transported by English vessels, the Staple Act of 1663 required "all colonial exports to Europe be landed through an English port before being re-exported to Europe."[202] England's strict protectionism effectively excluded most rivals from its colonies—Holland, which owned several commercial vessels and whose colonies were adjacent to the English, being the most adversely affected.[203] In 1663, England accorded a charter to the Royal African Company (formerly operated as the Company of Royal Adventurers) to trade in African slaves. The charter empowered with the "entire and only trade for the buying and selling, bartering and exchanging of for or with any negroes, slaves, goods, wares and merchandises."[204] The Royal African Company captured valuable portions of the African coasts on behalf of England for the international slave trade. These forts became vital for England in expanding commercial and national interests in Africa.[205]

3.4.3.2 Steady Shifts in English Colonial Jurisprudence on Slavery

Having embraced the transatlantic slave trade as the modality for realising colonial exigencies, the colony of Virginia naturally looked to England for legal guidance; but England, still sceptical of reforming the Common Law in its mainland to embrace slavery, in turn looked to rival European powers with the hope of deriving the much-needed vocabulary necessary to convert desired labour populations from the status of personhood into mere chattel property in its colonies. While the enslavement of Africans had been persistent across Virginia even prior to the arrival of "20 and odd Negroes," it was nevertheless not until March 1659 that the colonial administration passed a trading law, which officially recognised slavery as a corollary of its taxation exigencies. The law, inter alia, provided that

> if the Dutch or other foreigners shall import any negro slaves, they, the said Dutch or others shall, for the tobacco really produced by the sale of the said negro, pay only the impost of two shillings per hogshead, the like being paid by our owne nation.[206]

This Act was the most explicit acknowledgement to date of the colonial administration's conception of Africans in the territory as chattel property rather than persons.

Prior to embracing the transatlantic slave trade, the colony of Virginia previously heavily relied on indentured servants brought to the territory from the British Isles (their terms of servitude typically lasted for seven years, after which they were accorded full rights as free men).[207] The arrival of Africans thus coincided with the presence of many English, Scottish, and Irish indentured servants who were still held in labour bondage, and who naturally detested the colonial administration. It did not take long before the colonial administration found itself faced with the problem of complicit cooperation between the indentured servants and African slaves for the attendant purposes of running away from the plantations. The Virginia parliament (the Burgesses) responded to this new challenge by enacting a new regulatory "Runaways Act," authorising extension of the terms of servitude of culprit indentured servants, and an increase of the gravity of corporal punishment to be melted down on any escaping slaves.[208]

Given that the Runaways Act of 1661 provided inter alia that any Christian who ran away with a slave was bound to serve extra time in proportion to the labour time lost by the caught runaway slave, it became uncertain whether Christians could accordingly be legitimately enslaved. Moreover, considering that Europeans at the onset of the transatlantic slave trade initially advanced the evangelising mission, namely, the lack of Christianity amongst Africans as well as the imperativeness of extending the Christian faith unto heathen Africans as justification for the slave trade, doubts continually abound as to whether conversion into Christianity correspondingly translated into one's emancipation from slavery. While acknowledging this nuance, the Virginia House of Burgesses passed an Act in 1667 whereupon it categorically rejected baptism into Christianity as a ground for exempting any slave's status in bondage:

> Whereas some doubts have arising whether children that are slaves by birth, and by the charity and piety of their owners made pertakers of the blessed sacrament of baptisme, should by virtue of their baptisme be made ffree; It is enacted … that the conferring of baptisme doth not alter the condition of the person as to his bondage or ffreedome; that diverse masters, ffreed from this doubt, may more carefully endeavour the propagation of christianity by permitting … slaves … to be admitted to that sacrament.[209]

In October 1670, the Burgesses passed a Slavery Status act, dubbed as Act XII, which clearly delimited the following category of persons as susceptible for enslavement, coupled with the terms of servitude: persons that came to the colony by sea (Africans from Africa) were bound to be enslaved for life; and those that came by land (Africans arriving from elsewhere in the Americas) were to have their terms of servitude delimited by their ages at time of arrival.[210] In effect, the Act observed that "all servants not being Christians imported into this country by shipping shalbe slaves for their lives." By contrast, those who came by land as boys or girls were to be enslaved for 30 years, and for 12 years if they were adults at the time of their arrival.[211] In practice, it was more of a difference without a distinction, as slavers recurrently traded slaves between Virginia and neighbouring states, without any consideration as to whether the slaves were shipped into the Americas or were born in the New World.

Virginia colonial laws and codes in general were outrightly racist in orientation, especially with regard to the framing of categories of freedom and servitude, Africans and their descendants being the unmistakable targets of enslavement, even when race was tactically not explicitly highlighted. Even as the 1667 Act rejected the possibility of emancipation of African slaves through conversion to Christianity, a new Act with more stringent rigours was enacted by Virginian lawmakers in 1682 with a new Christian nativity clause, aimed at ensuring that descendants of slaves born in the New World retained the hereditary status of slaves. The Act inter alia provided that "all servants … whether Negroes, Moors, Mollattoes or Indians, who and whose parentage and native country are not Christian at the time of their first purchase of such servant by some Christian … [shall] be slaves."[212] The purport of this new legislation was obviously to empower slave owners with an open-ended right of ownership of all descendants of slaves. Since all persons already enslaved in the Americas supposedly came from non-Christian backgrounds, it went without saying per the legislation that all of their descendants, including slaves imported from other New World colonies, were by analogy also slaves by heritage.

The colony of Virginia was in fact a classic testing and fertile ground for the rigours of primitive accumulation. It evidenced some of the most glaring instances of the violence of capital accumulation. Profits were all that really mattered to the colonial administration as it sanctioned and codified jurisprudential doctrines on plantation slavery. While the mulattoes in the colony were fathered by slave owners, coming from professed Christian nations (the marker for entitlement to rights), Virginian lawmakers, in their quest for an expanded labour force in plantations, nonetheless opted for an inconsistent position that ensured that offspring of slave mothers were slaves from birth. This was a decisive break from Common Law in mainland England, which provided that all children born out of wedlock naturally assumed the status of their fathers. If this doctrine was to apply, the entire mulatto population (which constituted well over a quarter of all persons classified as black) would have been free peoples right from birth. Unwilling to consider such a likelihood, Virginia lawmakers completely abandoned the common law doctrine and adopted the Roman law rule of *partus sequitur ventrem*,[213] which essentially provided that the child follows the condition of the mother.[214]

While the Roman rule of *partus sequitur ventrem* enabled Virginia lawmakers to overcome the challenge of according rights to mulatto populations, it is noteworthy that the doctrine was initially construed by Roman law to govern livestock and animals rather than humans.[215] It was apparently for this reason that English jurists found the rule to be invaluable for realising the exigencies of an expanded labour force, and hence increased production, given that by explicitly reducing women and their offspring to the rank of animals, they were accordingly excluded from the realm of rights reserved for humans. As William Blackstone famously observed, "Of all tame and domestic animals, the brood belongs to the owner of the dam or mother; the English law agreeing with the civil, that *partus sequitur ventrem* in the brute creation, though for the most part in the human species it disallows that maxim."[216]

Although most enslaved African women who bore children for slave masters did not consent to sexual encounters, they unfortunately did not have any recourse through the legal system, as blacks were legally prohibited from testifying against any white person in a court of law.[217] Given that labour was indispensable for economic production, all forms of resistance or rebellion from slavery were accordingly treated as grave crimes deserving of maximum punishment. Beside the *partus sequitur ventrem* rule, two codes, one in 1680 and another in 1691, followed in Roman law's wane and conceptualised slaves in Virginia within the same frame as wild creatures, whose possible killing by their owners did not necessitate any trial or even a hearing by a court of law. The 1680 Act specifically made it legal for slave owners to kill any slaves that spark any form of "Negro insurrections" or ran away from the plantation.[218] A follow-up Act in 1691 broadened the scope of offences to include recalcitrance and unjustified absences from work. In effect, it became legal to kill any "negroes, mulattoes, and other slaves unlawfully absent[ing] themselves from their masters and mistresses service" by guns or other any other necessary means.[219]

3.4.3.3 John Locke, the Law of Nature, and the Transatlantic Slave Trade

John Locke was arguably not just the leading crusader but the main reference point for civil liberties and limited government between the 17th century and the first half of the 19th century. He incarnated the English revolutionary ideals on the imperativeness of property rights and civil liberties. His reputation as a champion of liberty and rights is severely compromised, however, not just by his stance on slavery but by involvement in the slave trade as well, especially in Virginia's neighbouring colony of Carolina as well. Many academics, while examining Locke's conception of liberty, frequently overlook the fact that he directly participated in the transatlantic slave trade—not just by validating it in writing but also by investing both money and resources in hopes of reaping economic gain. While as a theorist he valorised limited government and liberty, this was nevertheless complicated by his secondary duties as secretary and policy adviser for the colony of Carolina,[220] and a shareholding investor in two slaving companies. Most of Locke's theoretical insights on slavery are contained in the *Second Treatise of Government* and the *Fundamental Constitutions of Carolina*.[221]

In the *Second Treatise of Government*, Locke formulated a theory of natural law that justified slavery on the basis of just war. Slavery, he observed came about as a consequence of a state of war "between a lawful conqueror and a captive."[222] Concurring with Roman law as well as some of his legal predecessors—the likes of Francisco Suarez and Hugo Grotius (1583–1645), who both justified slavery on grounds of it being a better option than death, Locke's observation that spared captives "forfeited [their] own lives" to their owner[223] certainly squared with the doctrine of *captis deminutio maxima*. A just war to Locke, one commentator has observed, constituted any "war fought in defense of one's possessions against an aggressor."[224]

As afore-noted, the classical legal conceptions of slavery oscillated between two contradictory doctrines, to wit: the ancient Aristotelian canon of natural slaves and born masters, on the one hand, and the Christian doctrine of slavery as a consequence of the fall of man by sin—championed by St. Thomas Aquinas—on the other hand. While the latter argument perceived *jus gentium* as a problem that occasioned the institution of slavery, the former endorsed the institution of slavery as a function of just wars. Although Grotius, who preceded Locke, strongly rejected Aristotle's notion of born-slaves, he nonetheless contemplated scenarios according to which freemen could be legitimately enslaved along the just war frame:

> There is no man by nature slave to another ... but it is not repugnant to natural justice that men should become slaves by a human fact, that is by virtue of some agreement, or in consequence of some crime ... If we consider the persons, not only they who surrender themselves, or submit by promise to slavery, are reputed slaves; but all persons whosoever taken in a solemn way, as soon as they shall be brought into a place whereof the enemy is master.[225]

Elsewhere, Grotius, like Aristotle, contended that once enslaved, the status of "slave" became hereditary. To him, victors of wars had almost infinite legitimate rights over their captors: "neither do only they themselves become slaves, but their posterity forever; for whosoever is born of a woman after she is a slave, is born a slave."[226] In spite of the frequently invoked argument that crimes of war deserved death, it was still inexplicable as to why spoils of war (slaves) could be legitimately transferred to third parties in a market exchange—persons who had no connection with the so-called "just war," and effectively lacked any ability to act or react otherwise.

Unlike Grotius, Locke's just war frame was very restrictive, as it limited slavery to defeated combatants and rejected hereditary enslavement. While observing that prisoners of war could be taken only from conflicts in which interested parties actually fought and came out victorious, for any slavery resulting from it to be just, Locke further provided that enslaved persons could actually regain their freedom by simply paying adequate damages to their captors.[227] In rejecting hereditary enslavement, Locke argued that since children of slaves had themselves never been slaves, captors could therefore not have any lawful title to them or their posterity, nor could they transfer captives as inheritance:

> For since a father hath not, in himself, a power over the life or liberty of his child; no act of his can possibly forfeit it: so that the children, whatever may have happened to the fathers, are freemen, and the absolute power of the conqueror reaches no farther than the persons of the men, that were subdued by him, and dies with them.[228]

As aforementioned, Locke directly participated in transatlantic slavery, and he did so in three ways: by investing income and shares in slave trading companies; by serving as policy advisor for two companies transacting in the slave trade in the New World[229]; and by participating in drafting the *Fundamental Constitutions of Carolina*, which sanctioned and enforced African slavery in the state. In the Royal African Company (RAC), which was formed in 1672 to conduct British trade on the African coasts and supply slaves to plantations in the New World,[230] Locke invested £540 (£340 in 1674 and an additional £200 in 1675). That same year, he invested another £200 in Bahamas Island Company—a sum which at the time constituted 10% of the overall company shares.[231]

How do we reconcile Locke as a crusader of liberties against his defence of slavery and participation in the transatlantic slave trade? In the first instance, Locke may have convinced himself that slave raids sponsored by slave companies along the African coasts were legitimate acts of just war. A more salient indicator, however, can be gleaned by digging into the motive behind his postulations. As many English traders and investors erected plantations in the New World colonies, many academics assumed the role of articulating doctrines that could reveal the best possible ways of realising optimum economic returns, as well as tailor England's foreign policy and national aspirations unto a legal frame. Locke's *Two Treatises* definitely fulfilled these anxieties. As pointed out earlier, liberty in Locke's framing (lives, liberty, and estates) ultimately meant a quest for economic growth and progress. The drive for trade monopoly amongst classical political economists generally favoured a mindset of "the ends justifying the means," and slavery just happened to be one of those means.

Locke's participation in the *Fundamental Constitutions of Carolina* was yet another instance of mismatch between his core belief and practice. The constitution essentially established a crucial distinction between religious freedoms and civil liberties—the attendant consequence being the legitimation of the exploitation of African slaves by the colonial elites for economic profit. Faced with concerns of slave proprietors in the colony of Carolina who feared that they could lose some of their ownership rights over slaves, given that many of them were converting to the Christian religion, the constitution insinuated that while religious freedoms extended to "negro" slaves, that largess did not apply to civil liberties. The relevant section in fact endowed every freeman of Carolina amongst other things with "absolute power and authority over his negro slave of what opinion or religion whatsoever."[232]

Despite Locke's direct involvement with the transatlantic slave trade, he neither directly connected his just war frame with Africa and the New World nor discussed the race of slaves. Notwithstanding the fact that he directly invested in the transatlantic slave trade, Locke consistently justified only the enslavement of prisoners of war, while at the same time taking a stand against slavery by purchase.[233] Even if Locke wrote in general terms and was not specific about African slaves, his just war frame nevertheless still implicated Africans with the same rigours. Going by it, resistance to slave raids on the African coasts could well be interpreted as unlawful combatant actions, susceptible to just war retaliation. But considering the fact that he limited his conception of legitimate slavery to spoils of war and rejected slave inheritance as illegitimate, even after participating in the transatlantic slave trade himself, it can be deduced that he ultimately understood chattel slavery in general as unjustifiable.

3.5 Abolition of Slave Trade

3.5.1 Britain's Leading Role in the Struggle to End Slavery

Having lost its vast 13 North American colonies following defeat in the American Revolutionary War of 1775–1783, England—in an effort to sustain national growth and standards of living—profoundly reformed its productive emphasis away from reliance on agricultural production and drifted towards mass industrial manufacturing.[234] This drive resulted from the industrial revolution, which decisively boosted and sustained technological change and increased productivity. The revolution quickly spread throughout Europe and America, and was at the centre of the late 18th and 19th centuries' international politics.

Economic historians have advanced a number of hypothesis to explain the factors that prompted this robust transformation. Joel Mokyr and Robert Allen have asserted that efficiency, innovative potentials, good labour standards, and a vibrant intellectual environment were pivotal for England achieving the industrial milestone.[235] Economic determinist thinkers have roundly countered these propositions. In *Capitalism and Slavery* (1944), Eric Williams observed that it was the proceeds from the transatlantic slave trade that stimulated the English economy and prompted the industrial revolution to begin in England.[236] While Williams's thesis focused on the importance of Caribbean sugar production, Edward E. Baptist perceived cotton as the most widely traded commodity in the 18th century.[237] In spite of their variations, both works interpreted England's leading campaign for the abolition of the slave trade in the 19th century as driven in part by humanitarian concerns, but also by the exigencies of industrial capitalism.

3.5.2 British Anti-Slavery Campaign: Towards Extension of the Right to Visit (Ships) to Combat the Slave Trade

Emerging from the Napoleonic Wars (1803–1815) as the undisputed sea power, Britain sought to use its prowess to shape global law and order. On top of its list of priorities was the imperativeness to suppress the transatlantic slave trade, which in the course of three centuries had become the principal mode of trading between the four corners of the Atlantic Ocean (Africa, Europe, North America, and South America). Having enacted a series of acts and measures abolishing the trade in slaves first domestically and later throughout the British Empire, Britain perceived its hegemony at sea as the invaluable tool to facilitate the enforcement of its new humanitarian commitment, or, more broadly speaking, for preserving *Pax Britannica*.[238] In spite of the obvious humanitarian rationale behind the British abolition campaign, enforcement at sea was nevertheless bound to clash with the Grotian doctrine of universal freedom of the seas—widely embraced by most European sovereigns and legal practitioners at the time as a sacrosanct universal right.[239]

Although it was already commonplace in Ancient times that oceans and seas were by nature open to all, as noted by Ulpian and Celsus,[240] a new wave of monopolistic claims by European powers that sparked off in the 12th century and prolonged right unto the Renaissance period resulted in states claiming exclusive rights over seas and maritime coasts both adjacent to their territories and in conquered extraterritorial lands. This was especially so in the 15th century following a series of papal bulls, as already observed, coupled with claims by the kingdoms of Portugal (over the East Atlantic and Indian Oceans), Britain (over North America, the Caribbean, and Asia), Spain (over the West Atlantic and Pacific Oceans), Denmark and Sweden (over the Baltic Sea), and the city-states of Venice (over the Adriatic Sea), Genoa (over the Gulf of Lions and Ligurian Seas), and Pisa—each laid claims to vast areas of the seas as sovereign domains.[241] Levying heavy tolls on foreign vessels in order to guarantee passage in claimed waters, maritime commerce and exploration not only became cumbersome and expensive but had the effect of excluding smaller countries from international trade.[242]

Frustrated with the exclusion of Holland from the East Indian trade, Hugo Grotius in 1605 published his seminal thesis titled *Mare Liberum*—wherein he propounded a doctrine of freedom of navigation in the high seas for all nations, based on the understanding that no country had any legitimate claim to appropriate high seas or to prevent other nations from the right of navigation or commerce in maritime waters (as Portugal purported to do with its claim of monopoly over the East Indies). Observing that "all land, sea and commerce are common property by international law,"[243] Grotius established that states

(Holland in this case) could legitimately resort to force where the natural right of maritime commerce was perturbed. The doctrine of freedom of navigation empowered all merchant ships to freely ply the oceans and high seas, as long as they posed no threat to international peace and security. Any antislavery policing at the high seas was by analogy perceived as interference with maritime commerce.[244]

Although the Vienna Congress of 1814–1815, which brought together eight major European powers (Austria, Britain, France, Portugal, Russia, Spain, and Sweden), set its primary goals on fostering a balance of power amongst European powers as the modality for guaranteeing peace in the post–Napoleonic Wars era, Britain nevertheless perceived it as an opportunity to push for the creation of an international jurisdiction for the suppression of the slave trade—which for centuries had not just afflicted humanity but more so severely decimated sub-Saharan Africa economically, socially, culturally, and politically.[245] Despite showing a lack of serious commitment to the cause, the Vienna delegates nevertheless settled on a symbolic declaration "Relative to the Universal Abolition of Slave Trade."[246] Upon declaring the slave trade as "repugnant to the principles of humanity and universal morality," the Treaty of Vienna became the first international legal instrument to show a commitment to eradicate the trade in slaves. But its relevance was not so much more than symbolic as it heavily relied on the good offices of states to legislate or prosecute the trade as a crime.[247]

Having convinced itself of the humanitarian imperativeness of abolition but unable to secure a forceful legal commitment from other sovereigns against the slave trade, Britain reverted to its navy prowess and sought to exercise maritime power to police vessels of all nations both in peace and in wartimes.[248] In effect, it sought to equate the slave trade with piracy—and by analogy extending the "right to visit" (otherwise known as the right to search) foreign ships at sea (which was already sanctioned in international law and applicable during wartimes), to peacetimes as well.[249] The doctrine was a right accorded to all maritime nations during wartimes to visit and search suspected ships at sea to ensure that they weren't involved in piracy or had any weapons or contraband on board, including ships supposedly neutral to the conflict or flying a flag of convenience to ascertain their neutrality.[250] In the 1810 British admiralty *Amedie* case, in which Britain seized an American ship transporting slaves, the English admiralty court of Tortola ruled in favour of the seizure, noting that since the African slave trade was repugnant to the principles of justice and humanity, the act of seizure was thus justified, unless the ship owners could proof that slavery was permitted by the municipal laws of the country whose flag the ship was flying.[251] An 1807 United States federal Act had already prohibited the importation of slaves. While Britain was able to extend the right of visit during peacetime in the *Amedie*, the case was nevertheless just an outlier and did not become standard practice. In fact, just seven years later in *Le Louis* case (1817), the same court contradicted its ruling in *Amedie* case by observing that the slave trade did not violate international law, and as a consequence, the right to visit was limited to wartimes. The court further pronounced that during peacetimes, states needed to always gain consent before visiting and searching foreign ships, even if the visit was for the purpose of combatting the slave trade.[252]

In spite of its immense efforts, the British attempt to extend the right to visit steadily faced a number of stumbling blocks. As aforementioned, it ran contrary to the Grotian spirit of universal freedom on the high seas. In addition, any policing at sea was perceived as an arbitral abuse to the treasured right of sovereignty—whereupon consent was no longer required to interfere in one's internal affairs. Furthermore, many merchants and even some African societies that had tailored all production processes to the slave trade had no direct economic substitute in the event where the trade was abruptly abolished.

Unable to secure a multilateral treaty to enforce the abolition of the slave trade, Britain resorted to bilateral agreements, and this proved far more successful. Britain reportedly signed well over 31 bilateral treaties with other nations across Europe, Africa, and the Americas—most of which contained what was termed as "equipment" clauses.[253] In these treaties, Britain frequently equated the slave trade with piracy, as was the case with its agreements with Austria, Brazil, France, Prussia, and Russia—thus, paving the way for perpetrators to be prosecuted with the same laws against piracy.[254] Signatories to bilateral agreements against slavery generally consented to the "right to visit" each other's merchant ships and free slaves—whenever applicable. The equipment clause was to the effect that any "ship outfitted with certain material would be considered as *prema facie* evidence of its actual employment in the slave trade."[255] Although it is observed that these efforts resulted in the freeing of over 80,000 Africans from slave ships, these accomplishments nevertheless came at the expense of many slavers dumping all slaves on board their ships into the sea, when pursued, in order to evade prosecution.[256]

The extension of the right to visit during peacetimes as well ran contrary to the Grotian doctrine of universal freedom of the high seas. France in particular was overly resistant to the British attempts, not so much because it opposed the abolition of transatlantic trade, but more so because it perceived Britain as using the humanitarian rhetoric as merely a technique to foster self-serving commercial, political, and military ambitions.[257]

3.5.3 Industrial Capitalism and British Abolition Campaign: Reading Eric Williams's Thesis

From humble beginnings, the English activism to end the transatlantic slave trade quickly garnered steam, first from civil society politicking and subsequently championed by governmental actions. Two Christian groups—the Quakers and the English Evangelical Protestants—in 1787 forged an alliance that gave birth to a 12-man "Committee for the Abolition of the Slave Trade," with the set goal of educating the public on the evils of slavery and the slave trade.[258] While three of the founding members (Granville Sharp, Philip Sansom, and Thomas Clarkson) hailed from the Evangelical Protestants, the remaining nine members (George Harrison, John Barton, Joseph Hooper, John Lloyd, Joseph Woods Sr., James Phillips, Richard Phillips, Samuel Hoare Jr., and William Dillwyn) were Quakers.[259] It is alleged that their stimulus stemmed from the activism of William Wilberforce (1759–1833)—a prominent antislavery philanthropist and independent member of parliament—who had vowed to introduce a bill on the abolition of the slave trade to the British House of Commons.[260] Collectively, their humanitarianism earned them the esteemed status of "slavery abolitionists."

Following the sustained campaign of abolitionists, the British parliament in 1807 passed the famous "Act for the Abolition of the Slave Trade," commonly dubbed as the Slave Trade Act.[261] Although it abolished the slave trade throughout the British Empire and commissioned the British government to take all necessary actions and press other European powers to do same, abolitionists were far from satisfied, as the act abolished the trade in slaves but not slavery as an institution.[262] In fact, slavery remained legal throughout the empire. It took almost three decades before abolitionists mustered enough support in parliament for the passage of the Slavery Abolition Act 1833, which abolished slavery all over the British Empire but for the exception of territories under the East India Company, Ceylon, and Saint Helena (which were all accorded a ten-year waiver).[263]

In 1933, sovereign countries the world over rallied behind Britain to celebrate the centenary anniversary of the 1833 Slavery Emancipation Act, which many historians believe not only foreshadowed the fulfilment of international justice and universal humanitarianism but, more importantly, marked the beginning of the end of the transatlantic slave trade.[264] Between the emancipation proclamation and centenary celebrations, there was near consensus amongst academics on the invaluable role of Britain in bringing the slave trade to an end. With a near global consensus on the significance of the 1833 Act as the triumph of enlightenment thinking that uplifted all of humanity as a whole, public speakers and prominent newspapers and columnists, in their various speeches and columns, with good reasons keenly revered British abolitionist protagonists, who collectively changed the trajectory of human history for the better.[265] Overall, academics until the 1940s typically conceived Britain's aggressive campaign for the international suppression of the slave trade from two key complementary angles: (1) as firmly driven by religious and humanitarian sentiments, and (2) as signifying a moral milestone in universal humanitarianism, hence, the groundwork for the protection and promotion of social justice and international human rights.[266]

In spite of the heralded humanitarian narrative of the antislavery campaign which over the course of a century had assumed a uniformed storyline, it seemed that voices revering the triumph of abolitionism hardly questioned or dug into the motives and goals that propelled British altruism and other leading campaigners. Convinced that the political act of abolition liberated all peoples the world over from the injustices of enslavement and violent exploitation, academics felt very little need to consider possible economic incentives behind the antislavery campaign. A decade following the centenary celebrations, a new school of thought dubbed as the Caribbean school—and championed by economic determinist scholars—emerged in the West Indies, questioning and dismissing the whole premise of British humanitarianism. Proponents of this school included Trinidadian political intellectuals C.L.R. James and Eric Williams, and fellow Guyanese activists Forbes Burnham and Walter Rodney.[267] For these scholars, in order to glean the real motives and goals of the antislavery campaign, one needed to read deep into the timing of the rise and fall of the slave trade in the countries that led the humanitarian drive—Britain especially. This novel thinking was symbolic for marking an unprecedented intellectual clash between narratives of descendants of former slave owners and descendants of former slaves.

How could one reconcile the long-standing defence of the institution of slavery as legitimate with the sudden abolitionist drive by the same countries to destroy the very economic order that they sacrificed immensely to create in the New World colonies? What could have specifically triggered the abrupt recognition of the humanity of persecuted black souls? These considerations naturally trigger the need to take a step backward and reconsider: What prompted the justification of the transatlantic slave trade in the first place, and whose interests did it serve? This leads to the parallel question: Whose primary interest was to be served in abolishing the transatlantic slave trade? How do we explain the fact that Britain in particular went from being the leading slaving nation in the world in the 17th and 18th centuries to becoming the leading proponent of international suppression of the trade in the 19th century?[268] These are some of the key questions that the Caribbean school confronted and sought to address in their examination of the great morality tale of antislavery humanitarianism.

In 1944, the Trinidadian Eric Williams published his magnum opus, *Capitalism and Slavery*, wherein he observed that both the rise and the fall of the transatlantic slave trade was precisely guided by capitalist interest rather than humanitarian sentiments. In order to buttress his point, Williams advanced two strong claims pertaining to the British abolition campaign in particular, to wit: (1) it is proceeds from the transatlantic slave trade that furnished the capital which was used to finance the industrial revolution in England, and (2) it is the exigencies of industrial capitalism that compelled Britain to lead the drive to destroy the slave system.[269]

Although focused on the transatlantic slave trade and the particularity of the sugar plantation system in the West Indies, *Capitalism and Slavery*, in its search for capitalism's essence and nature at the crossroads of the 19th century and beyond, uncovered a fitting nexus between mercantilist practice and industrial capitalism. For Williams, while the humanitarian sensibilities of England and its history of the transatlantic slave trade were two epochs apart, they nonetheless corresponded to two phases in a peculiar linear capitalist transition, namely, from mercantilism to *laissez-faire* capitalism.[270] The history of the abolition of the transatlantic slave trade, to him, revealed how in spite of moral ascendancy and mutation in form, profit-making remained the driving force of capitalism. In the first three chapters of the book, he buttressed the fact that, contrary to popular opinion, the transatlantic slave trade was principally an economic rather than a racial scheme.[271] In Chapters 4 and 5, he provided that the transatlantic slave trade was the singular capitalist arrangement that enabled Britain to overtake all countries in the world economically, and further that proceeds from the trade financed the industrial revolution.[272] Later in the book, he made the case that the abolition of the slave trade championed by Britain was not a humanitarian act, but rather a function of the need to meet the exigencies of industrial capitalism.[273]

For Eric Williams, growing up at a time when Trinidad and Tobago was still a British colony, and in a space of inclusion versus exclusion, where race was the determining barometer for privileges or deprivation respectively—conditions which propelled him to get involved in politics in the first place—he found it hard to reconcile the image of England as the torch-bearer of morality, justice, and liberty, with the reality in the colonies.[274] Upon observing in the preface of *Capitalism and Slavery* that the purpose of the book was to deconstruct "the role of negro slavery and slave trade in providing the capital which financed the industrial revolution in England,"[275] Williams proceeded in the body of the work to compare the English economy before its involvement in the African slave trade, and the country at the peak of the trade in the 18th century—reaching the conclusion that the scheme provided extraordinary accumulation of capital which tremendously stimulated the economy and provided the necessary finance for industrial innovation, hence the industrial revolution. In his words:

> Britain was accumulating great wealth from the triangular trade. The increase of consumption goods called forth by the trade inevitably drew in its train the development of the productive power of the country. The industrial expansion required finance. What man in the first three quarters of the eighteenth century was better able to afford the ready capital than a West Indian sugar planter or a Liverpool slave trader?[276]

John Stuart Mill reportedly observed that the English Caribbean production was a very vital engine for English domestic growth.[277] Thomas Malthus concurred, observing that the transatlantic slave trade produced goods that tremendously stimulated the English economy between the 16th and the 18th centuries.[278] Robin Blackburn in *The Making of New World Slavery* (1997) also concurred with the imperativeness of the slave trade in enabling economic growth in Britain and Europe.[279] But unlike Williams and the Caribbean School, Blackburn did not attribute all of Britain's economic growth to the transatlantic slave trade. To him, Britain was already on the path of progress, with the slave trade's contribution helping rather than eclipsing the process.[280]

Although Blackburn's thesis compellingly underscored the importance of economic exchanges of New World plantation owners in enhancing industrialisation in metropolitan Britain, it nevertheless failed to evaluate the impact of the slave trade.

Being a system of economic exploitation that separated labourers from their means of production, progenitors of the transatlantic slave trade reaped mammoth profits that enabled them to accelerate national growth. Conceiving the transatlantic slave trade as the primary source of accumulation of capital amongst countries championing the commerce across the New World, Williams provided that proceeds from the slave trade not only were ploughed back to stimulate banking and finance, but were used to erect vast plants with powered new productive forces, and cumulatively propelled the industrial revolution.[281] He further observed that:

> Many of the eighteenth century banks established in Liverpool and Manchester, the slaving metropolis and the cotton capital respectively, were directly associated with the triangular trade. Here, large sums were needed for the cotton factories and the canals which improved the means of communications between the two towns.[282]

Contributions of the slave trade to European economies certainly had a ***domino*** or ***multiplier*** effect—namely, the possibility for capital to be doubled.[283] In 1788, the idea of abolishing the transatlantic slave trade was first floated in the British parliament—a proposal which, not surprisingly, naturally polarised opinion amongst members of parliament. In order to reach an informed decision, the parliament sought the opinion of experts and merchants directly involved in the trade. James Penny, a prominent slave merchant at Liverpool, warned that

> should the trade be abolished, it would not only affect the commercial interests, but also the landed property of the county of Lancaster, and more particularly the town of Liverpool, whose fall, in that case would be as rapid as its rise has been astounding.[284]

Williams concurred with Penny's assessment on the imperativeness of the transatlantic slave trade to the economic survival of not just Liverpool but all its environs: "it was only the capital accumulation of Liverpool which called the population of Lancashire into existence and stimulated the manufacturers of Manchester ... all of that capital accumulation came from the slave trade."[285]

Williams derived inspiration for *Capitalism and Slavery* from C. L. R. James's seminal work *The Black Jacobins*, chronicling the successful slave revolution against the French in Saint Dominique, which brought about the independent nation of Haiti.[286] James's work made a connection of capital accumulation and growth from Saint-Dominique to France, similar to the one Williams established between England and its West Indies colonies. The results of both books were stringently similar. *The Black Jacobins* was both an economic thesis underscoring the tremendous contribution of the transatlantic slave trade in enabling French (European) growth, but also a political manifesto on Black Nationalism—celebrating unsung martyrs who, despite their enslavement and chains, fought ceaselessly and overthrew their captors and exploiters, and forcefully asserted their own emancipation and independence.[287] One less-discussed element amongst academics at the time, which James forcefully highlighted in the book, was the fact that the Haitian slavery revolution was the springboard for black and Caribbean nationalism. The exploited had at long last rejected the subjugated position affixed to them, and they embraced their own destiny—and became masters of their own affairs and economic development.[288]

James located the origins of industrial revolution to the American Revolution of 1783. He observed that the secession of the 13 colonies that constituted the United States, contrary to popular perception, was somewhat more of an economic blessing rather than a disadvantage for Britain, following the transition of the country from monopolistic mercantilism towards a regime of free trade or *laissez-faire*. The period 1789–1838, when antislavery discourse cogently became good domestic politics across England, precisely coincided with American independence.[289] Up until that epoch, slavery had gained popular acceptance throughout Britain as a normal mode of production and way of life.[290] Not only was slavery and slave trade ingrained in British colonies, by 1783, Williams concurred that "all classes in English society presented a united front in regard to the [transatlantic] slave trade."[291] While Portugal sparked and led the trade in Africans as slaves to the New World, Britain steadily came to surpass the Portuguese and, at the dawn of the 18th century, already dominated the transatlantic slave trade.[292]

With the production processes of the British economy heavily built around slavery and the mercantile economy, Britain, in the aftermath of the United States—its biggest colonial possession in the New World—successfully seceding from its empire, saw its gains from the slave trade significantly curtailed. Its remaining West Indian plantation colonies could not meet up in time with the economic needs of the ever-growing British population. To Williams, "the West Indian economic system was so unprofitable that for this reason alone its destruction was inevitable."[293] Britain's resolve to meet and sustain vibrant national output, consumption exigencies, and economic growth seemed to rest on the making of ample use of its maritime supremacy as well as championing the cause for free trade.[294] As C. L. R. James observed, Britain suddenly "found that by the abolition of the mercantile system with America, they gained instead of losing. It was the first great lesson in the advantages of free trade."[295]

Overall, the works of Eric Williams and C. L. R. James importantly showed that the humanitarianism that attacked economic interests of slavers fostered new arguments that justified new economic interests of Europeans as well as the exploitation of Africa and West Indies. Collectively, the Caribbean school cogently illustrated that the transition from mercantilism to *laissez-faire* capitalism was not in isolation or based on contrary ideology, but rather went hand-in-hand along the same structural goal of meeting profit margins. Following the secession of the United States, Britain promptly looked beyond human slave labour and invested heavily in industrial machines to power production processes, especially in textiles and cotton services. Being the first major global power that was forced to rely on alternative economic processes to sustain growth, England had the best potential to transition into an industrial economy, and the best way for achieving the goal depended intensely on how efficiently it could harness the channels of industrial production and free trade. As Eric Williams illustrated, the capital for mammoth investments that revolutionised the English production economy into what became known as the industrial revolution came from the country's aggressive involvement in the transatlantic slave trade.[296]

Given that industrial capitalism was a more profitable mode of production—as the revolutionising of labour by machines resulted in greater output yield—the slave trade system, which naturally involved intensive human labour, naturally became perceived as detrimental to English national growth. The British antislavery campaign, Williams observed, was accordingly self-serving politics by which Britain certainly benefited more in economic terms, by willingly acknowledging the inhumanity and injustices of the slave trade and fighting to eradicate it. Consistent with Marxist thinking, Williams's thesis showed that pursuant to mutation in production forces (from reliance on human labour to reliance on machines), although industrial capitalism was stimulated by mercantilism, it nevertheless increasingly outgrew mercantilism and progressively destroyed it. Convinced that the industrial commercial scheme was inherent in the antislavery campaign, Williams provided that "The rise and fall of mercantilism is the rise and fall of slavery."[297] Another scholar has succinctly concurred thus: "economic interests built up the slave systems; the application of enlightened principles destroyed them."[298] This claim fitted neatly with the nexus located between the steady evolution of British humanitarianism and the practicalities of sugar plantations in the West Indies:

> The attack on the West Indian monopoly falls into three phases: the attack on the slave trade, the attack on slavery, the attack on preferential sugar duties. The slave trade was abolished in 1807, slavery in 1833, the sugar preference in 1846. The three events are inseparable. The very vested interests which had been built up by the slave system now turned and destroyed that system.[299]

It is worth reiterating that the transatlantic slave trade was sustained in the first place for the purpose of accumulating capital and maximising profits. Qualifying the British antislavery humanitarianism as "the greatest propaganda movement of all times," Williams argued that the transatlantic trade could be logically sustained only as long as it fulfilled its original purpose. The reverse was bound to be true once there was an alteration in productive forces and a more gainful mode of production.[300] With an in-depth focus on the West

Indian sugar plantation monopoly of Britain, Williams justified the collapse of the British slave trade as a consequence of falling profits:

> The capitalists had first encouraged West Indian slavery and then helped to destroy it. When British capitalism depended on the West Indies, they ignored slavery or defended it. When British capitalism found the West Indian monopoly a nuisance, they destroyed West Indian Slavery as a first step in the destruction of West Indian monopoly.[301]

While Williams's thesis largely received rave reviews, a number of commentators have nonetheless also attacked his hypothesis over the decades. These includes Seymour Drescher, Stanley L. Engerman, Paul Robert Thomas, Roger T. Anstey, and Philip R. P. Coelho.[302] They contend, amongst other things, that Williams hyped and overplayed the significance of the West Indian plantations to the advent of British industrialisation. To them, given that most West Indian colonies were relatively small islands, it went without saying that they collectively were not just a fraction of British gains from the slave trade, but paled in comparison to the United States—wherefrom Britain reaped most of its profits.[303] The Caribbean colonies mostly produced sugar. As Edward Baptist has recently shown in *The Half Has Never Been Told* (2016), it is cotton, which was produced by slave labour and had greater market value, that was the dominant global commodity until the 19th century.[304] Using that premise to justify why the industrial revolution sprouted in the cotton and textile sectors, Baptist's thesis certifies cotton as the oil of the day in transatlantic slavery times. Irrespective of whether proceeds were accrued through sugar production, cotton, or any other product produced by African slave labour, it seems to me that Williams's thesis was on point in asserting that it is the profits from the transatlantic trade that provided "the main streams of accumulation of capital in England which financed the industrial revolution."[305]

Be it as it may, the antislavery campaign proved very useful for Britain during the scramble for Africa. Considering its long-standing activism for the abolition of the transatlantic slave trade, Britain more than any other European power ultimately derived moral, political, and legal legitimacy to frame its colonial drive in Africa as a mission for progress and civilisation. While economic variables were primary in the antislavery drive as rightfully pointed by Williams, it is also a fact that without their intervention, the transatlantic slave trade would have persisted, thus not only perpetuating the vicious cycle of misery but the depopulation of sub-Saharan Africa.

3.6 Concluding Remarks

While the story of how international law has condemned, fought, or sought to eliminate slavery from international life is commonplace, the story of how international law promoted, justified, and validated slavery and the slave trade during the 16th to 18th centuries is less pronounced. Such an account is imperative not only for the tremendous human impact it had on the millions subjected to slavery, but for its overall impact on the economic trajectory of the world (also social, political, and cultural) as a whole and Africa in particular. While many notable ancient, medieval, and enlightenment scholars frequently advanced arguments that legitimated the institution of slavery, especially on grounds that slavery was an appropriate punishment for war captives, I submit that slavery laws were false universals—given that the justice and liberty, which classical political economists propagated and which permitted the institution of slavery, were strictly geared at protecting property interests of slave owners. Consequently, economic, social, and political structures that resulted from these conceptualisations, while augmenting the surplus value for slavers, nonetheless plunged the enslaved into the worst forms of exploitation and denial of human dignity. Slavery, one scholar has noted, "might have been socially regressive, but economically it made sense (to those exploiting the slaves)."[306]

The transatlantic trade, in direct contradistinction with previous economic processes that obtained in sub-Saharan Africa, was adversely detrimental to the subcontinent. It discouraged entrepreneurial spirit, political institutions, and families, and encouraged anarchy, in exchange for European articles that only benefited the ruling class and middlemen who played agency roles on behalf of slavers. It also encouraged trade and development only in specific regressive areas, namely the trade in people as legitimate property in exchange for whatever goods that were deemed to meet the value of slaves. The sustained exploitation of Africa hampered the continent's evolution towards a vibrant industrial society. As the economic gap between Europe and Africa progressively widened, products which otherwise would have been produced locally became substituted with European manufactured goods, thus plunging the continent on a path of dependency.[307]

The economic determinism of the Caribbean school certainly foreshadowed some of the pioneering third world voices in the anti-colonial movements and Third World Approaches to International Law (TWAIL). According to these scholars, the humanitarianism of abolition was driven more by the exigencies of industrial revolution as a more gainful mode of production, rather than as genuine altruism to end the violence and exploitation of Africans in all forms. Notwithstanding, I contend that the connection which contemporary economic determinist scholars established between humanitarianism and economic interests behind the antislavery drive ought not to be seen as playing down the positive contribution of abolitionists in ending the inhumane scourge of exploitation through slavery. It seems to me that their intent was geared at putting history in its proper context, rather than cherry-picking narratives that were widely prevalent in academic writings and discourses prior to their observations.

In Chapter 4, this study shows that while the slave trade paved the way for industrial capitalism, the new mode of production was more of a distinction without a difference in terms of violence and sufferings inflicted by European powers on African peoples in their pursuit for profits. Sub-Saharan Africans were essentially enslaved by another name, and they were roundly colonised, exploited, and violently compelled to extract the raw materials under their subsoils, for the powering of the nascent factories that were revolutionising growth across Europe.

Notes

1 Jean Allain, (Cambridge University Press, 2000) at 31–33.
2 Karl Marx, (Charles H. Kerr & Co., 1906) at 667.
3 Marx, *Capital: Critique of Political Economy* at 145.
4 Lawrence Clayton, *7 History Compass* (2009) at 1529.
5 Philip S. Foner, (Rowman & Littlefield Publishers, 2005) at 11.
6 Karl Marx, (Progress Publishers, 1966) at 163.
7 Eric Williams, (University of North Carolina Press, 1944) at 20.
8 The term "New World" has become commonplace in academia. Although European colonisers conceived the Americas as a New World, this was a purely Eurocentric understanding, as local inhabitants who had lived there since time immemorial retained their understanding of the continent as their natural habitat.
9 James A. Rawley, (University of Nebraska Press, 2005) at 5.
10 Rawley, *The Transatlantic Slave Trade* at 4.
11 Babacar M'baye, *11 The European Legacy* (2006) at 608. [*Emphasis mildly added*].
12 Seymour Drescher & Paul Finkelman, (Oxford University Press, 2012). The Bible endorses slavery and even purports to regulate it by advising people how to own slaves, how to treat them, and even how to use them sexually (see: Leviticus 25:44–46, Exodus 21:2–6, Exodus 21:7–11, Exodus 21:20–21, 1 Timothy 6:1–2, Ephesians 6:5, Luke 12:47–48); *Cambridge New American Standard Bible* (2011) at 97, 98, 101, 164, 271, 292–293. Slavers frequently invoked the Biblical verse Genesis 9:25 to justify that "negroes" were descendants of a curse race and biblically ordained to be slaves of other races: "Cursed be Canaan! The lowest of slaves will he be to his brothers" (New International Version (2011)).
13 Eric Williams, (University of North Carolina Press, 1944); C.L.R. James, (The Dial Press, 1938); Walter Rodney, (Pambazuka Press, 2012); Samir Amin, *9 Journal of Peace Research* (1972); Robin Blackburn, (Verso Books, 1997).
14 Drescher & Finkelman, "Slavery" at 890.
15 Slavery has been the rule rather than the exception in human history. It has been observed that all great empires—including the Egyptian, Mongolian, Macedonian, Roman, British, Ottoman, and American empires—built their edifice on the shoulders of slaves. *See*: Jean Allain, (Martinus Nijhoff, 2013) at 105.

According to Article 1(1) of the *Convention to Suppress the Slave Trade and Slavery(otherwise known as the Slavery Convention)*, "slavery is the status or condition of a person over whom any or all of the powers attaching to the right of ownership are exercised." Slave trade on its part is defined in (2) of the same article as:

> all acts involved in the capture, acquisition or disposal of a person with intent to reduce him to slavery; all acts involved in the acquisition of a slave with a view to selling or exchanging him; all acts of disposal by sale or exchange of a slave acquired with a view to being sold or exchanged, and, in general, every act of trade or transport in slaves.
>
> (Article 1(1) & (2) *Slavery Convention, 1926*)

16 To him, ***dominium*** was absolute power by design, entrusted with

> the capacity to derive the full economic value of a thing, to use and enjoy its fruits, as well as to use it up, to alienate it, but perhaps most significantly, as the Danish legal historian C.W. Westrup notes, it had a psychological meaning of

inner power over a thing beyond mere control. If it is difficult to explain why the Romans would want to invent the idea of a relation between a person and a thing, it becomes impossible to comprehend why they should want inner psychic power over it unless we understand that, for most purposes, the thing on their mind was a slave.

[*Emphasis mildly Added*] (*See*: Orlando Patterson, (Harvard University Press, 1982) at 31)

17 Patterson, *Slavery and Social Death* at 13.
18 J.E. Penner, (Oxford University Press, 2012) at 242–245.
19 Aristotle, *Politics* (transl. Benjamin Jowett); (Clarendon Press, Oxford: 1885) at 3–4.
20 Ibid at 6, 16, Chapter 5.
21 Ibid at 9–11, 19–22.
22 Ibid at 17–18. *See also*: Chapter 5.
23 Cf: Allain, *Slavery in International Law* at 13.
24 Aristotle, *Politics* at 6–7.
25 Darrell Dobbs, 56 *The Journal of Politics* (1994) at 79, 87.
26 Aristotle, *Politics* at 33–36, 116.
27 Ibid at 123–126.
28 Muldoon, *3 Ave Maria Law Review* (2005) at 75.
29 Ibid at 75.
While Aquinas differs significantly from Aristotle, it is possible that Aristotle had the same conception of natural law. He may have convinced himself that the ancestors of natural slaves digressed from the edicts of natural law, and their descendants were as a consequence natural victims of their heritage.
30 "*Sevitus est constitutio qua quis domino alieno contra naturam subicitur*" Cf: Allain, *Slavery in International Law* at 14.
31 W. W. Buckland, (Cambridge University Press, 1963) at 54. [*Mild Emphasis*]
32 Alan Watson, (Johns Hopkins University Press, 1987) at 7.
33 William D. Philips, (Manchester University Press, 1985) at 15; Buckland, *A Textbook of Roman Law* at 70–71.
34 Allain, *Slavery in International Law* at 16.
35 Ibid at 16.
36 Ibid at 16–17.
37 Watson, *Roman Slave Law* at 134–135. Elsewhere, Watson contended that the Roman law conception of the institution of slavery was seen as beneficial to both slave owners and slaves on at least three fronts: it fashioned paternalism as slaves were incorporated into the household of their masters, it brought about progress given that slaves learnt trades and discipline, and finally it had economic benefits—gains earned by masters conceived as a fair token for their goodwill gesture (Watson, *Roman Slave Law* at 8–12).
38 This position was strongly upheld by classic scholars—the likes of Aristotle, John Locke, Francisco Suarez, Hugo Grotius, etc.
39 Watson, *Roman Slave Law* at 8.
40 John Wright, (Routledge, 2007); Patrick Manning, (Cambridge University Press, 1990).
41 Rawley, *The Transatlantic Slave Trade* at 8.
42 Douglas A. Farnie, *15 The Economic History Review* (1962) at 210
43 Farnie, 'The Commercial Empire of the Atlantic' at 210.
44 Tom Brass, *35 Capital & Class* (2011) at 26.
45 Brass, 'Unfree labour as Primitive Accumulation?' at 26.
46 Edward E. Baptist, (Hachette, 2016); Walter Johnson, (Harvard University Press, 2013); Adam Rothman, (Harvard University Press, 2005).

47 Baptist, *The Half Has Never Been Told*; Johnson, *River of Dark Dreams*; & Rothman, *Slave Country*.
48 Gregory E. O'Malley, (North Carolina Press, Chapel Hill: 2014) at 218.
49 Patrick Manning, (Cambridge University Press, 1990) at 124.
50 Sidney W. Mintz, *2 Review (Fernand Braudel Center)*; (1978) at 98.
51 Temperley, 'Capitalism, Slavery and Ideology' at 98.
52 Gregory Clark, (Princeton University Press, 2008) at 57.
53 Paul Finkelman, (Oxford University Press, 2012) at 106.
54 Vernon Valentine Palmer, *53 Louisiana Law Review* (1995) at 363.
55 Cedric J. Robinson, (Zed, 1983).
56 James A. Rawley, (University of Nebraska Press, 2005) at 2.
57 Rawley, *The Transatlantic Slave Trade* at 3.
58 Ibid at 4. *See also*: "Ports of the Transatlantic Slave Trade."
59 Rawley, *The Transatlantic Slave Trade* at 2.
60 Manning, *Slavery and African life* at 52–53, 98, 102.
61 David Eltis, *58 William and Mary Quarterly* (2001) at 41.
62 David Eltis, Stephen D. Behrendt, David Richardson, Herbert S. Klein (Cambridge University Press, 1999) at 5.
63 Thomas Walter Wallbank, *15 Van Nostrand* (1964); Cf: Umozurike, 'The African Slave Trade' at 337.
64 Manning, *Slavery and African Life* at 171.
65 Ibid at 102–105, 113.
66 Umozurike, 'The African Slave Trade' at 338.
67 Nathan Nunn, 123 *The Quarterly Journal of Economics* (2008) at 142. See also, Chapurukha Kusimba *21 African Archaeological Review* (2004) at 66.
68 Nunn, 'The Long-Term Effects of Africa's Slave Trades' at 142.
69 David Easton, (Harvard Pub., 1957) at 171. *[Emphasis added]*.
70 Samir Amin, *10 The Journal of Modern African Studies* (1972) at 507–511.
71 Rawley, *The Transatlantic Slave Trade* at 11.
72 Ibid at 11.
73 Ibid at 11.
74 Ibid at 11.
75 Frederick Cooper, *20 Journal of African History* (1979) at 107.
76 Clark, *A Farewell to Alms* at 57.
77 Samir Amin, *9 Journal of Peace Research* (1972) at 119.
78 Umozurike, 'The African Slave Trade' at 338.
79 Amin, 'Underdevelopment and Dependence in Black Africa' at 511.
80 Wil Hout, (Edward Elgar Publishing Ltd, 1993) at 1, 52–60; Hunt Davis, *72 African Affairs* (1973) at 394; Joshua Settles & Ferlin McGaskey, *Working Paper, University of Tennessee Honors Thesis Project* (1996).
81 Samir Amin, *10 The Journal of Modern African Studies* (1972) at 505–506.
82 Amin, 'Underdevelopment and Dependence in Black Africa' at 510.
83 Amin, 'Underdevelopment and Dependence in Black Africa' at 506–511.
84 Ibid at 516–520.
85 Christopher Prior, *10 Historical Perspectives* (2007) 1–16; Jeremy I. Levitt, (Hart Publishing, 2008); Trevor-Roper H, (Thames and Hudson, London: 1966).
86 Trevor-Roper, *The Rise of Christian Europe* at 9; See also: Hegel & Rauch, *Introduction to The Philosophy of History*; Prior, 'Writing another Continent's History' at 2–3, 12.
87 Lwazi Siyabonga Lushaba, (Codesria Publishing, 2009) at 9.
88 Charles Gabriel Seligman, (Thornton 1930) at 59–61.
89 Rodney, *How Europe Underdeveloped Africa* at 9–11, 50, 103–104.
90 Kari Polanyi Levitt, *1 Estudios Críticos del Desarrollo* (2011) at 57.
91 Samir Amin, *10 The Journal of Modern African Studies* (1972) 503–524 at 505, 510.

92 Fernand Braudel, (Harper and Row, 1972) at 420.
93 Jack Goody, *22 Economic History Review* (1969) 393–405.
94 Rodney, *How Europe Underdeveloped Africa* at 56.
95 Ibid at 33–70.
96 Ibid at 8–9.
97 Ibid at 8–9, 35, 121.
98 Ambe Njoh, (Aldershot, Brookfield USA: 1999) at 45, citing William Tordoff, (Indiana University Press, 1984).
99 Rodney, *How Europe Underdeveloped Africa* at 41–42.
100 Rodney, *How Europe Underdeveloped Africa* at 8–9, 42–44, 55.
101 Amin, 'Underdevelopment and Dependence in Black Africa' at 510.
102 Samir Amin, *9 Journal of Peace Research* (1972)105–120 at 109.
103 Amin, 'Underdevelopment and Dependence in Black Africa' at 510. It is alleged that the entire cabinet of Ghana by 1067 were Muslims, learned in the Arabic scriptures. Some of these writings have survived as of this writing.
104 Robert Smith, *14 The Journal of African History* (1973) at 613.
105 Smith, 'Peace and Palaver' at 613.
106 Rodney, *How Europe Underdeveloped Africa* at 36–39, 44–47.
107 Ibid at 37–39.
108 Ibid at 37–39.
109 Ibid at 38–39.
110 Patrick Manning, (Cambridge University Press, 1990) at 124.
111 Nunn, 'The Long-Term Effects of Africa's Slave Trades' at 142.
112 Elias & Akinjide, *Africa and the Development of International Law*; R. P. Anand, *15 International and Comparative Law Quarterly* (1966) 55–75; Gathii, 'A Critical Appraisal of the International Legal Tradition.'
113 Onuma Yasuaki, *2 Journal of the History of International Law* (2000) at 61. *See also*: Martti Koskenniemi, (Universiteit Utrecht—Faculteit Geeseswetenschappen, 2011).
114 Taslim Olawale Elias has explained that in various parts of Africa, "there emerged broadly similar rules of customary law, which makes it possible to speak of the existence of a universal body of principles of African customary law that is not essentially dissimilar to the broad principles of European law" (Taslim Olawale Elias, (Manchester University Press, 1972) at 220.
115 John Spencer Trimingham, (Oxford University Press, 1959) at 28–30.
116 Alan Frederick Charles Ryder, (Longmans, 1969) at 73; François Bontinck, *1 Études d' Hisloire Africaine* (1970) at 48–49.
117 The most notable voyages were undertaken by: Henry the Navigator on the West African coast (1394–1460), Christopher Columbus in the Americas (1492–1493), Vasco da Gama on the Cape of Good Hope and the sea route to India (1498), and Ferdinand Magellan's expedition to the West Indies (1519–1522).
118 Hugh Thomas, (Simon & Schuster, 1997) at 48–50, 53, 76.
119 Most African communities unswervingly resisted the slave trade, but were often poorly equipped to combat slave raids—led by middlemen agents—who were fortified with European riffles and chains.
120 A. Saunders, (Cambridge University Press, 1982) at 138, 197, 250–260.
121 Johannes Postma, (Greenwood Press, 2003) at 5.
122 Rawley, *The Transatlantic Slave Trade* at 10.
123 Ibid at 10.
124 Junius P. Rodriguez, (ABC-CLIO, 1997) at 261; Basil Davidson, (Victor Gollancz Ltd, 1961) at 53; Saunders, 'The Depiction of Trade as War as a Reflection of Portuguese Ideology' at 219.
125 Muldoon, 'Spiritual Freedom—Physical Slavery' at 84.
126 Joseph Canning, (Routledge, 1996) at 5.

127 Saunders, 'The Depiction of Trade as War as a Reflection of Portuguese Ideology' at 222.
128 Robert Williams, *8 Arizona Journal of International and Comparative Law* (1991) at 56, 63.
129 Thomas, *The Slave Trade* at 39.
130 Ibid at 65–66, 398.
131 Walter Ullmann, *11 Virginia Journal of International Law* (1970) 356–371.
132 Brian Tierney, (Brill, 1998) at 15, 85.
133 Saunders, 'The Depiction of Trade as War as a Reflection of Portuguese Ideology' at 220.
134 Thomas, *The Slave Trade* at 70–72.
135 Ibid at 70–72, 112.
136 Muldoon, 'Spiritual Freedom—Physical Slavery' at 83.
137 Papal bull *Illius Qui* of 19 December 1442. *See*: Jeremy Watt, "The Incongruous Bull: In Supremo Apostolatus."
138 Muldoon, 'Spiritual Freedom—Physical Slavery' at 82–83.
139 Saunders, 'The Depiction of Trade as War as a Reflection of Portuguese Ideology' at 219–223.
140 Basil Davidson, (Brown & Co., Boston: 1961) at 39.
141 Sayre Archie, (Naval Institute Press, 1972) at 12.
142 The bull further empowered Afonso V to

> invade, search out, capture, vanquish, and subdue all Saracens and pagans whatsoever ... and to reduce their persons to perpetual slavery, and to apply and appropriate to himself and his successors the kingdoms, dukedoms, counties, principalities, dominions, possessions, and goods, and to convert them to his and their use and profit.
>
> (Cf: Brian D. Mclaren, (Convergent Books, 2016) at 77)

See also: Muldoon, 'Spiritual Freedom—Physical Slavery' at 83.
143 Muldoon, 'Spiritual Freedom—Physical Slavery' at 84.
144 Rawley, *The Transatlantic Slave Trade* at 21.
145 Thomas, *The Slave Trade* at 66.
146 Ibid at 66; H. Vander Linden, *22 The American Historical Review* (1916) at 3.
147 Horst Pietschmann, *15 Coloquios de Historia Canario Americana* (2002) at 1145–1146.
148 Linden, 'Alexander VI and the Demarcation of the Maritime and Colonial Domains'
149 Ernest Nys, (Thorin et Fils, 1894) at 64–67.
150 Andrew Fitzmaurice, (Oxford University Press, 2012) at 840–842; Robert Miller, *42 Idaho Law Review* (2005–2006) at 4. In the 1823 US Supreme Court case of *Johnson v. M'Intosh*, the court found that even though the Amerindians were formerly in clear possession and ownership of the lands, the supposedly transfer of their property rights to the Europeans was neither with their consent nor even with their knowledge. See *Johnson v. M'Intosh* (1823).
151 Miller, 'The Doctrine of Discovery' at 6.
152 Lewis Hanke, (Southern Methodist University Press, 1949) at 32–33, 42, 91.
153 Allain, *Slavery in International Law* at 22–23.
154 Hanke, *The Spanish Struggle for Justice* at 34, 50; Timothy J. Yeager, *55 The Journal of Economic History* (1995) 842–859.
155 See Luciano Pereña, (Mapfre, 1992) at 37.
156 Extract from 'The Requirement' (1513) in Lunenfeld Marvin, *Discovery, Invasion, Encounter: Sources and Interpretations* (1492), D.C. Heath and Co. Lexington, 1991 at 190. Cf: Evans, 'Where Lawlessness Is Law' at 12–13.

Another scholar, Christopher Weeramantry has illustrated at length how the Law of Nations in the 16th and 17th centuries was largely Christian in character. According to him,

> When international law commenced its modern career in the 16th and 17th centuries, it was cast largely in the Graeco-Judeo-Christian mould. Since then it has moved towards greater universalization. Many more universal perspectives drawn from all the world's cultural traditions can and must be fed into it as it develops to suit the needs of the 21st century.
>
> (Christopher Weeramantry, (Martinus Nijhoff Publishers, 2004) at 2–3.)

157 Yeager, 'Encomienda or Slavery?' at 843–844.
158 The mortality of Amerindians was due in large part to their lack of immunity to European gems and diseases. *See*: Allain, *Slavery in International Law* at 22.
159 Bartolomé de Las Casas, (Penguin Books, 1992) at 92. Cf: Allain, *Slavery in International Law* at 23. [*Emphasis mildly added*].
160 James Brown Scott, (Clarendon Press, 1934) at xiii–xiv.
161 Anthony Pagden & Jeremy Lawrance, (Cambridge University Press, 1991) at 248.
162 Pagden & Lawrence, *Vitoria: Political Writings* at 250–251, 278, 315.
163 Brown Scott, *The Spanish Origins of International Law* at 45.
164 Ibid at xli.
165 Francisco Suarez, (Clarendon Press, 1944) at 348.
166 Lawrence Clayton, 'Bartolome´de Las Casas and the African Slave Trade' *7 History Compass* (2009) 1526–1541 at 1531.
167 As far back as 1516, he was still in total support of the enslavement of Africans.
168 Blackburn, *The Making of New World Slavery* at 132.
169 Clayton, 'Bartolomé de Las Casas and the African Slave Trade' at 1529.
170 Rawley, *The Transatlantic Slave Trade* at 13.
171 William M. Denevan, (University of Wisconsin Press, 1992) at xxix.
172 Allain, *Slavery in International Law* at 28.
173 Rawley, *The Transatlantic Slave Trade* at 9.
174 Blackburn, *The Making of New World Slavery* at 136.
175 Vincent T. Harlow, (Oxford University Press, 1926) at 307.
176 Williams, *Capitalism and Slavery* at 9.
177 Isacio Pérez Fernández, (Mundo Negro-Esquila: 1991). Cf: Lawrence Clayton, *7 History Compass* (2009) at 1529.
178 Andrea Weindl, *10 Journal of the History of International Law* (2008) at 230.
179 Weindl, 'The Asiento de Negros and International Law' at 230–231.
180 Martin Luther, (Concordia Publishing House, 1958) at 1–5.
181 Alberico Gentili, (Clarendon Press, 1933) at 12–16. Cf: Allain, *Slavery in International Law* at 37.
182 As he put it,

> we cannot approve perpetual imprisonment either, if the victor has any other means of insuring the permanence of the victory which he has won. For the end of victory is to be able to enjoy it. And perpetual imprisonment means that one must not be set free except for an intolerable price or on conditions which are otherwise unfair.
>
> (Gentili, *De Iure Belli Libri Tres* at 327)

Cf: Allain, *Slavery in International Law* at 37.

183 Gentili, *De Iure Belli Libri Tres* at 328. Cf: Allain, *Slavery in International Law* at 37.

184 Ibid at 37.
185 Ibid at 38.
186 Ibid at 330. Cf: Allain, *Slavery in International Law* at 38.
187 Blackburn, *The Making of New World Slavery* at 228
188 Daughter of Powhatan, a local Native Amerindian leader in Virginia.
189 Blackburn, *The Making of New World Slavery* at 228; Peter C. Mancall, (University of North Carolina Press, 2018) at 225.
190 Blackburn, *The Making of New World Slavery* at 228.
191 Pory noted thus:

> Having mett with so fitt a messenger as this man of warre of Flushing, I could not but imparte with your lordship ... these poore fruites of our labours here.... The occasion of this ship's coming hither was an accidental consortship in the West Indies with the Tresurer, an English man of warre also, licensed by a Commission from the Duke of Savoye to take Spaniards as lawfull prize. This ship, the Treasurer, wente out of England in Aprill was twelvemoneth, about a moneth, I thinke, before any peace was concluded between the king of Spaine and that prince. Hither shee came to Captaine Argall, then governour of this Colony, being parte-owner of her. Hee more for love of gaine, the root of all evill, then for any true love he bore to this Plantation, vict-ualled and manned her anewe, and sent her with the same Commission to raunge the Indies.
>
> (Lyon Gardiner Tyler, *Narratives of Early Virginia, 1606–1625* (Charles Scribner's Sons Ltd, New York: 1907) at 228.)

192 Gad J. Heuman & James Walvin, (Psychology Press, 2003) at 764.
193 Winthrop D. Jordan, (University of North Carolina Press, 2013) at 53; Heuman & Walvin, *The Slavery Reader* at 764.
194 William Thorndale, *33 Magazine of Virginia Genealogy* (1995) at 168–170.
195 Davidson, *Black Mother* at 64.
196 Daniel Pratt Mannix & Malcolm Cowley, (Viking Press, 1962).
197 While England during the decade 1690–1700 exported 87,052 Africans into its American colonies, that number rose to 184,965 between 1741 and 1750, 375,016 between 1761 and 1770, and 398,719 between 1791 and 1800. *See*: David Eltis & David Richardson, (Yale University Press, 2010) at 19–21.
198 Rawley, *The Transatlantic Slave Trade* at 129–130.
199 Philip D. Curtin, (University of Wisconsin Press, 1972) at 362–364.
200 Edward E. Baptist, (Hachette, 2016); Walter Johnson, (Harvard University Press, 2013); Adam Rothman, (Harvard University Press, 2005).
201 Rawley, *The Transatlantic Slave Trade* at 130.
202 LaHaye, 'Mercantilism'
203 LaHaye, 'Mercantilism'; Rawley, *The Transatlantic Slave Trade* at 130.
204 Rawley, *The Transatlantic Slave Trade* at 132.
205 Ibid at 133–134.
206 Act XVI on Free Trade in Virginia, of March 1659. Cf: William Waller Hening, (J. & G. Cochran Printers, 1821) at 245.
207 Philip S. Foner, "The International Slave Trade" at 9.
208 The law provided thus:

> in case any English servant shall run away in company of any negroes who are incapable of making satisfaction by addition of a time, it is enacted that the English soe running away in the company with them shall at the time of service to their owne masters expired, serve the masters of the said negroes for their absence soe long as they should have done by this act if they had not beene slaves, every christian in company serving his proportion; and if the negroes be

lost or dye in such time of their being run away, the christian servants in company with them shall by proportion among them, either pay [four] thousand five hundred pounds of tobacco and caske or [four] yeares service for every negroe soe lost or dead.

(Runaways Act, CII, of March 1661. *See*: Hening, *A Collection of all the Laws of Virginia* at 116–117)

209 Act II of September 1667 on the status of baptised slaves. *See*: Hening, *A Collection of all the Laws of Virginia* at 260.
210 Act XII of the Slavery Status Act, of October 1670. *See*: Hening, *A Collection of all the Laws of Virginia* at 282.
211 Act XII of the Slavery Status Act, of October 1670. *See*: Hening, *A Collection of all the Laws of Virginia* at 283.
212 Cf: Hening, *A Collection of all the Laws of Virginia* at 491–492.
213 The maxim is loosely translated as "that which is brought forth follows the womb."
214 Wilbert E. Moore, *26 The Journal of Negro History* (1941) at 185–187; Finkelman, "Slavery in the United States: Persons or Property?" at 111.
215 Finkelman, "Slavery in the United States: Persons or Property?" at 111.
216 Blackstone, *Commentaries on the Laws of England* at 390.
217 Finkelman, "Slavery in the United States: Persons or Property?" at 112.
218 Act X, of 8 June 1680. *See*: Hening, *A Collection of all the Laws of Virginia* at 481.
219 Act XVI (Act for suppressing outlying Slaves) of April 1691. *See*: Hening, *A Collection of all the Laws of Virginia* at 86–87.
220 In 1673, Locke assumed a new position as Secretary to the Council of Trade and Plantations in the state of Carolina—accordingly becoming a stake broker between merchants, administrators, proprietors, plantation owners and businessmen. (Barbara Arneil, *55 Journal of the History of Ideas* (1994) at 592).

As to the impact of Locke in the administration of Carolina, one scholar has noted that "his influence in [the colony's] detailed management seems to have been almost paramount, and the zeal shown by him in endeavouring to secure the property of the settlement was amazing. Down to the autumn of 1672, he continues his informal, but onerous, office of secretary to the proprietors". Henry Richard Foxbourne, (HS King, 1876) at 245.

221 Brad Hinshelwood, *41 Political Theory* (2013) 562–590; Locke, *Second Treatise of Government.*
222 Locke, *Second Treatise of Government* at 24.
223 Ibid at 23. [*Emphasis mildly added*].
224 Wayne Glausser, *51 Journal of History of Ideas* (1990) at 207.
225 Hugo Grotius, (Liberty Fund Books, 2005) at 1360. Cf: James Farr, 'Locke, Natural Law and New World Slavery' *36 Political Theory* (2008) 495–522 at 502.

As to why the fate of prisoners depended on the goodwill of their captors, Grotius provided that "as the goods of every particular prisoner, by the right of war, belongs to the captors, so the goods of the people in general belong to the conquerors, if they please" (Cf: Farr, 'Locke, Natural Law and New World Slavery' at 502).

226 Grotius, *The Rights of War and Peace* at 1362. Cf: Farr, 'Locke, Natural Law and New World Slavery' at 502
227 Locke, *Second Treatise of Government* at 1186–1189.
228 Ibid at 189.
229 Glausser, 'Three Approaches to Locke and the Slave Trade' at 200.
230 While most slaving companies in the British colonies catered to state interests and included many noble elites within their ranks, the RAC lobbied mostly businessmen, and its charter clearly stated that the corporation was "a monopoly for the

trade of gold, silver, Negroes, slaves" etc, and profit-making as primary goal. (Cf: Glausser, 'Three Approaches to Locke and the Slave Trade' at 200).
231 Maurice Cranston, (Oxford University Press, 1957) at 115; Glausser, 'Three Approaches to Locke and the Slave Trade' at 200–201.
232 *See*: Glausser, 'Three Approaches to Locke and the Slave Trade' at 203.
233 Farr, 'Locke, Natural Law and New World Slavery' at 505.
234 Patrick Karl O'Brien & Roland Quinault, (Cambridge University Press, 1993) at 220–222.
235 Joel Mokyr, (Yale University Press, 2012); Robert Allen, (Cambridge University Press, 2009).
236 Williams, *Capitalism and Slavery.*
237 Baptist, *The Half Has Never Been Told.*
238 Christopher Lloyd, (Routledge, 2012) at ix.
239 J. S. Reeves, 'Two Conceptions of the Freedom of the Seas' *22 The American Historical Review* (1917) 535–543 at 540–543.
240 Ruth Lapidoth has quoted Ulpian as noting that "*mare quod natura omnibus patet*" (that is, that the seas belonged to everybody by nature), and Celsus as reaching the same conclusion thus: "*maris communem usum omnibus hominibus ut aeria*" (that is, the sea, just like the air is common to all mankind). *See*: Ruth Lapidoth, *6 Journal of Maritime Law and Commerce* (1974–1975) at 261.
241 G. Gidel, (Méllotée, 1932) at 130–133; Ian Patrick Barry, *33 Hofstra Law Review* (2004) at 306.
242 Barry, 'The Right of Visit, Search and Seizure of Foreign Flagged Vessels' at 306.
243 *See*: Lapidoth, 'Freedom of Navigation-Its Legal History and its Normative Basis' at 263–264.
244 Allain, *Slavery in International Law* at 58; Reeves, 'Two Conceptions of the Freedom of the Seas'.
245 Jerome Reich, *53 The Journal of Negro History* (1968) at 140
246 Joaquín Alcaide Fernández, (Oxford University Press, 2012) at 131.
247 The delegates committed themselves to bringing "to an end a scourge which has for a long time desolated Africa, degraded Europe, and afflicted humanity." *See*: British and Foreign State Papers, volume 10 (HMSO, London: 1820–1822) at 95. *See also*: David Eltis, *25 The Economic History Review* (1972) 55–64; Edward Hertslet, Lewis Hertslet (Eds.), (Butterworth, 1840) at 8–10.
248 William Beach Lawrence, (Little Brown & Co., 1858).
249 Christopher Lloyd, (Routledge, 2012) at 53–58; Ian Patrick Barry, *33 Hofstra Law Review* (2004) at 313–314.
250 Lloyd, *The Navy and the Slave Trade* at 54–58, 62, 158.
251 *The Amedie Case*, 12 English Reports (1810), Para. 240.
252 *Le Louis Case*, 165 English Reports (1817) at 1477–1478.
253 Allain, *Slavery in International Law* at 66–67. Jean Allain lists some of the contracting countries as including Portugal, Denmark, France, Spain, Netherlands, Sweden, Argentina, Colombia, Mexico, Peru, Brazil, Bolivia, Tuscany, Chile, Venezuela, Haiti, Uruguay, Texas, Austria, Prussia, Russia, the United States, The Kings and Chiefs of Cape Mount (Africa), Equator, Muscat, Arabs of the Gulf, New Granada, Zanzibar, and Egypt. *See*: Allain, *Slavery in International Law* at 66.
254 For instance, Article 2 of the *Treaty between Great Britain, Austria, France, Prussia, and Russia, for the Suppression of the African Slave Trade*, of 20 December 1841.
255 Allain, *Slavery in International Law* at 67. In the same paragraph, Allain further explained that examples of equipment that corroborated participation in slave

trade included such things as: chains, slave-deck, shackles, bolts or handcuffs, huge amount of food and water, etc.

256 Allain, *Slavery in International Law* at 67.

257 Ibid at 68.

258 J. R. Oldfield, *35 The Historical Journal* (1992) at 331–332; Hugh Thomas, (Simon & Schuster, 1997) at 514–517.

259 Oldfield, 'The London Committee and Mobilization' at 332; Thomas, *The Slave Trade* at 514–517.

260 Oldfield, 'The London Committee and Mobilization' at 332; Thomas, *The Slave Trade* at 514–517.

261 Slave Trade Act of 25 March 1807. See: Roger Anstey, (Macmillan, 1975) at 412.

262 Roger Anstey, *87 English Historical Review* (1972) at 331–332.

263 *See*: Davis, D. B., (Oxford University Press, 1984) at 108.

264 W. E. Lecky, for instance, qualified the British emancipation act as "amongst the three or four perfectly virtuous pages comprised in the history of nations." *See*: W. E. Lecky, (Appleton, 1890) at 165.

265 *The London Times* for instance authored a column titled as "The Centenary of Wilberforce". See: *The London Times*, of 29 July 1933.

266 Holger Lutz Kern, *6 Journal of the History of International Law* (2004) 233–258.

267 While two of these statesmen went on to become heads of state (Eric Williams was the prime minister of Trinidad and Tobago from 1962 to 1981, while Forbes Burnham became president of Guyana from 1980 to 1985), the other two suffered major tragedies as a result of their political activism. Despite their earlier friendship, C. L. R. James clashed with Williams politically after the latter became prime minister and didn't live up to expected Pan-Africanist socialist ideals, and the former was forced to self-exile himself from Trinidad. Walter Rodney, on his part, was assassinated in his native Guyana in 1980 for his Pan-Africanist activism. Speaking at a public rally in Guyana in 1984, before an estimated crowd of about 5,000 people, Prime Minister Forbes Burnham re-echoed the sentiments of James and Williams when he proclaimed that Britain ended the slave trade in the West Indies not for humanitarian reasons but because it was no longer profitable. *See*: Seymour Drescher, *26 History and Theory* (1987) at 181.

268 Allain, *Slavery in International Law* at 59.

269 Williams, *Capitalism and Slavery* at Preface, 105.

270 Williams, *Capitalism and Slavery*, *See* Chapter 7.

271 Ibid at 3–84.

Although the transatlantic slave trade is now noted for the horrific racism of Europeans on Africans, it is not racism but rather economic interests that sparked the commerce. The racism in fact developed out of the exigencies of the trade rather than started it. See: Williams, *Capitalism and Slavery* at 7–29.

272 Williams, *Capitalism and Slavery* at 85–107.

273 Ibid at 108–208.

274 Eric Williams, (Markus Wiener Publishers, 1969) at 11–13, 34–36.

275 Williams, *Capitalism and Slavery* at Preface.

276 Ibid at 98.

277 See: David Eltis & Standley L. Engerman, (2000) at 123.

278 Thomas Robert Malthus, (Roger Chew Weightman, 1809) at 539–541.

279 Blackburn, *The Making of New World Slavery* at 572.

280 Ibid at 573.

281 Williams, *Capitalism and Slavery* at 52–63, 105.

282 Ibid at 99.

283 Standley L. Engerman, *46 The Business History Review* (1972) at 435.

284 David Eltis & Standley L. Engerman, *60 The Journal of Economic History* (2000) at 123. The cities of Liverpool and Lancashire—which for long were amongst Britain's leading economic centres—were largely built from the proceeds of the African slave trade.
285 Williams, *Capitalism and Slavery* at 63.
286 C. L. R. James, (The Dial Press, 1938). Eric Williams jokingly indicated that a readers of *Capitalism and Slavery* could so easily find the summary of his book in three pages (pages 38–41) of the *Black Jacobins*: "the thesis is stated clearly and concisely and, as far as I know, for the first time in english" (*See*: Williams, *Capitalism and Slavery* at 268).
287 For Haiti to preserve their independence and freedom, it had to repel the two biggest powers at the time: France and Britain.

> Fearful that the idealism of the revolutionary movement would destroy the slave trade and slavery, the French planters of Saint Dominique in 1791 offered the island to England, and were soon followed by those of the Windward Islands. Pitt accepted the offer, when war broke out with France in 1793. Expedition after expedition was sent unsuccessfully to capture the precious colony, first from the French, then from the Negroes … Britain lost thousands of men and spent thousands of pounds in an attempt to capture Saint Dominique. She failed, but the world's sugar bowl was destroyed in the process and the French colonial superiority smashed forever.
>
> (Williams, *Capitalism and Slavery* at 148–149)

288 At the close of the 18th century, resistance by slaves against their owners became commonplace across the American plantations, although virtually all of them were successfully quashed. The successful Haitian revolution nevertheless became a pointer to the risks involved in sustaining the institution of slavery, as similar drives for freedom were most likely imminent in the near future.
289 Allain, *Slavery in International Law* at 60.
290 Slavery was so central to the agrarian economies of the New World and European growth, to the extent that any call for its abolition was seen as tantamount to the abolition of private property, and by analogy national economies. Any such violation going by Locke's definition of property would amounted to a denial of the right of pursuit of happiness.
291 Williams, *Capitalism and Slavery* at 39.
292 Eltis, 'The Volume and Structures of the Transatlantic Slave Trade' at 20.
293 Williams, *Capitalism and Slavery* at 135.
294 Allain, *Slavery in International Law* at 59.
295 C. L. R. James, *The Black Jacobins* at 38.
296 Williams, *Capitalism and Slavery* at 98.
297 Ibid at 136.
298 Temperley, 'Capitalism, Slavery and Ideology' at 98.
299 Williams, *Capitalism and Slavery* at 136. The imperativeness of West Indian Sugar to British economy has been vindicated by many scholars. In "Trade: Discovery, Mercantilism and Technology" (2004), C. Knick Harley, for instance, observes that: "In the eighteenth century, two American crops—sugar produced on the slave plantations of the West Indies and Tobacco from Virginia and Maryland—played a greater role in British (and European) trade than did all trade to the East" (C. Knick Harley, (Cambridge University Press, 2004) at 177).
300 Williams, *Capitalism and Slavery* at 177–179.
301 Ibid at 169.
302 Seymour Drescher, (University of Pittsburgh, 1977); Stanley L. Engerman, *46 Business History Review* (1972) 430–443; Paul Robert Thomas, *21 Economic History*

Review (1968) 30–45; Roger T. Anstey, *21 Economic History Review* (1968) 307–320; Philip R. P. Coelho, *10 Explorations in Economic History* (1973) 253–280.
303 Engerman, 'The Slave Trade and British Capital Formation' at 441–442.
304 Baptist, *The Half Has Never Been Told.*
305 Williams, *Capitalism and Slavery* at 52.
306 Howard Temperley, *75 Past & Present* (1977) at 95. [*Emphasis mildly added*].
307 Joshua Settles & Ferlin McGaskey, *Working Paper, University of Tennessee Honors Thesis Project* (1996) at 2.

References

Allain, Jean: *A Century of International Adjudication: The Rule of Law and its Limits* (Cambridge University Press, Cambridge: 2000).

———: *Slavery in International Law: Of Human Exploitation and Trafficking* (Martinus Nijhoff, Leiden/Boston: 2013).

Amin, Samir: 'Underdevelopment and Dependence in Black Africa—Origins and Contemporary Forms' *10 The Journal of Modern African Studies* (1972) 503–524. (Republished in: *9 Journal of Peace Research* (1972) 105–120).

Anand, Ram Prakash: 'Attitude of the Asian-African States Toward Certain Problems of International Law' *15 International and Comparative Law Quarterly* (1966) 55–75.

Anstey, Roger: 'A Re-interpretation of the Abolition of the British Slave Trade: 1806–1807' *87 English Historical Review* (1972) 304–332.

———: *The Atlantic Slave Trade and British Abolition, 1760–1810* (Macmillan, London: 1975).

Aristotle: *Politics*, Benjamin Jowett (transl.) (Clarendon Press, Oxford: 1885).

Arneil, Barbara: 'Trade, Plantations, and Property: John Locke and the Economic Defense of Colonialism' *55 Journal of the History of Ideas* (1994) 591–609.

Baptist, Edward E.: *The Half Has Never Been Told: Slavery and the Making of American Capitalism* (Hachette, New York: 2016).

Barry, Ian Patrick: 'The Right of Visit, Search and Seizure of Foreign Flagged Vessels on the High Seas Pursuant to Customary International Law: A Defense of the Proliferation of Security Initiative' *33 Hofstra Law Review* (2004) 299–330.

Basil, Davidson: *The African Slave Trade: Pre-Colonial History: 1450–1850* (Brown & Co., Boston: 1961).

Blackburn, Robin: *The Making of New World Slavery: From the Baroque to the Modern 1492–1800* (Verso Books, New York: 1997).

Bontinck, François: 'La Première Ambassade Congolaise à Rome' *1 Études d' Hisloire Africaine* (1970) 37–73.

Brass, Tom: 'Unfree Labour as Primitive Accumulation?' *35 Capital & Class* (2011) 23–38.

Braudel, Fernand: *Capitalism and Material Life, 1400–1800*, Miriam Kochan (transl.) (Weidenfeld and Nicolson, London: 1973).

Buckland, W. W.: *A Textbook of Roman Law from Augustus to Justinian* (Cambridge University Press, Cambridge: 1963).

Canning, Joseph: *A History of Medieval Political Thought: 300–1450* (Routledge, London: 1996).

Clark, Gregory: *A Farewell to Alms: A Brief Economic History of the World* (Princeton University Press, Princeton/Oxford: 2008).

Clayton, Lawrence: 'Bartolome´de Las Casas and the African Slave Trade' *7 History Compass* (2009) 1526–1541.

———: *Cambridge New American Standard Bible* (2011) (selected Verses: *Leviticus 25:44–46, Exodus 21:2–6, Exodus 21:7–11, Exodus 21:20–21, 1 Timothy 6:1–2, Ephesians 6:5, Luke 12:47–48*).

Coelho, R. P. Philip: 'The Profitability of Imperialism: The British Experience in the West Indies, 1768–1772' *10 Explorations in Economic History* (1973) 253–280.

Cooper, Frederick: 'The Problem of Slavery in African Studies' *20 Journal of African History* (1979) 103–125.

Cranston, Maurice: *John Locke: A Biography* (Oxford University Press, Oxford: 1957).

Curtin, D. Philip: *The Atlantic Slave Trade: A Census* (University of Wisconsin Press, Madison: 1972).

Davis, D. B.: *Slavery and Human Progress* (Oxford University Press, Oxford: 1984).

Davis, Hunt: 'Interpreting the Colonial Period in African History' *72 African Affairs* (1973) 383–400.

Denevan, William M.: "Native American Populations in 1492: Recent Research and a Revised Hemispheric Estimate" in William M. Denevan (ed.), *The Native Population of the Americas in 1492* (University of Wisconsin Press, Madison: 1992). 17–37.

Dobbs, Darrell: 'Natural Right and the Problem of Aristotle's Defense of Slavery' *56 The Journal of Politics* (1994).

Drescher, Seymour: *Econocide, British Slavery in the Era of Abolition* (University of Pittsburgh: Pittsburgh: 1977).

———: 'Eric Williams: British Capitalism and British Slavery' *26 History and Theory* (1987) 180–196.

Drescher, Seymour & Finkelman, Paul: "Slavery" in Bardo Fassbender & Anne Peters (eds.), *The Oxford Handbook of The History of International Law* (Oxford University Press, Oxford: 2012) 890–916.

Easton, David: 'The Perception of Authority and Political Change' in Carl J. Friedrich (ed.), *Authority 179—Nomos I* (Harvard Pub., Massachusetts: 1957) 170–196.

Elias, Taslim Olawale *The Nature of African Customary Law* (Manchester University Press, Manchester: 1972).

Elias, Taslim Olawale & Akinjide, Richard: *Africa and the Development of International Law* (Martinus Nijhoff, Dordrecht/Boston: 1988).

Eltis, David: 'The Volume and Structures of the Transatlantic Slave Trade: A Reassessment' *58 William and Mary Quarterly* (2001) 17–46.

Eltis, David, Behrendt, Stephen D., Richardson, David & Klein, Herbert S.: "Introduction", in *Teachers' Manual: The Trans-Atlantic Slave Trade. A Database on CD-Rom* (Cambridge University Press, Cambridge/New York: 1999).

Eltis, David & Engerman, L. Standley: 'The Importance of Slavery and the Slave Trade to Industrialising Britain' *60 The Journal of Economic History* (2000) 123–144.

Eltis, David & Richardson, David: *The Transatlantic Slave Trade Database* (Yale University Press, New Haven: 2010).

Engerman, L. Standley: 'The Slave Trade and British Capital Formation in the Eighteenth Century: A Comment on the Eric Williams Theses' *46 The Business History Review* (1972) 430–433.

Evans, Julie: 'Where Lawlessness Is Law: The Settler-Colonial Frontier as a Legal Space of Violence' *30 Australian Feminist Law Journal* (2009) 3–22.

Farnie, A. Douglas: 'The Commercial Empire of the Atlantic: 1607–1783' *15 The Economic History Review* (1962) 205–218.

Farr, James: 'Locke, Natural Law and New World Slavery' *36 Political Theory* (2008) 495–522.

Fernández, Isacio Pérez: *Bartolomé de Las Casas Contra Los Negros* (Mundo Negro-Esquila: Madrid/México: 1991).
Fernández, Joaquín Alcaide: “Hostes Humani Generis: Pirates, Slavers, and Other Criminals” in Bardo Fassbender & Anne Peters (eds.), *The Oxford Handbook of the History of International Law* (Oxford University Press, Oxford: 2012) 120–144.
Finkelman, Paul: “Slavery in the United States: Persons or Property?” in Jean Allain (ed.), *The Legal Understanding of Slavery: From the Historical to the Contemporary* (Oxford University Press, Oxford: 2012) 105–134.
Fitzmaurice, Andrew: ‘Discovery, Conquest and Occupation of Territory’ in Bardo Fassbender & Anne Peters (eds.), *The Oxford Handbook of the History of International Law* (Oxford University Press, Oxford: 2012) 840–859.
Foner, Philip S.: “The International Slave Trade” in Cecilia Conrad, James Stewart, John Whitehead & Patrick L. Mason (eds.), *African Americans in the U.S. Economy* (Rowman & Littlefield Publishers, New York: 2005) 9–13.
Foxbourne, Henry Richard: *The Life of John Locke* (HS King, London: 1876).
Gathii, James Thuo: ‘Imperialism, Colonisation and International Law’ *54 Buffalo Law Review* (2007) 1013–1066.
Gentili, Alberico: *De Iure Belli Libri Tres: The Translation of the Edition of 1612*, John C. Rolfe, Coleman Phillipson (eds.) (Clarendon Press, Michigan: 1933).
Gidel, G.: *Le Droit International Public de la Mer: Le Temps de Paix* (Méllotée, Châteauroux/Paris: 1932).
Glausser, Wayne: ‘Three Approaches to Locke and the Slave Trade’ *51 Journal of History of Ideas* (1990) 199–216.
Goody, Jack: ‘Economy and Feudalism in Africa’ *22 Economic History Review* (1969) 393–405.
Grotius, Hugo: *The Rights of War and Peace*, Book 3, Richard Tuck (ed.) (Liberty Fund Books, Indianapolis: 2005).
Hanke, Lewis: *The Spanish Struggle for Justice in the Conquest of America* (Southern Methodist University Press, Dallas: 1949).
Harley, C. Knick: “Trade: Discovery, Mercantilism and Technology” in R. Floud & P. Johnson (eds.), *The Cambridge Economic History of Britain since 1700* (Cambridge University Press, Cambridge: 2004) 175–203.
Harlow, Vincent T.: *A History of the Barbados* (Oxford University Press, Oxford: 1926).
Hegel, Georg Wilhelm Friedrich & Rauch, Leo: *Introduction to the Philosophy of History: With Selections from the Philosophy of Right* (Hackett Pub. Co: Indianapolis, 1988).
Hening, William Waller: *A Collection of All the Laws of Virginia, from the First Session of the Legislature in the Year 1619* (J. & G. Cochran Printers, Richmond: 1821).
Hertslet, Edward & Hertslet, Lewis (eds.): *Hertslet's Commercial Treaties: A Complete Collection of the Treaties and Conventions, and Reciprocal Regulations, at Present Subsisting between Great Britain and Foreign Powers, and of the Laws, Decrees, and Orders in Council, Concerning the Same, So Far as They Relate to Commerce and Navigation, to the Repression and Abolition of the Slave Trade, and to the Privileges and Interests of the Subjects of the High Contracting Parties* (Butterworth, London: 1840).
Heuman, Gad J. & Walvin, James: *The Slavery Reader* (Psychology Press, New York: 2003) at 764.
Hinshelwood, Brad: ‘The Carolinian Context of John Locke's Theory of Slavery’ *41 Political Theory* (2013) 562–590.

Hout, Wil: *Capitalism and the Third World* (Edward Elgar Publishing Ltd, Vermont/Hants: 1993).
James, C. L. R.: *The Black Jacobins: Toussaint L'Ouverture and the San Domingo Revolution* (The Dial Press, New York: 1938).
Johnson, Walter: *River of Dark Dreams: Slavery and Empire in the Cotton South* (Harvard University Press, Boston: 2013).
Johnson v. M'Intosh 21 U.S. (8 Wheat.) 543 (1823).
Jordan, Winthrop D.: *White Over Black: American Attitudes toward the Negro, 1550–1812* (University of North Carolina Press, Chapel Hill: 2013).
Kern, Holger Lutz: 'Strategies of Legal Change: Great Britain, International Law, and the Abolition of the Transatlantic Slave Trade' *6 Journal of the History of International Law* (2004) 233–258.
King, J. R. & Luther, Martin: *Luther's Works*, Joroslav Pelikan (ed.) (Concordia Publishing House, Saint Louis: 1958).
Kusimba, Chapurukha: 'Archaeology of Slavery in East Africa' *21 African Archaeological Review* (2004) 59–88.
Koskenniemi, Martti: *Histories of International Law: Dealing with Eurocentrism* (Universiteit Utrecht—Faculteit Geeseswetenschappen, Utrecht: 2011).
Lahaye, Laura: "Mercantilism" in *The Concise Encyclopedia of Economics, Library of Economics and Liberty* (2008). Available online: http://www.econlib.org/library/Enc/Mercantilism.html Last Accessed 3 March 2023.
Lapidoth, Ruth: 'Freedom of Navigation—Its Legal History and Its Normative Basis' *6 Journal of Maritime Law and Commerce* (1974–1975) 259–272.
Las Casas, Bartolomé: *A Short Account of the Destruction of the Indies* (Penguin Books, London: 1992).
Lawrence, William Beach: *Visitation and Search: Or, an Historical Sketch of the British Claim to Exercise a Maritime Police over the Vessels of All Nations in Peace as Well as in War with an Inquiry into the Expediency of Terminating the Eighth Article of the Ashburton Treaty* (Little Brown & Co., Boston: 1858).
Lecky, W. E.: *History of European Morals: From Augustus to Charlemagne* (Appleton, New York: 1890).
Le Louis Case, 165 English Reports (1817).
Levitt, Jeremy I.: *Africa: Mapping New Boundaries in International Law* (Hart Publishing, Oxford/Portland, Oregon: 2008).
Levitt, Kari Polanyi: 'Mercantilist Origins of Capitalism: Decline of Western Hegemony' *1 Estudios Críticos del Desarrollo* (2011) 51–87.
Linden, H. Vander: 'Alexander VI and the Demarcation of the Maritime and Colonial Domains of Spain and Portugal, 1493–1494' *22 The American Historical Review* (1916) 1–20.
Lloyd, Christopher: *The Navy and the Slave Trade: Suppression of African Slave Trade in the Nineteenth Century* (Routledge, London/New York: 2012).
Lushaba, Lwazi Siyabonga: *Development as Modernity, Modernity as Development* (Codesria Publishing, Dakar/Oxford: 2009).
Malthus, Thomas Robert: *An Essay on the Principle of Population, as It Affects the Future Improvement of Society* (Roger Chew Weightman, Washington City: 1809).
Mancall, Peter C.: *The Atlantic World and Virginia, 1550–1624* (University of North Carolina Press, Chapel Hill: 2018).
Manning, Patrick: *Slavery and African Life: Occidental, Oriental, and African Slave Trades* (Cambridge University Press, Cambridge: 1990).

Mannix, Daniel Pratt & Cowley, Malcolm: *Black Cargoes: A History of the Atlantic Slave Trade, 1518–1865* (Viking Press, New York: 1962).

Marvin, Lunenfeld: *Discovery, Invasion, Encounter: Sources and Interpretations (1492)* (D.C. Heath and Co., Lexington: 1991.

Marx, Karl: *Capital: Critique of Political Economy*, Frederick Engels (ed.) (Charles H. Kerr & Co., New York/Toronto: 1906).

———: *The Poverty of Philosophy* (Progress Publishers, Moscow: 1966).

M'baye, Babacar: 'The Economic, Political, and Social Impact of the Atlantic Slave Trade on Africa' *11 The European Legacy* (2006) 607–622.

McLaren, Brian D.: *The Great Spiritual Migration: How the World's Largest Religion Is Seeking a Better Way to Be Christian* (Convergent Books, New York: 2016).

Miller, Robert: 'The Doctrine of Discovery in American Indian Law' *42 Idaho Law Review* (2005–2006) 1–122.

Mintz, Sidney W.: 'Was the Plantation Slave a Proletarian' *2 Review (Fernand Braudel Center)* (1978) 81–98.

Mokyr, Joel: *The Enlightened Economy: An Economic History of Britain 1700–1850* (Yale University Press, New Haven: 2012).

Moore, Wilbert E.: 'Slave Law and the Social Structure' *26 The Journal of Negro History* (1941) 171–202.

Muldoon, James: 'Spiritual Freedom-Physical Slavery: The Medieval Church and Slavery' *3 Ave Maria Law Review* (2005) 69–94

———: *The Expansion of Europe: The First Phase* (University of Pennsylvania Press, Philadelphia: 1977).

Njoh, Ambe: *Urban Planning, Housing, and Spatial Structures in Sub-Saharan Africa: Nature, Impact, and Development Implications of Exogenous Forces* (Aldershot, Brookfield, Wisconsin: 1999).

Nunn, Nathan: 'The Long-Term Effects of Africa's Slave Trades' *123 The Quarterly Journal of Economics* (2008) 139–176.

Nys, Ernest: *Les Origines du Droit International* (Thorin et Fils, Paris/Brussels: 1894).

O'Brien, Patrick & Quinault, Roland: *The Industrial Revolution and British Society* (Cambridge University Press, Oxford: 1993).

Oldfield, J. R.: 'The London Committee and Mobilization of Public Opinion against the Slave Trade' *35 The Historical Journal* (1992) 331–343.

O'Malley, Gregory E.: *Final Passages: The Intercolonial Slave Trade of British America, 1619–1807* (University of North Carolina Press, Chapel Hill: 2014).

Palmer, Vernon Valentine: 'The Origins and Authors of the Code Noir' *53 Louisiana Law Review* (1995) 363–407.

Papal bull *Illius Qui* of 19 December 1442. *See*: Jeremy Watt, "The Incongruous Bull: In Supremo Apostolatus." Available online: https://scholarworks.iu.edu/dspace/bitstream/handle/2022/3341/Final+Draft+Jeremy+Watt+Essay.pdf?sequence=1 Last Accessed 10 July 2017.

Patterson, Orlando: *Slavery and Social Death* (Harvard University Press, Boston: 1982).

Penner, J. E.: "The Concept of Property and the Concept of Slavery" in Jean Allain (ed.), *The Legal Understanding of Slavery: From the Historical to the Contemporary* (Oxford University Press, Oxford: 2012) at 242–245.

Pereña, Luciano: *La idea de justicia en la conquista de América* (Mapfre, Madrid: 1992).

Pietschmann, Horst: Atlantic History. History between European History and Global History' *15 Coloquios de Historia Canario Americana* (2002) 1144–1171.

Postma, Johannes: *The Atlantic Slave Trade: Greenwood Guides to Historic Events, 1500–1900* (Greenwood Press, Westport, Connecticut: 2003).
Philips, William D.: *Slavery from Ancient Times to the Early Transatlantic Trade* (Manchester University Press, Manchester: 1985).
"Ports of the Transatlantic Slave Trade": Available online: http://www.liverpoolmuseums.org.uk/ism/resources/slave_trade_ports.aspx Last Accessed 31 August 2017.
Prior, Christopher: 'Writing Another Continent's History: The British and Pre-Colonial Africa, 1880–1939' *10 Historical Perspectives* (2007) 1–16.
Rawley, James A.: *The Transatlantic Slave Trade: A History* (University of Nebraska Press, Lincoln/London: 2005).
Reeves, Jesse S.: 'Two Conceptions of the Freedom of the Seas' *22 The American Historical Review* (1917) 535–543.
Reich, Jerome: 'The Slave Trade at the Congress of Vienna—A Study in English Public Opinion' *53 The Journal of Negro History* (1968) 129–143.
Robinson, J. Cedric: *Black Marxism: The Making of the Black Radical Tradition* (Zed, New York/London: 1983).
Rodney, Walter: *How Europe Underdeveloped Africa*, Revised edition (Pambazuka Press, Cape Town/Dakar/Nairobi/Oxford: 2012).
Rodriguez, Junius P.: *The Historical Encyclopedia of World Slavery* (ABC-CLIO, Santa Barbara: 1997).
Rothman, Adam: *Slave Country: American Expansion and the Origins of the Deep South* (Harvard University Press, Boston: 2005).
Ryder, Alan Frederick Charles: *Benin and the Europeans, 1485–1897* (Longmans, London: 1969).
Saunders, A: *A Social History of Black Slaves and Freedmen in Portugal, 1441–1555* (Cambridge University Press, Cambridge: 1982a).
———: 'The Depiction of Trade as War as a Reflection of Portuguese Ideology and Diplomatic Strategy in West Africa, 1441–1556' *17 Canadian Journal of History* (1982b) 219–234.
Scott, James Brown: *The Spanish Origins of International Law: Francisco de Vitoria and His Law of Nations* (Clarendon Press, Oxford: 1934).
Seligman, Charles Gabriel: *Races of Africa* (Thornton Butterworth, London: 1930).
Settles, Joshua & Mcgaskey, Ferlin: *The Impact of Colonialism on African Economic Development* (Working Paper, University of Tennessee Honors Thesis Project: 1996). Available online: http://trace.tennessee.edu/utk_chanhonoproj/182 Last Accessed 27 February 2013.
Slavery Convention, of 25 September 1926 (League of Nations: A.VI/S.C.I, 22 September 1926).
———: *The London Times*, of 29 July 1933.
Smith, Robert: 'Peace and Palaver: International Relations in Pre-Colonial West Africa' *14 The Journal of African History* (1973) 599–621.
Suarez, Francisco: *Selections from Three Works of Francisco Suárez, S. J.: The Photographic Reproduction of the Selections from the Original Editions*, Henry Davis (ed.) (Clarendon Press, Michigan: 1944).
Swarztrauber, Sayre Archie: *The Three-Mile Limit of Territorial Seas: A Brief History* (Naval Institute Press, Annapolis: 1972).
Temperley, Howard: 'Capitalism, Slavery and Ideology' *75 Past & Present* (1977) 94–118.

Tierney, Brian: *Foundations of the Conciliar Theory: The Contribution of the Medieval Canonists from Gratian to the Great Schism* (Brill, Leiden/New York/Cologne: 1998).
———: *The Amedie Case*, 12 English Reports (1810).
Thomas, Hugh: *The Slave Trade: The Story of the Atlantic Slave Trade: 1440–1870* (Simon & Schuster, New York/London/Sydney: 1997).
Thomas, Paul Robert: 'The Sugar Colonies of the Old Empire: Profit or Loss for Great Britain?' *21 Economic History Review* (1968) 30–45.
Thorndale, William: 'The Virginia Census of 1619' *33 Magazine of Virginia Genealogy* (1995) 168–170.
Tordoff, William: *Government and Politics in Africa* (Indiana University Press, Bloomington: 1984).
———: *Treaty between Great Britain, Austria, France, Prussia, and Russia, for the Suppression of the African Slave Trade*, of 20 December 1841, in *20 British and Foreign state papers* (1841).
Trevor-Roper, H.: *The Rise of Christian Europe* (Thames and Hudson: London, 1966).
Trimingham, John Spencer: *Islam in West Africa* (Oxford University Press, Oxford: 1959).
Tyler, Lyon Gardiner: *Narratives of Early Virginia, 1606–1625* (Charles Scribner's Sons Ltd, New York: 1907).
Umozurike, U. O.: 'The African Slave Trade and the Attitudes of International Law Towards it' *16 Howard Law Journal* (1970–1971) 334–350.
Ullmann, Walter: 'The Medieval Papal Court as an International Tribunal' *11 Virginia Journal of International Law* (1970) 356–371.
Vitoria, De Francisco: 'On the American Indians' in A. Pagden & J. Lawrance (eds.), *Political Writings* (Cambridge University Press, Cambridge: 1991).
Wallbank, Thomas Walter: *Contemporary Africa: Continent in Transition* (Van Nostrand, Princeton: 1964).
Watson, Alan: *Roman Slave Law* (Johns Hopkins University Press, Baltimore: 1987).
Weeramantry, Christopher: *Universalising International Law* (Martinus Nijhoff Publishers, Leiden: 2004).
Weindl, Andrea: 'The Asiento de Negros and International Law' *10 Journal of the History of International Law* (2008) 229–257.
Williams, Eric: *Capitalism and Slavery* (University of North Carolina Press, Chapel Hill: 1944).
———: *Inward Hunger: The Education of a Prime Minister* (Markus Wiener Publishers, Chicago: 1969).
Williams, Robert: 'Columbus's Legacy: Law as an Instrument of Racial Discrimination against Indigenous Peoples' Rights of Self-Determination' *8 Arizona Journal of International and Comparative Law* (1991) 51–76.
Wright, John: *The Trans-Saharan Slave Trade* (Routledge, London: 2007).
Yasuaki, Onuma: 'When Was the Law of International Society Born—An Inquiry of the History of International Law from an Intercivilizational Perspective' *2 Journal of the History of International Law* (2000) 1–66.
Yeager, Timothy J.: 'Encomienda or Slavery? The Spanish Crown's Choice of Labour Organization in Sixteenth-Century Spanish America' *55 The Journal of Economic History* (1995) 842–859.

4 Industrial Capitalism, Concepts of Improvement, and the Civilising Mission Metaphor in Africa

4.1 Introduction

The 19th century was marked by the industrial revolution and a remarkable wave of humanitarian sensibility by Europeans towards non-Europeans—frequently based on doctrines of social evolution and civility. In close parallel to the abolition movement that was making giant strides in bringing the slave trade in Africa to a close was another ideological campaign by European intellectuals to improve and lead non-European societies towards progressive transformation. The foundations of this drive stemmed from ideas of improvement articulated by Scottish intellectuals in the preceding century, based on the stadial theory which placed Europe—believed to be the epicentre of achievement—at the top of a hierarchical world system, and less progressive non-European societies at the bottom.[1] In the 19th century, James Mill and his son John Stuart Mill fused the stadial theory and classified peoples and societies into a simplified binary classification of civilised versus uncivilised.[2] The term "civilisation" was imperative in contrasting European societies that had made significant advancements in government, modes of economic production, commerce, laws, culture, and civility from societies of savages and barbarians that were either far behind on the ladder of human progress or whose advancement was painfully stagnant.

Although 19th-century international lawyers did not explicitly use the stadial order terminologies, they nonetheless appropriated the binary logic of civilised versus uncivilised—from which they deduced a corollary concept of *standard of civilisation* to denote the superiority of western civilisation over non-western societies. Seen as having been left behind on the ladder of progress, international law doctrines in the 19th century justified settler colonisation, with the goal of civilising the behaviours of the colonies, rendering them politically civil and economically productive. The standard of civilisation was further used to good effect to revisit prior categories of natural law. Upon revisiting prevalent categories of natural law that postulated for universal rights and equality, 19th-century international lawyers countered with positivist doctrines whereupon rights in the international society were only accrued based on the fulfilment of the newly formulated standard of civilisation.[3]

DOI: 10.4324/9781003265740-4

Central to international law framing of the standard of civilisation was the re-visitation of the nation state as a legal construct with regard to doctrines of territorial sovereignty and property rights. While natural law doctrines on the universality of rights and equity were commonplace at the close of the 18th century, 19th-century international lawyers on their part were more focused on the sources of said rights. The key questions centred on whether or not rights in the international society were inherent to humans by nature, or were created by nation states.[4] Their conclusion to these new sets of questions paved the way for legal vocabularies that justified new imperialism. Affiliating the standard of civilisation with the primacy of the state, positivists observed that rights were a privilege reserved for sovereign nations. Those that fell short of the standard needed to attain rights by subjecting themselves under a European sovereign.[5] Under this scheme, non-Europeans were nurtured by Europeans towards civility, and effectively excluded from the realm of rights within the international society, until such a time that they were deemed as having attained a satisfactory level of maturity and civilisation.[6]

The drive for new imperialism was primarily driven by the industrial revolution in Europe, commercial ambitions, and the extraterritorial quest for raw materials. It was an age of diffusion of doctrines from politics to commerce.[7] Being the last continent yet to be colonised by Europeans, Africa became the subject of European ambitious colonial expansion, power politics, and vigorous discussion amongst international lawyers between 1870 and 1900. Following the landmark Berlin conference, called by the German chancellor Otto von Bismarck in the winter of 1884–1885 for 14 recognised members of the family of nations, to establish uniform principles upon which European sovereignty could be extended unto Africa, a new professional association of international lawyers dubbed *Institut de Droit International* responded affirmatively by articulating a new concept dubbed *territorium nullius*, which enabled the legitimate appropriation of Africa's lands and European settler colonisation.[8]

4.2 From Conjectural History to Civilisation Metaphor

4.2.1 Scottish Enlightenment

In 1696, Thomas Aikenhead, an 18-year-old Scottish medical student from the University of Edinburgh, reportedly claimed that theology was "a rhapsody of feigned and ill-invented nonsense."[9] Arrested and prosecuted under Scotland's Blasphemy Acts of 1661 and 1695, Aikenhead was found guilty of the crimes of heresy and profanity, and executed on 8 January 1697.[10] While Scottish justice at the time of the judgement was heavily informed by Christendom as the basis for deciding the fate of humankind, the country nonetheless phenomenally witnessed a radical transformation half a century later, thanks to a philosophical and scientific movement that later became dubbed as the Scottish Enlightenment.[11] Crowned by groundbreaking philosophies of remarkable thinkers such as Adam Smith, Adam Ferguson, David Hume,

Francis Hutcheson, and James Hutton, the Scottish Enlightenment profoundly influenced discourse in social sciences—most notably, politics, economics, sociology, history, law, and society. The scope of the Scottish Enlightenment has been delimited to the "the period between 1726 (when Francis Hutcheson's "Inquiry into the Origin of Our Ideas of Beauty and Virtue" was first published) and 1816, when Adam Ferguson died."[12]

Deriving inspiration from four main sources, to wit: the Bible, classical literature, modern works of philosophy, and travel accounts,[13] the Scots expressed deep concern regarding the process of modernisation and improvement, tacitly perceiving the prevailing ideology of governance as counterproductive to economic growth. Although Scotland prided itself with top European universities and renowned intellectuals, it nonetheless significantly lagged behind in terms of socio-economic development by 1707, when it unified with England to form the United Kingdom. Noticing that England was prospering economically, in stark contrast to Scotland, the enlightenment intellectuals arrogated for themselves the duty to deconstruct universal rules of economics and advancement, as well as advance ideas and insights that could transform the country from a poor agrarian society into a modernised economy.[14] Contrary to conventional approaches, their philosophical investigations had the commonality of portraying all human causes as producing peculiar effects, the questioning of religious givens and their normative effects, and the conception of men from the lenses of reason rather than captives of the Bible. They moreover entertained debates over reason, and postulated theories for the advancement of societies—with the attendant goal of driving the economy towards improvements, and expanding freedoms for the populace.[15]

In *Account of the Life and Writings of Adam Smith* (1793), Dugald Stewart qualified the sophisticated writings of 18th-century Scottish intellectuals as conjectural history, while distinguishing them from philosophical traditions and narrative histories that prevailed in the preceding centuries.[16] Conjectural history to Stewart in effect depicted the sort of history that triumphed in the absence of direct evidence. As he observed,

> we are under a necessity of supplying the place of fact by conjecture; and when we are unable to ascertain how men have actually conducted themselves upon particular occasions, of considering in what manner they are likely to have proceeded, from the principles of their nature, and the circumstances of their external situation.[17]

What were conjectural histories all about, and what did they seek to achieve? Faced with the unknown about the transitional process in previous accounts of human progression and causes of differentiation between backward tribes and advanced societies, enlightened thinkers felt compelled to conject the process of how "men are likely to have proceeded from savagery to civilization."[18] In other words, conjectural history was geared at deconstructing the process and modality of progress. It replaced the primacy of religion as a solution to unresolved societal questions with scientifically explained rationales that were intrinsic in human nature. Locating the origins of that process to man's state in the backward antiquities, humans living in uncultivated ages or still living in such a state of nature were variously dubbed as "savages" and "barbarians."[19]

In a series of lectures delivered to English students in 1751, Adam Smith famously conceptualised a theory of history for all human civilisations based on four sequential stages of hunter-gatherers, pastoralists, agriculturalists, and commerce—an idea that became central in the 18th century for the articulation of theories of progress and the imperativeness of appropriating foreign lands.[20] The process of social evolution from savagery to civility was an inevitable process which mankind was bound to charter before attaining progress.[21] While Europe had transitioned into the highest stages of agriculture and commercial society, non-European societies were still lagging behind in primitive stages of savagery and barbarism. As already noted in Chapter 2 of this study, Adam Smith advanced the concept of division of labour as the modality for profit-making, better social well-being, improvements, modernity, and liberty.

For Scottish Enlightenment thinkers, the imperativeness of economic improvement was an inevitable corollary to the necessity to defend liberty as a sacred right. In fact, the scholarships of David Hume and Adam Smith were in some respect tacit responses to an earlier thesis by Thomas Hobbes (1588–1679) which admonished for limits to civil liberties, upon portraying man as ruthless by nature and driven solely by self-interests.[22] As Hobbes observed,

> if any two men desire the same thing, which nevertheless they cannot both enjoy, they become enemies; and in the way to their end (which is principally their own conservation, and sometimes their delectation only) endeavour to destroy or subdue one another.[23]

His strong support of absolute monarchy for the preservation of law and order in *Leviathan* (1651) fuelled European monarchs with a sense of invisibility, and was perceived by his critiques as empowering sovereigns to violate peoples' basic rights with impunity.

The origins of *Leviathan* has been traced to Hobbes's frustration with the vicious, costly violence and lawlessness that characterised the decade-long English civil war (1642–1651). In response, Hobbes wrote *Leviathan*, supposedly as a counterargument to the 17th-century social contract thinking that allowed people to depose abusive governments.[24] The bloody violence and deaths from the English civil war convinced Hobbes that the social contract theory had the real danger of plunging countries into perpetual chaos and lawlessness, as it rolled humans back into a throwback state of nature. Hobbes noted that a state of nature was characterised by lack of government, with the attendant consequence being that life was "nasty, brutish and short."[25] As a remedy, Hobbes advocated for total submission and obedience to traditional authority, as it was sometimes necessary to limit liberties in order to preserve the greater good—namely peace, law, and order.[26]

In two epic works, *A Treatise of Human Nature* (1740) and *Enquiries Concerning the Human Understanding and Concerning the Principles of Morals* (1777), Hume differed with Hobbes, contending that man's nature was not static but conditioned by moral exigencies. Hence, all human actions to him were motivated by individual experiences.[27] In spite of his affirmation of a non-static human nature, he nevertheless observed a common behavioural pattern amongst humankind. In fact, he conceptualised the "universal man" based on moral philosophy—an idea that human behaviour was uniform in all societies.[28]

Given that human behaviour is uniform in every society, people are accordingly akin to reacting in similar ways to similar situations.[29] The human mind is saturated with mental contents (ideas) which closely resemble one another. The conception of one idea, he observed, naturally triggers another that is closely related or contiguous with it, thus resulting to the articulation of customary norms.[30] For Hume, the pathway to modernity rested in understanding this complex human nature, and assuming our duty for improvement of societies: "The end of all moral speculations is to teach us our duty"[31] Like Adam Smith, he was a strong critic of mercantilism, and a defender of free trade. He observed that for domestic production to be profitable, it necessarily needed to adapt to the "spirit of industry" by laying the groundwork for foreign trade:

> Where a great number of commodities are raised and perfected for the home-market there will always be found some which can be exported with advantage. But if our neighbours have no art nor cultivation, they cannot take them, because they will have nothing to give in exchange. In this respect, states are in the same condition as individuals. A single man can scarce be industrious where all his fellow-citizens are idle. The riches of the several members of a community contribute to increase any riches, whatever profession I may follow.[32]

4.2.2 Civilisation Metaphor

At the turn of the 19th century, the erstwhile conventional stadial categories of hunter-gatherers, pastoralists, agriculturalists, and traders, devised by Scottish Enlightenment scholars, were squeezed into a more simplified binary differentiation of civilised versus uncivilised by political economists and international lawyers. It became the standard barometer (measured in terms of progress) for gauging the gap between Europeans and non-Europeans, and the appropriation of lands of the latter. James Mill (1776–1836) and his son, John Stuart Mill (1806–1873), are credited[33] for affording the scientific distinction between the civilised and the uncivilised.[34] They invoked these binary terms as a simplified way of replicating the stadial order. In his seminal essay titled "Civilisation" (1836), Stuart Mill construed civilisation as the antithesis of savagery and barbarism.[35] Unlike non-Europeans who were still lagging behind, the Mills observed that material progress had catapulted Europe to civilisation—the apex of progress and stadial order.[36] The wide gap which was established between Europeans and non-Europeans in the 19th century became the basis of formulating doctrines of occupations and the justification of settler colonisation, supposedly to civilise the behaviours of the uncivilised, reform their productive forces, and enable them to climb the imperative ladder of progress.

For Stuart Mill, industrial commerce was not only the ultimate last stage of the stadial order, but moreover the most important stage of achievement. Heavily captivated by Britain's advancement as a result of the industrial revolution, he sought to investigate ways of sustaining that achievement, as well as deconstructing an economic solution that could enable improvement in societies inhabited by savages and barbarians.[37] He was confident that British colonisation was bound to bring countless benefits to non-Europeans, as they were eventually going to benefit from the benevolence of the empire and economic growth thanks to industrial activity and increased commerce.

Within the new binary categorisation of the Mills, Africa incarnated the uncivilised. The overwhelming consensus amongst 19th-century European publicists was that the world was squarely divided between the savage, barbarism, and civilised peoples.[38] To that effect, Lewis Henry Morgan (1818–1881)—an American lawyer-anthropologist—provided that the natural sequence of progress amongst all tribes of humankind showed that savagery preceded barbarism and barbarism preceded civilisation.[39] European colonial intervention in non-European territories was interpreted in international law as a humanitarian act in so far as it brought law, order, and reason to a previously uncivilised people. This idea was very much in line with the Kantian notion of development (Kantian cosmopolitanism), which conceived progress as a prerequisite for a peaceful and orderly world.[40]

4.3 Industrial Capitalism, Revitalisation of Primitive Accumulation on a Global Scale, and the Civilising Mission in Africa

4.3.1 Primitive Accumulation Revitalised

The lessons of plantation capitalism revealed two things at the dawn of the 19th century: firstly, that imperialism was the most successful political method for bringing different parts of the earth under economic and political control for wealth creation. And secondly, that a theoretical articulation of a mode of production was inevitable for any legal vision of establishing colonial states and extraterritorial empires by analogy.[41] In fact, the 19th century on many counts, was very emblematic of the 16th century. For the first time since the 16th century, this epoch was the pivotal moment when things were profoundly remade in the international society, prompting practical ramifications and shifts in interpretation in the disciplines of political economy and international law-making. Specifically, things sparked off with the international economic system achieving a new and potent dimension, thus propelling a new ordering for global governance. Marked by a spirit of European expansionism and new trade exigencies, the 19th century was driven by economic and political factors that triggered robust shifts in scientific debates, especially in political economy discourse and international law. Nineteenth-century international lawyers in fact had the puzzling task of revisiting prior categories as well as creating new norms of trade and doctrines for acquisition of titles (property rights), reminiscent of the tasks that Francisco de Vitoria (1460–1546), Bartolomé de Las Casas (1484–1556), and Alberico Gentili (1552–1608) had in the 16th century.

On an abstract level, the 19th century kicked off with an entrenched persuasion amongst European academics to the effect that there was a fundamental distinction between Europeans and people of European extraction on the one hand and the savage "others" (non-Europeans) on the other. Europe and people of its extraction were the standard bearers of excellence and progress, and the basis for "the others" to emulate in order to measure up with progress.[42] With the thriving of industrial capitalism, international law assumed a new guise as a law with a civilising mission. In fact, the scientific term "civilisation" was variously invoked by political economists and publicists alike, as an equivalence of the classical idea of progress, which by extension essentially meant advances in economic development and the perfecting of social life.[43]

In Marxian rendition, the centrality of the 19th century marked a crucial revitalisation, namely the revival of primitive accumulation on a global scale. A mode of production for Marx corresponded to peoples' "relations of production, and definite stages of development of their material productive forces."[44] The Marxian conception of primitive accumulation on a global scale, as aforementioned, presents readers not only with a historical argument but a continuity one as well. Unlike Smith, Marx limited his conception of original accumulation not to a static moment, but rather to the structural manifestation of the concept as a continuous process, especially the nature of its reproduction and expansion—in different places and over different eras. As already stated in Chapter 2, the imperativeness of profit-making has historically conditioned the conceptual west to devise three momentous capitalist modes of production schemes: plantation capitalism (16–18th century), industrial capitalism (19th century), and development capitalism (20th century and beyond).

Having moreover observed that sub-Saharan Africa was one of the most adversely affected regions of the world in each of the aforementioned three watershed schemes, the previous chapters of this study were dedicated to the manifestation of the first scheme and its implication for the subregion. The following chapters (Chapters 4–6) are tailored to unmasking the transition from the first scheme unto the second, especially the nexus between the quest for extraterritorial growth, colonialism, and shifts in international law. In this chapter, I examine the key factors that caused European powers to steadily abandon plantation (mercantilist) capitalism while simultaneously embracing industrial capitalism as the preferred mode of production for their international relations.

While the Americas and Africa collectively constituted the periphery of the world system in the 16th century when primitive accumulation on a global scale was first launched, they nonetheless played diametrically different roles. While the Americas were colonised by European invaders, its inhabitants dispossessed of property rights and the territory appropriated for settler colonisation, sub-Saharan Africa was spared from these intrusions and instead conditioned to play the vital role of supplying the labour manpower necessary to transform the New World. With the advent of industrial capitalism at the turn of the 19th century, sub-Saharan Africa—having been determined to be abundantly endowed with the natural resources necessary for industrial capitalism—was promptly reconditioned by European powers to replace the Americas not just as the centre of the global periphery, but more so as the new site for settler colonisation.

As noted in Chapter 3, the revolutionising of labour by machines that marked the advent of the industrial revolution in England, and translated to greater yields and profits, quickly spread to the rest of western Europe, with industrial capitalism by analogy (otherwise dubbed in this study as the Second Primitive Accumulation Scheme on a global scale) being swiftly embraced throughout the 19th century as the more convenient, hence preferred mode of production. To be precise, as the economic interests that built up the slave trade system increasingly became unnecessary (from reliance on human labour to reliance on machines which yielded more profits), the inhumanity and injustices of the slave trade correspondingly increasingly became highlighted by European political economists, policy makers, and international lawyers. There was overwhelming consensus amongst Europeans on the imperativeness of industrial capitalism, based on the projected assumption that since the new mode of production was endowed with enlightened principles, it was accordingly bound to deliver justice and advancement across Africa.

From the standpoint of its progenitors, the Second Primitive Accumulation Scheme was essentially both a rejuvenation and an extension of the idea of progress to the remaining backward peoples of the globes—hence, European intervention for its realisation was perceived as bound to put all of humanity on the path of improvement. Heralded for its emphasis on legitimate trading, the progenitors of the new mode of production variously conceptualised it as epitomising the spirit of freedom and the catalyst for the civilising mission. Unlike the precolonial mode of production that was marred by slavery and unfree labour especially for affected Africans, the new scheme was a humanitarian project, with the promise to spread light and enlightenment unto the so-called backward places of the world. For sub-Saharan Africa, the promise implied that once they became proficient in the novel mode of production, they could subsequently exchange their output with the core of the world system in international trade, not only as free peoples but theoretically as equals.[45]

From a Marxian standpoint, the celebratory proclamations of industrial capitalist progenitors were as pretentious as they were misleading. The entire scheme was variously perceived by 19th-century Marxists as exploitation and legalised plunder, disguised as liberalism. Lamenting on the structural violence frequently melted out on annexed populations, the leftist scholar Foucault advanced a critique of the ethical consciousness of colonial labour, noting that forcing peoples into industrial capital labour was by all intents and purposes tantamount to giant "houses of confinement."[46] For contemporary Marxists, the extraterritorial manifestation of industrial capitalism was essentially an affirmation of capital as power and the capitalist mode of production as exploitative. Capital's power resided in the exploitation of labour relations and extraction of surplus value (profits).[47] The desire to extract surplus value naturally propelled the necessity to control labour processes, which by analogy also triggered capitalists to arrogate exclusive rights over the means of production.

As already pointed out, Marxists do not generally subscribe to the categories of abstract liberties (political freedoms) typically highlighted by political economists and international lawyers. The measure of liberty for Marxists is instead on the fulfilment of human freedoms. Going by this consideration, contemporary Marxists perceived the Second Primitive Accumulation Scheme as falling short of the two key criteria that are indispensable for real freedom, namely freedoms from means of labour, and freedom of producers to sell their own labour power.[48] While the structural system helped create a wage system across Africa, it nevertheless caused many in the continent to lose property rights and be confined to perpetual proletariats in the international division of labour.[49] In fact, far from enjoying real freedoms, Africans were suddenly dispossessed in the process, with the most valuable and resourceful lands being transferred to the European-administered colonial state.

In the face of 19th-century European extraterritorial aggressive colonial expeditions, Lenin and Rosa Luxemberg resurrected the concept of primitive accumulation laying emphasis on the dynamics of imperialism borne out of industrial capitalism which was prevalent in their lifetimes. Their scholarship was less focused on the foundation of the concept as originally propounded by Marx. By contrast, they dwelled extensively on the continuous character of the industrial capitalist mode of production and its propensity to cement the dominance of the global bourgeois class over the already-exploited proletariats of the universe. Upon concurring with Marx that capitalism (the capitalist mode of production) once mature creates conditions for its own existence and continuity, both thinkers variously observed that mature capitalism was in a constant search for non-capitalist spaces to invade and destroy less productive and less profitable modes of production, whereupon it could then transform those conquered spaces into the novel capitalist mode of production. As Luxemberg noted,

> Marx dealt in detail with the process of appropriating non-capitalist means of production as well as with the transformation of the peasants

> into a capitalist proletariat ... Yet we must bear in mind that all this is treated solely with a view to so-called primitive accumulation. For Marx, these processes are incidental, illustrating merely the genesis of capital, its first appearance in the world; they are, as it were, travails by which the capitalist mode of production emerges from a feudal society. As soon as he comes to analyse the capitalist process of production and circulation, he reaffirms the universal and exclusive domination of capitalist production.[50]

In *Imperialism: The High-Stage of Capitalism* (1938), Lenin variously qualified the prevalent 19th-century prominence of monopolies, finance capital, and the export of capital into new non-European spaces as a violent exploitative necessity for its progenitors, which given its unethicalness could be achieved only through imperialism. He termed this particular stage of capitalist mode of production as the second phase of global imperialism.[51] Noting that "the capitalist colonial policy of previous stages of capitalism is essentially different from the colonial policy of finance capital," Lenin predicted that new drive for capital accumulation through monopolies was inevitably going to result to rivalry wars (the great wars) as monopoly competitors struggled to outwit one another.[52]

> The question is: what means other than war could there be *under capitalism* of removing the disparity between the development of productive forces and the accumulation of capital on the one side, and the division of colonies and "spheres of influence" for finance capital on the other?[53]

Rivalries amongst competing capitalists notwithstanding, once a capitalist power successfully instituted its cartel in a new space, not only were production processes going to be completely transformed into the whims of the capitalists, but capitalism was by analogy bound to metamorphose into imperialism.[54] This conception was reminiscent of the colonial drive that effectively brought all non-European territories under European control by the close of the 19th century.

Given that the ultimate goal of the capital accumulation process was to generate profits and growth for its progenitors, this imperative by implication necessitated the conversion of the conquered populations into cheap labour and their spaces into new capitalist markets for finished goods. The new exploitative labour relations, uneven markets, and unfair new exchange relations between the colonisers and the colonised was a classic manifestation of a phenomenon that David Harvey, as previously mentioned, qualified as *accumulation by dispossession*.[55] Collectively, these structural schemas formed the foundation of the revitalised international division of labour, which, analogous to the First Primitive Accumulation Scheme, once more facilitated an unfair international social relation for redistribution of wealth that clearly favoured the metropoles and was, according to contemporary Marxists, detrimental to the peripheries by design. In general, contemporary Marxists have habitually identified striking parallels between the processes which I term in this study as the First and Second Primitive Accumulation Schemes on a global scale, namely: their defining character, triggered by historical conjecture; and the monopolisation of violence (use of force) to compel all and sundry into the capitalist modes of production. It is thanks to the confluence and interplay of these processes that international law vindicated and legitimated the scramble for Africa and the colonisation mandate (protectorates) as a necessary duty of the civilised unto the uncivilised of the world.

Violence, as aforementioned, was the principal technique of reproduction of the industrial capitalist mode of production. Seen as tailored by design on expropriating natural resources and accumulation of capital in the colonies, the Cameroonian historian and philosopher Achille Mbembe, in *On the Postcolony* (2001), qualified the particularity and manifestation of coercion during the colonial encounter as "founding violence."[56] Founding violence for Mbembe signified the foundational extraterritorial colonial scheme in the 19th century that was arrogated by European colonising countries in annexed territories, whereupon they instituted and legitimated a regime of expropriation and extraction of the latter's resources, primarily to benefit the metropoles. Founding violence was, by this construction, the pivotal technique for reproduction of original accumulation in the colonies—the instrument for domination, control, dispossession, subjugation, and ultimately law-making.[57] With the overriding goal being the constitution or reconstitution of social relations of labour based on the exigencies of the colonisers, this foundational structural order was inevitable for the crystallising of the colonial system and the thriving of industrial capitalist mode of production.[58] International law by analogy was borne, shaped, and reshaped out of these peculiar techniques of violence.

4.3.2 Colonial State as Guarantor of the Industrial Capitalist Mode of Protection

Since the conquest of the Americas in the 16th century, a strong synergy has been formed between capital accumulation and international law and prevails to the present. It is principally thanks to the crystallising of primitive accumulation schemes and the sturdy legitimation of capitalist mode of production relations over the centuries, that Europeans steadily fortified the institution of nation states as principal actors of international law. Both this chapter and Chapter 5 of this study highlight how 19th-century colonial conquests, especially in Africa, were justified as intended to realise the humanitarian objectives of extending civilisation unto the less fortunate peoples of the world, that were perceived as still languishing in backwardness. European intervention was crucial not just to guide the backwards reform of their political institutions and legal systems, but moreover to train them in the productive mode of production associated with civility—a pivotal prerequisite necessary for any polity to be fully admitted into the family of nations. Having subdued Africans, European powers conceived the institution of centralised colonial states as the best modality to realise these paramount humanitarian duties.

Meanwhile, European academics for centuries acknowledged the prevalence of political institutions and kingdoms throughout sub-Saharan Africa. In the 19th century however, there was almost near consensus amongst European intellectuals and politicians to the effect that African institutions were chiefly backward and lacking in modernity, when compared to European nation states. In addition, African relations of production were perceived to be a drawback to progress given that the population still variously relied on subsistence agriculture and the furtherance of the slave trade, which had in due course been deemed as an illegitimate international trade.[59] In the face of these challenges, European intervention was necessary in order to reform the political institutions of the continent towards the modern ideals of progress, namely the industrial capitalist relations of production. Since such an intervention could not be carried out from a distance, strong protectorate states needed to be set up across the continent in order not only to effectively stamp out backward ills in these societies, but moreover to drill them on the path of civility and progress.[60] That is, although African political entities were clearly acknowledged as not being *res nullius*, European powers nonetheless identified a set of deficiencies, whereupon they conceived the application of "civilisation mission" on these societies to enable them to conform to modernity in due course. In the sections that follow, I submit that Africa's supposed deficiency with regard to the standard of civilisation paved the way for international lawyers to frame Africa as *territorium nullius*, thereby empowering European powers to annex and set up colonial states termed protectorates throughout the continent.

While the second global capitalist accumulation scheme was momentous, it was not unexpected from a Marxian standpoint. Marx emphasised the continuous propensity of primitive accumulation, noting that primitive accumulation, once triggered, creates the necessary conditions for the system's endurance, reproduction, and continuity.[61] In *Philosophy of the Encounter* (2006), Louis Althusser expounded on the inevitability of colonial impulses in the face of a new capitalist mode of production:

> It so happens that this encounter took place, and took hold, which means that it did not come undone as soon as it came about, but lasted, and became an accomplished fact, the accomplished fact of this encounter, inducing stable relationships and a necessity the study of which yields "laws"—tendential laws of course ... what matters about this conception is less the elaboration of laws, hence of an essence, than the aleatory character of the "taking-hold" of this encounter, which gives rise to an accomplished fact whose laws it is possible to state.[62]

Althusser's contention unravelled the prevailing belief amongst contemporary Marxists to the effect that mature capitalism had an incessant impulse for territorial and extraterritorial expansion; thus, in the face of fertile conditions, primitive accumulation was certainly always going to revive itself as the driving modality for social relations. Once triggered, primitive accumulation penetrates non-capitalist spaces not just to invade, but more so to procure its natural resources, to destroy non-profitable labour or production processes, and to co-opt all social relations into the nascent capitalist mode of production. A new capitalist mode of production could take off only from a primitive accumulation process, which imperatively lays down the necessary groundwork (pre-conditions) for social relations and ordering. The propensity for profits according to Marx implied that a more profitable labour modality once devised was bound to confront the prevailing labour order, then steadily dominate and replace it as the overriding capitalist mode of production.[63] That is, the capitalist mode of production naturally seeks to dominate rather than co-exist. This explains why the production modes of the colonised are habitually abandoned once they are annexed by an external power. It is upon the destruction of African pre-existing political institutions and prevailing modes of production that a legal rationale was articulated for the necessity of the colonial state to fill the void and safeguard the professed rights and well-being of the colonised African populations. A gap in sovereign duty was perceived as a justified reason for invasion and dispossession.

The colonial state in fact emerged as the hegemonic superstructure for the guarantee of law, order, and the exigencies of industrial capitalism.[64] With the governance of Africans strictly on obligations, the colonial state was a classical superstructure of "'might makes right." Prior to the legitimation of colonial protectorates for Africa at the 1884–1885 Berlin conference, there had been a fierce scramble for African resources and territories by European non-state actors, which if unchecked could have easily generated a catastrophic international war. Actions of non-state actions were deemed to be legal as long as African collectivities gave their consent, as evidenced in cession treaties. There was consensus amongst Berlin conference delegates to the effect that the presence of colonial protectorate states was going to end the arbitral scramble and rivalries amongst the non-state actors, safeguard property rights for all, guarantee free trade, and, most importantly, institute regimes of law and order. Given that the centralised colonial state was laying the groundwork for a civilised nation state where none supposedly previously existed, European powers by analogy deemed it imperative to fortify the nascent state with exorbitant powers and duties. The new state and its administration needed to be the judge, judiciary, and executioner in all aspects of life in the colonies. Amongst other things, it was not only entrusted with the tutelage duty to train colonised subjects, but moreover to serve as the extraterritorial law-making organs of the metropole whereupon it could monitor, supervise, adjudicate, and discipline colonised subjects where necessary.[65]

The process of engagement of Africa into an industrial capitalist mode of production during the scramble, partition, and protectorate encroachments largely relied on coercion, both directly and indirectly (carrot-and-stick diplomacy). The overriding consensus was that a state worthy of the name ought to be the sole monopoly owner of arbitrary powers and legitimate use of force.[66] The application of a mixture of direct (lethal force) or indirect (for instance, persuasion and treaty negotiations) coercion in European colonial quests largely depended on whether or not they not faced resistance from targeted African communities. The different approaches notwithstanding, either technique was firmly geared at appropriating African natural resources, incorporating the annexed territories under the sovereignty of the metropole, and subjected colonised populations unto an industrial capitalist mode of production. One scholar has conceived of both approaches as two sides of the same coin, noting that

> even the most subtle form of power based on persuasion [required] a machinery of coercion to discipline the transgressor; on the other hand, even the most brutally coercive systems [had an] element of persuasion in their modes of power in order to elicit some kind of collaboration from the dominated.[67]

This study on examining the barrage of cession treaties that European powers entertained with African rulers in the 19th century, which supposedly transferred proprietary rights from the latter unto the former, concurs with Sanyal's observation, noting in addition that while indirect coercion was not only a direct corollary to lethal force, its very essence assumed the guise of subtle coercion, and its primary purpose geared at minimising the cost of colonisation. One scholar has contended that since primitive accumulation is naturally going to face resistance in new spaces, violence is accordingly legitimate as a last resort, since land and resources are imperative for economic growth, while resistances by backward peoples is in effect a drawback to progress and advancement.[68] Violence in such instances is necessary in the short run, for as Niobar put it, while land and resources are freely available to all, advanced peoples who are able to render it productive ought to be entitled to use all necessary means in order to achieve this noble goal.[69]

Given the dynamics of exclusion and inclusion for Africans and their third world counterparts on the one hand, and Europe on the other hand, from or into the family of nations respectively, it can be deduced that the barrage of 19th-century progressive legal articulations were not just synonymous to terroristic laws but in fact amounted to bloody legislations, as devised by Marx. The more Africans resigned themselves to new labour roles of primary production forced upon them, the more a global class order was firmly cemented, and international division of labour structurally revived. Prior to the institution of colonial state and protectorates, the primary of livelihood amongst African collectivities oscillated between a mixture of land ownership and inheritance entitlements, food crops farming, and artisanry.[70] Using varying sets of bloody legislations to discipline Africans, European powers under the auspices of the colonial state continually divorced indigenous populations from their means of production, while simultaneously converting the dispossessed to become labourers for the colonial administration.

The new capitalist mode of production conditioned the continent's lands and labour processes to divert to mining extraction and the production of cash crops such as cocoa, coffee, tea, and rubber, rather than food crops. The *Cambridge Advanced Learner's Dictionary* defines a cash crop as "a crop that is grown mainly to be sold, rather than used by the people who grew it or those living in the area it is grown in."[71] Not only are cash crops essentially monoculture in nature rather than mixed cropping, as was the case in precolonial Africa, but they are in addition purely luxury goods. Unlike food crops whose prices are determined by producers, cash crops by their very nature are destined for export and workers (their producers) cannot directly bargain the price for which they sell their labour power to the core, but instead rely on the purchasing price set by the latter's economy.[72] While sub-Saharan Africa under the new dispensation was fortified as the periphery of the world system through its concentration on primary production and new market for finished goods, Europe on its part solidified itself as the core through its concentration on industrial manufacturing and sale of finished goods. While political economists even in the 19th century heralded the international division of labour as a mutually beneficial process, an economy roundly rooted on unskilled primary extraction tasks, such as mining and cash crops production, cannot effectively compete with one whose concentration is grounded on skilled tasks and whose commodities for exchange are finished goods. In international trade, the exchange between lowly priced primary commodities against expensive finished goods can at best further widen rather than lessen the uneven gap between the periphery and the core, thus perpetuating the trajectory of development versus underdevelopment.

4.4 Harmonisation of the Civilising Mission, and Conceptual Image of Africa

Although the Law of Nations had been taught for centuries at universities across Europe, it was only in the 19th century that international law evolved into an autonomous academic discipline and was taught independently from other branches of law or philosophy. Hitherto, the personalities that are today revered as seasoned publicists not only had no tenure as publicists, but, most remarkably, actually belonged to varying disciplines such as theology, legal science, philosophy, and economics. It has been observed that the only way they distinguished themselves was by interpreting or writing extensively on international relations or issues affecting nations (Law of Nations).[73]

Driven by the zeal to be autonomous, assertive, and a voice to stand out in international relations, publicists increasingly sought to codify international law doctrines. With intellectual works both in law and neighbouring disciplines depicting the spaces of non-Europeans as strikingly backward and in need of interventions for them to be economically and politically resourceful, international lawyers, who up to now had operated independently, embarked on a collective venture in order to formulate unique uniform legislative reforms on broader international law issues, as well as to afford solutions to the looming concerns surrounding the European encounter with the non-Europeans.[74] A group of liberal thinkers led by Gustave Rolin-Jaequemyns (1835–1902), Tobias Michael Carel Asser (1838–1913), and John Westlake (1828–1913) published the first international law journal—*Revue de Droit International et de Législation Comparée* in 1868—as a professional forum for liberal legislative reform in Europe.[75] In response to inhumane conduct in the Franco-Prussian war of 1870–1871, these thinkers began working on a charter with Jean Gaspar Bluntschli (1808–1881) and eight other men for what in 1873 became the *Institut de Droit International* in Ghent, becoming the first professional association of international lawyers. Conceiving international law as positive morality or law improperly so-called, the *Institut*'s primary goal was to function as "the scientific organ for the common legal consciousness of the civilized world."[76] Specifically, Article 1 of the statute of the *Institut* inclined the organisation to "*favoriser le progress du droit international, en s'efforçant de devenir l'organe de la conscience juridique du monde civilisé.*"[77]

The innovation with the statute of the *Institut* was the conception of international law as an expression of popular consciousness, and its eventual extension beyond Europe—in contradistinction to earlier attempts to restrict the realm of international law to Europe and the Christian world.[78] The power of these international lawyers ultimately rested in their self-proclaimed pronouncements that they were inherently empowered to formulate binding rules for the international society. James Lorimer (1818–1890)—a Scottish advocate and professor of public law at University of Edinburgh, argued that the international space was inhabited by two dialectically opposite species of mankind, to wit: the progressive (civilised) and the non-progressive races (subdivided into savages and barbarians). Faced with this contradiction, it was incumbent on the progressive to ascertain as to what mechanisms or positive law were best suited to apply to the backward non-progressive races to bring them out of darkness.[79] Conceiving transnational humanitarianism thus as a duty, Bluntschli—Lorimer's colleague at the *Institut*—concurred by admonishing the civilised nations to develop and harmonise the spirit of the common laws of humanity:

> One is authorized to intervene to ensure respect for the individual rights that have been recognized as necessary … whenever these happen to be violated in the struggle between the citizens of a single state. One is authorized to intervene when the violation of international law constitutes a general danger … an oppressed minority could, under such circumstances, provoke foreign intervention not in the name of the state but in the name of international law.[80]

In accordance with their newfound positivist creed, international lawyers certified two separate regimes: one for governing relations amongst civilised sovereigns (or members of the family of nations) under formal equality, and the other governing relations between civilised sovereigns with uncivilised non-Europeans under inequality, granting privileges to the former.[81] It has been observed that the doctrine used in erecting these boundaries was the standard of civilisation, and was interpreted to legally determine those that belonged to the family of nations from those that did not.[82] Any nation that failed to meet the standard was by definition uncivilised.[83] A non-civilised polity could be admitted into the sovereign family of nations only if other sovereign nations had effectively and clearly recognised it as meeting the civilisation standard (the doctrine of recognition). The international community was accordingly strictly restricted to civilised nations which in fact had all achieved a particular level of economic development. Given the nature of this configuration, many questions arose, some of which remained unanswered. For instance, who or what decided what "civilisation" meant? Were civilisation and non-civilisation both mutable? In other words, could the civilised relapse back to a state of uncivilised, in the similar sequence as the process through which the uncivilised evolved to a state of civility? What were the legal results of using the standard of civilisation as the trendsetter of international law and consequently progress? Moreover, in what ways could the vocabulary as a "standard" buttress the exploitation of the non-European territories by the colonisers in the name of progress?[84]

It has been observed that the power to define is the power to declare, to identify, and to recognise, thus the ability to cultivate international legal standards.[85] In the 19th century, European academics qualified non-Europeans as a socio-cultural problem whose predicaments and any hope for advancement could be redressed only through western-model ideas of progress and civilisation. This fact is succinctly expounded by Ziauddin Sardar, who has argued that to understand Eurocentrism, we must first deconstruct its definitional power:

> The west defines what is for example, freedom, progress and civil behavior; law, tradition and community; reason mathematics and science; what is real and what it means to be human. The non-Western civilizations have to accept these definitions or be defined out of existence.[86]

International law in the 19th century in essence defined the non-western societies in general and Africa in particular as economically backward by contrasting it with modernity that incarnated civilisation or progress—a phenomenon that Anthony Anghie has termed as the "dynamic of difference."[87] While legitimating colonisation as a right, international law employed both inclusive and exclusionary metaphors framed in terms of binary dualities such as advanced versus backwards, civilised versus uncivilised, primitive versus progress, light versus dark, known versus mystery, found versus lost, tamed versus wild, etc.; all of these vindicated the rights of Europeans but through the same process, placed Africa and the rest of non-European territories on a bar ladder of progress which they needed to meet before enjoying similar rights. The encounter with sub-Saharan Africa was projected by some writers as a cultural collision—a scuffle with primitivism, as they purportedly revealed that African economic development was stagnant, and the continent had been left behind in stadial ladder of human development. Although European scholars concurred that sub-Saharan Africa had achieved the agricultural phase in the stadial order, they nevertheless still perceived the subcontinent as having little or no semblance with a civilised identity whether in geopolitical, socio-economic, or environmental outlooks.[88] It was believed that the subcontinent had not succeeded in formulating a concept of improvement and advancement. The land was thus depicted as needing thorough economic development to improve the well-being of its indigenous inhabitants. Unlike temperate Europe or the western world that was free from diseases, fertile, and productive, the African tropics were grossly dangerous—its nature widely infested by pests and disease, coupled with the barbaric activities of African "natives."[89]

As European intellectuals adopted the binary categories of civilised versus uncivilised, a growing number of discourses steadily assumed racial expressions, vindicating the hegemony of Europeans over other races. The 19th century in general witnessed an exceptional harmonisation of prejudice in some academic circles as scientific discourse. In the words of Anthony Anghie, the racialisation of the vocabulary of the period was manifested "not only in the explicit distinctions between the civilized and uncivilized, advanced and barbaric, but also in the integration of these distinctions into the very foundations of the discipline, namely the ostensibly neutral concepts of law, society and sovereignty."[90] The task of educating inferior races in political theory, civil life, and statehood was framed as a natural White man's burden: the great historical assignment.[91]

In making the case for the inevitable domination of Africa by the West, some intellectuals linked the projected economic stagnation of the continent to the supposedly natural biological and cultural inferiority of its peoples. This was the case, for example, with the ideological movement which emerged around 1870 in England and the United States known as Social Darwinism, claiming a mastery in the understanding of primitive societies. Led by Herbert Spencer (1820–1903), Thomas Henry Huxley (1825–1895), and Francis Galton (1822–1911), the school fostered the concept of "survival of the fittest" as a solution to primitive societies; which essentially implied that the Caucasian race was superior to all others both biologically and in terms of human development as a result of having a far superior culture, and was thus destined to rule over inferior peoples who might be impervious to progress. In *Dictionnaire du Darwinisme et de l'évolution*, Patrick Tort describes the concept thus:

> Social Darwinism is a form of sociology, the postulates of which are: As Man is part of nature, the laws of human society are, directly or almost directly, those of the law of nature; That the laws of nature are the

> survival of the fittest, the struggle for life and the laws of heredity; That it is necessary for the well-being of society to make sure these laws are properly applied in society.[92]

Thomas R. Malthus's book: *Essay on Population* (1798)[93] half a century after publication proved to be decisive in stimulating both the best and the worst in intellectual imaginations given its ability to inspire varying ideas on evolution, population, and social struggles. Two scholars, Charles Darwin (1809–1882) and Herbert Spencer, read the book around the same time and arrived at two parallel yet very contentious outcomes. Darwin was a naturalist and Spencer was a sociologist; hence, each saw the world from their respective lens of specialty. The two contentious works were Darwin's *Origin of Species* (1859) and Spencer's *Principles of Biology* (1864).[94] Provoked by Malthus's essay, Darwin, who had spent years in South Pacific observing and analysing plant and animal life formulated the concept of natural selection as an explanation for his own observation that these organisms were naturally logged in the "struggle of existence," with only favourable variants of each species surviving while unfavourable variants were destroyed. The book immediately became an intellectual sensation.

Five years after Darwin's epic publication, Spencer radically converted his idea of natural selection from natural sciences into a social norm by introducing his now infamous catchy concept of "survival of the fittest."[95] Spencer asserted that human societies were social organisms wherein mankind shared the same "survival of the fittest" biological and natural laws pattern as plants and animals, given that humans were unavoidably faced with pressure of balancing between population growth and an endless struggle for existence. Accordingly, a class struggle in the international society was inevitable for any given mode of production to be completely transcended. As a remedy, Spencer observed that the mentally upright, the most rational, the most physically fit, and the most productive amongst humans not only survive as a natural principle, but ought to survive, for only they could transmit value to existence and guarantee social improvement or perfection.[96] The school also depicted Africa and its people to the European metropolitan public as unfavourable variants whose very existence was a combination of shock and a drawback to progress. Social Darwinists interpreted the global social space as a proof that Europeans were stronger and superior beings, with the colonisation of "the others" being the survival of the fittest test.

Social Darwinists writings over time provided an influential ideological backbone for some scholars to postulate a wide gap between material development of Europeans and the "other" which was both empirically verifiable and physically obvious. The image of Africa, for instance, took many forms—it was visual as well as verbal. It appeared in separate but often overlapping academic disciplines.[97] One common denominator across these disciplines was the identification of Africa as a dark continent in need of light—that is, civilisation. The term "dark continent" came into popular usage through three infamous travel publications: one by David Livingstone, *Expeditions into the Dark Continent* (1876); and two others by Henry Morton Stanley, *In Darkest Africa* (1890) and *Through the Dark Continent* (1878).[98] While Livingstone's book, on one hand, was both a political and an economic plea for Europeans to reason with him about the devastation of the slave trade, on the other hand it served as a promissory note for them to realise that by embracing legitimate trade, Europeans would certainly reap even more profits than what they were obtaining from the slave trade.

In *Through the Dark Continent*, Stanley recounted his journey along the Zambezi River in the following words: "I felt my heart suffused with purest gratitude to Him whose hand had protected us, and who had enabled us to pierce the Dark Continent from east to west, and to trace its mightiest river to its ocean bourne."[99] In *Africa and the Victorians: The Official Mind of Imperialism*, Robinson and Gallagher found that recorded accounts of European explorers in Africa too often mocked and denigrated rather than offered a factual representation of the continent.[100] While it was generally believed that nature logically pitted man against man, this unfortunate reality was nonetheless believed to be for the greater good. This view was shared by Henry James Sumner Maine (1822–1888)—the Regius Professor of Civil Law at the University of Cambridge. Maine not only acclaimed the theory of natural selection but stated that life itself was a permanent struggle.[101]

4.5 Advent of Industrial Capitalism and Demise of the Slave Trade in Africa

Following the advent of triangular trade, sub-Saharan Africa steadily adjusted to the core to the labour needs of the world economy by dismantling its traditional economic structures and re-orientating their entire domestic patrimonies towards the international slave trade. The trade ruthlessly continued for over three centuries "with an attitude of callous indifference" until the mounting activism from abolitionist campaigners rose against it in the 19th century.[102] Despite uncountable attempts, a host of obstacles had prior to the 19th century effectively prevented Europeans from penetrating into sub-Saharan Africa's interiors, to wit: fierce resistance from African slave trade middlemen who became quite affluent by plying both the coasts and the interiors, thus functioning both as the contact point and bargaining agents between slave merchants and Africans; and tough topography and tropical diseases, especially malaria. And because many Europeans who dared to venture into the interior ended up dying mostly as a result of malaria, from which they had no immunity, sub-Saharan Africa famously became dubbed as the "White man's grave."[103] The only exception was southern Africa, where people were sparse and scattered along small communities, coupled with the fact that it had a Mediterranean-type climate and thus only temperate diseases.[104] As Europe traded with Africa principally along the coasts, Arabs dominated the slave trade (Arab slave trade) within the interiors, especially in eastern Africa.

Africans in retrospect had immunity from European and Arab germs, thanks to time-immemorial relations with these groups. This was one of the main reasons why societies in sub-Saharan Africa did not suffer population extinctions in spite of the wave of export of its peoples through the slave trade.

In spite of the minimal contacts with the African interiors and Arab influence in eastern Africa, the economic and socio-political order for most of sub-Saharan Africa was solidly anchored on the transatlantic trade. Over the centuries, coherent networks and commercial posts for the demand and supply of slaves in exchange for European articles had become well-fortified. As observed in the previous chapter, the trade in humans robbed the continent of essential manpower, labour, and brotherhood, and most importantly integrated the continent into the global market economy on disadvantageous terms, thus occasioning an endless progression of underdevelopment for the continent. But despite the banality of the trade, every attempt at its abolition in sub-Saharan Africa was interestingly met with sustained resistance. In the absence of the trade, kingdoms and middlemen that made a living by waging wars on their neighbours and capturing prisoners of war principally to be sold to the slave trade, and thus making many enemies in the process, would become volatile without a slave force and, in retrospect, would become vulnerable to vengeful attacks.[105] The slave trade encouraged local elites to increase the number of slaves owned, not for productive purposes but for confinement as a buffer stock in wait of better market prices. Powerful Africans had grown accustomed to owning slaves. At one moment, one 18th-century noble in Benin was said to have owned up to 10,000 slaves at the same time.[106] Such attitudes not only hindered trade in non-slave products but slowed economic growth across the continent.

Given that the slave trade achieved a mammoth global economic hype for some over a very long period of time, those who ventured to stop it after being met with fierce resistance quickly discovered that the slave trade could be ended only if Africa was provided with an equal or more lucrative alternative trade. Merchants observed that even with the introduction of a new trade, there was no way Africans could voluntarily submit to it especially if it was not immediately as profitable as the slave trade. Just as was the case with African middlemen acting as facilitators in the old trade, retailers in any new trade had to be well-remunerated, which in turn could be used in extracting labour from the African masses.[107]

Propelled by huge capital accumulated from the transatlantic slave trade, European powers at the dawn of the 19th century witnessed a profound revolution in production techniques, first in the British cotton industry and steadily in virtually every other sector (coal, steel, iron, construction, etc)—a process that became known as the industrial revolution. Characterised by the abandonment of old methods of production, this remarkable breakthrough in industrial capitalism rapidly spread to France, Holland, Belgium, and the United States.[108] Given that industrial capitalism was marked by a great power rivalry both at the state level and between merchants from competing countries, the upshot of this transformation naturally was hardly going to limit itself to the competing countries. Industrial capitalism quickly played out beyond the European borders as every emerging industrialising nation resorted to extra-territorial sources for the quest of raw materials.

One of the primary techniques of industrial capitalism involved expanding from the western temperate regions into equatorial and tropical regions of the world inhabited by non-Europeans in order to procure raw materials for nascent industries and to grow luxurious cash crops which could perform best only in warmer regions.[109] Within a short spate of time, the search for natural resources led to Africa, the Caribbean, and the Pacific regions being re-engaged along new trade patterns and paradigms. How was this nouvelle drive going to impact the livelihood and the economic and political development of the people in those tropical regions? What kinds of international relations were Europeans going to entertain with the non-Europeans? For international lawyers, these concerns were addressed by conceptualising a world in which everyone benefited. The logic of the civilising mission was to entrust Europeans with the duty to help non-Europeans by teaching and uplifting them to modernity. The consensus amongst international lawyers was that the colonisation of non-European territories would extend the fruits of civilisation unto these peoples, thereby improving their overall well-being.

4.6 Missionary Activities as the Groundwork for Legitimate Commerce in Africa

If ever there was one individual to whom the colonial origins of Africa can be directly traced, that person would be David Livingstone (1813–1873), the Scottish pioneer medical missionary with the London Missionary Society (LMS) who profoundly influenced European peoples' thoughts and imaginations about Africa and Africans in the 19th century. As the anti-slavery campaign garnered global steam across Europe and the United States, many Christian missionary societies became convinced that a thorough understanding of the African hinterlands was imperative to combatting the scourge of the slave trade and winning new souls for the church. Consistent with the tradition by most religious societies in the 19th century, LMS in 1841 commissioned Livingstone to Africa as part of an evangelisation crusade to convert heathen tribes into the Christian faith.

When Livingstone faithfully began his ministerial assignment, hardly did he know that the journey would inadvertently change the trajectory of African history in general as well as fuel the ultimate rationale for the colonisation of the continent. His focal vision was to penetrate into the African interiors, pave and map it out for Europeans to follow after him, and civilise the continent.[110] He conceived of missionary and religious duties as not confined to evangelisation and winning of souls but instead as encompassing the whole spectrum of human relations and advancement. He contended that a good missionary must preach but also enlighten new brethren by introducing the arts and sciences of civilisation to them.[111] In fact, he saw the living conditions, social, economic, political, and spiritual needs of Africans as inseparable from the evangelisation campaign—mankind needed to be one another's brother keeper.[112]

Moving forward from the predicament of the times, Livingstone found a strong nexus between the slave trade and commerce as a humanitarian duty. Given that the slave trade was created and sustained through the demand for European goods, legitimate commerce could so easily undo this predicament. Although Livingstone was neither an international lawyer nor a political economist, he nonetheless complemented and aided the colonisation purposes of these disciplines by "[fusing] moral purpose with the civilizing functions and values of commerce."[113] By advocating for Christianity, Commerce, and Civilisation—what eventually became known as the three "C's"—as a remedy to curb the slave trade across Africa and open up the continent for legitimate trade, Livingstone effectively afforded the humanitarian vernacular on which European scholars relied to justify the European colonisation of Africa.

What was legitimate commerce per Livingstone? What did it entail, and for whose interests? The three "C's" was very catchy, not least because it offered the best dual possibility to date to the European metropolitan reading public on how to supposedly frame Africa's humanitarian needs. Moreover, trade and private property rights in accordance with the three "C's" assumed a revitalised prominent place in new global economic relations. The metaphor of civilisation was methodically turned into the best-known mannerism for European intervention in Africa, given that international lawyers had already internalised the metaphor by framing the standard of civilisation.[114]

On arriving in Africa, Livingstone was appalled by the atrocities committed by slavers—whom he qualified in his diaries as disgusting and inhumane. Slave wars had caused Africans to be at perpetual animosity against neighbours—as stronger tribes constantly made prey out of their weaker defeated neighbours. It was very easy for Europeans and even Arabs to recruit militias from either ethnic grouping under the pretext of fighting the enemy.[115] Around the shores of the river Zouga in 1851, Livingstone found a community known as Makololo that was more complicit in the slave trade than the other villages that he had come across. Interestingly, almost everyone in that community wore European clothing and owned European items both personally and in their households, all acquired as proceeds for their capture and sale of fellow Africans. Noticing that European items were highly priced in this part of the world and were in fact the main if not the only motivation for people engaging in the slave trade, Livingstone, as evidenced by his mail of 17 October 1851, bitterly lamented that it was a pity that these items could not be traded through legitimate commerce.[116] He immediately began sending reports and accounts of his experiences across Africa to Europe, outlining his convictions and clamouring for legitimate commerce, whereby "natives" could amiably trade agricultural produce and handicraft works with European manufactured goods, as the one best way to eradicate the scourge of the slave trade. In his words, "if the slave market were supplied with articles of European manufacture by legitimate commerce, the trade in slaves would become impossible."[117]

Through his routine letters and later his home visit in 1857, when he gave a series of public lectures including one at the Cambridge City Hall, Livingstone initially and forcefully summed up his recommendation for new engagement between Europe and Africa as opposed to the slave trade in two terms: legitimate commerce, and Christianity. These two admonitions, he contended, were key remedies to two entrenched evils, to wit: the slave trade and paganism. Persuaded by his advocacy, Livingstone during his 5 December 1857 Cambridge lecture admonished Europeans in the following words:

> I beg to direct your attention to Africa. I know that in a few years, I shall be ... in that country, which is now open; do not let it be shut again! I go back to Africa to make an open path for commerce and Christianity, do you carry out the work which I have begun? I leave it with you.[118]

Livingstone stood firm in his conviction that Africa's true salvation rested on its fertile soil and was going to see the day with agricultural development.[119] This position is at odds with the arguments of dependency scholars who see the continent's natural resources as a resource curse and a magnet for external economic exploitation. It can nevertheless be deduced from Livingstone's interactions and proclamations that he candidly perceived the empowerment of Africans especially through trade as a practical test for true Christianity.

Over time, after encountering further practical experiences, Livingstone reconsidered his cardinal principles and added "civilisation" to the initial two "C's", explaining that Commerce and Christianity could not be achieved unless Europeans first educated Africans and taught them new methods of agriculture and hygiene, as well as talked them out of pagan beliefs and practices such as polygamy.[120] Livingstone in effect made a solid case to Europeans that the doors of the "dark" continent were wide open for enlightenment and the best tools that could chase away the prevailing darkness in Africa were his three "C's"—all of which, if implemented, would uplift Africans morally, prepare them for political and economic development, and, most importantly, culminate into a supposedly righteous government characterised by the guarantee and protection of the civil rights of persons. European potential investment on industrial capitalism in Africa was conceived of as a humanitarian act in that it had the ultimate effect of working as a cure against the slave trade, thus bestowing Africans with an alternative lifestyle.[121]

Livingstone differed from other missionaries in that he conceived of the duty of Christianity as encompassing the whole continuum of human society and activities. In a space that was dominated by inhumane activities and mayhem as a result of the slave trade, he became convinced that with a change in trade emphasis, Europe could reap even more profits while preserving African lives on the continent. His entire crusade as summed up in the three "C's" afforded a clear-cut formula for humanitarian sensibility, thus utterly providing scholars with the badly needed positivist creeds to vindicate the activities of European companies that were either operating on the continent or seeking influence. It has been observed that the identification of Christian civilisation as being in conformity with international law in due course enabled the discipline to widen its scope of interaction and action across Africa.[122]

All things considered, what was conspicuously missing in the three "C's" was a fourth "C": Colonisation, especially considering that this was the end game of the other three. Taking a close look at the three "C's," one is left with the impression that Livingstone, like other missionaries on the African continent, seemed to reject anything uniquely African as abominable and primitive, while endorsing everything European as not only civilised but in accordance with the will of God. On the whole, missionaries in Africa effectively became agents of colonisation, aiding in the pacification of relations between the European powers and Africa. In the years following the colonisation of the continent, missionaries despite occasional discrepancies with colonial administrators, generally vindicated colonialism and European lordship over Africa as a fulfilment of biblical revelation, namely the proliferating of light onto pagans. This belief was solidly grounded on different levels of economic development. Admonishing Africans to be submissive to European authority, to exercise humility, and to be patient, missionaries frequently reminded their followers that Europeans had come to Africa for the unique mission of saving them and preparing them for progress and salvation not only for the future, but even in the afterlife.[123] Frederick Cooper has persuasively hammered on this point, stating that,

> The idea of Africa as a slave-ridden continent oppressed by its own tyrants and kept off the path to Civilization, Christianity, and Commerce, was crucial to missionary propaganda from the 1860s on, the rallying cry of anti-slavery movements for the rest of the century, and a major component of the knowledge of Africa available to the reading publics of Europe.[124]

As international law later in the century sought to situate new impending international relations, especially within the context of industrial revolution and the encounter between Europeans and Africans, the conception of cultures as advanced or backward, superior or inferior, became a crucial informing mechanism. Accordingly, since European will was God's will, Africans could redeem themselves and advance only by self-converting themselves into the image of Europe—similar to the exigencies outlined by the three "C's."[125]

Although Livingstone was never a planter of flags, preferring pacific persuasion rather than imposition, it has been doubted how else he thought to achieve his goals except through political annexation.[126] To an extent, he was pretty much a coloniser like many others, or at the very least was an unconscious colonialist. Despite the fact that he in his dealings never qualified Africans as inferior, he was utterly convinced of the superiority of Europeans vis-à-vis Africans and in fact reached the same ideological conclusion shared amongst European radical social scientists that the economic and political future of African rested in European intervention and paternalism. One observer, Cecil Northcott, for instance has commented thus:

> Livingstone was a colonialist and was not ashamed of it. He was in Africa to offer the benefits of the White man's civilization, and no latter day beliefs in the black man's freedom, liberation and independence may be read into his actions.[127]

While there is no doubt in Livingstone's genuineness in the quest for legitimate commerce and betterment of Africans, it is also a fact that he longed for a British colony for Brits on the continent, around which "natives" could gladly settle.[128] At his 1857 Cambridge lecture which attracted an audience comprising of geographers, lawyers, researchers, government officials, and even visitors to the city, he emphasised that the Christian mission in Africa was in essence a fulfilment of the work of geography: "The end of the geographic fact is but the beginning of the missionary enterprise."[129] Like geographers, missionaries were vital for originality—they were men on the spot, Europe's eyes and ears, where journalists and other experts were rare.[130]

Whatever opinion we may deduce about Livingstone, it is still hard to gauge his ambition on colonisation with certainty, as he died before he could ever have the opportunity to comment on European colonialism in Africa within the context of his three "C's." Be that as it may, Livingstone's influence in Africa ought to be read as indirect, for as already noted, not only did he not plant flags, he did not live to see his dreams come true or go out of control. The slave trade was very much alive by the time he died despite being declared illegal in many international legal instruments. Evidently, central Africa was eventually opened up to European trade and commerce, yet it remains unsettled as to whether it is exactly what he bargained for. He specifically clamoured for legitimate commerce. Although the slave trade was completely stamped out in sub-Saharan Africa by 1900, the vision and reality of legitimate commerce cannot be appreciated in isolation but in conjunction with actual practice.[131]

4.7 Doctrinal Ascendancy of Positivism over Natural Law in the Wake of Industrial Capitalism[132]

Up until the 19th century, the Law of Nations was heavily informed by Christianity and primarily driven by natural law. Since all human activity according to natural law was bound by an overarching morality, sovereign states were in retrospect also bound by principles of natural law and the enforcement of natural justice.[133] For most natural law jurists such as Samuel Pufendorf, Vitoria, and Grotius, the law of nations was comprehended as universal in scope and extendable to all humankind. In his book *Introduction to the Principles of*

Morals and Legislation (1789), Jeremy Bentham coined the term "International Law" as a preferred term, while attempting to convey what the Law of Nations had meant up to the 18th century and what it had in store for the future.[134]

Natural law acquired its prominence by emphasising equal rights. In *Elements of International Law* (1836), Henry Wheaton nevertheless posed the question whether there was a uniform Law of Nations, to which he answered that

> there certainly is not the same one for all the nations and States of the world. The public law, with slight exceptions, has always been, and still is, limited to the civilized and Christian people of Europe or to those of European origin. This distinction between the European law of nations and that of the other races of mankind has long been remarked by the publicists. Grotius states that *jus gentium* acquires its obligatory force from the positive consent of all nations, or at least of several.[135]

Wheaton's contention contradicted Samuel Pufendorf, the German jurist, who in 1677 contended that natural law was the foundation of international law and cut across all religious confessions.[136] In spite of the differentiation, both Wheaton and Pufendorf nevertheless perceived Christianity to be at the foundation of natural law and, by extension, one of the primary sources of the Law of Nations.

Following the wave of enlightenment writings which were characteristically secular and their popular reception, the strong influence of Christianity on international law began to severely weaken in the 19th century. Wheaton essentially perceived the Law of Nations as following two different parallel streams of natural law and positive law.[137] He was not alone in this line of thinking. In *Commentaries on the Law of Nations* (1839), his contemporary, William Oke Manning, reached a similar conclusion by remarking that the law of nations was not a uniform discipline, but rather constituted from three main sources, to wit: natural law, customs, and conventions.[138] While for him, natural law was synonymous with divine law, customs and conventions epitomised positive international law. Wheaton and Manning's identification of a diametrically opposing two-tier international law clearly mirrored a growing trend amongst many 19th-century international lawyers who embraced a positive conception of international law and projected the discipline as a framework for the structuring and regulation of international society. Following the new positivist framing, the non-Christian nations of Japan and Turkey were perceived by European nations throughout the century as qualified members of the family of nations.

Slowly but surely, positivism was envisaged as a tactical and pragmatic remedy for overcoming the discipline's Christian underpinnings, replacing dogmatism with legal scientific knowledge—that is, a belief in sovereign states as guarantor of rights rather than the belief in a Christian God. States effectively became the judge, jury, and executioner of their own sovereign conducts, both at home and abroad. As civilised entities, they were "*justi hostes*" and could ascertain "*justa causa*" for themselves.[139] Although positivism stood for exorbitant rights of the sovereign states, it also placed a lot of importance on the limits of sovereignty, ensuring that the "Law of Nations claimed no higher authority than that which nations agreed between themselves."[140]

For positivist international lawyers, positivism was not a rejection of natural law, but rather its amendment, so that international law could meet the test of time. In fact, in spite of its decline, many 19th-century international lawyers—the likes of Westlake, James Lorimer, and Oppenheim—frequently revisited natural law's framework as inspiration for positive law.[141] As natural law weakened in influence, positivism cultivated a peculiar identity by merging the natural law conceptions of *just war* and the classical idea of progress into the standard of civilisation—which was then promoted as an all-encompassing humanitarian package from the civilised to those in need. Whereas under natural law the mere existence of a community was sufficient for a polity to be part of *jus gentium*, under positivism one could become a member of the community of states or family of nations only by first meeting the standard of civilisation.[142] As a result, positivism instigated a strict shrinking in the international society from a world of all to a society for the privileged few—the certified civilised. Consequently, it is only by stretching that 19th-century international law is now projected as a global regime.[143]

Because of the humanitarian overtones, the standard of civilisation was rarely criticised or challenged in the 19th century. In the view of one scholar,

> everyone arbitrarily bestows to the expression "civilization" a subjective sense after their own Weltanschauung, so that each religious domination or philosophical school cherishes a peculiar conception of civilization. When European international law scholars speak about civilization or civilized states, they do so likewise from the subjective standpoint of their own Weltanschauung.[144]

Overall, universality with positivism was a function of culture, and not an inherent right. It was a restrictive privilege stringently reserved for advanced cultures that had achieved a satisfactory level of progress. Put differently, for those who were born into civilisation, universality was an event, but for those that born unto non-civilisation, universality was a process.[145]

4.8 Territorium Nullius in Africa

The standard of civilisation was imperative in the 19th century not just as an arbiter of international law for establishing which societies belonged to the family of nations from those that did not, but was moreover used as a justification for establishing sovereignty over entities outside of the community of states. Fused from the stadial order of societies, the standard of civilisation by placing Europe at the hierarchical apex of civilisations and into the corpus of the family of nations, impliedly allowed Europeans to justify colonisation "through the projection of their understanding of sovereignty onto societies which they judged to be inferior."[146] In a speech before the French National Assembly in 1885, the former French prime minister, Jules Ferry—an ardent promoter of colonial expansion—while admonishing his country to embark on an aggressive *mission civilisatrice* in Africa, declared that "superior races have an inherent duty to civilize inferior races."[147] J. de Hornung concurred, and asserted that "*les civilisés doivent donner l'exemple d'une justice supérieure … les nations civilisées doivent aider les 'races inférieures' à entrer dans le système politique des Etats.*"[148] Following the scramble of Africa orchestrated by European corporations which was endemic in the 1870s and 1880s, the German chancellor, Otto von Bismarck, convened a conference at Berlin in the fall of 1884–1845, whereupon he invited all recognised members of the family of nations. The gathering was billed as a pre-emptive measure against potential conflict and outright war amongst colonial competitors, and for the delegates to codify core principles upon which European sovereignty could be extended to Africa.[149] The scope and implication of the Berlin conference is explored in depth in Chapter 6.

In the aftermath of the Berlin conference, the *Institut de Droit International* embarked on a drive to translate the resolutions of the conference into authoritative norms of international law. In 1887, one of its members, F. de Martitz, a professor of law at Tubingen, was commissioned to draft a report on the proceedings of the conference within the broader meaning of international law. In his report, titled "*Projet de déclaration*," he observed that following the General Act of the Berlin conference, there was an effective shift from the classical Roman law concept of *res nullius* (also known as *terra nullius*) to a new concept dubbed *territorium nullius*.[150] As to what this embodied, he explained that:

> all regions which do not find themselves effectively under the sovereignty or the Protectorate of one of the States which form the community of the law of nations, no matter whether this region is inhabited or not, will be considered as *territorium nullius*.[151]

The differentiation stemmed from the fact that while *res nullius* applied only to unoccupied lands, *territorium nullius*, as implied from Berlin Act's requirement of effective occupation, extended to occupied territories of the uncivilised.

Defined as "the formal taking of possession of lands previously uninhabited, or inhabited by a barbarous or semi-civilized people,"[152] the doctrine of *terra nullius* was crucial to Britain for the colonisation of Australia. Fitzmaurice has explained that Martitz found an imperativeness for the new construction of *territorium nullius* because the *res nullius* doctrine would have otherwise been inapplicable to Africa, since it was inhabited and its indigenous peoples had long established effective property rights over their territories.[153] Why was there any need to extend European sovereignty unto Africa, given that the effectiveness of their political organisations was a well-known fact? John Stuart Mill had earlier contended that civilised peoples had evolved to "live in fixed dwellings in cities or villages and engage in commerce, agriculture, and manufacture; none of these attributes ... [could be] observed amongst the savages except in primitive forms."[154] The new phrasing derived from the dual Latinism—*terra* (land) and *territorium* (territory)—effectively permitted European colonisers "to establish imperium, or sovereignty, over territories while acknowledging local property rights."[155]

African societies, just like European nations, were not monolithic societies. Different kingdoms and collectivities naturally had different administrative styles. For instance, while the Ashanti and Kumasi regions were composed into confederations of rulers (nations), the Benin empire was renowned as a distinctively cultural reformist government. The Dahomey kingdom, on the other hand, was noted as a military dictatorship.[156] The sharp cultural distinction between the advanced and the backward could not make much sense except when matched with the different levels of economic development and the evidence of political organisation. It was assumed by Europeans that African tribal leaders were generally despotic, incompetent, and superstitious. This combination of negatives was at odds with three basic conditions necessary for economic growth and progress famously laid down by Adam Smith, to wit: peace, easy taxes, and a tolerable administration of justice.[157]

While the question of indigenous sovereignty and political organisations prompted some international lawyers to object to the doctrine of *territorium nullius*, Westlake on his part did not consider this fact to exonerate Europeans from the duty of the civilising mission. To him, the presence or absence of governance was really not the issue; instead, the crucial question was whether the political institution in place could accommodate the comfort and needs of Europeans:

> When people of the European race encountered American or African tribes, the prime necessity is a government under the protection of which the former may carry on the complex life to which they have been accustomed in their homes ... Can the natives furnish such a government, or can it be looked for from the Europeans alone? In the answer to that question lies, for international law, the difference between civilization and want of it.[158]

The presence of a government or political organisation thus made sense to Westlake only if it adequately sheltered Europeans and protected both western lives and their property rights. This to him was the minimum requirement for proof of civilisation.[159] For polities that were unwilling or unable to meet this standard because of the imperfections of its civilisation or other deficiencies, Westlake observed that civilised states could freely annex it as a moral duty in order to safeguard trade, peace, order, and freedom in the international space.[160]

As for the fate of the colonised subjects in the aftermath of conquest, Westlake asserted that international law naturally leaves the treatment of "natives" to the conscience of the civilised state to which sovereignty is awarded.[161] Bluntschli concurred, noting that "international law depends on humanity's consciousness for its rights."[162] Lorimer added that all colonisation did was to lend a helping hand to the improvement of economic conditions of all those who were subjected to it.[163] In *The Dual Mandate in British Tropical Africa*, Lord Frederick Lugard argued that since the industrial world was dependent on raw materials; civilised humanity was in retrospect endowed with a universal right of discovery to develop every undeveloped resource wherever it happened to be. If the natives had no intellectual ability to care for their resources, he affirmed, it would be incumbent on civilised humanity to care for it.[164] If the pathway of the deer, as funnily remarked by Azikiwe, is the only realistic way to realise constructive progress, that deer must logically surrender its path.[165] By intruding thus on "native" lands, European powers were in effect asserting a *de facto* sovereignty over them. By overthrowing African despotic rulers and replacing them with European sovereignty, it was assumed that colonial powers were in so doing extending the fruits of civilisation to the world's backward peoples.[166]

4.9 Concluding Remarks

The advent of the industrial revolution in the 19th century was a defining moment in international relations, and by analogy international law. As machines promptly replaced human labour, thereby doubling production and profits, the transatlantic slave trade which had defined international relations between the four corners of the Atlantic (Africa, Europe, and the Americas) during the previous two centuries quickly became perceived by European powers as a costly and less efficient mode of production. The resultant global campaign to abolish the slave trade while cloaked as a humanitarian mission was nevertheless stringently tied to the imperativeness of fulfilling the exigencies of the nascent industrial mode of production. With sub-Saharan lands richly endowed with badly needed natural resources to power the factories in Europe, international law doctrines promptly revisited prior categories of the idea of progress, justifying settler colonisation, under the guise of civilising the behaviours of Africans, and rendering them politically civil and economically productive.

A new fierce scramble for control of the continent's lands resulted in Africa being partitioned amongst the European powers and governed by the latter as administrative provinces. While abolitionists championed the imperativeness of "legitimate trade" as the best modality for curbing the international slave trade across Africa, the eventual implantation of these ideals through colonial governance confined Africa into the periphery of the world system, and its peoples in conditions of servitude as labourers. In fact, while colonial governance was framed as a civilising mission, it was in effect a system of exploitation, whereupon Africans were forcefully compelled to furnish European factories with natural resources extracted from their subsoils. In Chapter 5, this study examines the non-state actors that foreshadowed the practical scramble for Africa, as well as the legitimacy of the barrage of cession treaties with African rulers that were evoked by Europeans to justify the colonisation of Africa.

Notes

1 Andrew Fitzmaurice, (Cambridge University Press, 2014) at 201–202.
2 Jennifer Pitts, (Princeton University Press, 2005) at 127–133.
3 Anthony Pagden, *31 Political Theory* (2003) at 171–172.
4 Andrew Fitzmaurice, *117 The American Historical Review* (2012) at 125; David Kennedy, *1 Accounting, Economics, and Law* (2011) at 10, 50.
5 Fitzmaurice, 'Liberalism and Empire in Nineteenth-Century International Law' at 124.
6 Makau Mutua & Antony Anghie, *Proceedings of the 94th Annual ASIL Meeting* (2000) 31–40; Anthony Anghie, *Imperialism, Sovereignty and the making of International Law*; Bhupinder S. Chimni, *8 International Community Law Review* (2006) 3–27.
7 David Kennedy, *65 Nordic Journal of International Law* (1996) at 391.
8 Fitzmaurice, 'Liberalism and Empire in Nineteenth-Century International Law' at 124.
9 Robert Chambers, (W. & R. Chambers, Bloomington, 1861) at 160–161.
10 Chambers, *Domestic Annals of Scotland* at 161.
11 The term "Scottish Enlightenment" came into popular usage in 1900, following the publication of *Francis Hutcheson: His Life, Teaching and Position in the History of Philosophy* by William Robert Scott, wherein he used the phrase "the Enlightenment in Scotland" to depict the immense contribution of Francis Hutcheson and his Scottish contemporaries to modern political economy discourse. William Robert Scott, (Cambridge University Press, 1900) at 257, 261.
12 Gerhard Engel, (Springer, 2013) at 253.
13 Roger L. Emerson, *19 Historical Papers* (1984) at 63.
14 "[I]n responding to the pressure of political events, the Scots found that they were groping for an alternative to a political language which did not make sense of their own political predicament. They could see that in a commercial world states had developed a complex provincial structure which the existing language of politics did not seem to recognise. What they sought was a language responsive to the economic, social and historical experience of provincial communities and realized that the virtue of a provincial citizen class was more likely to be released by economic and cultural institutions than by a national parliament remote from the provincial citizen's world" (Nicholas Phillipson, (Cambridge University Press, 1981) at 26. Cf: Neil Davidson, 4 *Journal of Agrarian Change* (2005) at 5).
15 William C. Lehmann (Springer, 2013) at XV–XXVI.
16 Dugald Stewart, (Charles Knight & Co., 1843). Cf: Simon Evnine, *31 Journal of the History of Philosophy* (1993) at 589.
17 Stewart, *Account of the Life and Writings of Adam Smith* at iv. Cf: Evnine, 'Hume, Conjectural History' at 589.
18 H. M. Hopfl, *17 Journal of British Studies* (1978) at 19–20.
19 Ibid at 24.
20 Adam Smith, (Liberty Fund, 1982) at 201.

21 Hopfl, 'From Savage to Scotsman' at 19.
22 Thomas Hobbes, (Cambridge University Press, 1991). While the social contract doctrine is often attributed to Hobbes, variants of the doctrine had already postulated by Marsilius of Padua in the 13th century.
23 Ibid at 90–97.
24 Ibid at Chapters 1 and 2.
25 Ibid at xi, 92.
26 Ibid at 92–95.
27 David Hume, (Oxford University Press, 1978). Cf: John Gingell, Adrian Little & Christopher Winch, (Routledge, 2003) at 90–103.
28 David H. Fischer, (HarperCollins, 1970) at 206.
29 "Mankind are much the same, in all times and places, that history informs us of nothing new or strange in this particular. Its chief use is only to discover the constant and universal principles of human nature". David Hume, *An Inquiry Concerning Human Understanding* (Bobbs-Merrill Educational Pub.: 1955) at 93.
30 Hume, *A Treatise of Human Nature*. Cf: Gingell, Little & Winch, *Modern Political Thought* at 91–92.
31 David Hume, (Sweet & Maxwell, 1965) at 25.
32 David Hume, (Walter Scott Ltd, 1906) at 68–69.
33 Pitts, *A Turn to Empire* at 127–133.
34 Ibid at 145.
35 James Mill, (Cambridge University Press, 2015) at 119.
36 Ivan Berend, (Cambridge University Press, 2012) at 2–7.
37 John Stuart Mill, (University of Toronto Press, 1981) Vol X, Nature, 402.
38 William Oke Manning, (S. Sweet, 1839) at 14–15.
39 Lewis Henry Morgan, (Belknap Press, 1964) at 5, 10–11.
40 Morgan, *Ancient Society* at 5, 10–11; Ernest Nys, (EF Bohn, 1894). Cf.: Martti Koskenniemi, (Universiteit Utrecht—Faculteit Geeseswetenschappen, 2011) at 152–153; Jeremy Moses, *Annual Meeting of the International Studies Association, Honolulu, Hawaii* (2005) at 13; Barry Buzan, (Cambridge University Press, 2004).
41 John Lonsdale & Bruce Berman, *20 Journal of African History* (1979) at 487; Robert B. Marks, (Rowman & Littlefield Inc., 2007) at 67.
42 Gerrit W. Gong, (Clarendon Press, 1984) at 9–14, 61–63.
43 François Guizot, *Histoire de la Civilisation en Europe: Depuis la chute de l'Empire Romain jusqu'a a la Révolution Française* (Ad. Wahlen, Brussels/Paris: 1843) at 12, 59.
44 Karl Marx, (Lawrence and Wishart, 1968) at 182.
45 Tom Brass, *31 Journal of Peasant Studies* (2003) 101–136.
46 Michel Foucault, (Vintage Books, 1988) at 35
47 Kalyan K. Sanyal, *6 Rethinking Marxism* at 117.
48 Tom Brass, *35 Capital & Class* (2010) at 24–26.
49 Rhys Jenkins, *8 Capital & Class* (1984) 28–57.
50 Robinson, "Introduction" to *Rosa Luxemburg, The Accumulation of Capital* at 364–365.
51 Vladimir Lenin, (International Publishers, 1938).

> Imperialism is capitalism in that stage of development in which the dominance of monopolies and finance capital has established itself; in which the export of capital has acquired pronounced importance; in which the division of the world among the international trusts has begun; in which the division of all territories of the globe among the biggest capitalist powers has been completed.
>
> (Lenin, *Imperialism: The High-Stage of Capitalism* at 99–100).
> [*Emphasis mildly added*].

52 Lenin, *Imperialism: The High-Stage of Capitalism* at 91–94.[*Emphasis mildly added*].
53 Ibid at 113. [*Emphasis mildly added*].
54 Ibid at 17–20.
55 Harvey, "Accumulation by Dispossession" at 154–160.
56 Achille Mbembe, (University of California Press, 2001) at 25.
57 Ibid at 25–29.
58 Ibid at 25–29.
59 Joan Vincent, (Transaction Books, 1988) at 137–154.
60 Vincent, "Sovereignty, Legitimacy, and Power" at 137–154.
61 Marx, *Capital: Critique of Political Economy* at 453–459.
62 Louis Althusser, (Verso, 2006) at 197. [*Emphasis mildly added*].
63 Marx, *Capital: Critique of Political Economy* at 461–463.
64 *See generally*, Marx, "Preface to a Contribution to the Critique of Political Economy."
65 Michael Heinrich, (Monthly Review Press, 2012) at 204.
66 De Angelis, 'Marx and Primitive Accumulation' at 1–3.
67 Sanyal, 'Capital, Primitive Accumulation, and the Third World' at 121. [*Emphasis mildly added*].
68 Herman Jeremias Nieboer, (Martinus Nijhoff, 1910) at chapters 1–3.
69 Nieboer, *Slavery as an Industrial System* at chapters 1–3.
70 Vincent, "Sovereignty, Legitimacy, and Power" at 137–154.
71 The *Cambridge Advanced Learner's Dictionary* (Cambridge University Press, 2014) at 111.
72 P. Kozel, (Routledge, 2006) at chapter 1.
73 Martti Koskenniemi, (Cambridge University Press, 2005) at 131; Alexis Heraclides, *16 Journal of the History of International Law* (2014) at 28.
74 Gbenga Oduntan, (Routledge, 2009) at 101.
75 Martti Koskenniemi, *The Gentle Civilizer of Nations: The Rise and Fall of International Law, 1870–1960* (Cambridge University Press, 2001) at 14.
76 Koskenniemi, *The Gentle Civilizer of Nations* at 42; Martti Koskenniemi, *16 European Journal of International Law* (2005) 113–124 at 120. Article 1 of the Institute's statute conceives the association as the "Juridical conscience of the civilized world"; John Austin, (The Law Book Exchange, 2005) at 37–38. The founding fathers of the Institut in 1873 were: Augusto Pierantoni from Naples (1840–1911), Carlos Calvo from Buenos Aires (1824–1906), David Dudley Field II from New York (1805–1894), Émile Louis Victor de Laveleye from Liege (1822–1892), Johann Kaspar Bluntschli from Heidelberg (1808–1881), Gustave Moynier from Geneva (1826–1910), Gustave Rolin-Jaequemyns from Ghent (1835–1902), James Lorimer from Edinburgh (1818–1890), Pasquale Stanislao Mancini from Rome (1817–1888), Tobias Asser from Amsterdam (1838–1913), and Wladimir Besobrassof from Saint-Petersburg.
77 *See* Koskenniemi, *The Gentle Civilizer of Nations* at 41.
78 Ibid at 49; Gustavo Gozzi, 'History of International Law and Western Civilization' *9 International Community Law Review* (2007) 353–373 at 354.
79 James Lorimer, (W. Blackwood, 1883) at 101–102.
80 Johann Caspar Bluntschli, (Guillaumin et cie, Paris: 1868—French edition: 1874) at 272. [*Emphasis mildly added*].
81 Arnulf Becker Lorca, *51 Harvard International Law Journal* (2010) at 477; Sally Engle Merry, *25 Law and Society Review* (1991) at 890.
82 Gong, *The Standard of Civilization* at 3, 9–14.
83 Ibid at 3–5.
84 Moses, 'Humanitarianism and International Law' at 3; Prabhakar Singh, *16 African Journal of International & Comparative Law* (2008) at 73, 74, 77.

85 Oduntan, 'International Laws and the Discontented' at 104, 106.
86 Ziauddin Sardar, (Zed Books, 1999) at 44–45.
87 Antony Anghie, *27 Third World Quarterly* (2006) at 742.
88 Anghie, *Imperialism, Sovereignty and the Making of International Law* at 5; Koskenniemi, *The Gentle Civilizer of Nations* at 101.
89 Michael Havinden & David Meredith, (Routledge, 1995); Mahamadou Diallo, (African World Press, 2001) 105–126; David Arnold, (University of Washington Press, 2006). *See also*: Lord Lugard, *The Dual Mandate in British Tropical Africa* (William Blackwood and Sons, 1922) 2–7.
90 Anghie, 'Finding the Peripheries' at 67–68.
91 Moses, 'Humanitarianism and International Law' at 7. The phrase, the "White Man's burden" was invented by Rudyard Kipling in his poem of the same name. (*See* Rudyard Kipling, (The Definitive Edition, 1982).
92 Patrick Tort, (Presses universitaires de France (PUF), 1996) at 1008–1009.
93 *See* Thomas Robert Malthus, (Macmillan, 1966).
94 Charles Darwin, (Murray, 1968); Herbert Spencer, (William Norgate, 1880).
95 Gregory Claeys, *61 Journal of the History of Ideas* (2000) at 223, 225–227.
96 Spencer, *The Principles of Biology* at 60–64. Spencer even sought to tie his work to Darwin's: "The survival of the fittest which I have here sought to express in mechanical terms," he wrote, "is that which Mr. Darwin has called 'natural selection' or the preservation of favoured races in the struggle for life." Spencer, *The Principles of Biology* at 65.
97 Felix Driver, *133 Past & Present* (1993) at 140; Lucy Jarosz, *74 Geografiska Annaler. Series B, Human Geography* (1992) at 110.
98 Henry Morton Stanley, (Charles Scribner, 1890); Henry Morton Stanley, (Harper & Brothers, 1878). For Livingstone's *Expeditions into the Dark Continent* (1876), see: Noah R. Bassil, *25 Critical Arts* (2011) 377–396.
99 Stanley, *Through the Dark Continent* at 467.
100 Dunlop, 'The Influence of David Livingstone' at 144; Ronald Edward Robinson & John Gallagher, (Macmillan, 1966).
101 Henry James Sumner Maine, (John Murray, 1875) at 26.
102 Sola Akinrinade & Toyin Falola, (Croom Helm Ltd, 1986) at 1.
103 Philip D. Curtin, *21 The Journal of Interdisciplinary History* (1990) at 64–69.
104 Curtis A. Keim, (Indiana University Press, 1995) at 115.
105 Akinrinade & Falola, "Africa and Europe: Prelude to the Partition" at 7.
106 Keim, "Africa and Europe before 1900" at 121.
107 Stephen Ocheni & Basil Nwankwo, *8 Cross-Cultural Communications* (2012) at 49.
108 Juhani Koponen, *2 Nordic Journal of African Studies* (1993) at 121.
109 Ramage, 'The Partition of Africa' at 221–222.
110 Keim, "Africa and Europe before 1900" at 125.
111 Fidelis Nkomazana, *12 PULA: Botswana Journal of African Studies* (1998) at 44.
112 Ibid at 44.
113 Richard Price, (Cambridge University Press, 2008) at 142.
114 Tetsuya Toyoda, *46 Alberta Law Review* (2009) at 1111.
115 John Stewart Dunlop, *75 The Scottish Geographical Magazine* (1959) at 145–147.
116 Jack Simmons, (English Universities Press, 1955) at 42.
117 Cf. Dunlop, 'The Influence of David Livingstone' at 147.
118 Cf. Nkomazana, 'Livingstone's Ideas of Christianity, Commerce and Civilization' at 44.
119 Ibid at 55.
120 Dunlop, 'The Influence of David Livingstone' at 148.
121 Nkomazana, 'Livingstone's Ideas of Christianity, Commerce and Civilization' at 45; Thomas L. Haskell, *90 The American Historical Review* (1985) at 340.

122 Mensah-Brown, 'Notes on International Law' at 107.
123 Peter P. Ekeh, *17 Comparative Studies in Society and History* (1975) at 97; Akinrinade & Falola, 'Africa and Europe: Prelude to the Partition' at 6.
124 Frederick Cooper, (Chapel Hill, 2000) at 27.
125 Ako Adjei, *50 American Journal of Sociology* (1944) at 190
126 Dunlop, 'The Influence of David Livingstone' at 148.
127 Cecil Northcott, (Lutterworth Press, 1973) at 74.
128 See: Dunlop, 'The Influence of David Livingstone' at 148; H. Alan C. Cairns, (Routledge & Kegan Paul, 1965) at 195.
129 Cf: William Monk (ed.), (Deighton, 1858) at 22.
130 Kiernan, 'Europe in the Colonial Mirror' at 49.
131 Dunlop, 'The Influence of David Livingstone' at 146.
132 An early version of this section was published in *Journal of African and International Law*. See: George Forji Amin, *6 Journal of African and International* Law (2013) 191–226.
133 Anghie, 'Finding the Peripheries' at 10–11.
134 Jeremy Bentham, (The Athlone Press, 1970) at 10; John Austin, (The Law Book Exchange, 2005) at 37–38; M. W. Janis, *78 The American Journal of International Law* (1984) at 405–407.
135 Henry Wheaton, (B. Fellowes, 1836) at 26.
136 Gustavo Gozzi, *52 Harvard International Law Journal* (2010) 73–86 at 75.
137 Wheaton, *Elements of International Law* at 56.
138 William Oke Manning, (S. Sweet, 1839) at chapter 1.
139 Gozzi, 'The Particularistic Universalism of International Law' at 75.
140 Evans, 'Where Lawlessness Is Law' at 14; Arnulf Becker Lorca, *51 Harvard International Law Journal* (2010) at 489.
141 John Westlake, *Chapters on the Principles of International Law* (Cambridge University Press, 1894); Lassa Oppenheim, (Longmans, London: 1905).
142 Gong, *The Standard of Civilization* at chapters 1 to 3.
143 Hedley Bull, (Columbia University Press, 1977) at 29–34; Charles H. Alexandrowicz, *37 British Yearbook of International Law* (1961) at 506–507.
144 Tsurutaro Senga, (AÖR Bd, 1897) at 136. Cf. Lorca, 'Universal International Law' at 502; Arnulf Becker Lorca, (Cambridge University Press, 2015) at 73.
145 Edward Keene, (Cambridge University Press, 2002) at 114.
146 Andrew Fitzmaurice, (Cambridge University Press, 2014) at 363.
147 Bernard Phan, (Armand Colin, 1999) at 14. [Quote translated from French by author].
148 J. de Hornung, 'Civilisés et barbares,' *17 Revue de Droit International et de Législation Comparée* (1904) at 552 (that is, "those who are civilized must act in line with superior justice ... civilized nations must help the inferior races return to the political system of states").
149 Fitzmaurice, *Sovereignty, Property and Empire* at 366.
150 Andrew Fitzmaurice, *38 Australian Historical Studies* (2007) 1–15 at 10.
151 *Annuaire de l'institut de Droit International*, 9e Année, (1888) at 247. Cf: Fitzmaurice, 'The Genealogy of Terra Nullius' at 10.
152 Thomas Alfred Walker, (Cambridge University Press, 1895) at 26.
153 Fitzmaurice, 'The Genealogy of Terra Nullius' at 13.
154 *See*: Arnulf Becker Lorca, *51 Harvard International Law Journal* (2010) at 84.
155 Fitzmaurice, 'The Genealogy of Terra Nullius' at 13.
156 C. H. Alexandrowicz, (United Nations Institute for Training and Research-UNITAR, 1975) at 33.
157 Jacob Viner, *35 Journal of Political Economy* (1927) 198–232 at 200.
158 Westlake, at 141–142; Anaya, Indigenous Peoples in International Law at 20.

159 Gong, *The Standard of Civilization* at 64.
160 Westlake, *Chapters on the Principles of International Law* at 142–143.
161 Ibid at 143.
162 Cf: Emmanuelle Jouannet, 'European Colonialism and Contemporary Neo-Colonialism: Notes on European International Law Treatises dating from 1850 to 1914' at 12.
163 Paul Muldoon, 17 *Social and Legal Studies* (2008) at 60, 68, 70; James Lorimer, (Blackwood & Sons, 1883) at 228. Lorimer, remarking on the French brutal war in Algeria, interestingly apportioned the blame to victims (Algerians) for failing to French people and property: "Had Algeria come to respect the rights of life and property, its history would not permanently deprived it of the right of recognition." See Lorimer, *The Institutes of the Law of Nations* at 161.
164 Frederick Lugard, (Archon Books, 1965); cf Ben N. Azikiwe, *16 The Journal of Negro History* (1931) at 290.
165 Azikiwe, 'Ethics of Colonial Imperialism' at 290.
166 Alam, 'Some Economic Results of the Civilising Mission' at 4.

References

Adjei, Ako: 'Imperialism and Spiritual Freedom: An African View' *50 American Journal of Sociology* (1944) 189–198.

Akinrinade, Sola & Falola, Toyin: 'Africa and Europe: Prelude to the Partition' in Amadu Sesay (ed.), *Africa and Europe: From Partition to Interdependence or Dependence?* (Croom Helm Ltd, London/Sydney/Dover, New Hampshire: 1986) 1–20.

Alam, Shahid: 'Some Economic Results of the Civilising Mission' (January 2005) at 2. Available Online: http://ssrn.com/abstract=950876 or http://dx.doi.org/10.2139/ssrn.950876 Last Accessed 3 May 2022.

Alexandrowicz, Charles H.: 'Doctrinal Aspects of the Universality of the Law of Nations' *37 British Yearbook of International Law* (1961) 506–515.

———: 'The Role of Treaties in the European-African Confrontation in the Nineteenth Century' in A. Kodwo Mensah-Brown (ed.), *African International Legal History* (United Nations Institute for Training and Research-UNITAR, New York: 1975) 259–302.

Althusser, Louis: *Philosophy of the Encounter: Later Writings, 1978–1987* (Verso, London/New York: 2006.

Anghie, Anthony: *Imperialism, Sovereignty and the Making of International Law* (Cambridge University Press: Cambridge, 2005).

———: 'Finding the Peripheries: Sovereignty and Colonialism in Nineteenth Century International Law' *40 Harvard International Law Journal* (1999) 1–80.

———: 'The Evolution of International Law: Colonial and Postcolonial Realities' *27 Third World Quarterly* (2006) 739–753.

Arnold, David: *The Tropics and the Traveling Gaze: India, Landscapes and Science, 1800–1856* (University of Washington Press, Seattle/London: 2006).

Austin, John: *Lectures on Jurisprudence, or the Philosophy of Positive Law*, Robert Campbell (ed.) (The Law Book Exchange, New Jersey: 2005).

Azikiwe, Ben N.: 'Ethics of Colonial Imperialism' *16 The Journal of Negro History* (1931) 287–308.

Bassil, Noah R.: 'The Roots of Afropessimism: The British Invention of the Dark Continent' *25 Critical Arts* (2011) 377–396.

Bentham, Jeremy: *Introduction to the Principles of Morals and Legislation*, J. H. Burns & H. L. A. Hart (eds.) (The Athlone Press, London: 1970).

Berend, Ivan: *An Economic History of Nineteenth-Century Europe: Diversity and Industrialization* (Cambridge University Press, Cambridge/New York/Madrid/Melbourne/Cape Town: 2012).

Bluntschli, Johann Caspar: *Le Droit International Codifié, Translated from German by Charles M. Lardy* (Guillaumin et cie, Paris: 1868—French edition: 1874).

Brass, Tom: 'Unfree Labour as Primitive Accumulation?' *35 Capital & Class* (2011) 23–38.

———: 'Why Unfree Labour Is Not: "So-Called": The Fictions of Jairus Banaji' *31 Journal of Peasant Studies* (2003) 101–136.

Bull, Hedley: *The Anarchical Society: A Study of Order in World Politics* (Columbia University Press, New York: 1977).

Buzan, Barry: *From International to World Society? English School Theory and the Social Structure of Globalisation* (Cambridge University Press, Cambridge: 2004).

Cairns, H. Alan C.: *Prelude to Imperialism: British Reactions to Central African Society 1840–1890* (Routledge & Kegan Paul, London: 1965).

Chambers, Robert: *Domestic Annals of Scotland: 1689–1748* (W. & R. Chambers, Bloomington, Indiana: 1861).

Chimni, Bhupinder S.: 'Third World Approaches to International Law: A Manifesto' *8 International Community Law Review* (2006) 3–27.

Claeys, Gregory: 'The Survival of the Fittest and the Origins of Social Darwinism' *61 Journal of the History of Ideas* (2000) 223–240.

Cooper, Frederick: 'Conditions Analogous to Slavery: Imperialism and Free Labour Ideology in Africa' in T. Holt & R. Scott (eds.), *Beyond Slavery. Explorations of Race, Labor, and Citizenship in Post Emancipation Societies* (University of North Carolina Press, Chapel Hill, London: 2000) 107–149.

Curtin, Philip D.: 'The End of the "White Man's Grave?" Nineteenth-Century Mortality in West Africa' *21 The Journal of Interdisciplinary History* (1990) 63–88.

Darwin, Charles: *On the Origin of Species by Means of Natural Selection, 1859* (Reprint: Murray, London: 1968).

Davidson, Neil: 'The Scottish Path to Capitalist Agriculture 3: The Enlightenment as the Theory and Practice of Improvement' 4 *Journal of Agrarian Change* (2005) 1–72.

De Angelis, Massimo: 'Marx and Primitive Accumulation: The Continuous Character of Capital's Enclosures' *2 The Commoner* (2001) 1–22.

Diallo, Mahamadou: 'The Literature of Empire and the African Environment' in Daniel M. Mengara (ed.), *Images of Africa—Stereotypes and Realities* (African World Press, Trenton/Asmara: 2001) 105–126.

Driver, Felix: 'Henry Morton Stanley and His Critics: Geography, Exploration and Empire' *133 Past & Present* (1993) 134–166.

Dunlop, John Stewart: 'The Influence of David Livingstone on Subsequent Political Developments in Africa' *75 The Scottish Geographical Magazine* (1959) 144–152.

Ekeh, Peter P.: 'Colonialism and the Two Publics in Africa: A Theoretical Statement' *17 Comparative Studies in Society and History* (1975) 91–112.

Emerson, L. Roger: 'Conjectural History and Scottish Philosophers' *19 Historical Papers* (1984) 63–90.

Engel, Gerhard: "David Hume and the Scottish Enlightenment" in Christoph Luetge (ed.), *Handbook of the Philosophical Foundations of Business Ethics* (Springer, Heidelberg/New York/London: 2013) 253–279.

Evans, Julie: 'Where Lawlessness Is Law: The Settler-Colonial Frontier as a Legal Space of Violence' *30 Australian Feminist Law Journal* (2009) 3–22.
Evnine, Simon: 'Hume, Conjectural History, and the Uniformity of Human Nature' *31 Journal of the History of Philosophy* (1993) 589–606.
Fischer, David H.: *Historians' Fallacies: Toward a Logic of Historical Thought* (Harper-Collins, New York: 1970).
Fitzmaurice, Andrew: 'Liberalism and Empire in Nineteenth-Century International Law' *117 The American Historical Review* (2012) 122–140.
———: *Sovereignty, Property and Empire 1500–2000* (Cambridge University Press, Cambridge: 2014).
———: 'The Genealogy of Terra Nullius' *38 Australian Historical Studies* (2007) 1–15.
Forji, Amin George: 'International Law, the Civilizing Mission and the Ambivalence of Development in Africa: Conceptual Underpinnings' *6 Journal of African and International Law* (2013) 191–226.
Foucault, Michel: *Madness and Civilization* (Vintage Books, New York: 1988.
Gingell, John, Little, Adrian & Winch, Christopher: *Modern Political Thought: A Reader* (Routledge, London/New York: 2003).
Gong, Gerrit W.: *The Standard of Civilization in International Society* (Clarendon Press: Oxford, 1984).
Gozzi, Gustavo: 'History of International Law and Western Civilization' *9 International Community Law Review* (2007) 353–373.
———: 'The Particularistic Universalism of International Law in the Nineteenth Century' *52 Havard International Law Journal* (2010) 73–86.
Guizot, François: *Histoire de la Civilisation en Europe: Depuis la chute de l'Empire Romain jusqu'a a la Révolution Française* (Ad. Wahlen, Brussels/Paris: 1843).
Harvey, David: "Accumulation by Dispossession" in David Harvey (ed.), *The New Imperialism* (Oxford University Press, Oxford: 2003) at 146–150.
Haskell, Thomas L.: 'Capitalism and the Origins of the Humanitarian Sensibility, Part I' *90 The American Historical Review* (1985) 339–361.
Havinden, Michael & Meredith, David: *Colonialism and Development: Britain and Its Tropical Colonies, 1850–1960* (Routledge, London: 1995).
Heinrich, Michael: *An Introduction to the Three Volumes of Karl Marx's Capital* (Monthly Review Press, New York: 2012).
Heraclides, Alexis: 'Humanitarian Intervention in International Law 1830–1939. The Debate' *16 Journal of the History of International Law* (2014) 26–62.
Hobbes, Thomas: *Leviathan*, Richard Tuck (ed.) (Cambridge University Press, Cambridge: 1991).
Hopfl, H. M.: 'From Savage to Scotsman: Conjectural History in the Scottish Enlightenment' *17 Journal of British Studies* (1978) 19–40.
de Hornung, J.: 'Civilisés et Barbares' *17 Revue de droit international et de législation comparée* (1904).
Hume, David: *An Inquiry Concerning Human Understanding: With a Supplement: An Abstract of a Treatise of Human Nature*, Charles William Hendel (ed.) (Bobbs-Merrill Educational Pub., Indianapolis: 1955).
———: *A Treatise of Human Nature*, L. A. Selby Bigge (ed.) (Oxford University Press, Oxford: 1978).
———: *Enquiry Concerning the Principles of Morals*, Alisdair Maclntyre (ed.) (Sweet & Maxwell, London: 1965).

———: *Political Discourses*, William Bell Robertson (ed.) (Walter Scott Ltd, London: 1906).

Janis, M. W.: 'Jeremy Bentham and the Fashioning of International Law' *78 The American Journal of International Law* (1984) 405–418.

Jarosz, Lucy: 'Constructing the Dark Continent: Metaphor as Geographic Representation of Africa' *74 Geografiska Annaler. Series B, Human Geography* (1992) 105–115.

Jenkins, Rhys: 'Divisions over the International Division of Labour' *8 Capital & Class* (1984) 28–57.

Jouannet, Emmanuelle: 'European Colonialism and Contemporary Neo-Colonialism: Notes on European International Law Treatises dating from 1850 to 1914' at 12. Available online: http://cerdin.univ-paris1.fr/IMG/pdf/European_Colonialism_and_Contemporary_Neo-Colonialism.pdf Last Accessed 8 January 2022.

Keene, Edward: *Beyond the Anarchical Society: Grotius, Colonisation and Order in World Politics* (Cambridge University Press, Cambridge: 2002).

Keim, Curtis A.: 'Africa and Europe before 1900' in Phyllis M. Martin & Patrick O'Meara (eds.), *Africa*, 3rd edition (Indiana University Press, Bloomington: 1995).

Kennedy, David: 'Some Caution about Property Rights as a Recipe for Economic Development' *1 Accounting, Economics, and Law* (2011) 1–62.

Kiernan, G. Victor: 'Europe in the Colonial Mirror' *1 History of European Ideas* (1980) 39–61.

Kipling, Rudyard: *The White Man's Burden: The United States and the Philippine Islands. 1899. (Rudyard Kipling's Verse)* (The Definitive Edition, New York/London: 1982).

Koponen, Juhani: 'The Partition of Africa: A Scramble for a Mirage' *2 Nordic Journal of African Studies* (1993) 117–135.

Koskenniemi, Martti: *From Apology to Utopia: The Structure of International Legal Argument* (Cambridge University Press, Cambridge: 2005a).

———: *Histories of International Law: Dealing with Eurocentrism* (Universiteit Utrecht—Faculteit Geeseswetenschappen, Utrecht: 2011).

———: 'International Law in Europe: Between Tradition and Renewal' *16 European Journal of International Law* (2005b) 113–124.

———: *The Civilizing Mission: International Law and the Colonial Encounter in the Late 19th Century* (Deutsche Rechtshistorikertag, Bonn: 2004), *draft*, 1–21.

Kozel, P.: *Market Sense: Towards a New Economics of Markets and Society* (Routledge, New York: 2006).

Lehmann, William C.: *Henry Home, Lord Kames, and the Scottish Enlightenment: A Study in National Character and in the History of Ideas* (Springer, The Hague: 2013).

Lenin, Vladimir: *Imperialism: The High-Stage of Capitalism*, first published: 1916), New Revised Translation (International Publishers, New York: 1938).

Lonsdale, John & Berman, Bruce: 'Coping with the Contradictions: The Development of the Colonial State in Kenya, 1895–1914' *20 Journal of African History* (1979) 487–505.

Lorca, Arnulf Becker: *Mestizo International Law: A Global Intellectual History 1842–1933* (Cambridge University Press, Cambridge: 2015).

———: 'Universal International Law: Nineteenth-Century Histories of Imposition and Appropriation' *51 Harvard International Law Journal* (2010) 475–552.

Lorimer, James: *The Institutes of the Law of Nations: A Treatise of the Jural Relations of Separate Political Communities* (William Blackwood & Sons, Edinburgh/London: 1883).

Lugard, Frederick: *The Dual Mandate in British Tropical Africa* (Archon Books, Hamden: 1965).
Maine, Henry James Sumner: *The Effects of Observation of India on Modern European Thought: The Rede Lecture Delivered before the University of Cambridge* (John Murray, London: 1875).
Manning, William Oke: *Commentaries on the Law of Nations* (S. Sweet, London: 1839).
Marks, Robert B.: *The Origins of the Modern World: A Global and Ecological Narrative from the Fifteenth to the Twenty-first Century*, 2nd edition (Rowman & Littlefield Inc., Boulder/New York/Toronto/Oxford: 2007).
Marx, Karl: *Capital: Critique of Political Economy*, Frederick Engels (ed.) (Charles H. Kerr & Co., New York/Toronto: 1906).
Marx, Karl & Engels, Friedrich: "Preface to A Contribution to the Critique of Political Economy" in Karl Marx and Frederick Engels (eds.), *Selected Works* (Lawrence and Wishart, London: 1968) at 182.
Malthus, Thomas Robert: *First Essay on Population, 1798. Vol. 14.* (Macmillan, London: 1966).
Mbembe, Achille: *On the Postcolony* (University of California Press, Berkeley: 2001).
Mensah-Brown, A. Kodwo: *African International Legal History* (United Nations Institute for Training and Research-UNITAR, New York: 1975).
Merry, Sally Engle: 'Law and Colonisation' *25 Law and Society Review* (1991) 889–922.
Mill, James: *Essays on Politics and Society Part I* (Cambridge University Press, Cambridge: 2015).
Mill, John Stuart: 'A Few Words on Non-Intervention' in John Stuart Mill (ed.), *Dissertations and Discussions: Political,Philosophical and Historical* (W. V. Spencer, Boston: 1967).
———: *Dissertations and Discussions: Political, Philosophical and Historical* (J. W. Parker, London: 1859).
———: "Essays on Ethics Religion and Society" in John Robson (ed.), *The Collected Works of John Stuart Mill* (University of Toronto Press, Toronto: 1981) 766–776.
Monk, William: *Dr. Livingstone's Cambridge Lectures* (Deighton, London: 1858).
Morgan, Lewis Henry: *Ancient Society* (Belknap Press, Cambridge, Massachusetts: 1964).
Moses, Jeremy: 'Humanitarianism and International Law: The Standard of Civilization in Contemporary International Relations' *Paper presented at the International Studies Association Annual Conference*, Honolulu, Hawaii, 1–5 March 2005, at 1–53.
Muldoon, Paul: 'The Sovereign Exceptions: Colonization and the Foundation of Society' *17 Social and Legal Studies* (2008) 59–74.
Mutua, Makau & Anghie, Antony: 'What Is TWAIL?' *Proceedings of the 94th Annual Meeting: American Society of International Law* (2000) 31–40.
Nieboer, Jeremias Herman: *Slavery as an Industrial System* (Martinus Nijhoff, Leiden: 1910).
Nkomazana, Fidelis: 'Livingstone's Ideas of Christianity, Commerce and Civilization' *12 PULA: Botswana Journal of African Studies* (1998) 44–57.
Northcott, Cecil: *David Livingstone: His Triumph, Decline and Fall* (Lutterworth Press, London: 1973).
Ocheni, Stephen & Nwankwo, Basil: 'Analysis of Colonialism and Its Impact in Africa' *8 Cross-Cultural Communications* (2012) 46–54.

Oduntan, Gbenga: 'International Laws and the Discontented: Westernization, the Development and the Underdevelopment of International Laws' in Amita Dhanda & Archana Parashar (eds.), *Decolonisation of Legal Knowledge* (Routledge, London/New York/New Delhi: 2009) 91–126.

Oppenheim, Lassa: *International Law, A Treatise* (Longmans, London: 1937).

Pagden, Anthony: 'Human Rights, Natural Rights, and Europe's Imperial Legacy' *31 Political Theory* (2003) 171–199.

Phan, Bernard: *Colonisations et Décolonisations Française* (Armand Colin, Paris: 1999).

Pitts, Jennifer: *A Turn to Empire: The Rise of Imperial Liberalism in Britain and France* (Princeton University Press, Princeton: 2005).

Price, Richard: *Making Empire: Colonial Encounters and the Creation of Imperial Rule in Nineteenth-Century Africa* (Cambridge University Press, Cambridge: 2008).

Ramage, B. J.: 'The Partition of Africa' *7 The Sewanee Review* (1899) 221–238.

Robinson, Joan: *"Introduction" to Rosa Luxemburg, The Accumulation of Capital* (Routledge & Kegan Paul, London: 1951).

Robinson, Ronald Edward & Gallagher, John: *Africa and the Victorians: The Official Mind of Imperialism* (Macmillan, London: 1966).

Sanyal, Kalyan K., 'Capital, Primitive Accumulation, and the Third World: From Annihilation to Appropriation' *6 Rethinking Marxism* 117–130.

Sardar, Ziauddin: 'Development and the Locations of Eurocentrism' in Ronaldo Munck & Denis O'Hearn (eds.), *Critical Development Theory: Contributions to a New Paradigm* (Zed Books, London/New York: 1999) 44–62.

Scott, William Robert: *Francis Hutcheson: His Life, Teaching and Position in the History of Philosophy* (Cambridge University Press, Cambridge: 1900).

Senga, Tsurutaro: *Gestaltung und Kritik der heutigen Konsulargerichtsbarkeit in Japan* (AÖR Bd, Berlin: 1897).

Singh, Prabhakar: 'From Narcissistic Positive International Law to Universal Natural International Law: The Dialectics of Absentee Colonialism' *16 African Journal of International & Comparative Law* (2008) 56–82.

Smith, Adam: *Lectures on Jurisprudence*, R. L. Meek, D. D. Raphael & P. G. Stein (eds.) (Liberty Classics, Indianapolis: 1978); (*Republished by*: Liberty Fund, Indianapolis: 1982).

Spencer, Herbert: *The Principles of Biology, 1864* (Reprint: William Norgate, London: 1880).

Stanley, Henry Morton: *In Darkest Africa, or the Quest, Rescue and Retreat of Emin, Governor of Equatorial* (Charles Scribner, New York: 1890).

———: *The Congo and the Founding of Its Free State: A Story of Work and Exploration* (Searle & Rivington, London: 1885).

———: *Through the Dark Continent or the Sources of the Nile Around the Great Lakes of Equatorial Africa and Down the Livingstone River to the Atlantic Ocean* (Harper & Brothers, New York: 1878).

Stewart, Dugald: *Account of the Life and Writings of Adam Smith* (Charles Knight & Co., London: 1843).

———: *The Cambridge Advanced Learner's Dictionary* (Cambridge University Press, Cambridge: 2014).

Tort, Patrick: *Dictionnaire du Darwinisme et de l'évolution. Tome 2* (Presses universitaires de France (PUF), Paris: 1996).

Toyoda, Tetsuya: 'Influence of Public Opinion on International Law in the Nineteenth Century' *46 Alberta Law Review* (2009) 1099–1113.

Vincent, Joan: "Sovereignty, Legitimacy, and Power: Prologomena to the Study of the Colonial State" in Ronald Cohen & Judith D. Toland (eds.), *State Formation and Political Legitimacy* (Transaction Books, New Brunswick/Oxford: 1988) at 137–154.

Viner, Jacob: 'Adam Smith and Laissez Faire' *35 Journal of Political Economy* (1927) 198–232.

Westlake, John: *Chapters in the Principles of International Law* (University of Michigan Press: Michigan, 1894).

———: *The Collected Papers on Public International Law*, Lassa Oppenheim (ed.) (Cambridge University Press, Cambridge: 1914).

Wheaton, Henry: *Elements of International Law: With a Sketch a Sketch of the History of the Science* (Carey, Lea and Blanchard: Philadelphia, 1836).

5 The Scramble for Africa

Non-State Actors and Acquisitions by Cession Treaties

5.1 Introduction: Prelude to Cession Treaties: Colonial Empire Builders as Forbearers of the Scramble for Africa

The drive by European corporations and merchants in the 19th century to expand processes of industrial capitalism unto non-European territories had a pivotal role in shaping international economic and legal order during the first half of the century and beyond.[1] An intense rivalry amongst European corporations trading across Africa resulted to a fierce scramble for lands on the continent. The scramble was chiefly championed by corporations and traders from eight European countries through commercialisation operations, to wit: Belgium, England (Britain), France, Germany, Holland, Italy, Portugal, and Spain. This chapter specifically revolves around the operations of three pioneer empire builders from three of these leading colonial nations, namely Leopold II of Belgium in the Congo, Cecil Rhodes of Britain in southern Africa, and Pierre Savorgnan de Brazza of France in Congo-Brazzaville—three remarkable men in the game of international power politics.[2] Although there was a whole host of explorers throughout the continent, emphasis is placed on these three personalities because they, more than many of their peers, are deemed to have given colonisation "a recognizable, human face ... which allowed citizens to understand overseas expansion as a series of extraordinary personal quests ... [thereby creating] huge public enthusiasm."[3] Avowed industrial capitalists, and driven by a mixture of "ego, courage and racism,"[4] the merchants were determined to go after riches to the end of the earth wherever these were found, first and foremost in their own personal rights but also for the benefit of their home states.

At quick glance, 19th-century empire builders—well-noted for their eccentricity—appear to have had little or nothing to do with neither international relations nor international law-making. However, their activism, quest for profits, lure for grandeur, and extraterritorial economic engagements enabled them to emerge as some of the principal drivers of both disciplines in the 19th century. Their actions inadvertently laid the groundwork for the modern African state system as we know it today. They were masterful in rallying support around private economic self-fulfilments, yet they were seen not as such but

DOI: 10.4324/9781003265740-5

rather as championing a higher noble purpose for humankind—the so-called opening up, development, and modernization of tropical Africa.

While Leopold II relied on phony self-created "international" associations (which in a real sense were anything but international) for legality towards his imperial ambitions, Rhodes's professed rights and privileges emanated from a charter accorded to his company by Britain;[5] and De Brazza—although solely responsible for negotiating trade and protection rights with African rulers—nevertheless received direct oversight from the French government.

Overall, non-state European corporations that were aggressively engaged in commercial operations across Africa successfully prompted their home states to prioritize extraterritorial expansion and relations as a matter of national policy in the 19th century. This chapter firstly locates the historical premise of the aforementioned leading empire builders, whose activities sparked the scramble for Africa. Following this biographical overview, the chapter turns to an examination of the legitimacy of contractual agreements—the so-called capitulation or cession treaties between European non-state actors and African rulers in the 19th century—especially considering that the treaties later became the legal basis according to which European powers justified the right to set up colonies and protectorates throughout Africa.

5.2 Empire Builders and Three Alternative Manifestations of International Relations

The operations and manoeuvres of empire builders as catalysts of the scramble for Africa followed three main different dimensions: (1) the ideology of the privilege to damage without accountability or compensation; (2) the formalisation of colonial international relations (local administration embracing the colonial); and finally, (3) the harbouring and dissemination of information out of Africa. While the actions of Leopold II and Cecil Rhodes best mirrored the logic of privilege to damage without accountability or compensation (by claiming an exercise of sovereign rights over the occupied), the operations of De Brazza and David Livingstone,[6] on the other hand, evidenced the formalisation of colonial international relations (local administration embracing the colonial). Both approaches tightly controlled the modalities by which information from areas under their spheres of influence was harboured and disseminated out of Africa.

5.2.1 The Privilege to Damage without Accountability or Compensation: Examining Leopold II and Cecil Rhodes

The operations of Leopold II and Cecil Rhodes are very revealing of how actors in the international society can articulate appealing projects that justify the humane duty to dominate, but whose outcome ultimately results to misery on the lives of the colonised. International law in these situations was invoked by concerned instigators to formalise a privilege to damage without accountability or payment of compensation.

5.2.1.1 Leopold II (Belgium)

Leopold II of Belgium is now remembered in academic circles as an astute king who masterminded one of the biggest mischiefs of the 19th century to become the poster child of the civilising mission in Africa. The scheme enabled him to carve out a personal kingdom for himself at the heart of Africa—precisely in the Congo—wherefrom he engineered a reign of brute terror and other human rights violations on its inhabitants, thereby reaping untold profits from their exploitation.[7] He has in recent decades been described using countless adjectives, but amongst those, none probably does him as much justice as the 1963 book by Neal Ascherson titled *The King Incorporated*.[8] A member of the London Geographical Society (LGS), Leopold had his eyes set on economic possibilities around the globe that the society could locate. In 1876, he organised an international geographical conference in Brussels for philanthropic, scientific, and commercial goals as well as to craft a common cooperative humanitarian platform for the exploration of the African interior, whereupon European powers supposedly could extend the blessings of civilisation unto Africa. The conference brought together prominent European geographers, explorers, merchants, publicists, and other scholars with interest in exploration and investment on the African continent. It further sought to crystallise the basis of the civilising mission and the philanthropic foundations that subsequently enabled the justification and legitimation of the scramble for Africa.[9] In his opening speech, Leopold II affirmed that "the subject which unites us today is one of those which deserve the highest degree to occupy friends of humanity ... to open to civilization the only part of our globe where it has not yet penetrated."[10] The king, moreover, is reported to have made the following proclamation in defence of humanitarianism for Africa:

> Our refined society attaches to human life—and with reason—a value unknown to the barbarous communities. When our directing will is implanted among them its aim is to triumph over all obstacles, and results which could not be attained by lengthy speeches may follow philanthropic influence. But if, in view of this desirable spread of civilization, we count upon the means of action which confer upon us the dominion and the sanction of right, it is not less true that our agents, nearly all of whom are volunteers drawn from the ranks of the Belgian army, have always present in their minds a strong sense of the career of honour in which they are engaged, and are animated with pure feeling of patriotism; not sparing their own blood, they would the more spare the blood of the natives, who would see in them the all-powerful protectors of their lives and their property, benevolent teachers of whom they have so great a need.[11]

Following this conference, a non-state international organization dubbed *l'Association pour l'Exploration et la Civilisation de l'Afrique centrale*, better known as *Association Internationale Africaine* (AIA), was founded, with Leopold II elected as its first president and Brussels its official headquarters. The association's mission revolved around four cardinal humanitarian engagements: coordination of national committees (beside the international committee, each participating country was encouraged to form a national committee),[12] the opening up of trading posts and bases across Africa for the development of commercial activities, the sharing of geographical knowledge, and the eradication of the slave trade.[13] With the objectives of the conference said to be purely scientific and humanitarian, the means for their realisation was envisaged to be strictly international, with focus on: "(1) the exploration of Africa from ocean to ocean and from the Zambesi to the Soudan, and (2) the establishment of scientific and relief stations within this territory."[14]

The goals of AIA may have been as pretentious as they were misleading. In spite of the seductive humanitarian postulations, AIA operated more as a shakedown vehicle to buy international legitimacy. Leopold's dreams of an overseas colony predated his ascension to the Belgian monarchy. The Congress of Vienna of 1815 merged Belgium (the Southern Netherlands) and Holland (the Northern Netherlands) to form one state, the United Kingdom of the Netherlands.[15] During the time of the union, which ended in 1830, Belgium contributed mostly as the commercial organ of the state whereas Holland fuelled the economy with excessive surplus imported from its colonies.[16] With the breakup of the union, the Belgian economy, deprived of the colonial privileges, began to dwindle, forcing the state to impose high taxes, tariffs, and import duties.

Coming to power in 1865, Leopold II, like his father before him, sought to replicate the erstwhile glorious luxuries and excesses—the fruits of imperialism as enjoyed by the state during the union with Holland—in order to line the Belgian treasury.[17] Already way back in the 1850s when Leopold was still the duke of Brabant, he ceaselessly engineered several failed attempts to acquire foreign colonies, even by outright purchase. As Roger Astey has provided, Leopold, conscious of the weakness of Belgium, strictly sought after soft targets—any territories already abandoned by European powers or those that had not yet been "discovered" or appropriated.[18] Some of these botched overseas attempts included the schemes to buy lands and concessions in the Philippines, Tonkin in the Far East, Argentine provinces, Sarawak in Malaysia, and Mozambique in Africa.[19] Acquiring foreign possessions, Leopold thought, was going to greatly uplift Belgian standing and grow trade, as well as counter adverse economic effects amongst other European powers.

Leopold might have utterly failed in his early attempts for overseas ventures, but in the process he became exceedingly shrewd and skilful for future endeavours. Not satisfied with constitutional restrictions on his authority as Belgian monarch, he began a new drive to carve out an extraterritorial kingdom in his individual name.[20] His dreams of a private African empire a decade later "might have been called hopelessly unrealistic except that he succeeded in transforming them into reality by a remarkable combination of energy, shrewdness, and luck."[21] Of all the AIA's national committees, the only one that was mildly active was the Belgian committee which, thanks to Leopold's stimulation, sent two private expeditions to Tanganyika by 1877, though with very little positive results. A year later, in January 1878, sub-Saharan Africa's economic and political history would assume a radical twist when Henry Morton Stanley, the British journalist (like Leopold, he was equally a very shrewd individual, and formerly known as John Rowlands)—who had recently travelled to the Congo basin and wrote elaborately about his "discovery" of the Congo River, the region's excessive natural riches and commercial value—returned to Europe. His writings had made their way to the *Journal Officiel de la République Française* amongst other top European newspapers, wherefrom Leopold is said to have learnt of the African hidden treasures. In addition, he was an early reader of the book *Across Africa* (1877) by Verney Lovett Cameron, an English explorer who is said to be the first European to cross equatorial Africa from coast (sea) to coast (sea).[22] The book colourfully celebrated tropical Africa's "incalculable wealth," "vast fortunes," and "almost unspeakable richness" which could be exploited at very minimal cost.[23] Both accounts were consistent with *The Times*, which ran a feature column picturing the interior of equatorial Africa as overflowing with fabulous richness in its subsoil.[24]

On arrival in Marseille, France, two emissaries from Leopold II cornered Stanley for a well-remunerated expedition assignment to return back to the Congo basin and its tributaries—an offer he accepted without hesitation. A year later, Leopold formed a new organization under his direction with identical aims as the AIA: *Comité d'études du Haut-Congo*, most probably because he feared that information of the discovery of the Congo River if unhampered was going to facilitate the gaining of access into the African interior for competing European states. Moreover, the new organisation would enable Leopold to discard from any responsibility towards AIA and assert absolute independence over his activities in central Africa. It was under the auspices and finances of this new organisation—whose name was promptly changed during the same year to become the *Association Internationale du Congo* (AIC)—that Stanley was dispatched back to the Congo as his personal flag-bearer for boundless commercial undertakings.[25] This involved setting up trading posts throughout the region and the negotiation of economic agreements with local leaders geared towards bestowing Leopold with an exclusive monopoly over the explored areas. With the employment of Stanley, Leopold's African empire project began to take form and substance.[26]

In later years after securing the Congo, Leopold allegedly lampooned how he was able to pull it off by employing Stanley with a deceptive description of his real job, despite all European powers expressing similar interests in the territory:

> I think that if I entrusted Stanley publicly with the job of taking over part of Africa in my own name, the English would stop me. If I consult them,

> they will again try to stop me. So I think that at first I shall give Stanley an exploring job which will not offend anybody, and will provide us with some posts.[27]

Stanley's successes forced other European merchants to start raising the flags of their metropolis in various regions of Africa.

5.2.1.2 Cecil John Rhodes (1853–1902)

In *Merchant Kings: When Companies Ruled the World, 1600—1900* (2010), Stephen R. Bown does Cecil Rhodes good justice by identifying him (together with five other "merchant kings" whose heroic commercial undertakings in non-European territories resulted to the expansion of European imperialism) amongst the greatest rogues of the gallery between the 17th and 20th centuries.[28] While the other five—Pietr Stuyvesant (Dutch West India Company), Jan Pieterzoon Coen (Dutch East India Company, VOC), Robert Clive (English East India Company), Aleksandr Baranov (Russian America Company), and George Simpson (Hudson's Bay Company)—conducted their operations exclusively in Asia and the Indies, only Rhodes British South Africa Company (BSA) was concentrated in Africa. In the footsteps of the five other merchants before him, Rhodes's acute ego for profit making and empire building across Africa resulted in the crushing of any people that stood on his way—indigenous Africans paying heavily with their lives and property.[29]

In a short 1902 eulogy piece celebrating Cecil Rhodes's role in the expansion of the British Empire to Africa, shortly after his death, one scholar noted that

> very few amongst the sons of men who, born not in the list of kings and warriors and philosophers, have power within them to change profoundly the maps and minds of humanity. They are yet more rare and happy to whom it is given to see in large measure their work accomplished while they live.[30]

Rhodes was born into an ordinary if not poor background, his father a simple vicar at a parish in Hertfordshire for the Church of England. Rhodes was sickly, and his parents were unable to afford his financial and medical needs. So, in 1870, thanks to money borrowed from his aunt, the family dispatched him on a ship to join his brother Herbert, who had settled in Natal, South Africa. This turned out to be his golden fleece, after he dabbled into the Kimberly diamond mines, ploughed back profits, and bought all the small mining operations in the region, reaping untold profits following the booming of diamond prices and a strategic partnership with the London-based Diamond Syndicate that gave him a global monopoly in the trade. The partnership resulted in Rhodes amalgamating a hold in De Beers Consolidated Ltd; hitherto known as De Beers Mining Company.[31]

In 1873 Rhodes briefly returned to England, leaving his venture with his business partner, Charles Rudd, to further his education at Oriel College, Oxford, but ultimately abandoned it after just one term. While at Oriel, Rhodes joined the Freemason secret society. The society's drive for power politics and imperial domination inspired Rhodes to envisage bringing the entire uncivilised world under the British Empire, wherein he would not only have a stake but also become a key player.[32] He envisaged a Cape to Cairo Railway scheme linking various British African possessions along the two extreme edges of the continent (lying 5000 miles apart) on a continuous red line, as the sole means to realize his grand objective of an exceptional settlement for white people.[33] Upon completion, it was going to unify the entire trading and settlement axis; thus serving as a cultural backbone of western civilization and grandeur, expectantly greater and more prosperous than the United States. While this dream never materialised, it was certainly not for lack of trying. While empire builders generally were mavericks, Rhodes was undoubtedly the mavericks' maverick. He was "bold," "brilliant," but also "brash," "brutal," and "bigoted."[34] At the tender age of 24, obsessed with Social Darwinism, he articulated his vision for the British expansionism in "Confession of Faith," which was never published during his lifetime. A paragraph from the work nevertheless featured in his last will and testament:

> I contend that we are the finest race in the world and that the more of the world we inhabit the better it is for the human race. Just fancy those parts that are at present inhabited by the most despicable specimens of human beings what an alteration there would be if they were brought under Anglo-Saxon influence, look again at the extra employment a new country added to our dominions gives.[35]

Whereas Leopold was very diplomatic but undeniably always shrewd in his empire pursuits, Rhodes didn't try as hard to disguise his intentions. Not only was he a firm believer in British imperialism, qualifying it as a "bread and butter question," he ultimately perceived the Anglo-Saxon colonisation of "the others" as the only means of evading civil war. Never shy to propagate his dogmas, he famously stated his overriding manifesto thus:

> I was in the East End of London yesterday and attended a meeting of the unemployed. I listened to the wild speeches, which were just a cry for "bread! bread!" and on my way home I pondered over the scene and I became more than ever convinced of the importance of imperialism. … My cherished idea is a solution for the social problem, i.e., in order to save the 40,000,000 inhabitants of the United Kingdom from a bloody civil war, we colonial statesmen must acquire new lands to settle the surplus population, to provide new markets for the goods produced in

> the factories and mines. The Empire, as I have always said, is a bread and butter question. If you want to avoid civil war, you must become imperialists.[36]

With his abundance of newly acquired wealth, Rhodes began looking for concessions beyond Cape, expanding as far as the eye could see, reaching faraway places such as Basutoland (Lesotho) and Zambezi. One of his biggest obstacles came from Lobengula, the powerful king of Ndebele of Matabeleland, who despite uncountable persuasions refused to grant Rhodes any mining concession within his territory. However, Rhodes managed to convince Lobengula using Francis Thompson—a Brit whom the king trusted—under the false pretence that fewer than ten white men were going to carry out mining at Matabeleland. The strategy had been well cooked in advance by the two men, and the clause in question was never inserted into the final agreement, which Lobengula signed. Instead, the "cession" document stated that per the concession, Rhodes was authorized to do anything necessary for the realisation of its operations.[37] Realizing that he had been deceived and the implication of the treaty, Lobengula wrote a letter dated 23 April 1889 to the English queen, for which he never received a reply. It read in part thus:

> They asked for a place to dig, and said they would give certain things for the right to do so ... Three months afterwards, I heard from other sources that I had given by that document the right for all minerals in my country ... I do not recognize the paper as it contains neither my words nor the words of those who got it.[38]

A similar deceptive agreement was signed with Lewanika, king of Lozi in Zambezi. Using these acquired concessions, Rhodes successfully applied for and was granted a royal charter by the British government to operate his *British South Africa Company* (BSA) in 1889. Almost single-handedly, BSA succeeded in imposing British influence throughout southern Africa, with nearly the entire region (except Mozambique and Angola, which became Portuguese colonies) becoming British colonial protectorates.[39] Under the auspices of BSA, Rhodes freely invaded territories northwards with his brutal militia, culminating with him becoming the only English person in the world to have not just one but two countries named after himself: Northern and Southern Rhodesia. The British premier, Robert Gascoyne-Cecil, 3rd Marquess of Salisbury, reportedly endorsed Rhodes's terror on the "natives" in the following words: "You take what you can, ask me later."[40] In 1890, Rhodes was elected as prime minister of the Cape Colony. He unapologetically set the foundation of his political regime on the following platform: "the native is to be denied the right to vote, and treated as a child."[41] This ultimately was Rhodes's great dream of the British Empire—his idea of the duty of the white race to civilize Africa.[42]

5.2.2 *The Formalisation of Colonial International Relations (Local Administration Embracing the Colonial): Examining De Brazza, Livingstone, and Henry Morton Stanley*

Contrary to Leopold II and Cecil Rhodes, whose approaches to the expansion of imperial rule to Africans were driven by imposition; De Brazza and Livingstone exemplify an opposite reality—an illustration of how international relations was able to pacifically co-opt the colonised, thus offering a pathway towards cognisable legal forms.

5.2.2.1 *Pierre Savorgnan de Brazza*

While Leopold II and Rhodes have recently witnessed growing scrutiny in academic circles; Pierre Savorgnan de Brazza is hardly discussed. He was nevertheless as much a colonialist as Leopold and Rhodes, but distinguished himself by his humane treatment of the people he conquered and with the best of intentions, did his utmost best to uplift the Africans under his control—consistent with the rhetoric of *mission civilisatrice*. While this act of nobility ironically made him the most ill-famed of the explorers in historical accounts, it has nonetheless won him an indelible place in the hearts and minds of Congolese whom he colonized. Not only is the country's capital, Brazzaville named after him, but a mausoleum was inaugurated in 2007 at the city in his honour; a direct contrast to the Democratic Republic of Congo which in the aftermath of its independence changed the name of its capital city from Leopoldville to Kinshasa; Rhodesia equally officially changed its name to Zimbabwe at independence[43] and its capital from Salisbury[44] to Harare—both countries not wanting to be haunted by the ill legacies of Leopold and Rhodes.

Following Leopold II's much-heralded 1876 international geographical conference, the French national branch of AIA commissioned Savorgnan de Brazza to lead an exploration mission deep into the hinterlands from the coast of Gabon, which was already under French control. Upon crossing the Congo River, De Brazza discovered that Stanley was aggressively signing unannounced treaties around the southern part of the river with African rulers on behalf of Leopold II, in what not only seemed to be at odds with the spirit of AIA but obviously looked like a disguised mission.[45] Upon uncovering this fact, De Brazza decided not to work within the framework of AIA but instead to pursue French colonial interests in the region, even before he could report back to his fatherland. To that effect, he independently concluded a barrage of treaties with African rulers in the name of France in what is present day Republic of Congo.[46] Like Stanley, he kept his activities a guarded secret when he signed treaties in 1880 with the rulers of Makoko, Congo Rapids, and Teke, all of whom by the agreements ceded their territories to France, thereby effectively undercutting Stanley from possibly moving any further northwards on behalf of Leopold.[47] For De Brazza, this was a unique opportunity to remedy France's poor competitive position in the Central Africa trade, which was principally due to lack of commercial posts. Although France never gave De Brazza the authority to conclude these treaties in the Congo, both chambers of the French parliament on 30 November 1882 nevertheless unanimously approved his agreements with King Makoko, who was acknowledged as the sovereign ruler of the Batekes. The ratification of De Brazza's treaties by the French state effectively incorporated the region earmarked by the treaties into *France d'Outre-mer*.[48] Unlike Leopold II and Rhodes, De Brazza, in accordance with the French imperial mindset, conceived colonization more in educational terms rather than economic; this explains the reason why the French government placed De Brazza's mission instead under the tutelage of the minister of public instruction—which at the time was headed by Jules Ferry.[49]

Despite avoiding employing brutal tactics in his quest for territory, De Brazza was not totally immune from the exploitation of Africans. It is alleged that for all the treaties that he signed across the region, all he paid back in return (depending on the size of the land) were jewelleries, pieces of coloured cloth, knives, and small mirrors.[50] Although there is no account of him molesting the "natives," the sanctity and free will of the treaties he collected is doubtful, giving that he surrounded himself with Senegalese sharpshooters in order to toughen his bargaining prospects.[51]

5.2.2.2 David Livingstone versus Henry Morton Stanley

The extent of Stanley's undertakings in the Congo region and legal implications will be further examined later in Chapter 6. In the interim, it is important to note that Stanley has been traditionally associated with two "discoveries": the Congo and finding David Livingstone. Livingstone who through his accounts and letters to Europe had become the source of information for many in the metropolitan reading public and journals, suddenly went missing without a trace around 1865. In 1869, the *New York Herald* newspaper commissioned Stanley to help find him, a mission he accomplished on 10 November 1871 when he found him and his entourage at Ujiji along the shores of Lake Tanganyika, reportedly greeting him with the words, "Dr. Livingstone, I presume?"[52] The veracity of the statement has been seriously debated in academic circles. It is strongly believed that Stanley—a reporter long noted for producing sensational articles, used his experience as a journalist to fabricate and drastically dramatise his encounter with the tongue-in-cheek phrase purely for a publicity stunt.

The encounter is probably more significant for the contrast between the two personalities than the actual meeting. Of the Europeans present in Africa during the era, Livingstone and Savognan de Brazza were amongst the most loved amongst Africans. Livingstone was generally seen to be very concerned with the welfare of the Africans he preached to. He treated them with respect, kept a minimal entourage, and never attempted to force Christianity on the populace, to which they returned the favour in kind.[53] However, despite his efforts it is said that he managed to convert only one African: Chief Sechele of the Kwena people.[54] A quick learner, Sechele got baptised, learnt the alphabet, and began reading the Bible,[55] but he lived a double life by secretly exalting his African culture contrary to Livingstone's teachings. He continued the ritual of rainmaking and privately strongly believed in polygamy just like his kinsmen. Although he initially heeded to Livingstone to divorce four of his five wives in order for all of them to be baptised, a year later one of his former wives was pregnant from Sechele, and despite pleading with Livingstone not to give up on him, Livingstone left his region for good.[56]

Stanley was the exact opposite of Livingstone. He was shrewd, didn't believe in rights for Africans, and perceived geographical science in purely economic terms and exploration in terms of life and death—with the stronger inevitably subjugating their captives into economic and political gains.[57] While the two men were both eloquent and charismatic, their first difference was without doubt also one of semantic construction. While Livingstone had admonished the civilised to help the unfortunate, Stanley subscribed to Social Darwinist thinking which construed Europeans and Africans in terms of the superior versus inferior. But what exactly was the difference between unfortunate and inferior? A holistic reading of the assertions suggests that while helping ultimately meant ruling, superiority over the inferiors necessitated sheer domination. Thus, where Livingstone saw a duty to serve, Stanley saw an urge to grab. In either case, however, the "natives" were ultimately bound to fall under European tutelage. Stanley's expeditions and activities were characterised by dreadful brutality on Africans—in what became known as the Congo atrocities.[58] His regiments profusely flogged Africans, slaughtered some, and burnt their villages—with those surviving transformed into virtual slaves. He justified flogging as in accordance with African customs, and he downplayed the killing of "natives" as an act of a just war. As he framed it, he never killed them if he could buy their peace.[59]

The encounter of the two personalities at Ujiji oddly became symbolic as a moment of transition from old imperialism giving way to the new—the failure of the pacific approach to trade and political relations and the advent of brutal methods to achieve the goals of empire building and trade monopoly.[60] During the six years that Stanley worked for Leopold, the two men inspired the worst of colonial excesses. Stanley was reportedly everything that Livingstone hated and rejected (Livingstone was allegedly embarrassed to be associated with him)—where Livingstone brought light, Stanley came after him with terror and corruption.[61]

5.3 Non-State Actors as Colonising Agents

Tempted by the zeal to generate capital and profits and to be competitive on a macro scale, 19th century European corporations through their aggressive undertakings across Africa foreshadowed the way for their home countries to prioritize extraterritorial expansion and relations as a matter of national policy. States, as aforementioned, were not key players throughout the scramble for Africa. Instead, it is ambitious transnational "merchant adventurers" who, although not principal actors of international law, initiated independent economic and political relations with local entities, which eventually culminated to what one scholar has termed as "private foreign policy."[62] As the private interests of corporations increasingly coincided with Eurocentric national programs and policy formulations, international law stepped into the fray to validate acquired titles and rights of exclusivity.[63] Contrary to conventional norms, transnational corporations were now officially mandated with decision-making powers to decide on sovereignty matters on behalf of their home states, starting with the annexation of territories. In this study, I term broadly term these entities as non-state actors.

While explorers such as Henry Morton Stanley and Lovett Cameron branded Africa as overflowing with unspeakable riches, others such as Joseph Thomson, who refused to acknowledge any economic motives behind the civilising mission project, contended that although Africa was without doubt going to appreciate European goods and textile—legitimate trade, so to speak—it nonetheless had nothing to offer in return.[64] Given the uncertainty and conflictual accounts as to the extent of the richness of Africa in terms of natural resources, most European governments did not want to gamble with public funds for imperial purposes.[65] In the midst of uncertainty, European states were nonetheless more than willing to support national chartered corporations, explorers and other commercial companies who could spearhead the transnational quest for wealth, and raw materials for industrialisation.

With the exponential rise of non-state actors across the continent as from the mid-1870s, each corporation, not surprisingly, celebrated every new territorial acquisition by hoisting its national flag on strategic positions to ward off all other potential conquerors. The merchants frequently clashed with fellow competitors from rival countries that were pursuing similar interests. Sola Akinrinade and Toyin Falola have observed that these actions instigated an unprecedented realm of political conduct between home states and host states.[66] Realizing that direct political control would have entailed direct responsibility to spend, the technique of company politics, which let corporations do the aggressive dirty annexations, afforded home states the invaluable advantage of being spared not only the cost of annexation but the potential disgrace of defeat from rivalry powers as well.[67] Whereupon things went out of control, any involved European power still preserved its diplomatic cards during any resulting treaty or political negotiations. European powers widely favoured the use of non-state actors as modality for acquiring lands in Africa, given the propensity of the approach in procuring exclusive trading rights and commercial monopoly, yet with very limited political and financial investment. Jean Stengers has concurred with Akinrinade and Falola that non-state actors shouldered economic, political, and financial responsibilities of annexation—performing these exceptional political and economic duties of states in return for commercial privileges and protection by their home governments.[68] The trading monopolies and commercial posts secured by these corporations in due course became the springboard on which states sealed territories into colonies or protective domains.[69]

5.3.1 Overview of Company Rule/Scramble Politics by Country

5.3.1.1 Britain: Royal Charter Company Politics

Having taken a firm stand against the slave trade, Britain led the drive for "free trade imperialism" in the 19th century.[70] Fearing that colonisation could quickly become a wanton burden to taxpayers if the state had to substantially invest in extraterritorial acquisitions, the British government resolutely granted royal charters which were splendidly accompanied with political rights and obligations only to corporations that proved that their earmark areas of operations were not just strategic but pivotal to British national interests.[71] For instance, considering the strategic importance of Cape Province in southern Africa and Egypt in northern Africa, Britain considered only charter applications for operations that had tangible plans to protect, defend, and expand on the concessions.

To meet the qualification of a royal charter, a company ought to have been capable of conducting political relations. It was a *quid pro quo* relationship whereby commissioned corporation safeguarded British economic interests in return for gaining political protection and monopoly that ultimately translated to an exercise of sovereignty. In the following sections, I briefly explore three key royal charters representing three different regions of Africa that came under the British protectorate: west, south and east Africa. While George Goldie's Royal Niger Company (RNC) was the dominant British colonising entity across West Africa, these same functions were performed by Cecil Rhodes's British South Africa Company (BSA) in southern Africa, whereas William Mackinnon's Imperial British East Africa Company (IBEA) dominated the eastern part of the continent.

5.3.1.1.1 ROYAL NIGER COMPANY (RNC)

Following the 1884–1885 Berlin Conference, Britain in 1888 granted a royal charter to George Goldie's newly renamed Royal Niger Company, which was already conducting operations across the Niger Delta. The corporation had begun operations since 1879 as the United African Company (UAC), specialising in buying and marketing palm oil and palm kernels from African traders.[72] A profitable trade, the corporation quickly expanded especially thanks to its amalgamation through purchase of smaller British trading entities which enabled it to become the biggest British conglomerate in West Africa. RNC's agents doubled as British administrators steering trade agreements and political alliances with local leaders until Britain could amass enough resources to officially exert presence on the ground.[73] Goldie's operations successfully prevented France and Germany from having any foothold in the area, despite their quests. The UAC's hegemony in the territory saw a leap in 1884 after the company roundly defeated a French rival corporation—the *Compagnie Française de l'Afrique Equatoriale*. In 1898, upon realising that Goldie and not Britain was controlling such a big chunk of territory, France began a military expedition to annex the area; but Goldie masterfully negotiated a treaty with them, thus effectively legitimising the region for Britain.[74]

5.3.1.1.2 BRITISH SOUTH AFRICA COMPANY (BSA)

BSA was to southern Africa, and perhaps even more so, what RNC was in western Africa. As already observed, this occurrence became a reality principally thanks to Cecil Rhodes's imperial obsessions. Having amassed huge fortunes from his previous mining ventures, Rhodes appointed himself as the crusader of British expansion in southern Africa. When BSA acquired a royal charter in 1889, Britain, just as it had done with RNC, enlisted BSA to conduct independent political relations on behalf of the metropole.[75] As Britain gained political channels yet avoiding costs, BSA on its part was able to enjoy sovereign protection over its ever-growing economic concessions.

5.3.1.1.3 IMPERIAL BRITISH EAST AFRICA COMPANY (IBEA)

While RNC and BSA obtained their royal charters as a result of their tremendous influence following already accrued economic and political concessions in western and southern Africa respectively, the reverse was true for William Mackinnon's Imperial British East Africa Company (IBEA), as not only did it not meet the requirements in place for a charter but was actively elevated into a stature of influence by the British government itself.[76] The decision to award IBEA with a royal charter was a counterweight measure against aggressive German activities across eastern Africa, especially around Tanganyika and Zanzibar and their imminent inland advancements. Although IBEA, which got its charter in 1888, eventually oversaw an area of roughly 640,000 km^2 covering present-day Kenya and Uganda, Mackinnon nevertheless never enjoyed the kind of independence accorded to Goldie and Rhodes, as direct government authorities, although working hand-in-hand with IBEA, had overriding oversight over most expansion initiatives. One such government personality, and perhaps the most instrumental, was Lord Frederick Lugard (1858–1945), who doubled as IBEA representative in Uganda region. He greatly exploited existing ethnic and religious clashes in the region for his imperial advantages.[77]

According to Robinson and Gallagher, prior to European arrival, Arabs who were already dominating trade across the region had converted a cross section of the population to Islam. After war broke out in 1867 between the Muslims and the Kabaka kingdoms (Mutesa and Mwanga—that is, kings of Buganda) lasting for close to a decade, Africans who had long detested the Arabs burnt down many of their homes and chased others from the region. In the late 1880s, the Kabaka Kings (Mutesa, Mwanga, Kabalega, Bunyoro [kabalega] and Buganda) variously requested European merchants to arrange for resident missionaries into their territories, hoping that this would undermine Arab influence across the region. Anglicans, Catholics, and Baptist missionaries soon arrived in significant numbers, and the population became divided along religious lineage. Lugard exacerbated the rivalries by giving weapons to either side, thus generating a proxy war which seriously weakened the different warring fronts. In the process, he was able to institute command over all of them, although only successfully as from 1892. Two years later, Uganda was declared a British protectorate.[78]

5.3.1.2 Leopold II and the Making of Etat Indépendent du Congo *(EIC)*

Leopold II's 1876 geographical conference is remarkable for laying down the template for the civilising mission, around which concerned European powers could commit themselves towards "helping" Africans. By all intents and purposes, AIA was anything but Leopold's private organisation. He administered the *Etat Indépendent du Congo* (EIC, or Congo Free State)—the brainchild of the organisation, not as a constitutional monarch but in personal capacity as the proprietor of an economic enterprise.[79] Leopold's administration over EIC was probably one of the biggest nuances of the 19th century—namely, that another country, so to speak was practically a private company *sui generis* of an individual. With profit maximisation at the state's foundational base, the entity met all the prerequisites of a transnational corporation, with all administrative operations geared at commercial ends.[80] Leopold II dispatched expeditions to EIC not in the name of the Belgian government, but rather under the auspices of his only-on-paper associations.

Leopold's reign was characterised by massive abuses on the lives and property of local inhabitants. Following the Berlin conference which legitimated Leopold's acquisitions, one of his first acts was to decree ivory and rubber trades as exclusive state monopolies.[81] Trading licences were thoroughly screened and dished out principally to expand trade in the region as well as meet the augmented demands of ivory and rubber. To that end, a brutal force dubbed *Force Publique* was formed specifically to facilitate the exploitation of the region.[82] Authorised corporations in the region were to be accountable to no one else but the king.

Right from the onset, Leopold II never seemed to envisage a colony in the true sense of the word, much less one for Belgium. It is suspected that what he wanted was a private overseas enterprise with no affiliation to the Belgian state or territorial sovereignty.[83] The Belgian state was actually one of the last states in Europe beside Turkey to recognize EIC. It is generally understood that Belgium feared that openly recognising the state would trigger financial responsibility. But in reality, Leopold II deliberately created the sensation that it was imperative for him to bear the troubles of EIC personally, thus discarding it from becoming a burden to Belgian taxpayers.[84] This seemed to be his strategy all along, especially from 1876 right up to the Berlin conference of 1884–1885 during the formative days of the corporate state as evidenced by his bogus self-fulfilling "international" associations. Given that Leopold II, as a private monarch of the entity, was supposedly bound to finance the operations of the state solely from his personal fortune, this became a natural recipe to enslave the Congolese indigenes. The brutality of EIC administration will be examined more explicitly in Chapter 6.

5.3.1.3 France: Direct Government Annexation

Unlike other European powers, France was not a big advocate of company politics. Most French expansionist annexations across Africa were carried out with direct government involvement—French corporations playing only a limited role. In fact, the most effective French corporations in sub-Saharan Africa were formed only after effective French colonization.[85] There were three prominent types of French companies: government conglomerates, commercial houses, and independent private initiatives.[86] With the French government typically not relinquishing political power to its trading transnational corporations, the latter depended largely on the former's colonial military apparatus for protection, security, free trade, and fair trade policies.[87] Such was the case, for instance, with *Société Victor Régis* operating around Dahomey in the palm oil trade. French corporations that had secured numerous trading posts such as Arthur Verdier were engulfed into the French colonial administration, rather than accorded sovereign powers to administer territories.[88]

5.3.1.4 Germany: Charter Reenactment Politics

Germany was in a totally different place as opposed to other European powers at the dawn of the industrial revolution. It has been observed that following the defeat of French troops under Napoleon III in 1870, fragmented German states united into one nation state in 1871 under the German Empire, and as a consequence, the country was more focused on creating national consciousness rather than on imperial quests.[89] The government initially vehemently rejected any colonial prospects under the rationale that since colonial quests were solely driven by commercial activities, any such drive must remain the exclusive reserve of private corporations and not state policy.[90] The attitude of its chancellor, Otto von Bismarck, in particular towards colonies was that keeping them was bound to involve high cost in administration, and considering that Africa was such an unchartered space and thus too high a risk, colonisation could possibly be economically unprofitable for the German populace.[91] Although Bismarck openly opposed formal colonisation, he nevertheless remained an avowed champion of private actors' incursions, encouraging German firms to compete and uncover potential treasures in the African interiors.

With unification having generated a whole new set of economic crises, it is the overemphasis on pan-Germanism that eventually, ironically, inspired the country to seek colonies in Africa to address domestic woes.[92] To that effect, commercial associations were born throughout Germany to articulate a framework for explorations in Africa—the likes of *The German Colonisation Society*

(1873), *The German African Society* (1876), and the *Deutsche Kolonialverein* (1882).[93] A number of German merchants in Africa were busy buying lands and signing treaties with African rulers, such as Carl Peters who secured a parcel of land close to 60,000 square miles in East Africa, and Adolf Lüderitz who procured a similar vast chunk at Angra Pequena (Namibia) in 1882—both hoisting the German flags in those territories.[94]

Having arrived late on the colonial scene, Germany had the luxury of first evaluating prior approaches employed by other rival powers before deciding on how best to formulate its own sound and workable annexation policy. Bismarck evaluated but considered the French policy of direct control as unnecessarily expensive, preferring the British model of charter company politics, which he found not only to be ideal but most importantly allowed the government to greatly minimise costs. While laying out his official policy for colonisation, Bismarck made it clear that the entire venture was an economic undertaking—and that the principal objective was for the establishment of "*entrepôts* for German manufacturers, and to insure to these manufacturers free access to new markets."[95] The government's role, he contended, ought to be one of providing a political and diplomatic cover for its private investors. The Woerman Corporation, headed by Adolf Woerman and based between central and West Africa, cautiously accepted the responsibility of fostering German colonial ambitions when in 1884 he reached an entente with coastal kings around Duala, establishing basis and posts for an imminent German colony in Cameroon.[96] However, Woerman preferred direct imperial authority by the German government, rejecting any possibility of the firm playing any independent political or sovereign roles.

Along the east coasts of the continent where German firms were more entrenched, such as the Hansing and O'Swald firms, Bismarck formed the *Deutsche Ostafrikanische Gesellschaft* (German East Africa Company; DOAG) as a chartered colonial organisation under the direction of Hermann von Wissmann and Carl Peters, to effectuate the annexations of what became Tanganyika, Zanzibar, Rwanda, and Burundi.[97] Considering the German lateness on the colonial scene, DOAG was empowered with wide-ranging political and administrative powers; whereupon it began entertaining hasty treaties on behalf of the German state.[98] Although DOAG succeeded in establishing few stations in the earmarked areas and warding off rivals, in actuality it achieved quite little and was never a viable force, mostly operating at a loss.[99]

5.3.2 Limitation of Non-State Actors as Sovereign Entities

European non-state actors achieved their broad goals in host states in the 19th century, by directly tying their interests to the needs of their home states. The prominence and domination of non-state actors instead of state actors in driving international relations—as evidenced with the scramble for Africa—without doubt foreshadowed new developments in the realm of international law making. While sovereign acts of non-state actors were noteworthy in host states, their resolve to solicit the canopy of their home states' governments in many regards proved their limitation as veritable actors of international law and international relations. They were neither able to fully exercise nor demonstrated capability of sustaining everlasting monopoly over territories under their control, until European states stepped in and instituted colonial protectorates. As one scholar has noted, "where business corporations have exercised an influence over political developments, they have tended to do so as instruments of their home governments rather than as independent actors."[100] It is deduced that by engaging their home governments, non-state actors presented themselves as instruments for the realisation of states' interests, rather than independent political actors in their own rights. Hence, private foreign policies as conducted by non-state actors in the 19th century had limited relevance except when they were ratified or endorsed by state actors. This begs the question whether the numerous cession treaties, which these entities entertained with African rulers, were legal and binding in international law.

5.4 Nineteenth-Century Cession Treaties with African Rulers and Ambivalence of International Law

Having embarked on settlement colonisation since the 16th century, Europeans steadily resorted to legitimating their presence in foreign lands by imposing treaties on non-European trading parties. With treaty clauses frequently drawn by European settlers, the said agreements were habitually unequal and unfair to the non-European contracting parties.[101] While the encounter between Europe and Africa in the 19th century was guided by positivist international law, the binding force of their relations were imbued in legal instruments variously dubbed as cession or capitulation treaties.[102] An examination of contractual agreements reached between European merchants and African rulers is crucial, given that these agreements in due time became the primary legitimating devises for colonial expansion. The new arrangements severely denigrated and downgraded the authority of rulers and political institutions on the African continent. Given the character of the contracting parties (African chiefs, European corporations, traders, explorers, etc.)—all of whom were considered by positivist international law as non-sovereigns—and the asymmetric imbalance between them, one is bound to be confronted with a series of pertinent questions. For instance, were the treaties binding? What was the process of bargaining, and what was the legal capacity of chiefs to entertain them? African rulers were projected by Europeans initiating the treaties as title holders of territories. Was this a true or false narrative?

5.4.1 Were the Treaties Binding? What Was the Bargaining Process?

International lawyers have habitually called to question the legality of European-African cession treaties in the 19th century, given the conceptual ambiguity that characterised these agreements, as well as the instruments' unconventional provisions. The debates have typically ranged from the legal personality of the signatories, to the authenticity of the documents and the scope of their territorial application—where authors have deemed the agreements to be valid legal instruments. Central to these questions is the desire to ascertain the legal character of the treaties. In the landmark *Cameroon vs. Nigeria* Bakassi Maritime boundary case, which centred on the merits of pre-colonial agreements between African local rulers and Europeans, the International Court of Justice (ICJ) ruled that the agreements did not qualify as treaties, for African political entities were not judged to be states at the time under international law.[103] The court seemed to have based its judgment on the meaning of treaties as embodied in Articles 51 and 52 of the Vienna Convention on the Law of Treaties, 1969—which envisages treaties between state entities—and invalidates any agreement that is grounded on coercion or duress.[104]

While the ICJ ruling in *Cameroon vs. Nigeria* case was clearly in line with the Vienna Convention on the Law of Treaties, the agreements between African rulers and Europeans that were central to the case were nonetheless entertained over eight decades before the Vienna Convention. Judge Max Huber ruled in the Permanent Court of Arbitration *Island of Palmas* case (1928) that "a judicial fact [of an agreement] must be appreciated in the light of the law contemporary with it," and not the law or doctrine in place at the time when the dispute arises.[105] Academics have indeed tended to dismiss 19th-century cession treaties based on other international law standards rather than the Vienna Convention. Relying on the standard of civilisation, international law at the dawn of the 19th century, as observed in Chapter 4, decisively perceived African political collectivities as lacking civilisation requirements to be sovereign states. Placed outside of the family of nations, African political entities accordingly lacked the capacity to entertain legally binding treaties in international law.

While Westlake's measure of the standard of civilisation was based on a society's ability to realize mass commodity production, William Edward Hall and Henry Wheaton settled on Christianity as the barometer for newcomers to be admitted to the family of nations.[106] For them, African political entities failed to meet either test. The treaties in question for the most part fell short of all these requirements. For these authors, the obligations and duties of the treaties were purely moral, not legal. Westlake in particular pointedly rejected cession treaties with African rulers as of no legal value, since "uncivilised" peoples to him—having no knowledge of the complex concepts of treaties and sovereignty—could by analogy not cede away the same thing that they had no knowledge of.[107] For authors that shared this belief, the agreements were mere "scraps of papers which neither imposed legal obligations nor conferred any rights."[108]

While the treaties for Westlake, W. E. Hall and Henry Wheaton, were technically not binding at the time of conclusion based on these shortcomings, they nevertheless acquired legal force over the years as a consequence of *fait accompli* (that is, reality on the ground).

International law habitually underscores territorial sovereignty as one of the key rights and duties of states—with every recognised collectivity enjoying political independence and freedom from external intervention. Based on the legal sanctity of territorial integrity, any European appropriation of lands in Africa for it to be legitimate was bound to be acquired through a contractual treaty of cession.[109] As already observed in the preceding chapter, 19th-century international lawyers devised an entirely new set of rules to colonise Africa than those that were applied in the Americas, given that African societies were already perceived to be governed by effective political organisations, and moreover as having long attained an agrarian stage of economic development. Although African rulers were also perceived as exercising "sovereign" authority[110] within their territories, political entities in Africa were nevertheless still habitually deemed as falling short of European standards for "civilised nations."

In *The Helena case* (1801), where Algerian authorities seized a European vessel along their shores and subsequently sold it to a different buyer, the English High Court of Admiralty, in its quest to establish whether it belonged to the original owner or the eventual buyer from Algerian authorities, posed and addressed the question whether the seizure was an act of piracy or had been carried out by a competent juridical authority. According to Judge William Scott:

> Certain it is that the African states were not considered many years ago, but have long acquired the character of established governments, with whom we have regular treaties, acknowledging and confirming to them the relations of legal states. ... Although their notions of justice, to be observed between the nations, differ from those which we have entertained, we do not on that account venture to call in question their public acts.[111]

In spite of Judge Scott's affirmation of the sovereignty of Algeria, the case was an aberration rather than a trend in European perception of African political entities. It is not obvious from the judge's ruling whether this standard applied mainly to North Africa or to the entire continent, considering that European relations with sub-Saharan Africa prior to this were mostly limited to the coasts.

Infamously dubbed as treaties of friendship and protection, the cession agreements purported to prove that land titles were legitimately acquired, and further that Africans were happily waiving away their rights to property because they longed to be incorporated into the community of nations so as to enjoy the blessings of civilisation. This notwithstanding the fact that the consent and free will of African rulers was for the most part obtained either through fraud, duress, or coercive measures; or in some cases, a combination of coercion and inducements. The aforementioned cases of loss of territories by King Lobengula of Matebele and Lewanika and King of Lozi in Zambezi vividly reveals how Cecil Rhodes in each case, robbed them of their lands using purely fraudulent "treaties." The trend was the rule rather than the exception amongst European explorers extracting the treaties across sub-Saharan Africa. It has been observed that interpreters—carefully employed by the corporations—were deliberately often dishonest with their translations. They used coded words such as "cede", "waiver", etc but explained them lightly to the rulers as "renting land" to hide the real mission of the deals.[112] Because of the technicality and coded rhetoric of the treaty language, it is all the more obvious that the rulers were deliberately kept in total darkness as to their intended scope and reach.

The lapses notwithstanding, cession treaties—duly contracted between African rulers and European entities—without doubt amounted to bilateral contractual agreements. However unjust the treaties may have been, the content of many of the agreements insinuated some degree of dialogue between contracting parties. Was this single fact sufficient to elevate the agreements to the level of *traités-lois*—that is, binding treaties (including general application)? Whether the bilateralism in the treaties amounted to a logical entente is a totally different thing. Be it as it may, the sanctity of the treaties nonetheless remains questionable, given that the agreements were typically initiated using gunboat diplomacy. Although many African rulers signed the treaties, many understood them solely as agreements for friendship and protection. Others recognised that explorers were according to the treaties authorised to "dig" limited parts of their soils for the extraction of minerals, but without any incursion or interference onto the lives of the populace. In either case, African rulers for the most part did not have say or leeway with respect to the treaty clauses.

In *Prelude to the Partition of West Africa* (1963), John D. Hargreaves contended that African-European relations at the dawn of the 19th century were partly driven by insecurity problems across Africa, with the concern paving the way for the proliferation of cession treaties.[113] Hargreaves's contention is grounded on the security challenges that afflicted sub-Saharan Africa, following the solidification of the slave trade as a mode of production. The economic climate in effect rendered African environments very unsafe right up till the 19th century. It was an age of endless conflicts and wars throughout sub-Saharan Africa, as various kingdoms invaded one another, subdued them, and captured prisoners of war purposely to market them in the slave trade. There seemed to be no end in sight. Faced with these security challenges, African rulers found themselves between a rock and a hard place, with rulers of communities facing imminent danger genuinely interested in the protection aspects of the treaties as a firewall, not just against enemy attacks but as a shield for political survival, as well. Thus, the more restless a place, the more willing its leaders were to entertain the treaties, for it was better for the White man to guarantee them protection—whether this eventually materialised or not—than be spinelessly susceptible to the anarchy of slave raids.[114]

In fact, the explorers, backed by armed militias, often announced their imminent arrival in advance, visiting the rulers' palaces on the appointed date with a contract already written out. The rulers were made to understand that if they refused to sign, their rival neighbours and other groupings would undoubtedly sign, thus benefiting from European protection.[115] It was accordingly understood that kingdoms that refused to sign were accordingly bound to become vulnerable to attacks. On the other hand, they would automatically enjoy a superior warring advantage in their region if they signed, as European militia would supply them with firearms and even fight for them if anyone ever attacked them. It is commonly understood that the mere threat of invasion by company militias forced many rulers to adhere to the treaties. While there is a gist of truth to this, in fact, the corporations avoided the use of force as much as possible, as each war was not just an unnecessary distraction from the pursuit of more territorial gains elsewhere, but moreover a plunder to already-gotten political and economic capital. In fact, "cession" treaties by nature were envisaged as a pacific approach to annexation, without warfare and the costly consequences that this could have entailed.[116]

While cession agreements were veritable bilateral agreements between the signatories; many academics—the likes of Mark Frank Lindley, George Peabody Gooch, and Harold Temperley—have observed that in practice, they were principally destined for rival European powers (and not the African signatories), to support effective rights over territorial claims.[117] As a result, in pre-emption against future disputes, maximum precaution was always taken to give the agreements the coloration of genuineness beyond reasonable doubt. In the event of disputes, the European party with a better claim was bound to become the rightful proprietor over territory. Having accrued rights through the agreements, however faulty these were, the instruments became a huge bargaining advantage between rival Europeans, especially when they were trying to exchange territory for expediency.[118] In *Souveraineté Territoriale par Traité*, Mamadou Hébie has observed that cession treaties between Europeans and non-European entities attained their utmost relevance not through adherence to prevailing international law, but rather as a consequence of their propensity for international law making, in situations where no clear legal rules previously applied.[119]

Despite the gunboat diplomacy nature of the treaties, many African rulers who participated in the treaties, so to speak, were nonetheless not just active participants in the ordeal, but others even had their own dubious agenda for personal gains. Even if the contextual meaning was beyond the comprehension of the rulers (as was often the case), the same was not true for the tacit implication of the treaties. Without doubt, African rulers understood that by affixing their signatures on a piece of paper brought forth by the Europeans, they were effectively either entering into an agreement for a new kind of relationship (where none existed before) or a different kind of relationship other than the one they had before (where the two parties already had some acquaintance).[120] Other dubious rulers motivated by personal gains on their part knew fully well that the whole shady atmosphere of the treaties, inducements, and even bribes—all finalised in solemn ceremonies—could not mean anything else except fraud, although it would forever remain doubtful as to how far they understood the extent of the fraud. This latter category of rulers marked a stark distinction with many others such as the Chief of Mohsi in Upper Volta, Khama I of Bechuanaland in southern Africa, the kings of Kosoko and Fante and Prempeh I of Asante (all in West Africa) who resisted or outrightly rejected the agreements either in part or in whole; opting to trade with anyone who stepped up to buy their commodities, entertain friendship with them, or offer better commercial bargains.[121] Despite the resistance, they were crushingly invaded anyway in military confrontations, brought under the British Empire in due course and replaced by puppets.

Theoretically, humanitarianism was front and centre in the treaties by virtue of the protection clauses. It has been observed that some African rulers such as the Mandara and Yoruba kingdoms entertained the treaties solely to preserve the political status quo and balance of power with their neighbours, and in the case of Buganda as an instrument to extend their absolute influence in the region.[122] Although European corporations were more concerned in protecting their business interests, the mere presence of the protection clause in the treaties was vital in importance whereupon any disputes arose. For Alexandrowicz, the unconventional nature of cession treaties does not in any way suggest that the agreements were illegal under international law. To him, "the very fact that the ruler's powers were capable of being limited in international law, must be considered evidence of the fact that he had the powers to make treaties, maintain foreign relations, cede territory and go to war."[123]

In "Treaty-Making in Africa" (1893), Frederick Lugard stated that European signatories typically justified their territorial claims on two counts, to wit: (1) that a treaty with a local leader had ceded rights to them; and (2) that the corporation had become morally and legally bound to protect the said African peoples and could not in good faith renege on that obligation.[124] The claim that Africans had entrusted their well-being on a given corporation for which it was bent on acting well on specific treaty pledges, at least at face value, showed a spirited commitment toward Africans. The new pledge in practical terms was nonetheless as hypocritical as it was misleading. For the most part, most Europeans did not intend to honour even the most generous parts of the agreements, as long as only the interest of Africans were at stake. For instance, Saadia Touval has cited a case of an African chief in the Gold Coast who signed one such treaty with a British corporation. After he was attacked, he invited protection, but the corporation ignored him, took advantage of the crisis, and instead shared the land between itself and a French corporation, the latter incorporating the new gotten land into its Togo concession.[125] The discarded ruler wrote to the English queen complaining, but the plea was unheeded.

European inducements ranging from provision of firearms, articles, and construction of a modern house, to a monthly allowance and military protection, in exchange for the treaties typically varied depending on the toughness of the chiefs, the usefulness of the land, and the degree of rivalry by the competitors. Some chiefs such as Lobengula signed double treaties with different companies especially where they were highly solicited, to play the Europeans against each other, knowing that in the event of an attack from a fellow African tribe, one or both of the corporations was going to step up and fight for them.[126] One African ruler who actually benefitted from European protection was the emir of Benoue—the French who had earlier signed a treaty with him fought on his side, not only defeating neighbouring tribes but moreover again helped him prevent an imminent invasion by Sir George Goldie's Royal Niger Company.[127] As Hébié has noted, some agreements amongst colonial powers specifically contained clauses prohibiting all forms of attacks against the independence and territorial sovereignty of some local political entities.[128] Such was the case with the 1862 agreement between France and Britain committing to preserving the sovereignty of the Sultanate of Zanzibar.

The decision whether or not to invoke the treaties during disputes was always dependent on the whims of Europeans.[129] In the same light, the decision to annex, divide, or even delimit a territory was the sole judgement of corporate entities. A signatory European corporation typically used the instrument as a pretext to overstretch its reach to cover all adjacent territories that had nothing to do with the initial treaty. This was aided by the open-ended treaty provisions, which practically enabled the corporations to do as they found fit. This notwithstanding that many adjacent communities to those that signed the treaties were sometimes communities with no traditional or cultural connection with each other. This explains why, unlike any other continent, over 35% of African borders follow straight lines—a clear evidence of colonial disregard of local needs and indigenous socio-political and cultural circumstances. The remaining 65% of the borders variously follow geographical landmarks and features.[130]

5.4.2 Were African Rulers Title Holders of Territories?

African cession treaties were strikingly similar in their political and economic overtones, regardless of which European nationals or corporations initiated them. Typically, Africans surrendered property and territorial rights, and European merchants stepped into their shoes assuming an exclusive monopoly in to the exclusion of all other Europeans or companies. Claims by signatory European merchants that African rulers were legitimate title holders of territories with ascendant rights to transfer property rights had no factual merits. To illustrate this, I firstly examine the conception of sovereignty and territorial rights in three separate treaties: in two instances where treaties were solely drafted by the companies, and in a third instance where an African ruler was able to opine on both elements (sovereignty and territorial rights) within the framework of customary law limits bestowed on his authority. I also examine what real value European signatories attached to the agreements by revisiting their own statements and confessions in the immediate aftermath of securing the treaties.

Companies typically enacted the treaties using standardised forms, wrote down the terms of agreement, and translated the documents to the chiefs—the latter's role becoming not much else except to append their signatures.[131] The standard form used by the Royal Niger Company read in part thus: "[I the Chief] hereby give to the company and its assigns, forever, full jurisdiction of every kind."[132] The witness column read in part thus:

> We the undersigned are witnesses to the marks (i.e., signatures) of the [chiefs] and also vouch for their understanding what they have signed ... [We] do hereby declare that the foregoing agreement was duly and correctly explained to the [chiefs] and they fully understand it.[133]

Henry Morton Stanley, acting on behalf of Leopold II, exhibited a very similar trend in his treaty with the kings and chiefs of Ngombi and Mafela. The terms of agreement read thus:

> **Article 1**. The chiefs of Ngombi and Mafela recognize that it is highly desirable that the International African Association should, for the advancement of civilization and trade, be firmly established in their country. They, therefore now, freely of their own accord, for themselves and their heirs and successors for ever, do give up to the said Association the sovereignty and all sovereign and governing rights to all their territories. They also promise to assist the said association in its work of governing and civilizing this country, and to use their influence with all the other inhabitants, with whose unanimous approval they make this treaty, to secure obedience to all laws made by the said association, and to assist by labor or otherwise, any works, improvements, or expeditions which the said association shall cause at any time to be carried out in any part of these territories.
>
> **Article 2**. The chiefs of Ngombi and Mafela promise at all times to join their forces with those of the said Association, to resist the forcible intrusion or repulse the attacks of foreigners of any nationality or color.
>
> **Article 3**. ... [The chiefs] ... solemnly affirm that all this country belongs to them; that they can freely dispose of it; and that they neither have already, nor will on any future occasion, make any treaties, grants, or sales of any parts of these territories to strangers without the permission of the said Association. All roads and waterways running through this country, the right of collecting tolls on the same, and all game, fishing, mining, and forest rights, are to be the absolute property of the said association, together with any unoccupied lands as may at any time hereafter be chosen.
>
> The International African Association agree to pay to the chiefs ... the following articles of merchandise, namely, one piece of cloth per month to each of the undersigned chiefs ...; and the said chiefs hereby acknowledge to accept this bounty and monthly subsidy in full settlement of all their claims on the said Association.[134]

Discrepancies were quickly noticed in cases where African rulers were given the leeway to contribute to the treaty provisions (a rare privilege), as was the case for example with the phraseology of the treaty with a Gambian chief who clearly stated that he did not have competence to sell the territory, instead affirming that proprietary rights rested with ancestors and for all.[135] This is in direct contrast to the model company clause which, Edward Hertslet has noted, often read thus: "All sovereignty of the before specified territory is now vested in the said king."[136] The example of the Gambian ruler mirrors well with the prevailing tradition in a number of western Africa communities at the time where power was not centralised but administered by a council of elders, with the king's role just one of first amongst equals.[137]

Another evidence that African rulers were leaders and not title holders of territories can be gleaned from the real value European signatories attached to the agreements, as evidenced by statements and confessions which they made in the immediate aftermath of securing the treaties. Frederick Lugard was without doubt one of the leading collectors of cession agreements. Although a relatively unknown personality when he served as the colonial governor of Hong Kong (1907–1912), Lugard nevertheless enjoyed stardom in Britain both during and after his later tenure between 1914 and 1919 as the colonial governor general of Nigeria, firstly for successfully amalgamating different parts of the Niger area into one country, but most importantly for his publication *The Dual Mandate in British Tropical Africa* (1922), which afforded the ideological backbone for outsmarting rival Europeans and for a more effective, more economical Indirect Rule policy management.[138] He also stood out as the most outstanding colonial official who wrote most authoritatively and extensively on cession treaties as well as his personal experiences while conducting such agreements. He expounded two diametrically contradictory pronouncements which cannot be reconciled except by reading them side by side. On one hand, he alleged that Africans customarily took treaty-making very seriously, and their conception of the tradition was perfectly in accordance with international law traditions. On the other hand, he admitted that the whole treaty atmosphere and seriousness of it was anything but a practical joke. While in ordinary circumstances the latter statement would nullify the former, it rather illuminates the whole regime of African cession agreements.

Beginning with Lugard's first pronouncement, he claimed that Africans in fact took treaty-making and treaty terms very seriously. He professed to have found a parallel match in Africa to the international law principle of *pacta sunt servanda* in the ritual of *blood brotherhood*. He described it thus:

> When I learnt its significance, it seemed to me that I had found the nearest equivalent possible to our idea of a contract (treaty). This is the ceremony of blood brotherhood. It is held in Africa amongst … the tribes as the most solemn and binding of contracts (treaties). The rite is performed in various ways always with the utmost solemnity and impressment.[139]

What exactly was blood brotherhood? Lugard explained that it was an African ritual of oath-taking—the most binding of contracts across the continent, wherein participants literally sucked each other's blood and swore by the sword to abide to an agreement while at the same time making pledges and invoking imminent consequences that would befall anyone that dared to renege on the agreement.[140] With European merchants, the rituals necessitated that they each recite their terms of engagement—the African elites swearing that they were going to abide to the terms of agreement, whereas Europeans assured them that their mission was not to oust them from their territory but rather to trade, excavate, or protect them against from attacks by enemies. As to the significance of the sword or spear as part of the process of blood brotherhood, Lugard explained thus:

> To the savage, the most precious thing in this world or the next are his spear and his arms of war; more precious than his own skin. They are his heirlooms, his sole possession—more thought of, more cared for than his wives—they are never out of his hands by day, they lie beside him at night. His oath is sworn on these, the gods of his existence. I fancy the inference is that if he turns traitor his own arms shall turn against him.[141]

Notwithstanding that there were incidences of foul play in the conclusion of cession treaties, one immediate consequence of Lugard's blood brotherhood claim was the demonstration that Africans did understand written contracts and their nature and considered them binding. Moreover, it fosters the suggestion that *pacta sunt servanda* was in the back of the minds of both the Africans and the Europeans. Given that these claims lend cession agreements—at least on face value—a façade of good faith, it becomes vital to ascertain the honest impression of the treaty initiators. Lugard famously dismissed the treaties out of anguish, as agreements produced in "cartloads."[142] While the depiction of cartloads is clearly a figurative expression, it nonetheless evidences what value its signatories really attached to the agreements—as cosmetic rather than genuine—a form of window-dressing.

As aforementioned, European explorers and corporations predestined their cession treaties for rival fellow Europeans as theoretical evidence of acquisition of title deeds rather than contracting African parties. However, amongst fellow Europeans, they conceived any genuine reliance on the agreements as valid legal instruments, as nothing more than a real practical joke. Such honest revelations typically came to light in adjudication situations where an African ruler had signed multiple treaties with different European personalities and one or more of the cession treaties were judged to be faulty against another seen as more authentic. Such was the scenario with Lugard, whose lucrative treaty with "Lord of Borgu" of Dahomey in the Niger area was judged to be faulty in the face of a similar agreement which the French entertained a few weeks later in the same territory with King Nikki, which led to Lugard fessing up out of annoyance about the practical irrelevance of the so-called treaties.[143]

Dahomey was a relatively diversified kingdom, especially in terms of religious and traditional affiliations. While Lugard's treaty was written on a form with the letterhead "For Muslims," the French agreement led by Captain Decoeur, on the other hand, purported to be with Nikki of Borgu-Dahomey.[144] Since King Nikki himself was not a Muslim, Lugard's agreement was deemed to be faulty and invalid, despite the latter's claim that Decoeur's treaty was illegal because he had obtained it through duress. France argued that Lugard's agreement was in effect between himself and a straw chief lacking legitimacy who had showed up solely for the occasion, as evidenced by the fact that throughout the solemn ceremony, he sat behind the wall as he communicated to Lugard with the aid of an interpreter.[145]

Frustrated by his loss to the French over Dahomey, Lugard became more forthright about the veritable nature of the treaties, most especially in his diaries wondering how anyone could rationally see "treaties" in which people purportedly gave away their entire lands and every rights in exchange for protection as remotely legitimate. Reflecting on his casual treaty with Waiyaki of the Kikuyus, Lugard wrote:

> [When I presented] him a flag and explained its use, I made a treaty, but as I do not believe in the printed treaty forms of the company by which a man gives away all his land and rights of rule to the company in exchange of their "government and protection," I made out my own treaty form. This company's treaty is an utter fraud. No man if he understood would sign it, and to say that a savage chief has been told that he cedes all rights to the company in exchange for nothing is an obvious untruth. If he has been told that the company would protect him against his enemies, and share in his wars as an ally, he has been told a lie, for the corporations have no intention of doing any such thing.[146]

A possible reading of Lugard's disclosure is that although all effort was made to give cession treaties an appearance of genuineness, in reality there were more aptly just window-dressing arrangements. Lugard's disclosure was far from being an isolated event. A fellow Brit, Harry Johnston ridiculed the fact that his own jagged agreements received seriousness as legal instruments, especially the treaty with the Edadamas which was concluded in a total state of drunkenness, with the "proceedings altogether too boisterous for serious treaty making."[147]

The treaties typically neither cited any African laws nor proved that they were in accordance with African customary practices. Even if the European companies managed to procure the consent of the chiefs—which was often invalidated by the duress applied, the consent of the populace was never sought or accorded. Did African social contracts entrust their leaders with exorbitant powers to dispose of territory or do with it as the leaders found fit? Did they have any standing to mortgage not only their present proprietary rights but also that of their posterity to strangers? Judging by the behaviour and actions of the rulers during the treaties' signings, it can be deduced that the rulers themselves not only recognised that they had no such authority but moreover conducted the deals in utmost secrecy in order not to provoke the rage of the population.[148]

Lugard frankly affirmed to the lack of seriousness during the treaty-making sessions, depicting the entire scenario as one of high-level clandestineness. The agreements were signed in the presence of the chief's supposed body council of advisers, but Lugard suspected that these individuals were more often than not the chiefs' most trusted friends or relatives.[149] Such outright secrecy, if anything, evidences the chiefs' evasion of the populations they were supposed to govern—an abuse of the natural social contract. Lugard did not see this factor to be any discrediting fact, however, for according to him, "a treaty was a dual purpose instrument, it allowed the Europeans to obtain a foothold in Africa and it enabled the African communities to join the universal family of nations."[150]

In sum, to the extent that the treaties were understood as exempting private law rights of "natives," they were private law contracts. However, whereupon they were understood or intended to surrender sovereignty in any way, they became public law arrangements.

Notes

1 Mieke Van der Linden, (Wolf Legal Publishers, 2014) at 61.

2 Given the closeness of their nomenclature, the Democratic Republic of Congo (Congo Free State, also formerly known as Zaire) and the Republic of Congo are commonly distinguished by their capitals: Congo-Kinshasa and Congo-Brazzaville, respectively. No German or Portuguese empire builder is included in this preliminary examination, given that these countries (or their nationals) did not overtly and aggressively join the scramble race until the dawn or after the Berlin conference in 1884–1885.

While actions and manoeuvres of Leopold II and Cecil Rhodes were very ruthless, De Brazza on his part, despite being as much of a colonial enthusiast, nevertheless saw his operations as a veritable *mission civilisatrice*, according to which Africans were going to enjoy similar rights and treatment as any other French citizen in metropolitan France.

3 Edward Berenson, (University of California Press, 2011) at 2–3. I borrow this depiction to qualify Leopold II, Rhodes, and de Brazza. Edward Berenson however used the phrase to qualify Rhodes and five other rogue empire merchants (they will be named in the following section) that appropriated non-European societies. Only the operations of Rhodes are of interest to this chapter, given that the other five merchants were not actively involved in Africa.

4 Gayle K. Brunelle, *XLV Canadian Journal of History/Annales canadiennes d'histoire* (2010) at 689.

5 Robert I. Rotberg, (Oxford University Press, 1988) at 289.

6 While David Livingstone's role in formulating the ideological vernacular for colonisation is crucial, I have included him here only as an outsider, given that he died just before the effective scramble for Africa took place, or at least caught steam.

7 Guy Vanthemsche, (Cambridge University Press, 2012) at 53.
8 Neal Ascherson, (Allen & Unwin, 1963).
9 John de Courcy MacDonnell, (Cassell, 1905) at 93.
10 John MacDonnell, (Negro Universities Press, 1905) at 94.
11 Joseph Conrad & Robert Kimbrough, (Norton, 2006) at 119.
12 Austria, Belgium, France, Germany, Holland, Italy, Portugal, Russia, Spain, and Switzerland formed national committees, but most of them existed solely on paper. In spite of this, the international committee met once annually, mostly to re-elect Leopold II as president. The national committees were supposedly expected to craft out independent strategies in accordance with the association's goals on how to open up Central Africa.
13 Norman Robert Bennett, (Africana Publishing Company, 1975) at 88–89.
14 Jesse S. Reeves, *3 American Journal of International Law* (1909) at 103.
15 Barry Turner, (Macmillan, 2015) at 194–196.
16 Turner, *The Statesman's Yearbook 2015* at 194–196.
17 Jean Stengers, (Longman, 1972) at 249–251.
18 Roger Anstey, *37 Revue Belge de Philologie et d'Histoire* (1959) at 498.
19 Unable to win public support for his schemes, he lamented thus:

II est navrant de penser qu'avec notre exubérance de forces et de capitaux, nous ne faisons rien ... Mon rêve est de créer une société belge universelle ayant son siège à Bruxelles et qui deviendrait petit à petit pour la Chine ce que la Compagnie des Indes de Londres est devenue pour l'immense empire indoustanique.

It is heartbreaking to think even for a moment that with our exuberance of forces and capital, we can afford to do nothing ... My dream is to create a universal Belgian company with its headquarters in Brussels and which would slowly but surely become for China what the London Indian Company has been for the immense Hindustani empire.

(Roger Anstey, 'Roeykens (A.). Leopold II et l'Afrique, 1855–1880' at 498)

20 Akinrinade & Falola, 'Africa and Europe: Prelude to the Partition' at 15.
21 Galbraith, 'Gordon, Mackinnon, and Leopold' at 372.
22 James A. Casada, *141 Geographical Journal* (1975) 203–215.
23 Verney Lovett Cameron & Daniel Oliver, (Harper & Brothers, 1877); Galbraith, 'Gordon, Mackinnon, and Leopold' at 369–370.
24 Auguste Roeykens, (Académie Royale des Sciences d'Outre-Mer, 1958) at 330.
25 Martin Ewans, (Routledge Curzon, New York/ London: 2002) at 87, 102–107.
26 Galbraith, 'Gordon, Mackinnon, and Leopold' at 377.
27 Ascherson, *The King Incorporated* at 104.
28 Stephen R. Bown, (Macmillan, 2010). *See also* Brunelle, [*Book Review*] 'Merchant Kings: When Companies Ruled the World 1600–1900' at 688.
29 Brunelle, [*Book Review*] 'Merchant Kings: When Companies Ruled the World 1600–1900' at 688–689.
30 Henry Cust, 'Cecil Rhodes.' *175 The North American Review* (1902) 99–114 at 99.
31 Ian R. Phimister, *1 Journal of Southern African Studies* (1974) at 76–78; Gordon Le Sueur, (Nast & Co. 1914) at 3–5.
32 Phimister, 'Rhodes, Rhodesia and the Rand' at 74–90; Robert I. Rotberg, *42 The Journal of Imperial and Commonwealth History* (2014) at 555–556; Sandy Phan, (Teacher Created Materials, Huntington Beach, 2012) at 13.
33 *See generally*, Princess Catherine Radziwill, (Cassell & Co, 2014).
34 These were the adjectives used to depict Rhodes in: A 2012 BBC TV Documentary presented by Jeremy Paxman, *Empire* (Episode 5: Doing Good).

35 Marvin Perry, Matthew Berg, & James Krukones, (Cengage Learning, 2010) at 21; Advice Viriri & Pascah Mungwini, *3 The Journal of Pan African Studies* (2010) at 34.
36 Cf: Vladimir Lenin, (first published: 1916), New Revised Translation, (International Publishers, 1938) at 76.
37 Ian R. Phimister, *1 Journal of Southern African Studies* (1974) at 75–77, 79; J. Cobbing, *3 Rhodesian History* (1972) 77–81.
38 Deryck Marshall Schreuder, (Cambridge University Press, 1980) at 241.
39 The British protectorate extended to the entire East Africa (British East African Protectorate); however, the latter region was procured not by Rhodes but William Mackinnon through his Imperial British East Africa Company.
    Although Namibia and Tanganyika were German colonies, they later fell to British trusteeship after the Second World War, following the defeat of Germany and the confiscation of all its colonies.
40 *See* 2012 BBC TV Documentary presented by Jeremy Paxman, *Empire* (Episode 5: Doing Good).
41 Ibid
42 Ibid
43 Cecil Rhodes actually arrogantly named two territories after himself, to wit: Northern Rhodesia (Zambia) and Southern Rhodesia (Zimbabwe); both of which abandoned the name at independence for African identities. With Zambia or former Northern Rhodesia obtaining independence in 1964, the name "Rhodesia" became limited to the former Southern Rhodesia until its independence in 1980.
44 Upon annexing the region, Rhodes named the capital after the British premier at the time, Robert Arthur Talbot Gascoyne-Cecil, 3rd Marquess of Salisbury.
45 Bennett, *Africa and Europe from Roman Times to the Present* at 88–89; George N. Sanderson, (Frank Cass, 1975) at 6.
46 Marcel Dubois & Auguste Terrier, (Challamel, 1901) at 581–583.
47 Henri Brunschwig, (Librairie Armand Colin, 1963) at 159–161.
48 Dubois & Terrier, *Les Colonies Françaises* at 583; Brunschwig, (Presses Universitaires de France, 2015) at 318.
49 Leonard Woolf, (Allen and Unwin, 1920) at 42.
50 Donals Vernon McKay, 'Colonisation in the French Geographical Movement 1871–1881' *33 Geographical Review* (1943) 214–232 at 225.
51 McKay, 'Colonisation in the French Geographical Movement' at 225.
52 Clare Pettitt, (Harvard University Press, 2007).
53 Andrew C. Ross, (Bloomsbury Publishing, London/ New York: 2002) at 63–84.
54 Ross, *David Livingstone: Mission and Empire* at 63–84.
55 According to Livingstone, it took Sechele just two days to learn how to read. Within a year after that, he managed to read all the Christian literature in Livingstone's possession, all by himself. To Livingstone who was a firm believer in the usefulness of education, Sechele's accomplishment was vivid testimony of the three "C's" prospects. *See* William Garden Blaikie, (Murray, 1888) at 57–59.
56 Ross, *David Livingstone: Mission and Empire* at 63–64; Stephen Tomkins, (Oxford University Press, 2013) at 72–74.
57 Henry Morton Stanley, (Searle & Rivington, 1885); Driver, 'Henry Morton Stanley and His Critics' at 138.
58 Jeannette Eileen Jones, (University of Georgia Press, 2011) at 51.
59 Driver, 'Henry Morton Stanley and His Critics' at 162.
60 Ibid at 165.
61 Ibid at 141, 165.
62 Stephen Cooney, *6 British Journal of International Studies* (1980) at 155.
63 Arnulf Becker Lorca, *51 Harvard International Law Journal* (2010) at 479.

64 Joseph Thomson, (Mifflin & Co., 1881) at 285; Koponen, 'The Partition of Africa: A Scramble for a Mirage.' at 133.
65 John S. Galbraith, *14 Victorian Studies* (1971) 369–388 at 370.
66 Sola Akinrinade & Toyin Falola, (Croom Helm Ltd, 1986) at 10–12.
67 Sola Akinrinade & Toyin Falola, "Africa and Europe: Prelude to the Partition" at 10–12.
68 Jean Stengers, (Oxford University Press, 1988) at 229; Galbraith, 'Gordon, Mackinnon, and Leopold' at 370.
69 Akinrinade & Falola, "Africa and Europe: Prelude to the Partition" at 12.
70 Ronald Robinson & John Gallagher, *6 The Economic History Review* (1953) 1–15.
71 Frederick Pedler (Cambridge University Press, 1975) at 95–126.
72 John E. Flint, (Oxford University Press, 1960).
73 Cooney, 'Overseas Companies As Transnational Actors' at 168.
74 Robinson & Gallagher, *Africa and the Victorians* at 402–407.
75 Rotberg, *The Founder: Cecil Rhodes and the Pursuit of Power* at 289.
76 J. Forbes Munro, (Boydell Press, 2003) at 408.
77 Robinson & Gallagher, *Africa and the Victorians* at 290–300.
78 Ibid at 199–202.
79 *See* generally: Ewans, *European Atrocity, African Catastrophe: Leopold II.*
80 Ewans, *European Atrocity, African Catastrophe: Leopold II* at 116, 138–139.
81 *Etat Indépendant du Congo Bulletin Officiel,* of 3 June 1906 at 226; Ewout Frankema & Frans Buelens, (Routledge, 2013) at 90.
82 Galbraith, 'Gordon, Mackinnon, and Leopold' at 371.
83 *Etat Indépendant du Congo Bulletin Officiel,* of 3 June 1906 at 226
84 Stengers, 'King Leopold's Imperialism' at 273–275.
85 Jean Suret-Canale, (Editions Sociales, 1958) at 268–271.
86 Ibid at Chapitre 1.
87 Ibid at 19–20.
88 Paul Atger, (Université de Dakar, 1962) at 4–6.
89 John E. Flint, (Humanities Press, 1972) at 112–114.
90 Henry Ashby Turner, (Cambridge University Press, 1967) at 47.
91 Hans Ulrich Wehler, *48 Past and Present* (1970) at 128.
92 Wehler, 'Bismarck's Imperialism: 1862–1890' at 121; Klaus J. Bade, (Oxford University Press, 1988) at 122, 124.
93 Shirley G. Ardener, (Government Press, 1968) at 24.
94 William Osgood Aydelotte, *5 The Cambridge Historical Journal* (291–313) at 291–294.
95 Daniel De Leon, *1 Political Science Quarterly* (1886) at 120.
96 Cooney, 'Overseas Companies As Transnational Actors' at 174.
97 Robert Cornevin, (Cambridge University Press, 1969) at 405; Erik Grimmer-Solem, *25 German History* (2007) 313–347.
98 Henri Brunschwig, (Presses universitaires de France, 1957) at 132–137.
99 Geoff Eley, *121 The English Historical Review* (2006) 867–869.
100 Robert Gilpin, *25 International Organization* (1971) at 418.
101 Kennedy, 'The Expansion of Europe' at 334.
102 C. H. Alexandrowicz (United Nations Institute for Training and Research-UNITAR, 1975) at 61.
103 *Bakassi Penisular Cameroon vs. Nigeria* case, (2002), ICJ Reports 405, para. 205.
104 Articles 51 & 52, of the Vienna Convention on the Law of Treaties, 1969. The relevant sections read thus:

Article 51: "The expression of a State's consent to be bound by a treaty which has been procured by the coercion of its representative through acts or threats directed against him shall be without any legal effect"

52: "A treaty is void if its conclusion has been procured by the threat or use of force in violation of the principles of international law embodied in the Charter of the United Nations."

105 *Island of Palmas Case* (The Netherlands vs. USA), Award of 4 April 1928, *2 Reports of International Arbitral Awards* (1928) at 845, 898.

106 Westlake, *Chapters on the Principles of International Law* at 141–142; William Edward Hall, (Clarendon Press, 1895) at 111–118. Wheaton, *Elements of International Law* at 52–56.

107 Lassa Oppenheim (ed.), (Cambridge University Press, 1914) at 142–145.

108 John Mugambwa, 'Treaties or Scraps of Paper? A Second Look at the Legal Character of the Nineteenth Century British/African colonial agreements' *20 Comparative and International Law Journal of Southern Africa* (1987) 79–93 at 79.

109 Malcolm N. Shaw, *13 Netherlands Yearbook of International Law* (1982) at 61.

110 While the authority of African rulers over their territories was not in doubt, the societies were nonetheless not considered to be sovereign, in a Eurocentric sense.

111 (The Helena (Heslop Master) ([1801] 4 C. Rob. 3), *British International Law Cases*, 1965, vol. 3, pp. 770–771). Cf: Hébie, *Souveraineté Territoriale par Traité* at 281.

112 Saadia Touval, *7 The Journal of African History* (1966) at 282.

113 John D. Hargreaves, (Macmillan, 1963) at 3–8.

114 Touval, 'Treaties, Borders, and the Partition of Africa' at 283.

115 Mamadou Hébié, *85 British Yearbook of International Law* (2015) 21–89.

116 Charles Ghequiere Fenwick, (Appleton-Century-Croft, 1965) at 410–412.

117 Mark Frank Lindley, (Negro Press, 1969) at 176; George Peabody Gooch & Harold Temperley (eds.) (HM Stationery Office, 1932) at 140–142.

118 Touval, 'Treaties, Borders, and the Partition of Africa' at 288.

119 Hébie, *Souveraineté Territoriale par Traité*, at chapters 2–3.

120 Touval, 'Treaties, Borders, and the Partition of Africa' at 284–285.

121 Sola Akinrinade & Toyin Falola, (Croom Helm Ltd, 1986) at 26–27.

122 Andrew D. Roberts, *3 The Journal of African History* (1962) 435–450 at 441–443.

123 C. H. Alexandrowicz, (A. W. Sijthoff, 1973) at 79.

124 Frederick Lugard, *1 The Geographical Journal* (1893) 53–55 at 54.

125 Touval, 'Treaties, Borders, and the Partition of Africa' at 290.

126 Example of such rulers included Lobengula and Mogho Naba Wadogo of Mossi (he signed treaties with both the French and the British).

127 John E. Flint, (Oxford University Press, 1960) at 175–177.

128 Hébie, *Souveraineté Territoriale par Traité* at 363.

129 Lindley, *The Acquisition and Government of Backward Territory* at 176; Gooch & Temperley, *British Documents on the Origins of the War* at 140–142.

130 Touval, 'Treaties, Borders, and the Partition of Africa' at 291.

131 Edward Hertslet, *The Map of Africa by Treaty* (His Majesty Stationery Office, London: 1904) at 133–135.

132 Scott R. Pearson, 'The Economic Imperialism of the Royal Niger Company' *1 Food Research Institute Studies* (1971) 69–88 at 77. [*Emphasis mildly added*].

133 Alexandrowicz, "The Role of Treaties in the European-African Confrontation"at 48. [*Emphasis mildly added.*]

134 Stanley, *The Congo and the Founding of its Free State*' at 195–196.

135 Hertslet, *The Map of Africa by Treaty* at 6.

136 Ibid at 7, 11.

137 Examples of such kingdoms include the Yorubas and the Oyos.

138 Frederick Lugard, (W. Blackwood, 1926).

139 Frederick Lugard, (W. Blackwood and sons, London: 1893) at 33.

140 Ibid at 33–35, 579–581.
141 Lugard, 'Treaty-Making in Africa' at 54; Lugard, *The Rise of Our East African Empire* at 33–35, 579–581.
142 Frederick Lugard, (W. Blackwood, 1926) at 15.
143 *See*: Flint, *Sir George Goldie and the Making of Nigeria* at chapters 1–3.
144 Margery F. Perham, (Collins Co., 1956) at 503–511.
145 Perham, *Lugard. Part 1, Years of Adventure* at 531–541, 702; Lindley, *The Acquisition and Government of Backward Territory in International Law* at 176.
146 Margery Perham (ed.), (Faber & Faber, 1963) at 318.c [*Emphasis mildly added*]
147 Harry Hamilton Johston, *The Story of my Life* (Bobbs-Merrill Co. 1923) at 195.
148 *See*: Bruce Fetter, (University of Wisconsin Press, 1979).
149 Alexandrowicz, "The Role of Treaties in the European-African Confrontation" at 48–49.
150 Alexandrowicz, "The Role of Treaties in the European-African Confrontation" at 48.

References

A 2012 BBC TV Documentary presented by Jeremy Paxman, *Empire* (Episode 5: Doing Good). (n.d.).

Akinrinade, Sola: 'Berlin and Afro-European Relations' in Amadu Sesay (ed.), *Africa and Europe: From Partition to Interdependence or Dependence?* (Croom Helm Ltd, London/ Sydney/ Dover/ New Hampshire: 1986) 21–33.

Akinrinade, Sola & Falola, Toyin: 'Africa and Europe: Prelude to the Partition' in Amadu Sesay (ed.), *Africa and Europe: From Partition to Interdependence or Dependence?* (Croom Helm Ltd, London/Sydney/Dover, New Hampshire: 1986) 1–20.

Alexandrowicz, Charles H.: *The European-African Confrontation: A Study in Treaty-Making* (Sijthoff, Leiden: 1973).

———: 'The Role of Treaties in the European-African Confrontation in the Nineteenth Century' in A. Kodwo Mensah-Brown (ed.), *African International Legal History* (United Nations Institute for Training and Research-UNITAR, New York: 1975) 259–302.

Anstey, Roger: 'Roeykens (A.). Leopold II et l'Afrique, 1855–1880' *37 Revue Belge de Philologie et d'Histoire* (1959) 498–503.

Ardener, G. Shirley: *Eye-Witnesses to the Annexation of Cameroon 1883–1887* (Government Press, Buea: 1968).

Ascherson, Neal: *The King Incorporated: Leopold II in the Age of Trusts* (Allen & Unwin, London: 1963).

Atger, Paul: *La France en Côte-d'Ivoire de 1843 à 1893: Cinquante ans d'Hésitations Politiques et Commerciales* (Université de Dakar, Dakar: 1962).

Aydelotte, William Osgood: 'The First German Colony and Its Diplomatic Consequences' *5 The Cambridge Historical Journal* (1937) 291–313.

Bade, Klaus J.: 'Imperial Germany and West Africa: Colonial Movement, Business Interests and Bismarck's Colonial Policies' in Stig Forster, Wolfgang Mommsen & Ronald Robinson (eds.), *Bismark, Europe and Africa: The Berlin Africa Conference 1884–1885 and the Onset of the Partition* (Oxford University Press, Oxford: 1988) 21–24.

Bakassi Penisular Cameroon Vs. Nigeria Case, (2002), International Court of Justice (ICJ) Reports 405.

Bennett, Norman Robert: *Africa and Europe from Roman Times to the Present* (Africana Publishing Company, New York: 1975).
Berenson, Edward: *Heroes of Empire: Five Charismatic Men and the Conquest of Africa* (University of California Press, Berkeley: 2011).
Blaikie, William Garden: *The Personal Life of David Livingstone: Chiefly from His Unpublished Journals and Correspondence in the Possession of His Family.* (Murray, London: 1888).
Bown, R. Stephen: *Merchant Kings: When Companies Ruled the World, 1600—1900* (Macmillan, London: 2010).
Brunelle, K. Gayle: *[Book Review]* 'Merchant Kings: When Companies Ruled the World 1600–1900' *XLV Canadian Journal of History/Annales canadiennes d'histoire* (2010).
Brunschwig, Henri: *L'avènement de l'Afrique Noire: Du XIXe Siècle à Nos Jours* (Librairie Armand Colin, Paris: 1963).
———: *L'Expansion Allemande Outre-mer, du XVe à nos Jours* (Presses universitaires de France, Paris: 1957).
Cameron, Verney Lovett & Oliver, Daniel: *Across Africa. Vol. 1* (Harper & Brothers, London: 1877).
Casada, A. James: 'Verney Lovett Cameron: A Centenary Appreciation' *141 Geographical Journal* (1975) 203–215.
Cobbing, J.: 'The Unknown Fate of the Rudd Concession Rifle' *3 Rhodesian History* (1972) 77–81.
Conrad, Joseph: *Heart of Darkness* (Brighthouse, London: 1923).
Conrad, Joseph & Kimbrough, Robert: *Hear of Darkness: An Authoritative Text, Backgrounds and Sources, Criticism*, 4th edition (Norton, New York: 2006).
Cooney, Stephen: 'Overseas Companies as Transnational Actors during the European Conquest of Africa' *6 British Journal of International Studies* (1980) 154–179.
Cornevin, Robert: "The Germans in Africa before 1918" in Lewis H. Gann & Robert Cornevin (eds.), *Colonialism in Africa 1870–1960* (Cambridge University Press, Cambridge: 1969).
Cust, Henry: 'Cecil Rhodes' *175 The North American Review* (1902) 99–114.
De Courcy Macdonnell, John: *King Leopold II: His Rule in Belgium and the Congo* (Cassell, Los Angeles: 1905).
de Leon, Daniel: 'The Conference at Berlin on the West-African Question' *1 Political Science Quarterly* (1886) 103–139.
Driver, Felix: 'Henry Morton Stanley and His Critics: Geography, Exploration and Empire' *133 Past & Present* (1993) 134–166.
Dubois, Marcel & Terrier, Auguste: *Les Colonies Françaises. Un Siècle d'Expansion Coloniale* (Challamel, Paris: 1901).
Eley, Geoff: 'Carl Peters and German Imperialism, 1856–1918: A Political Biography' *121 The English Historical Review* (2006).
Etat Indépendant du Congo Bulletin Officiel, of 3 June 1906.
Ewans, Martin: *European Atrocity, African Catastrophe: Leopold II, the Congo Free State and Its Aftermath* (Routledge Curzon, New York/ London: 2002).
Fenwick, Charles Ghequiere: *International Law* (Appleton-Century-Croft, New York: 1965).
Fetter, Bruce: *Colonial Rule in Africa: Readings from Primary Sources* (University of Wisconsin Press, Wisconsin: 1979).

Flint, John: 'Chartered Companies and the Scramble for Africa' in Joseph C. Anene & Godfrey N. Brown (eds.), *Africa in the Nineteenth and Twentieth Centuries: A Handbook for Teachers and Students* (Humanities Press, London: 1972) 110–115.

———: *Sir George Goldie and the Making of Nigeria* (Oxford University Press, Oxford: 1960).

Frankema, Ewout & Buelens, Frans: *Colonial Exploitation and Economic Development: The Belgian Congo and the Netherlands Indies Compared* (Routledge, London/ New York: 2013).

Galbraith, S. John: 'Gordon, Mackinnon, and Leopold: The Scramble for Africa, 1876–84' *14 Victorian Studies* (1971) 369–388.

Gilpin, Robert: 'The Politics of Transnational Economic Relations' *25 International Organization* (1971) 398–419.

Gooch, George Peabody & Temperley, Harold William Vazeille: *British Documents on the Origins of the War, 1898–1914. Vol. 8* (HM Stationery Office, London: 1932).

Grimmer-Solem, Erik: 'The Professors' Africa: Economists, the Elections of 1907, and the Legitimation of German Imperialism' *25 German History* (2007) 313–347.

Hargreaves, D. John: *Prelude to the Partition of West Africa* (Macmillan, London: 1963).

Hébié, Mamadou: *Island of Palmas Case* (United States vs. The Netherlands), 2 U.N. Rep. International Arbitration Awards (1928).

———: *Souveraineté Territoriale par Traité : Une Étude des Accords entre Puissances Coloniales et Entités Politiques Locales* (Presses Universitaires de France, Paris: 2015a).

———: 'The Role of the Agreements Concluded with Local Political Entities in the Course of French Colonial Expansion in West Africa' *85 British Yearbook of International Law* (2015b) 21–89.

Hertslet, Edward: *The Map of Africa by Treaty*, 3 vols., 3rd edition Harrison and Sons, London: 1909).

Jones, Jeannette Eileen: *In Search of Brightest Africa: Reimagining the Dark Continent in American Culture, 1884–1936* (University of Georgia Press, Athens: 2011).

Johston, Harry Hamilton: *The Story of My Life* (Bobbs-Merrill Co., Indianapolis: 1923).

Koponen, Juhani: 'The Partition of Africa: A Scramble for a Mirage' *2 Nordic Journal of African Studies* (1993) 117–135.

Lenin, Vladimir: *Imperialism: The High-Stage of Capitalism*, (first published: 1916), New Revised Translation (International Publishers, New York: 1938).

Le Sueur, Gordon: *Cecil Rhodes: The Man and His Work* (Nast & Co., New York: 1914).

Lindley, F. Mark: *The Acquisition and Government of Backward Territory in International Law: Being a Treatise on the Law and Practice Relating to Colonial Expansion.* (Negro Universities Press, New York: 1969).

Lorca, Arnulf Becker: 'Universal International Law: Nineteenth-Century Histories of Imposition and Appropriation' *51 Harvard International Law Journal* (2010) 475–552.

Lugard, Frederick: *The Dual Mandate in British Tropical Africa* (Archon Books, Hamden: 1965)

———: *The Rise of Our East African Empire: Early Efforts in Nyasaland and Uganda* (W. Blackwood and Sons, London: 1893b).

———: 'Treaty-Making in Africa' *1 The Geographical Journal* (1893a) 53–55.

McKay, Donals Vernon: 'Colonisation in the French Geographical Movement 1871–1881' *33 Geographical Review* (1943) 214–232.
Mugambwa, John: 'Treaties or Scraps of Paper? A Second Look at the Legal Character of the Nineteenth Century British / African Colonial Agreements' *20 The Comparative and International Law Journal of Southern Africa* (1987) 79–93.
Munro, J. Forbes: *Maritime Enterprise and Empire: Sir William Mackinnon and His Business Network, 1823–93* (Boydell Press, Suffolk: 2003).
Pearson, R. Scott: 'The Economic Imperialism of the Royal Niger Company' *1 Food Research Institute Studies* (1971) 69–88.
Pedler, Frederick: 'British Planning and Private Enterprise in Colonial Africa' in Peter Duignan & L. H. Gann (eds.), *Colonialism in Africa* (Cambridge University Press, New York: 1975) 95–126.
Perham, F. Margery: *Lugard. Part 1, Years of Adventure* (Collins Co., London: 1956).
———: *The Diaries of Lord Lugard* (Faber & Faber, London: 1963).
Pettitt, Clare: *Dr. Livingstone, I Presume?: Missionaries, Journalists, Explorers, and Empire* (Harvard University Press, Boston: 2007).
Phan, Sandy: *Cecil Rhodes: The Man Who Expanded an Empire* (Teacher Created Materials, Huntington Beach, California: 2012).
Perry, Marvin, Berg, Matthew & Krukones, James: *Sources of European History: Since 1900* (Cengage Learning, Boston: 2010).
Phimister, R. Ian: 'Rhodes, Rhodesia and the Rand' *1 Journal of Southern African Studies* (1974) 74–90.
Radziwill, Princess Catherine: *Cecil Rhodes Man and Empire-Maker* (Cassell & Co., New York/ London/ Melbourne/ Toronto: 2014).
Reeves, S. Jesse: 'The Origin of the Congo Free State, Considered from the Standpoint of International Law' *3 American Journal of International Law* (1909) 99–118.
Roberts, D. Andrew: 'The Sub-Imperialism of the Baganda' *3 The Journal of African History* (1962) 435–450.
Robinson, Ronald & Gallagher, John: 'The Imperialism of Free Trade' *6 The Economic History Review* (1953) 1–15.
Roeykens, Auguste: *Leopold II et l'Afrique, 1855–1880. Essai de Synthèse et de la Mise au Point* (Académie Royale des Sciences d'Outre-Mer, Paris: 1958).
Ross, C. Andrew: *David Livingstone: Mission and Empire* (Bloomsbury Publishing, London/ New York: 2002).
Rotberg, I. Robert: *The Founder: Cecil Rhodes and the Pursuit of Power* (Oxford University Press, Oxford/ New York: 1988).
Sanderson, George N.: 'The European Partition of Africa: Origins and Dynamics' in Roland Oliver & G. N. Sanderson (eds.), *The Cambridge History of Africa, Volume 6: 1870 to 1905* (Cambridge University Press, Cambridge: 1985) 1–54.
Schreuder, Deryck Marshall: *The Scramble for Southern Africa, 1877–1895: The Politics of Partition Reappraised* (Cambridge University Press, London: 1980).
Shaw, N. Malcolm: 'Territory in International Law', *13 Netherlands Yearbook of International Law* (1982) 61–91.
Stanley, Henry Morton: *In Darkest Africa, or the Quest, Rescue and Retreat of Emin, Governor of Equatorial* (Charles Scribner, New York: 1890).
———: *The Congo and the Founding of Its Free State: A Story of Work and Exploration* (Searle & Rivington, London: 1885).

———: *Through the Dark Continent or the Sources of the Nile Around the Great Lakes of Equatorial Africa and Down the Livingstone River to the Atlantic Ocean* (Harper & Brothers, New York: 1878).

Stengers, Jean: 'King Leopold's Imperialism' in R. Owen & B. Sutcliffe (eds.), *Studies in the Theory of Imperialism* (Longman, London: 1972).

———: 'Leopold II and the Association Internationale du Congo' in Stig Forster, Wolfgang Mommsen & Ronald Robinson (eds.), *Bismarck, Europe and Africa: The Berlin Africa Conference 1884–1885 and the Onset of Partition* (Oxford University Press, Oxford: 1988) 248–276.

Suret-Canale, Jean: *L'Afrique Noire Occidentale et Centrale*, Tome I (Editions Sociales, Paris: 1958).

The Helena (Heslop Master) ([1801] 4 C. Rob. 3), *British International Law Cases*, 1965, vol. 3.

Thomson, Joseph: *To the Central African Lakes and Back: The Narrative of the Royal Geographical Society's East Central African Expedition, 1878–80. Vol. 2* (Mifflin & Co., Houghton/ London: 1881).

Tomkins, Stephen: *David Livingstone : The Unexplored Story* (Oxford University Press, Oxford: 2013).

Touval, Saadia: 'Treaties, Borders, and the Partition of Africa' *7 The Journal of African History* (1966) 279–293.

Turner, Barry: *The Statesman's Yearbook 2015: The Politics, Cultures and Economies of the World* (Macmillan, London: 2015).

Turner, Henry Ashby: 'Bismark's Imperialist Venture: Anti-British in Origin?' in Lewis H. Gann & Peter Duignan (eds.), *Colonisation in Africa 1870–1960* (Cambridge University Press, Cambridge: 1967) 121–147.

Van der Linden, Mieke: *The Acquisition of Africa: The Nature of Nineteenth-Century International Law* (Wolf Legal Publishers, Oisterwijk: 2014).

Vanthemsche, Guy: *Belgium and the Congo, 1885–1980* (Cambridge University Press, Cambridge: 2012).

Viriri, Advice & Mungwini, Pascah: 'African Cosmology and the Duality of Western Hegemony: The Search for an African Identity' *3 The Journal of Pan African Studies* (2010) 27–42.

Wehler, Hans Ulrich: 'Bismarck's Imperialism: 1862–1890' *48 Past and Present* (1970) 119–155.

Westlake, John: *Chapters in the Principles of International Law* (University of Michigan Press: Michigan, 1894).

———: *The Collected Papers on Public International Law*, Lassa Oppenheim (ed.) (Cambridge University Press, Cambridge: 1914).

Wheaton, Henry: *Elements of International Law: With a Sketch a Sketch of the History of the Science* (Carey, Lea and Blanchard: Philadelphia, 1836).

Woolf, Leonard: *Empire and Commerce in Africa, a Study in Economic Imperialism* (Allen and Unwin, London: 1920).

6 Public Law Arrangements

The Pursuit for Free Trade, the Berlin Conference 1884–1885 and the Partition of Africa

6.1 Introduction: Free Trade as a Universal Right

There is a long-standing consensus amongst academics that trade is indispensable to international relations. Given that trade, unlike war, makes nations less likely to have conflicts, constituent members of the international community are habitually admonished to tailor relations with other nations around commerce—a process that is considered to bring about substantial benefits for all concerned parties. As noted in Chapter 2, this sentiment was central to Hugo Grotius's seminal *Mare Liberum* (1609), wherein he expounded the renowned theory of the "freedom of the seas," or the "right of the Dutch to participate in the East Indian Trade."[1] In his 1748 epic work *L'Esprit des Lois* (*The Spirit of the Laws*), the French lawyer Baron de Montesquieu reaffirmed Grotius's idea with a more succinct rationale, namely that humans are naturally driven by aggressive belligerency because of the need to address the problems of scarcity and choice.[2] While Montesquieu's treatise is most renowned for the concept of separation of powers, which has become the bedrock of many constitutions the world over, it is worth noting that it also dwelled extensively on the duality of commerce and conquest as two alternatives for realising the exigencies of states. Per Montesquieu's characterisation, commerce was the trigger of *bonne moeurs*—the undisputable catalyst for the prevention of war, given that it compelled trading parties to become mutually dependent on each other, based on their various needs.[3] Robert Howse (2006) observed that the consideration of commerce compelled Montesquieu to perceive the conquest of Egypt and India by Alexander the Great of Ancient Greece as a sign of progress since it propelled trade between these three entities.[4]

As Europeans scrambled for territories in Africa at the dawn of the 19th century, the necessity to formulate new principles of free trade for the international society once more took central stage. Leopold's geographical conference (1876), which brought together prominent European geographers, explorers, merchants, publicists, and other scholars with interest in exploration of and investment in the African continent, advocated for the central coastlines and gulfs of sub-Saharan Africa to be "internationalised." This imperative was based on two-dimensional objectives: first, to enable Europeans to trade freely

DOI: 10.4324/9781003265740-6

and benefit from economic opportunities that Africa afforded; and second, to assign European nations that assumed this task the additional duty of civilising "natives" within their spheres of influence.[5] Drawing inspiration from the Danube regime—the second-longest river in Europe, dubbed as "the king of European rivers," the infamous Berlin Conference of 1884–1845 resulted in a new regime of international free trade. The Danube regime doctrine stems from centuries of fighting by European powers over the river—because of its immense utility, for its exclusive monopoly, and control by European powers. Despite the overt discords, contentious parties nevertheless managed to put aside their differences and formulate the doctrine of freedom of navigation over the watercourse in the Paris Treaty of 30 May 1814.[6] The agreement, otherwise known as open door politics, had the dual significance of paving the way for the Vienna Congress of 1815 and the Danube becoming an international waterway. Acting on the principles agreed at the Paris treaty, delegates from Great Britain, Austria, France, Portugal, Prussia, Russia, Spain, and Sweden resolved at the Vienna conference that from then on, the Danube watercourse was to "be entirely free, and shall not, in respect to commerce, be prohibited to anyone."[7]

Considering that there has been mounting debate amongst publicists on the status of the Berlin Conference in international law, this study—in an attempt to shed light on what it was actually all about and what is was not—takes a composite look at the prevailing literature and submits that there are at least three broad ways to read the proceedings of the conference of 1884–1885 and its accompanying act. Firstly, the gathering and its act can be read as a multilateral political congress aimed at formalising common economic interests of its attendees, with the eventual political mandate of protectorates a largely unintended consequence. Secondly, the conference should be seen not as intended to curb the scramble for Africa, but rather the opposite—as intended for the legitimisation of the scramble as a function of international law by codifying uniform rules—whereupon delegates could afford a "safety valve" for orderly scramble, void of "unsavoury consequences."[8] Finally, it should be understood as a forum principally intended for institution and codification of a free trade regime across Africa that could combat monopolistic practices, such that merchants, explorers, and all other actors from supposedly civilised countries could operate without interference or stumbling blocks from fellow members of the community of nations.

6.2 The Confluence between the Scramble and the Partition of Africa

European rivalries in the scramble for Africa culminated in concerns over how to institute an international free trade and navigation regime in sub-Saharan Africa that would benefit all competing countries.[9] With the intensification of rivalries, European statesmen began envisaging the need for imminent remedies to guarantee an international free trade regime and the right of passage over Africa's strategic regions. The scramble and the eventual partition of Africa were indeed two separate phases of the same economic process. While the scramble enabled European extraterritorial expansion into Africa, the partition formalised the territorial acquisitions. It has been observed that while the scramble was effectuated through aggressive competitive struggles between non-state actors, the partition on its part was a negotiated settlement by home governments of corporations as pre-emption against rivalries going out of control and the propensity of an outright conflict.[10] Although Leopold II in normal circumstances would have been easily dismissed or pushed out of rivalry with a broad brush, the protective policies of France and Portugal nonetheless made him relevant, as he in theory was willing to guarantee free trade to all nations, thus forcing other powers such as Germany and Britain to negotiate and collaborate with him. That notwithstanding, all the powers perceived him not just as weak but also as the lesser evil that could be pushed whenever the need arose.[11]

6.3 In Search of International Free Trade Remedies: Origins of the Berlin Conference

As the rivalries for the scramble for Africa intensified, Bismarck, who had assumed the function of a pragmatist, made it a duty to diffuse the tensions before there could be any miscalculations. In asserting such omnipotence at the helm of European political affairs, he was seen as playing as much to the German audience as he was to the European public.[12] He had come to the realisation that claims of rival powers simply could not be willed away or argued out of existence. For him, the best remedy to deal with European quest for control of territories across Africa and the accompanying squabbles was for the concerned parties to come together, whereupon they could forge an international settlement—backed up with a binding legal instrument.

It is observed that it was after the flopping of his initial dual proposal for partnership with other European powers to counter Britain that Bismarck resorted to the last possible card remaining in the game of power politics for an international objectification of claims to titles, namely, remedy via negotiation to render the territorial acquisitions in Africa effective in international law.[13] Following the immense success of the 1815 Congress of Vienna in pacifying European discords, international conferences suddenly became the typical instrument for conducting further European international diplomacy and regional affairs.[14] Vienna was in fact respectively followed by Aix-la-Chapelle (1818), Carlsbad (1819), Troppau (1820), Laibach (1821), Verona (1822), London (1832), and Berlin (1878). At the height of rivalries, the *Institut de Droit International* at a session in September 1883 at Munich also sought to afford a long-standing solution. In a report titled *La Question du Congo devant l'Institut de Droit International*, Gustave Moynier proposed in part that the only way the Congo could be judiciously exploited to benefit the international community was for a free trade regime with free access to all instituted all over the territory—be it over land, air, or sea.[15] The execution of outlined principles, he continued, in order to come to fruition ought to be ratified by way of an international treaty, administered under the auspices of the *Institut*. His colleague at the *Institut*, Émile Louis Victor de Laveleye, endorsed the proposition and recommended that the said mandate take the form of an international commission mirrored after the Danube commission: "*Internationaliser le Congo … serait peut-être moins facile que la neutralisation des bouches du Danube.*"[16]

While the idea of a dialogue congress beyond the *Institut* in the wake of the rivalries was first raised at a meeting in London on 27 April 1884 during a casual corridor encounter between the French and German ambassadors as both parties expressed their dissatisfaction with the Anglo-Portuguese treaty entertained just two months prior, it was private couriers between Bismarck and Baron Alphonse de Courcel, the French Ambassador to Germany, that really set the ball rolling.[17] In the first of a series of telegrams between the two in April 1884, Bismarck asked Courcel whether France could in principle support the concept of free trade over all unoccupied territories of the world not yet under the control of a recognised sovereign power.[18] On 26–27 April 1884, Courcel was invited to Bismarck's Varzin estate for discussion on a preliminary agenda for such a conference. This gathering as well as other cables between Bismarck and Jules Ferry constituted the *travaux préparatoires* of the Berlin Conference. Bismarck and Courcel settled on three key items as tentative agenda, thus[19]:

- That the meeting should rule on the effectiveness of new occupations. This was construed as a measure to limit many British annexations existing solely on paper, as well as for the examination of questionable AIC treaties which Henry Morton Stanley constantly boasted about.
- That the principle of freedom of navigation over the Congo and Niger Rivers be "based on the system of administration adopted for the Danube."
- That the principle of commercial freedom over the Congo basin firmly excludes the Gabon estuary (which also included French Congo).

Before the conference would be convened, Bismarck and Jules Ferry had rephrased the tentative agenda as freedom of commerce, dispute settlement, and the Congo question.[20] After deliberating between Paris and Berlin, both men resolved that Bismarck should host the conference at Berlin. In separate communications, Bismarck and Jules Ferry agreed on whom to invite to the conference, with a consensus arrived at on 14 countries, excluding AIC, whose sovereignty was hotly contested at the time by prominent countries and could have overshadowed the proceedings. For instance, prior to the conference, the French cabinet mockingly ridiculed Henry Morton Stanley's treaties as irrelevant agreements that at best were concluded by a private individual and not a constituted sovereign state, thus every area he had claimed in the eyes of some members of the French cabinet were still *res nullius*.[21] Belgium was, however, allowed to attend. This proved controversial, as its delegates were in practice also Leopold's official representatives.[22] Moreover, Stanley and Henry Shelton Sanford, although part of the American delegation, were two more of Leopold's proxies. The wordings of the invitations stated in part that the conference was going to dwell on the "*definition des formalités à observer pour que les occupations nouvelles sur les côtes de l'Afrique soient considérés comme effectives*."[23]

The British presence, especially from Bismarck's perspective, was expected to be a trap, as Bismarck had accused the British fictitiously attempting to institute a Monroe Doctrine of a sort in Africa.[24] Expectedly, a united stand was going to be arrived at, whereby whoever laid claims anywhere on the African continent had to prove not just legality but effectiveness as well. Accordingly, in the course of the conference, cession treaties, although just a mere scrap of papers as previously noted, would suddenly become the most treasured trophies to which any state could lay claim. Jules Ferry, while fully in support of the concept of the conference, also countered Bismarck and clearly pointed out that he did not want such a gathering to become an arena of conflict with Britain, as the latter was in a sound position to cause other difficulties for France elsewhere in the world.[25]

Cognisant of the antagonism from the other powers, and sceptical of the goals of the conference, Britain upon receiving an invitation inquired and was informed that the gathering would focus strictly on codifying "principles unanimously laid down by the jurists and judges of all lands, including England." Granville, appearing to be well satisfied, committed to the event.[26]

In between the stakes and prospects of an all-out war and the successes of 1884–1885 gathering in articulating a common framework for the protection of each other's interest across Africa, the convener of the conference, Bismarck, is said to have emerged as the most powerful statesman in Europe during the century.[27] Not since the Treaty of Paris of 1763 which ended the Seven Years' War and Third Carnatic War had any European leader been more decisive; yet in the midst of the tensions, Bismarck managed to preserve the balance of power across Europe as well as to evade an imminent war.[28]

6.4 The Conference

Variously dubbed as the "Berlin Conference," the "Berlin West African Conference," the "Berlin African Conference," or the "Congo Conference," the gathering's goals were undoubtedly as mysterious as they were controversial. When the conference kicked off on 15 November 1884—stretching all the way through 26 February 1885, communities back in Africa were going about their lives and business as usual, without any clue that thousands of miles away, across the oceans in Europe, aliens were restfully congregated in a festive mood at Bismarck's Reich Chancellery mapping out those communities' destinies and eventual fate in the international society. With representatives invited from much of the perceived civilised world, the conference from the lenses of members of the family of nations, "commanded [an] almost universal assent."[29] The majority of the delegates did not have any knowledge of actual conditions in Africa and had never even set foot over there; hence, they relied solely on the expert advice of explorers—most of which was skewed in favour of their motherlands and individual interests.[30]

Although Africa was the agenda, no African was invited.[31] Overall, the gathering and its General Act has now gone down into history as one of the most famous, most talked-about and most contentious conferences. The polemics notwithstanding, the forum without doubt was one of the most consequential moments in the history and development of international law during the century, not just for its strict diplomatic procedure but moreover for the ostensible aspirations with which the delegates conceptualised and codified international jurisprudence.[32] Not only was the conference "diplomatic in form, it was economic in fact; ostensibly international in its bearings"—its outcome accordingly bound to generate universal ramifications.[33] It legitimated the scramble for Africa as a fulfilment of international law, and helped to write a new chapter in the history of international obligations,[34] thus marking the first time ever that colonisation was codified through an international treaty as a binding legal practice for the international society. It is through this process that modern African sovereign states, institutions, and their current boundaries were born, and not surprisingly with varying repercussions. By endorsing the scramble for Africa, the Berlin Act brought to full circle the fate of cession treaties—which until then had remained the subject of contentions and speculations. It reinvigorated the spirit of the concert of Europe which obliged fellow Europeans to respect the vital interests of others, where one's own interests were not directly affected.[35] Although Africa featured as the overriding theme of the conference, the primary emphasis was first and foremost the strengthening of European international affairs.

In at least two major ways, the Berlin Conference stood out from all previous international workshops from the 18th and 19th centuries. Firstly, unlike the concert of Europe that had neither any written rules nor permanent institutions, the Berlin Conference, in the absence of an international organisation for states, arrogated for itself the role of an international Chamber of Arbitration—presenting and mandating what it perceived as orderly rules for international behaviour in Africa. It effectively became the arbiter of looming conflicts, of prior cession treaties, and the maker of binding rules and definite principles for eventual colonial occupation. Secondly, Berlin may very well have been both the first-ever international humanitarian conference and international treaty drawn up to spell out the obligations and responsibilities of the "advanced" towards the "backwards." Emerging as a testament of the civilised world's peaceful *modus vivendi* (meeting of the minds), the eventual Berlin Act enabled its signatories to maintain a unified concept of colonial legal order.[36] The conference's agenda revolved around economic, juridical, and socio-political (humanitarian) questions surrounding the dispossession of Africans of political autonomy, and in replacement incorporating their collectivities into the sovereignty of European governments.[37]

6.5 Issues at the Conference and the "General Act"

The goals of the conference were set along three cardinal points: how to effectively respond to European non-state acquisitions across Africa, the resolution of conflicting claims surrounding the Congo basin and the formalisation of annexation rules for all future acquisitions. The results of the conference were codified in a General Act—a cardinal instrument that functioned on one hand to regulate colonial operations under a doctrine of *règles uniformes*, and formal establishment of European spheres of influence on the other hand.[38] It was a maiden code for international law practice with regard to colonisation. Structured into 38 articles judiciously spaced out in seven chapters, the Act was characterised by its progressive spirit. The Act was ratified by all participants except the United States, which in protest over its lead delegate's inability to secure definite rights for "natives" asserted a reservation to subsequently accept or reject the conclusions of the conference.[39]

6.5.1 Trade and Navigation

As already observed, the paramount goal of the conference was to internationalise the key regions of Africa, notably the Congo and Niger basins, in whose terrains European rivals had a commercial stake by establishing free trade and navigation zones. It is naturally probing to ascertain why focus should be placed on these two regions, in spite of the continent's dense mast. It is assumed that this was as a result of expositions by explorers, geographers, and missionaries who had collectively certified the earmarked areas as the key to uncovering Africa's hidden treasures—as having not just the most commercial potentials but also the nucleus to every prospective trade routes and gateway into the interiors. Given this imperativeness, many conference delegates perceived these regions as the common heritage of the civilised.

The conference thus kicked off with this most crucial item, notably deliberations over a draft declaration on free trade in Central Africa, and French reservations thereto. The overriding trend amongst most attendees was making the territory a free trade zone and for it to be neutral both during war and peace times.[40] Most delegates found it very convenient to entrust that task to Leopold's AIC, as it was purportedly set up in the first place to do just that: the guarantee of fair treatment, free access, and exemption from customs duties to all nations. The idea of a neutral Congo basin was boasted by support from Belgium's established status in international law as a neutral state, thus consistent with all territories under the control of its monarch, the irony notwithstanding. These principles appeared workable for the most part during times of peace but weren't respected during the first belligerent episode—the Congo basin wasn't neutral during World War I after being attacked by Germany in 1914.[41]

Prior to the conference, AIC had disingenuously opened hitherto inaccessible territories "on the basis of unrestricted freedom of trade to everybody."[42] These were the principles that had motivated the United States to recognise the association and its flag on 22 April 1884 as that of a friendly government over African states that had willingly submitted to it for protection and their own benefit; against the backdrop of Leopold's promise of an open-door policy to American traders throughout the region.[43] In the same vein, Bismarck, in a secret treaty with Leopold II on 8 November 1884, at the very eve of the conference, also recognised AIC and its boundaries as those of a friendly state. In return, German traders were to be accorded fair treatment, and most favoured nation protection throughout AIC's territory.[44] This fitted neatly with what Bismarck had always wanted—protecting German interests overseas without having to bear the cost of administration.

In his opening speech, Bismarck proposed for participants to adopt a universal right of free trade over all the unoccupied lands of the world that were not yet under the control of any sovereign power.[45] He further informed the assembly that on a personal note, it did not matter so much for him about whichever European power eventually got hold of whichever African territory, as long as the country in question was committed to guaranteeing free trade for all others: "I only want free trade in the Congo, and I do not care which country claims sovereignty, provided that it guarantees this principle to me."[46]

France made concessions to the principle of free trade only after an exception was made to the Gabon basin on the one hand, which included its own half of the Congo, and its colonial settlements in Senegal and Guinea on the other hand. Germany's secret treaty with AIC was found to have unacceptably encroached on French rights in the Gabon basin as it extended to territories where De Brazza had signed well-acclaimed treaties. Germany reneged on its support to AIC after France agreed to extend the principle of the Congo basin to the Indian Ocean.[47]

Articles 1–3 of the General Act of the Berlin Conference specifically dealt with liberalisation of free trade in the Congo basin, converting the region into an international regime. While Article 1 provided that the "trade of all nations shall enjoy complete freedom" throughout the Congo basin, Articles 2 and 3 respectively added the following emphasis: "all flags, without distinction of nationality, shall have free access … to the coastlines, the rivers and all waters of the Congo and its tributaries"; "[Imported water shall be] subject to no other taxes than such as may be levied as fair compensation for expenditure in the interests of trade."[48]

While Germany, for instance, favoured no custom duties and tariffs, France argued that colonial administrations imperatively needed to collect taxes and transit tariffs at least sufficient enough to compensate for commercial expenses; otherwise they were going to go bankrupt.[49] Although Article 5 of the General Act guaranteed equality of treatment to all traders of all countries, with monopolies and special privileges expressly prohibited, France nevertheless objected to a *laissez-faire* customs-free open-door policy, based on the belief that owning a territory without imposing customs and tariffs was going to be tantamount to having a house without any authority over it.[50] A certain degree of custom duties and tariffs was warranted, France contended, because nations that opened up territories could achieve the goal only by incurring huge budgetary expenses.

As a corollary to the free trade regime, the second item on the agenda not surprisingly centred on freedom of navigation—a concept which, as I have already noted, was first proclaimed at the Vienna Congress of 1815, recognising the Danube and navigable waters linking states as a free domain for all including non-river nations, and these rights bound to be protected by international law. But unlike the Danube regime, Bismarck wanted freedom of navigation in Africa even over rivers that crossed only one state.[51] There was strong opposition to the idea, with the eventual consensus limited to the Congo and Niger Rivers only; in addition to rights over transit facilities, and taxes restricted to duties for services rendered. The internationalisation of these rivers and access points was to remain in place both during peacetimes and wartimes, except for the transportation of war contrabands.[52] Given that free trade was acclaimed as the inevitable catalyst to render global justice, peace, and law and order in general; the attempt at neutralising the Congo basin probably stood out as the least contentious item of the conference. The underlining provisions were contained in Articles 10, 11, and 12 of the General Act.[53]

*6.5.2 **Humanity***

Anyone who reads the proceedings of the General Act of the Berlin Conference without any *a priori* knowledge is certainly bound to be mesmerised and impressed with the fact that humanitarian considerations towards Africans occupied a prominent place in the deliberations.[54] Humanitarian articulations were grounded on the rationale that primitiveness and backwardness were not just an African problem but that of the international society at large. Being the canopy of civilised nations, international law expectedly could not be indifferent while a cross-section of humanity was under threat, for backwardness anywhere was a threat to progress everywhere. The conference was thus compelled to find solutions to the looming needs of Africans, and these were framed in the Berlin Act in terms of obligations and prohibitions. While the obligation clauses were concerned with "native" welfare and abolishment of the slave trade, the prohibitive clauses on their part involved bans on sale of firearms and liquor to Africans. Most importantly, even the determination of scope of humanitarian intervention was strictly based on elements that could advance the purposes of internationalisation and free trade and the prevention of acts seen as inimical to industrial capitalism, such as the slave trade.

*6.5.3 **Obligations***

6.5.3.1 Native Welfare

The Berlin gathering marked the first time ever that the United States participated in an international conference convened by a European power.[55] Its delegation to the conference nursed the belief that the "natives" in Africa would adore their colonisation by Europeans, as soon as they realised that the dominion over them by the White man unavoidably meant peace, economic development, and open commerce—all useful for their own welfare: "the civilization and the dominion of the white man means for them peace and freedom and the development of useful commerce, free to all the world."[56]

Article 6 charged signatories to guard over the welfare of "native" tribes, and care for their moral and material well-being.[57] Following the conference, Westlake echoed the same sentiment, affirming that "natives" ought to count themselves blessed and lucky for coming under the compassionate authority of Europeans:

> natives have on their governors more than the common claim of the governed, they have the claim of the ignorant and helpless on the enlightened and strong; and that claim is the more likely to receive justice, the freer is the position of the governors from insecurity and vexation.[58]

John A. Kasson, the lead US representative, unsuccessfully clamoured for a form of right of self-determination[59] for African "natives," having insinuated that protectorates could fulfil their stated humanitarian goals by guaranteeing, protecting, and promoting "native" rights. The voluntary consent of "natives" to come under European protection especially where they did not provoke any aggression, he contended, ought to be the minimum condition to be fulfilled for colonial occupation to be recognised as a legal fact.[60] But the conference vehemently refused to issue a statement of principle in regard to this juridical concern. In normal circumstances, this refusal would have been real scandal, given one would have expected such a request to in fact be the primary raison d'être of the conference. This is even more so because consent is not just a *grundnorm* in the discipline of international law, but pioneers of cession treaties (the immediate acts that that triggered the conference) had framed their titles as originating from consensual treaties of protection. One potentially important aspect of the adaptation of Kasson's position would have been that all the so-called cession treaties would have automatically come under scrutiny and verification, at which point many of the acquisitions would have been probably invalidated.

Consistent with his quest for "native" self-determination, Kasson in addition wanted a clear principle whereby cession treaties could become legitimate only if initiated by "natives" and not provoked by Europeans, since there was always going to be a cloud of fraud in the latter scenario.

Religion was also seen as inevitable for the salvation of "natives," with the topic featuring loosely but spot-on on the agenda. While the spread of Christianity was a foregone conclusion, the Ottoman representative also successfully appealed for religious freedom to be extended to all faiths and confessions, and not just Christianity; to which a consensus agreement was a stroke in favour of the opinion—with the whole continuum of religious freedom thus extended to missionaries from all civilised nations.[61]

6.5.3.2 Slave Trade Abolition

The most salient manifestation of humanitarianism in defence of "native" rights was the stringent commitment amongst attendees to unequivocally stamp out the slave trade, with an unprecedented manifestation of an urgent need "to exert all energies for the amelioration of the native races by suppressing the export of slaves."[62] Although the transatlantic slave trade had been formally outlawed through national and international instruments prior to the conference, it nonetheless continued unabated. Worst still, there was no abolitionist activism towards the Arab slave trade running concurrently on the continent. Thus, despite the significant presence of Arabs across Africa, especially on the eastern parts of the continent at the dawn of the Berlin Conference, the idea of an eventual peaceful co-existence with them was vehemently rejected as impossible because of their unapologetic acquiescence of the slave trade.[63]

Article 9 of the Berlin Act instituted what amounted to a new "just war" doctrine against the slave trade in conformity with international law, mandating signatory states into seeing

> that the operations, which, by sea or land, furnish slaves to trade, ought likewise to be regarded as forbidden, the Powers which do or shall exercise sovereign rights or influence in the territories forming the Conventional basin of the Congo declare that these territories may not serve as a market or means of transit for the trade in slaves, of whatever race they may be. Each of the Powers binds itself to employ all the means at its disposal for putting an end to this trade and for punishing those who engage in it.[64]

It is germane to point out that although this altruistic anti-slave trade campaign was without doubt an act of humanitarianism; it was nevertheless first and foremost driven and compelled by commercial motivations and profit margins for industrial capitalism. Borrowing a page from Eric Williams's thesis, it can be observed that with the slave trade having evolved into an economic impediment for industrialisation, it soon became obvious that the more industrialised a country was becoming, the more vocal it was in the antislavery crusade. Britain being at the helm of this index ensured that whatever agreement that was eventually reached on free trade at the very minimum guaranteed the express prohibition of slavery in general and the slave trade in particular. In a November 1884 circular to its delegates at Berlin, the British foreign office instructed them to bear the following in mind throughout the conference deliberations:

> I have, however, to direct your attention to the consideration that commercial interests should not, in the opinion of Her Majesty's Government, be looked upon as exclusively the subject of deliberation; while the opening of the Congo markets is to be desired the welfare of the

> natives should not be neglected; to them it would be no benefit, but the reverse, if freedom of commerce, unchecked by reasonable control, should degenerate into license. Her Majesty's Government trust that this would be borne in mind, and that such precautions will be adopted for the regulation of legitimate commerce as may tend to insure, as far as possible, that its introduction will confer the advantages of civilization on the natives, and extinguish such evils as the internal Slave Trade, by which their progress is at present retarded. The principle which will command the sympathy and support of Her Majesty's Government will be that of the advancement of legitimate Commerce, with security for the equality of treatment of all nations, and for the well-being of the native races.[65]

Although the slave trade abolition discourse at governmental level was increasingly gaining grounds across Britain, public discourse on the subject was still frequently at odds with the administration and the antislavery societies—many influential voices preferring a gradual tread. Sir Travers Twiss—the British legal expert at the conference—for instance opined that the abolition of the slave trade should be limited to the export of slaves based on his rationale that any infringement on the internal slave trade was going to "disorganize the social system of the natives."[66] Colonial powers with territories around the Congo basin also undertook to stringently "watch over the preservation of native tribes, and to care for the improvement of the conditions of their moral and material well-being, and to help in suppressing slavery and especially the slave trade."[67]

Despite the strong stand against the slave trade, implementation was nevertheless left to the bona fide largess of signatories. The delegates moreover deliberately decided not to elevate the slave trade to the same level of gravity as piracy, for fear that it would have rendered "slavers liable to seizure at sea irrespective of the flag they flew, thus giving the warships of all nations the right to interfere with commercial shipping."[68] In fact, the slave trade agreement was not finalised in the Berlin Act but left opened for further dialogue in the future.[69] The Brussels Agreement of 1890, for instance, was specifically convened to amend certain provisions of the Berlin Act on the slave trade, firearms, and ban on liquor.[70]

6.5.4 Prohibitions

There were two contentious prohibitions in the General Act as part of the package on humanitarianism, notably bans on sale of firearms and of liquor to Africans.

6.5.4.1 Firearms

Firearms had been very vital in the past for mercantilist capitalism, facilitating the needs and purposes of the slave trade. They enabled divisions to be fomented between communities and tribes, battles to be fought, and prisoners of war to be captured for the slave trade. Between the 16th and 19th centuries, European firearms such as muskets had become the most revered and most solicited European article amongst African elites. It is observed that they served at least three critical functions: were expedient for wars, were symbols of prestige and class, as well as for hunting and capital investments.[71] With the advent of industrial capitalism, European powers found themselves in a totally different place, given that firearms' widespread availability would have encouraged Africans to stage resistance, thus rendering conquests much harder. Accordingly, the delegates at Berlin framed the ban as a humanitarian cause with the main intent of preventing the mutual destruction of native tribes.[72]

6.5.4.2 Liquor

Given that the colonisation of Africa was framed as a civilising mission, it was argued that the possible importation or sale of liquor to Africans was bound to be a disservice to this cherished ideal, as it was going to inflame bad passions amongst "natives," thus ultimately demoralising and degrading them.[73] Leading the charge, the Missionaries and Aborigines' Protection Society condemned any such attempt as immoral, unproductive, and, more importantly as contrary not only to the spread of civilisation but also to progress and economic development.[74]

In the years following the conference, the prohibition on liquor proved to be controversial at the very least and unrealistic at best. Not only was European liquor hugely solicited amongst Africans, but it also made up for crucial administration revenue through customs duties levied on imported goods.

Holland and Germany in particular raised serious objections to the ban, as it was amongst their most externally traded items. It actually took a different convention and agreement two decades later at Brussels (1906) to impose limited restrictions on the trade, but its implementation proved grossly ineffective. Since trade naturally follows traffic in leading commercial articles, colonial powers in the aftermath of the conference quickly devised a strategy to market liquor within their protectorates without raising eyebrows by affixing high taxes on the item under the pretext that this was an attempt to prevent the demoralisation of "native" tribes.[75] Another strategy was the lowering of taxes on locally produced liquor with the attendant effect that it attracted the localisation of brewery industries and foreign direct investment. Consequently, any attempt at kowtowing to the ban would have driven commerce away from one's protectorate into territories of other powers.

6.6 Occupation, Protectorates, and Effective Occupation as Remedy for *Territorium Nullius*

For delegates at Berlin, formal colonies were an unintended outcome, the opposite of what they had wished for. The overriding desire all along was to establish commercial rather than political nation states. Not surprisingly, therefore, what became independent African nations eight decades later, during colonial times were commercial posts of the metropoles, satisfying necessary factors of production.

While exploring the politics and legality of classic transnational appropriations, Jörg Fisch noted that prior to the Berlin Conference, two methods had been in place to settle arising disputes, to wit: *a priori* demarcation and *a posteriori* demarcation.[76] Under these approaches, the determining factor was limited to respect of borders and not actual occupation itself. However, following the Berlin Conference, an entire new standard was devised: the concept of effective occupation. The latter was a policy aimed at preventing fictitious occupations especially by Britain—which had claim territories solely on paper.

The principle of effective occupation as embodied in the General Act was the most manifest outcome of the spirit of internationalism. Although a novelty, it could nevertheless indirectly trace its routes to Grotius. The indeterminacy of natural law had caused European nations to make an avalanche of limitless claims in foreign countries to the exclusion of all others, with the only recourse to disputes being the goodwill of the pope or his representatives. This is the problematic that Grotius faced when he emerged on the scene in the 17th century as a young lawyer. He made his mark by formulating what was basically a doctrine of "effective occupation" to the effect that whoever claims ownership of property must be in possession of it; otherwise, it belongs to all.[77] In *A Treatise on International Law* (1880), William Edward Hall mirrored this sentiment when he observed that discovery alone was not a sufficient legal ground to justify acquisition of territory, except where it was backed by intent and effective control.[78]

Although all the provisions of the Berlin Act were noteworthy, Chapter VI on the aforementioned principle of effective occupation, titled "Declaration Relative to the Essential Conditions to Be Observed in Order that New Occupations on the Coasts of the African Continent May Be Held to be Effective," ultimately embodied the most crucial resolve of the conference. The provisions of Articles 34 and 35 are crucial:[79]

> Article 34. Any Power which henceforth takes possession of a tract of land on the coasts of the African continent outside of its present possessions, or which, being hitherto without such possessions, shall acquire them, as well as the Power which assumes a Protectorate there, shall accompany the respective act with a notification thereof, addressed to the other Signatory Powers of the present Act, in order to enable them, if need be, to make good any claims of their own.
>
> Article 35. The Signatory Powers of the present Act recognize the obligation to insure the establishment of authority in the regions occupied by them on the coasts of the African continent sufficient to protect existing rights, and, as the case may be, freedom of trade and of transit under the conditions agreed upon.

Article 34 was explicit on squarely limiting the principle to the coasts, and inapplicable to the interiors, thus only by stretching was the Act subsequently interpreted as applying to all of Africa. Despite the ambiguity, there is nevertheless a basis for such a manoeuvre. By providing that any nation that takes possession of a coastal territory or name any such parcels of land as its protectorates, the Act was making sure that it gave European powers enough flexibility to do as they found fit. This fact has been more succinctly expressed by Jörg Fisch, who observed that Chapter VI was crucial for the Berlin Act, principally because it accorded European sovereigns a two-sided leverage. On the one hand, it depicted Africa as "*terra nullius*,"[80] but only if the colonising country deemed it that way. On the other hand, it allowed the colonising country to treat "native" rulers as sovereigns if it equally chose to do so.[81] Depending on the colonising power, realism therefore fell anywhere in between.

A closer reading of Chapter VI clearly reveals that the principle had two counts—one diplomatic and the other being effectiveness. Regarding the first count contained in Article 34, any power claiming territory was mandated to notify all the other signatories of the Berlin Act. The second count embodied in Article 35 required the occupying power to institute sufficient authority over the acclaimed territory—vibrant enough to evidence presence and apt maintenance of not just law and order, but administration of justice as well.[82]

Beneath the principle of effective occupation, another very remarkable standard as exemplified in Article 34 was the exigency of occupations to be protectorates. Hence, for appropriations to become legitimate, there was in addition the exigency for a full governmental infrastructure over the said territories. Although different European countries prior to the conference had varying legal understandings of occupations and protectorates or related concepts, Berlin managed to institute a uniform demarcation and conceptualisation around them.[83] While Germany was still in the process of articulating appropriate colonial terminologies; to the French, there was little ambiguity, as *les colonies* had long been understood to infer to *les protectorats*. Britain on the other hand was in a very different place, as the two words had diametrically different legal meanings and status. Since English law automatically applied to colonies (occupied territories) but not to protectorates, slavery for instance could be prohibited in the former but not in the latter.[84]

The conception of occupations as protectorates was very significant because whereas "occupation" per se did not mandate any duties on the occupier, a protectorate by definition, at the very minimum, imposed specific conditions on the protector. Consequently, the new standard ultimately enabled the eventuality of not just an effective administration but also the execution of the realm of humanitarian engagements agreed to at the conference.

In the ordinary meaning of the term, a protectorate would presuppose the presence of an existing state.[85] Within the realm of the Berlin Conference, the concept denoted to the exact opposite—territories deemed to constitute *territorium nullius*—the overriding consensus becoming that territories could be occupied only when conceptualised as lacking proper sovereign authority. Accordingly, 19th-century publicists habitually made a distinction between original and derivative acquisitions—the former denoting new claims and the latter former claims.[86] In its broad meaning, original acquisitions presupposed that the land in question was ownerless prior to occupation; and in its narrow meaning, that its owner was not sufficiently recognised as such at that point in time at least by international law. By contrast, there had to be a recognised former owner for derivative acquisition to occur—the act becoming legitimate only if the previous owner voluntarily escheated the property to a new owner, for instance either by sale or gift.[87] It seems to me that the difference between original and derivative acquisitions was at best a distinction without a difference, given that either way, the land finished up as *territorium nullius* at the disposal of Europeans.

The principle of effective occupation, as previously stated, was principally directed against Britain, which was fond of paper annexations, backed by its detached indirect rule policy. Britain on its part sought to reduce the scope of the principle to as meaningless as possible, and did in fact succeed to a good extent, as the standard was limited solely to new acquisitions and strictly to the coasts. In the immediate aftermath of the conference, Sir Edward Malet succinctly reported the following to the British government: "no attempt was made … to interfere with existing maxims of international law. Dangerous definitions had been avoided."[88] British fear had been that there was going to be premature demarcations if obligations were allowed to apply to the interiors of the continent.[89] Thanks to the ambiguities, it was still left for each power to ascertain the effectiveness of its occupation, with the informing of other powers being the only supervening control.[90]

6.7 Westlake and Status of Capitulation Treaties in the Aftermath of the Berlin Conference

In the preface of *Chapters on the Principles of International Law*, Westlake acknowledged a fact that became very apparent throughout the volume, namely that it was the Berlin Conference and the rules in its General Act that primarily moved him into writing the book.[91] While some consensus seemed to have emerged amongst European publicists and policy-makers over cession treaties in the aftermath of the Berlin Conference as veritable instruments of international law, Westlake, as already pointed out, sharply dissented. Although he never disputed the professed right of Europeans to annex territories in Africa, he nonetheless concluded that the conference never satisfactorily addressed the question of territorial sovereignty especially with regard to cession treaties with African rulers.

Westlake's disparity stemmed mainly from the fact that he applied a totally different test than other publicists on the conception of private property.[92] Westlake felt that most publicists had accepted that claim without qualification. That to him was a scandal given that such a consideration could have been vital in determining both duties and entitlements of a colonising state. To that effect, he found it imperative to distinguish between ***dominium*** and ***imperium***,[93] for the two notions obviously played two different yet parallel "parts in the system of acts and purposes which makes up civilized life."[94]

Eighteen principles in total, Westlake's predominant concern is perhaps most evident in the first three, to wit: (1) European civilization was the most advanced stage of achievement, privileged with rights and duties for its states and men; (2) the consent of the international society to the rules prevailing in it is the consent of the men who are the ultimate members of that society; (3) consent is binding on the conscience of men and the international society is not voluntary but necessary.[95] Although he recognised the Berlin Act as a binding legal instrument,[96] the deal breaker for him nevertheless rested with Africa's perceived failure to meet civilisational standards. As aforementioned, Westlake was adamant that the presence or absence of governance for him was really not the issue. Instead, the crucial question was whether the political institution in place could accommodate the comfort and needs of Europeans. Given that "a stream cannot arise higher than its source," capitulation treaties with African rulers were accordingly, to him, of no legal consequence.[97] A society from his vantage point needed to be civilised and governed by a sovereign in order to have any capacity to entertain treaties. Since international law perceived Africans to be uncivilised, it went without saying that they were thus categorically incapable of comprehending the complex elements of sovereignty. It is a logic which William Edward Hall comfortably corroborated, adding that the "backwards" necessarily had to join the family of nations in order to acquire the capacity to entertain treaties.[98]

In one sense, these dissenting variances, even without any alteration on the Berlin Act, were ultimately defeated by *fait accompli*. Even if that was not the case, Westlake's contentions were in fact way more imperialistic and unequivocally aggressive than the Berlin Act itself. The "inflow of the White race," he affirmed, "cannot be stopped where there is land to cultivate, ore to be mined, commerce to be developed, sport to enjoy, curiosity to be satisfied."[99] He interpreted Kasson's advocacy for more "native" rights and consent as grossly misconstrued, for, although a civilised polity ought to take precaution and treat uncivilised peoples decently; the securing of the latter's consent to him was a step too far—a negative one too, and definitely not a ground to invalidate European title to possession. "Natives'" lack of consent was at best a "good ground of objection on the part of any [other civilised] power" interested in colonial conquest, and not the other way round.[100] Furthermore, although the doctrine of effective occupation was literally limited to the coasts of the continent, Westlake contended that it was undeniably intended to be applicable over the entire African continent, based on the rationale that since Africa was still to be mapped out, the limitation was one of time, not space—that is, confined to the best-known areas at the time of the treaty:

> the rules which the African conference of Berlin laid down in Articles 34 and 35 of its General Act, though limited in their expression to the

acquisition of territory on the coasts of Africa, embody the shape which the law as to the original acquisition of title has taken under the influence of these views. Few doubt that their principles are applicable generally.[101]

6.8 Did the Berlin Conference Partition Africa or Not?

At the close of the Berlin Conference, Bismarck in his concluding remarks praised the Berlin Act as the triumph of peace over war: "you have sought for the means to withdraw a great part of the African continent from the vicissitudes of general politics, and confine the rivalry of nations to the peaceful competition of trade and industry."[102] Despite the authenticity of his claim, one question naturally still looms, namely: Did the Berlin Conference partition Africa or not? Conventional wisdom and even some reputable scholars erroneously answer this question in the affirmative. It has been shown by J. D. Hargreaves and Matthew Craven that in reality, Berlin as a conference did not partition Africa, but sparked the framework through which this occurrence was later realised in the decades that followed, through a barrage of endless bilateral negotiations and agreements.[103] Thus, while the conference was not aimed at averting the partition of Africa, it was nevertheless geared at precipitating the process through the adoption of rules bound to regulate existing and eventual territorial squabbles for the scrambling nations. To be precise, territorial disputes were not specifically dealt with at Berlin. Instead, various boundary differences were dealt with in separate bilateral agreements in later years.[104] In fact, the partition of Africa was completed only in 1914.

In the next section, I briefly highlight some of the bilateral agreements that occasioned the veritable partition of Africa post Berlin Conference.

6.9 Examples of Bilateral Agreements Leading to Partition in West and Central Africa

Given that the gulfs of West and Central Africa were prominent in the proceedings of the Berlin Conference, it is imperative to deconstruct how these regions accordingly evolved into European-style nation states. Immediately following the conference, Germany and its trusted ally, France, reached a protocol in December 1885 that resulted to the former to waiving all claims over the Guinea area to the latter. Along the same gulf, two other allies, Britain and Portugal, in May 1886 resolved their differences over what became Guinea Bissau, with Portugal henceforth certified as the territory's protector.[105] In June 1885, Britain and Germany came to an amicable agreement over their frontier between Cameroon and Nigeria set at Rio del Rey. France and Britain reached an exchange deal with France conceding the Gold Coast to Britain in August 1889, while in return, Britain surrendered all claims in Côte d'Ivoire in 1892 despite its long-standing commercial engagements in the area.[106] Leopold II on his part concluded varying treaties variously with France, Portugal, Germany, and Britain between 1885 and 1908, mapping out the full boundaries of the Congo Free State.

6.10 Colonial Global Governance in Africa: A Comparative Overview

Following the Berlin Act and a series of subsequent bilateral agreements, the de facto sovereign authority of African collectivities became formerly rested on European "protectors" who proceeded to institute protectorates.[107] Alexandrowicz has afforded the following definition for a protectorate:

> A protectorate means a split of sovereignty and its purpose is to vest in the protector rights of external sovereignty while leaving rights of internal sovereignty in the protected entity. In this way, the protector shelters another entity against the external hazards of power politics.[108]

Europeans engaged two crucial agencies, Chiefs and Middlemen, to forge a liaison between local peoples and the colonial administration. Accordingly, they became the first local auxiliaries of colonial governance. All colonial protectorates either co-opted or relied on them in varying degrees in places where they already existed. Also, new ones were created where none existed before.

Although the projected character and image of protectorates served to fulfil the international law exigencies of civilisation, Albert Sarraut, who served as the French governor of Indochina, noted that however beautifully designed any colonial policy was, it could barely escape the temptation of selfish profit-making disguised as human solidarity.[109] Colonisation was conceived not as an option but as an imperative necessity to drive the metropole economy by exporting surplus capital from the colonies.[110] In fact, one sentiment shared by all colonial powers was the belief that protectorates were worthless except when they were commercially profitable. This is not to suggest, however, that the protectorates were all the same. Far from that, they were each unique and tailored to meet other varying goals. Thus, some were clearly more humanitarian or brutal than others. To shed more light on this, it is imperative to explore the different approaches that enabled European colonial governance across the different protectorates on the continent. I limit this overview to four systems of protectorates under four different colonial powers. The chosen colonial systems are: (1) the French policy of assimilation in Senegal, (2) the British policy of Indirect Rule in Nigeria, (3) Leopold II's Company's rule in the Congo Free State, and (4) the German policy of Indirect Rule in Cameroon.

6.10.1 The French Assimilation Policy in Senegal

If ever there was a country that was radically reshaped by revolution, France would certainly meet the test. Following its popular revolution that began on 14 July 1789 with the Storming of the Bastille and lasting until 1799, France emerged with a stringent fidelity to the ideals of "*Liberté, égalité, et fraternité*."[111] These ideals were instrumental in orientating the country's domestic and international relations. They also contrasted France from other European nation states that for the most part remained typical old-fashioned monarchies. In the aftermath of the revolution, Bossy d'Anglas, who at the time was an influential French politician, proudly proclaimed that there could be only "one right way of administering; and if we have found it for [France], why should [the colonies] be deprived of it?"[112] The rationale was that rights ought to extend to everyone who was born French or who became one. To that effect, France, guided by philosophical theories such as the enlightenment impression of *bon sauvage* derived from Jean-Jacques Rousseau's writings,[113] conceived its 19th-century *mission civilisatrice* campaign not by the letter (in contradistinction with other European powers) but in the spirit of the term, and its policy in its colonies dubbed "assimilation" was one of assimilating African subjects into French identity, fraternity, and elevating them into the full ranks of French citizenship.[114]

In principle, assimilated Africans were equal with all other Frenchmen, subject to the enjoyment of equal rights under the law. Although French scholars variously celebrated French colonisation as "*la paix Française*" and "*L'oeuvre civilisatrice*,"[115] the policy nevertheless had the potential drawback of cultural assassination. Frantz Fanon and other postcolonial writers have observed that since Africans were expected first of all to abandon their African values in order to achieve assimilation, sooner or later, they began to feel not just a sense of loss, but conflict with their own identities.[116] For a good grasp into assimilation policy proper, it would be imperative to examine the application of the policy in its oldest African colony, Senegal. A country of six major ethnicities (Diola, Manding, Pulaar, Serer, Soninké, and Wolof), Senegal was the first but also the most advanced experiment of assimilation in Africa.[117] Very progressive in application, the Senegalese approach was never applied by the same measure elsewhere in Africa, until after 1945.[118] But even in the other Francophone African colonies, France exercised a high degree of acceptance and willingness to incorporate acculturated Africans.[119] It has been observed that although assimilation was projected as a badge of emancipation, to be free in this sense meant one had to unshackle oneself from Africanism.[120] After independence, many Senegalese tried very hard to reconnect with their long-lost roots. It was within this guise that the concept of *negritude* was devised by the country's first president, Léopold Sédar Senghor, as a mode of restoring the black value system and African culture that had been damaged by assimilation.[121]

6.10.1.1 Administrative Organisation in Colonial Senegal

The French protectorate system was generally one of direct administration—centralising conformity.[122] Commenting on French cession treaties, Henri Lorin, a notable French parliamentarian and advocate of direct rule in the colonies, noted thus in 1906:

> Si l'on etudie [la fortune Française placée à l'étranger], on s'aperçoit que les plus gros placements ont été faits partout en fonds d'Etat ... Or très rarement l'émission de ces emprunts a été suivie de commandes à l'industrie Française ou de concessions à notre commerce.[123]

Since colonies were geared at eventually becoming an integral part of *France d'Outre-mer*, Jules Ferry launched the French colonial policy for protectorates in Africa in 1885 by informing the French parliament that administration was going to be direct, in conformity with *droit public* and the spirit of the French Revolution.[124] Assimilation, he contended, was the only realistic way to guarantee genuine progress for all peoples. Projected as the only means for integrating "natives" into the "bosom of the big French family," the policy of assimilation had two parallel aims: (a) the psychological order, which was cultural absorption; and (b) the legal and political order, which was direct administration.[125] Overall, not only was the French colonial policy mapped out as an extension of its domestic policy; in its application, it combined elements of nationalism, commerce, and science into one single objective.[126] Thus, for years to come, the colonial policy proved to be a useful mechanism of pacifically securing African collaboration—as both the colonising and the colonised aspired to a common fatherland. Direct rule enabled Africans from different ethnic groupings to work together in everyday life thus leading to a strong sense of national consciousness.

Although France first conquered Senegal in 1659, its influence was predominantly limited to Saint-Louis and Gorée. It was not until the 19th century that the entire region came under full French control, beginning with the incorporation of two other communes, Dakar and Rufisque. These four regions were collectively known as *Les Quatre Communes*. The origins of the *Quatre Communes* can be traced to the heavy presence of French traders along the Senegalese coasts as far back as 1659. Beginning in 1817, the Saint-Louis and Gorée regions began to witness urbanisation according to European standards.[127] In 1848, the second French republic adopted a liberal colonial policy to offer each of its colonies, including Senegal, the power and right of representation in the French national assembly—with elections opened to all residents who could prove a five-year continuous residence in the communes.[128] In 1872, Senegal acquired the same municipal prerogatives as all the other French communes, that is, *communes de plein exercice*.[129]

The history of the *Quatre Communes* sheds more light into the process of French colonial policy and administration. It divulges that political and civil rights were imperatively tied to economic production and achievement. Thus, inhabitants in a locality were accepted as civilised, assimilated, and *evolués* only upon attaining an acceptable level of economic development.

Although the legal foundations of assimilation policy in Senegal were laid down in varying measures through different legislations and decrees in 1794, 1830, 1833, and 1848; it was only during the period 1871–1900 (at the climax of the manifestation of industrial capitalism) that the policy witnessed its most conscious application.[130] Prior to the 19th century, Senegalese who did not want to be assimilated simply moved out of the communes into adjacent localities. However, following the Berlin Conference, the entire basin became colonised, and people found themselves trapped with the limited choice of either submitting to French rule or relocating to neighbouring British or Portuguese territories. Most people nevertheless chose to stay under French authority, since they were generally seen as more approachable and humanitarian compared to the other Europeans.

In 1794, France, by virtue of a decree order dated *16 Pluviôse, An II*, abolished slavery throughout its overseas possessions and instead conferred basic civil liberties on the liberated subjects.[131] On 5 November 1830, France, through a new orders-in-council converted Senegal into an integral part of France—extending the *Code Civil* (French fundamental law) to be applicable over the territory. Probably because of the ambiguity of the 1830 law, a new decree of 24 April 1833 clarified the scope of rights in overseas possessions as encompassing civil and political rights to assimilated persons—which, in the case of Senegal, translated to all peoples born or living in the *Quatre Communes*.[132] Another law of 27 April 1846 expanded civil and political rights to include the right of representation, with Senegal henceforth mandated to send representatives to the national assembly in metropolitan France.[133] All adults who could prove a residency of five years in any of the communes were eligible to take part in the elections as voters. There was generally no development of core civil rights as observed in France, such as freedom of press, right of trade unions, or free speech.[134]

Upon perceiving the existence of African institutions and their customary systems of justice as undeserving of reforms and detrimental to the goals of creating one grand French fatherland driven by civilisation, France dismantled the most prevalent traditional institutions and deposed their rulers, replacing them with subservient new *chefferies* strictly answerable to the colonial administration. Even the king of Dahomey, who under the British system of indirect rule would have been an ideal collaborator, was also deposed.[135] Replaced by puppet chiefs, each deposed ruler saw his former kingdom partitioned into several small units and placed under different "native" heads—a clear divide and rule tactic. It has been observed that there were four main techniques of deposing and replacing African rulers: firstly, upon being judged or condemned for failing to observe civilisational values; secondly, upon being accused of involvement in the slave trade or other primitive acts; thirdly, by preventing the replacement of an unwanted chief by a successor after death; and finally, through physical or outright removal.[136]

The sole role of new chiefs was to function as the nominal *porte-paroles* of the colonial administration, and to execute tasks such as the collection of taxes for which they received a small annuity, the recruitment of a labour force for the colonial administration, service as messengers of French instructions, and exercising the duties of organisers of crops cultivation or other relating farming.[137] They could not therefore oversee administrative justice, punish defaulters, or control any administrative budgets. In fact, they had no authority of their own.[138]

6.10.1.2 Economic Organisation

Jules Ferry reportedly squared the African colonial project in a specific economic configuration, affirming that "Colonial policy is the daughter of industrial policy."[139] In *La Mise en Valeur des Colonies Françaises*, Albert Sarraut noted that in order for Senegal and other African colonies to be meaningful to France, they ought to exist as estates or enterprises for the French state.[140] A proponent of assimilation, Sarraut felt that there ought to be a price tag for the privilege to become French, thus he opined that the *pacte colonial* ought to be one that was going to benefit not just the colonised but the colonisers as well.[141]

In its capacity as the capital of French West Africa, Senegal became the hub for France's agricultural produce, especially peanuts, palm kernel, and cotton. Beginning in 1890, Rufisque stood out amongst the four communes as the leading agricultural producer. On its part, the strategic location of Saint-Louis meant that it commanded trade along the Senegal River, thus generating significant income for the economy through tariffs and custom duties.[142] Peanut was very valuable both as an edible delicacy and for the production of cooking oil, soap, and wax. Following the successes of agricultural schemes, a trading post was constructed in 1831 at Bekel to facilitate the penetration to adjacent lands for expansion of crops cultivation. New forts were built to coordinate commercial activities. The industrial revolution inspired the resident French governor to embark on an ambitions grand plan to annex territories from Gambia and Sudan to Bamako and Timbuktu. With the exception of Sudan, all these plans came to fruition.[143] There was very little industrial processing in Senegal, with most of the agricultural produce shipped in raw state to Marseille or Bordeaux.

The economy was sustained by extracting labour from the populace, albeit in different measures. All Senegalese outside the communes were dubbed as *indigenat* and as a result were governed by the *Code de L'Indiginat* (native code).[144] On the other hand, the inhabitants of the communes— *les originaires* or *evolués* (assimilated Africans)—were guaranteed full political, social, and economic protection. It was a quid pro quo relationship—benefits (rights) juxtaposed with responsibilities. As beneficiaries of French civilisation, *les originaires* needed to take the lead in making a series of sacrifices to justify their French citizenship. As a civil duty, all *evolués* were legally compelled to do a *prestation*, which in essence was 12 days of mandatory free labour each month to the administration, or its money equivalence (taxes).[145] *Indiginats* on their part ought to pay hut and poll tax—which was made exorbitant in order to force them to do the monetary equivalent of work for the administration or work in colonial cultivation. All of these were clear tactics to drive the population into a wage economy.

6.10.2 British Indirect Rule in Nigeria

In the aftermath of the colonial era, Britain boasted that it never went to Africa to transform Africans but rather to train and share their skills and values with the continent, in hope that Africa could one day be in a position to run not just their own communities but also economic and political institutions with the acquired tools.[146] While this is hyperbole at best, there is nonetheless a gist of truth to the assertion based on its colonial policy of indirect rule. Since this policy necessitated Britain to keep most African political institutions intact, indigenes in British colonies naturally became more assertive at independence compared with those from other European colonies. This outcome was nevertheless a pure unintended occurrence. The policy from inception was devised as an efficient way of engaging "natives" and saving administrative costs so that they did not become a burden to British taxpayers, while at the same time bringing vast areas of Africa under British rule for the satisfaction of national economic needs. The reliance on chiefs and chosen elites for the execution of vital tasks of "native" administration tacitly meant that the latter considerably acquired noteworthy managerial skills.

Following the British acquisition of vast territories both before and after the Berlin Conference by the Royal Niger Company (RNC) of George Goldie, the drive to institute a protectorate in the region was met with the challenge of framing an administrative policy that could unify the different ethnicities, save cost, and guarantee the rule of law and order while also safeguarding British economic and political pursuits. It is within these considerations that indirect rule was conceived as the most appropriate colonial policy, which from Britain's vantage point was going to do dual justice to both the colonial administration and the Africans as well.[147] The territory later came to be known as Nigeria.

The British protectorate of Nigeria officially began in 1885 with the establishment of the British Oil Protectorate, which by analogy effectively ended the political sovereignty of Delta states and surrounding collectivities.[148] The very name Nigeria evidenced the economic relevance of the country to British industrial economy. The location of the territory is still the subject of anyone's guess in the British metropolitan reading public; the name was coined by Flora Shaw, the wife of the pioneer governor of the new country in 1897, in an op-ed for *The Times*, to depict the geographical and jurisdictional location of the Royal Niger Company—an area which hitherto had been referred to by various titles, including the Niger Empire, the Niger Sudan, the Central Sudan, and the Hausa Territories.[149] Nigeria thus simply meant the Niger Area—an attempt to put face to the unknown.

What was indirect rule? Going by its nomenclature, it was the exact opposite of direct rule. It was a policy that consisted of identifying influential local leaders and traditional structures and configuring them to execute colonial directives over the population. It also involved creating chiefs and tribes in areas where none existed.[150] It was a practice of adapting colonial governance to the local administration in the same structure that the Brits found it. In other words, it was a local command structure typically qualified as "native administration," with the specific role of dealing with the "native" population. For Lugard, Africans needed order before development, and the best method for realising this was going to be through the institutions of chiefs and emirs.[151] Prior to instituting indirect rule in Nigeria, Lugard through a series of columns and opinions in British journals had criticised the prevailing British colonial systems of administration in Africa as ununiformed, inefficient for the expansion of British trade, and not cost efficient, given that it allowed for three different administrative patterns, to wit: chartered company administrations, crown colonies, and full protectorates.[152]

Indirect rule as applied in Nigeria consisted of receiving instructions from British colonial administrators and executing them by disseminating the received orders to the rest of the population. It was the "nearest approximation to the British ideal system" because it guaranteed "order, organization and a progressive stage of African evolution."[153] Against this backdrop stood a crucial irony, namely an acknowledgement of the capacity of African political institutions to exercise attributes of governance. The tacit acknowledgement by analogy self-nullified the crucial rationale of the Berlin Act, vindicating the imperativeness of European protectorates as indispensable for the redemption of African political units from a state of anarchy. It also put the whole civilising mission rationale into question, considering that by relying on uneducated African chiefs and not European administrators, it went without saying that the overriding emphasis was not geared at educating Africans in practical terms.

Be it as it may, the policy was a British counterresponse to the insistence of effective occupation as mandated by the Berlin Act of 1884–1885. Considering the vastness of Nigeria and other claimed territories on the continent, it became apparent to Britain that any attempt at employing a corresponding number of administrators was not only a nearly impossible task. Moreover, even if that was feasible, any established protectorate would possibly crumble on its heels with expensive costs. "Native" chiefs were particularly conducive across Nigeria because they generally commanded respect amongst the populace, were accustomed to the terrain of their jurisdictions, and their collaboration was thus invaluable to any system of law and order.

The assumption that all African societies were ruled by chieftaincy was seriously flawed. Following the colonisation of Nigeria, Lugard soon found out that many societies in southern Nigeria had no chieftaincy institutions but were instead ruled by a rotating council of elders. Lugard not surprisingly created chieftaincy in such localities and imposed their authority on the populace.[154] Indirect rule saw its easiest application in the north of the country, given that it was already ruled by emirs who commanded immense authority.

6.10.3 Congo Free State (1885–1908): Corporate Policy, Red Rubber, and the Heart of Horror

One of the most noteworthy items from the 1884 Berlin Conference proceedings was the invocation of over 450 cession treaties supposedly signed between Henry Morton Stanley and African rulers in the Congo region,[155] as a testimonial affirmation that the latter by these instruments voluntarily surrendered their sovereignties in exchange for the "benevolent" protection of Leopold II. This occasioned one of the biggest nuances of the Berlin Act, namely the legitimation of *Association Internationale du Congo* (AIC) as a *sui generis* protectorate under the protection of Leopold II, a private individual.[156] The state was

> advertised as an area of free trade and humanitarianism, but obviously was intended to enable economic profits from the extraction of resources, and hence it practically turned out to be a private venture of the Belgian King, shaped by monopoly capitalism and brutal violence.[157]

The new state was 80 times the size of Belgium, one-twelfth of Africa's total landmass, the same size as Western Europe and separated from Belgium by over 10,000 miles. On 29 May 1885, three months following the Berlin Conference, Leopold II celebrated the diplomatic acquisition by naming the colony as the *Etat Indépendent du Congo* (that is, the Congo Free State), and assuming the majestic title of *Roi-Souverain de l'Etat Indépendant du Congo* (King Sovereign of the Congo Free State). The designation enabled him to differentiate his new procurement from his other role as the Belgian monarch.[158] Paradoxically, throughout his life, he never set foot on the Congo territory.

Leopold's first act as King Sovereign was the issuance of a real estate decree on 1 July 1885 pronouncing all "vacant" lands as the *Domaine Privé* (private property) of the state, which, practically speaking, meant ownership of every land in the entire colony.[159] In order to enforce this order, colonial administrators immediately began forcing Congolese to surrender their lands to the state—lands which for generations had been their primary source of livelihood and their most precious natural gift. It was a treasure upon which every Congolese community traditionally exploited for food, habitat, cultivation, grazing, and hunting. But with the advent of the new state, peasants were now strictly restricted to small fields immediately adjacent to their huts.[160]

There was actually no legal connection between the Congo state and Belgium except for the fact that they had a common sovereign, who acted as an absolute monarch in the former and a constitutional king in the latter, given that his powers were formally limited by the fundamental law of the Belgian state.[161] Gustav Rolin-Jacquemyns of *Institut de Droit International*, in a stimulating write-up, welcomed the new "state" as "an international investiture."[162] In reality, the "protectorate" was anything but international. Contrary to its "liberty" sounding name, the colony was neither free nor really a state. As earlier noted, it met all the attributes of a transnational corporation, with Leopold as its owner and chief executive officer. All administrative operations were moreover geared at commercial ends. Although Leopold repeatedly heralded his Congo project as one of meeting two landmark humanitarian fulfilments—protection of international free trade and the moral and material well-being of "natives"[163]—in actuality, the Congo Free State was nothing but a heroic civilisational fraud—a deceptive scheme of sheer proportions.[164] While Adolf Hitler and Josef Stalin were notorious in the 20th century for inhumaneness, in fact, Leopold II in the prior century had set the most outstanding European standard for cruelty, as he callously masterminded a machinery of large-scale human massacres across the Congo. The violence in Congo was exacerbated by the fact that Leopold was compelled to finance his costly imperial projects through local taxation, as he did not want to bother the Belgian government for fear that they could express the desire to take over control.[165]

Contrary to popular belief, the institution of control over the territory was actually not an easy coastal ride for Leopold. In *Colonialism in the Congo* (2005), Thomas J. Watson pointed out that while many communities such as the Baloki and Bobangi frequently resisted Leopold's authority and cooperation, the fiercest revolt came from the Yeke people in the Katanga region, whose king, Msiri, not only fought relentlessly but also vowed that he was never going to under any circumstance hand his land (sovereignty) to Leopold: "I am the master here," he declared. "And as long as I live, the kingdom of Garangaze [Katanga] shall have no other."[166] In order to combat the ever-increasing pockets of resistance, Leopold decided to constitute a well-fortified force known as *Force Publique*, which was completed in 1888 with 8,000 strong men, becoming the biggest and most brutal military force of any European colony in Africa. In time, it was 18,000 strong, given that fear was primordial into making the Congo state profitable. Well remunerated by the standards of the time, the force armed to the teeth with guns and *chicotte* whips, was comprised of Belgian and other Europeans as commanding officers and Africans as field troops.[167]

Leopold soon reached the conclusion that the regime of free trade mandated by the Berlin Act was the biggest impediment hampering the state's ability to reap efficient profits, to which he sought to make amends. In 1889, he convened an international antislavery conference in Brussels supposedly for the practical fulfilment of humanitarianism—more specifically, to drastically stamp out the slave trade once and for all in Central Africa. It quickly turned out that the real goal was to institute and legitimise absolute monopoly on the territory so that other Europeans could now be prevented from competing with Belgian concessionary companies. In order to trade, they henceforth had to succumb to excessive tariffs, custom duties, and exploitation taxes. Leopold justified these measures on the ground that the state needed huge financial capital in order to honour its civilisation objectives towards the natives.[168] Being the shrewd technician that he was, he was once again able to get virtually everything that he asked for. Immediately following the conference, he issued a new decree that forbade Africans from selling their produce, especially ivory and rubber, to any other person or entity except the government. In fact, they could harvest these commodities only for the purposes of selling it to the state. This was based on the rationale that since all land in the Congo Free State belonged to the state, any produce therefrom by analogy belonged to its sovereign king.[169]

Summarily put, Leopold's system of administration was one of pure domestic extraction and geared for international trade. He relied heavily on the collection and sale of ivory to generate income during the gestation years of the state. Although the state on the average was able to make an annual gain of approximately 85 million Belgian francs, this paled in comparison to what it would generate once the trade in rubber suddenly came into vogue.[170] In 1887, John Boyd Dunlop—an obscure Scottish trader who would soon found Dunlop Pneumatic Tyre Company—discovered that natural rubber could be used to make inflatable tyres and other items such as "hoses, tubing, gaskets, insulation for the telegraph, telephone, and electrical wiring."[171] Not only was rubber now one of the most important vectors of the industrial revolution, its trade was going to have dire consequences at its source—namely, the Congo Free State, where it was plentiful with its vine spreading all over its dense forests. This discovery immediately changed the economic outlook of the Congo State, as its citizenry were plunged into the unspeakable nightmare of rubber enslavement and senseless deaths. The term *red rubber* is often used to depict the massive amount of Congolese blood that was spilled in order to realise its production and trade.[172]

As the price of rubber skyrocketed and, as a consequence, elevated the product into a lucrative commodity, arbitrary rules geared at forcefully committing "natives" for its collection without pay were developed and validated with legal underpinnings such as administrative taxation and labour policy. The administration thus posited as an agent of centrally planned creative violence. Not only did it give direct orders for acts of violence to be inflicted on the population, but public callousness was vindicated as an imperative to realise the state's development objectives. The crucial importance of rubber to the state's solvency necessitated the employment of any means necessary.[173]

As an inductive tactic, Leopold introduced a taxation policy known as *impôt indigene*, whereby villagers were heavily taxed. Given that they had no money to pay, the administration provided them the tedious option of collecting rubber for the state, fittingly determined by fixed quotas. Forced labour was legally justified as the most efficient mode of taxation, prompted by the lack of a monetary economy—and based on the rationale that since any economic development project ultimately benefitted the "natives," it was only logical for them to foot the cost of their colonisation and civilisation.[174] Moreover, Congolese were typically projected as lazy in nature. If the new state was to progress, it went without saying that its peoples had to embrace a culture of hard work. Forced labour accordingly emerged as a vital educative measure.[175]

Suspicious of unknown eventualities in the future, Leopold created a private domain of 25,000 hectares within the Congo Free State known as "*domaine de la Couronne*" (and outside the rubric of the *domaine privé*) whose records were a guarded secret.[176] Cognisant of the fact that he needed professionals in order to maximise production, Leopold enlisted the Anglo-Belgian India Rubber Company (ABIR) for assistance, according it wide-ranging powers which included amassing as much forest land as they needed to expand production, the right to subdue "natives" into labour by any means necessary, the right to raise an armed force of their own if necessary, or freely securing the services of *Force Publique* if this was a less costly option.[177]

The punishment for failing to meet the quotas was not just fierce, but brutal and bloody, ranging from harsh beatings in lenient situations to the maiming of hands in cases deemed as serious violations.[178] The practice of hand-cutting began out of Belgian administrators' fears that agents of the *Force Publique* were probably using bullets for personal use such as hunting rather than the supervision of natives harvesting rubber. To ensure that they used it solely for rubber-related delinquencies, the state instituted a system of legitimate violence and began ordering the forces to cut off the right arm of any rubber-harvesting defaulters, and to bring the chopped hands over to the Belgian commanders as a precondition to receiving their wages.[179] The tactic was also a form of deterrence and modality for the enforcement of state rules and needs. Many villages began escaping the terror to other European protectorates. In order to prevent this emigration trend and mass exodus, women and children were held hostage in guarded camps, where many were frequently raped by the guarding forces until the men satisfied their required weekly rubber quota to the state.[180] Thanks to these unorthodox methods, before long Leopold began reaping astronomical profits. The Congo Free State at the same time greatly enhanced Belgian exchange on the international market, especially given that the two countries were, technically speaking, a one indivisible territory—tied together by their sovereign king; even if violence was directed only at one end and resulting profits syphoned to the other end.[181]

From an economic standpoint, however, the Congo Free State was a veritable success as it rose to become the world's top supplier of rubber and the most profitable of any European African protectorates.[182] As the population shrunk and many escaped, those remaining were overworked. *Force Publique* forces also increasingly became stationed in villages to guard against population desertions. Although Leopold destroyed all state records, it has nevertheless been estimated that over 15 million Congolese died as a result of his atrocities—representing about 60% of the territory's population at the time.[183]

Leopold's administration largely escaped scrutiny during the first five years of the formative state. Instead, many pundits got carried away with his ever-growing lavish humanitarian pronouncements, erroneously praising the colonial project as a model for the European civilising mission. One of those persons deeply fascinated with the colony was George Washington Williams, a black American politician and historian who, carried away with Leopold's humanitarian pronouncements, in 1890 made an adventurous trip to the colony expecting to encounter grandiose moral and social progress in the heart of Africa, borne out of the fruits of European Christian civilisation. His initial vision was to learn the secret of the colony's success, after which he planned to develop a policy paper which he hoped the US government could then use to elevate the plight of the downtrodden black population in America. Contrary to his keen anticipation, he could barely control his shock upon bumping unto a manifest reign of terror being orchestrated on the inhabitants by Belgian administrators.[184] He wrote two open letters—one to Leopold II, titled "An Open Letter to His Serene Majesty Léopold II, King of the Belgians and Sovereign of the Independent State of Congo," and the other to the US government. In the latter, he petitioned the United States to convoke all the countries that signed the Berlin Act to reconvene in order to address the severe violations. In the former, he deployed the inhuman brutality of Leopold's agents on Congolese peoples and reminding Leopold that he was manifestly guilty of many crimes against humanity. He concluded by admonishing for any other European country to take over control of the territory and above all for concerned individuals the world over to mobilise and reverse the brutal situation.[185] Williams died under controversial circumstances in England while on his way back to the United States. Although his accounts failed to gain any traction when they were initially published in 1890; his recommendations nevertheless became one of the guiding frameworks during the next decade upon which anti–Congo State humanitarian activists relied to build their cause. The movement importantly arrived at a similar conclusion to that of Williams, namely, the fierce need for an imminent transfer of the Congo State from Leopold to the Belgium state or any other European power, and a call for an immediate end to the brutality and massacres across the Congo.

The most resourceful personalities with first-hand knowledge of Leopold's atrocities were European missionaries, especially those living in rubber districts. Missionaries in the state were not just from Belgium but emanated from several western countries. In fact, the freedom to preach throughout the Congo state became the only part of the Berlin Act that Leopold truly honoured. These missionaries largely remained indifferent to the state violence on the populations, however. Given that the missionaries emanated from varying denominations and were each competing to win souls for Christ; their general attitude was one of nonchalance—for fear of being expelled from the lucrative large territory. Instead, they habitually adopted the approach of encouraging Africans to surrender their lives to Christ, so that even if they lost their lives in the state villainy, they could at least find salvation in the afterlife, which was in fact the ultimate and real freedom.[186] The first priest who broke the silence was Edvard Vilhelm Sjöblom —a Swedish missionary who in 1896 spoke openly in Sweden not just about the mutilation of hands but other gruesome atrocities as well:

> If the rubber the Congolese collect does not reach the required amount, the sentries attack them, kill some, and bring the severed hands to the District Commissioner. One sentry said: "The commissioner has promised us if we have plenty of hands, he will shorten our service." The hands were often smoked to preserve them till shown to the District Commissioner.[187]

Being an isolated voice, Sjöblom was largely disregarded just as Williams before him. But it was only a matter of time before the cry would gain traction.

Edmund Dene Morel, a British journalist and politician, became the first person to successfully connect the key dots of Leopold's operations and atrocious massacres in the Congo. Like everyone before him, he had ignored all the previous indications of alleged mayhems that repeatedly popped up since the 1890s. He however got his epiphany late in the 1890s while working as a clerk for *Elder Dempster*, a Liverpool shipping firm positing as the principal shipping agent for the Congo Free State's shipments between Antwerp and Boma-Congo.[188] Morel was particularly intrigued by the strange nature of the shipping inventories. For a state that prided itself as the citadel of the civilising mission and international free trade, ships returning from Congo were always full of tons of rubber and other natural resources, but those returning did not carry any noticeable commercial items, nor manifested transporting items for a normal civil government. When Morel followed his intuition and looked through the accounting books of ships destined for the Congo Free State and noticed that they transported nothing else but guns, chains, machetes, and other warfare items; he concluded not only that no commercial dealings were going on, but that "natives" were surely subjected to enslavement or prison-like conditions.[189]

> On the face of the import statistics, the natives were getting nothing or next to nothing. How then was this rubber and ivory being acquired? Certainly not by commercial dealing. Nothing was going in to pay for what was coming out.[190]

Morel later visited Congo to confirm his suspicion. But before he could ever set foot on the Congolese soil, he had gathered enormous evidence which prompted him to conclude that he had effectively stumbled upon the "secret society of murderers."[191] Worried that his employer was more worried about profits rather than human rights abuses caused by the rubber trade, as he had never once questioned the strange dealings, Morel sought to rely on other external forces and worldwide activists who shared the same humanitarian plight so that they could collectively effectuate change.

As fate would have it, Morel soon found an indispensable ally in his Congo humanitarian crusade in the person of Sir Roger Casement—the new British consul to the Boma in Upper Congo—who was still to assume duty. Like Morel, Casement's involvement was a pure act of chance and coincidence.

Following Leopold's monopolistic trade practices against other European traders, the initial assignment which the British government handed Casement upon dispatching him to Upper Congo was to secretly investigate the treatment of British subjects over there. Upon arrival, Casement realised that there was an even more appalling crisis, namely: state enslavement, suppression, and brutality of the "natives." The British government accordingly commissioned him with a new assignment—to produce a report vividly detailing the treatment of Africans in Upper Congo where he was based. He immediately opened his investigations, recording countless eyewitness accounts, interviewing victims who were everywhere with maimed hands, taking pictures as evidence, and collecting the diaries of missionaries who were willing to anonymously disclose evidence of the red rubber atrocities. The report was finalised in 1904 with detailed accounts of the gruesome carnages. As he unmasked "the caricature of noble principles on which Leopold II, King of the Belgians, founded the Congo state,"[192] people of goodwill the world over were left in a state of real shock. One very intriguing thing in the report was the author's contrast of the horror in Upper Congo in 1904 with the normal livelihood he experienced during his maiden visit to the area in 1887. The country had within a few years transformed into an unbearable concentration camp. The Polish-British writer Joseph Conrad, who also visited the colony about the same time, best qualified the atrocities as the *Heart of Darkness* (1899)—accounting that the so-called state was nothing but robbery with absolute barbarism, aggravated murder on a large scale, and the direct opposite of civilisation at the very least.[193] The Casement Report amongst other things read thus:

> A careful investigation of the conditions of native life around (Lake Mantumba) confirmed the truth of the statements made to me—that the great decrease in population, the dirty and ill-kept towns, and the complete absence of goats, sheep, or fowls—once very plentiful in this country—were to be attributed above all else to the continued effort made during many years to compel the natives to work for rubber. Large bodies of native troops had formerly been quartered in the district, and the punitive measures undertaken to this end had endured for a considerable period. During the course of these operations there had been much loss of life, accompanied, I fear, by a somewhat general mutilation of the dead, as proof that the soldiers had done their duty.[194]

The impact of the report was immediate and far-reaching. A vibrant and sustained international campaign against Leopold's regime led by Casement and Edmund Dene Morel, known as the Congo Reform Association, was born. Slowly but surely, it gathered steam and successfully began to turn the tides against Leopold, as they continually publicised the brutality of the Congo state, published columns in reputable journals, and successfully elevated the subject to an issue of international politics.[195] Even at the heart of the Congo Reform Movement campaign, Leopold was still able to reap over 43 million Belgian francs from the rubber trade.[196] Leopold suffered yet another backlash, however, when few sources from within the ranks of the traders vented their discontent by anonymously supplying information to the Congo Reform Association.[197] A separate Belgian investigation commission set up following the backlash from Casement's report corroborated many of the abuses, and highlighted other cases of excessive taxes, forced labour, and blatant brutality on "natives" both by the colonial administration and concessionary companies.[198]

Thanks to the Congo Reform Association, the Belgian state at long last voted in both chambers of parliament to force Leopold to hand over the

Congo Free State in 1908. Legally speaking, this marked the first time that a juridical tie was established between Belgium and the Congo state. At the time of the takeover, several problems had occurred as a result of the intense repression. There was enormous antagonism amongst peoples, especially between the brutalised and *Force Publique* mercenaries working for Leopold; populations had been severely decimated, leading to demographic imbalances, while rubber was going extinct in several areas. After the takeover, however, the most brutal forms of repression were outlawed or regulated while labour taxes were gradually replaced with taxes in coins.[199] There were significant improvements at the level of administration and population welfare. Although the Belgian regime curtailed the most ruthless forms of physical abuse, the denial of rights nonetheless remained ingrained and commonplace, including the use of the *chicotte*.[200]

6.10.4 Germany and Indirect Rule in Cameroon

After 1880, the influx of explorers and missionaries especially from Britain, Germany, Portugal, France and America, intensified on the coasts of what is today known as Cameroon, along the Duala estuary, with each competing for utter dominance. Although the two leading foreign nationals were from Britain and Germany, the Germans whose prominent presence in the area dated to 1868 following the building of the Woermann firm for tropical products along the river Wouri, saw British advancement across the Niger region as imminently heading to Duala, and thus petitioned their government to annex the territory in other to protect their trading interests or send a resident consul.[201] In response, Bismarck dispatched Gustav Nachtigal, the German consul-general for Tunisia, to honour the petition of the traders.

Despite informing Britain of the mission, although claiming that his assignment was strictly to investigate the welfare of German trade in the area, Nachtigal was nonetheless under Bismarck's strict instructions to annex the territory and Togoland for Germany.[202] Arriving in *Kamerunland* on 14 July 1884, and with C. Woermann & Co. having arranged the necessary groundwork, Nachtigal immediately signed treaties of cession with two coastal kings: Bell and Akwa, hoisting the German flags in the region.[203] On 17 August 1884, a similar agreement was signed with the King of Bimbia. Following the Berlin Conference and signing of bilateral agreements between Britain and France—whereupon the latter ceded all claims, Germany consolidated its hold over the entire *Kamerun* protectorate, which lasted for 32 years until the German defeat in 1916 (in Kamerun) during the First World War.[204] It was not until 1899 that the *Kamerun* interior was opened up for trade and colonial administration when Germany decisively defeated ever mounting sporadic resistances.[205]

Generally, the German colonial ideology in Africa was guided by two conceptions: *emigrationist* and *economic*. While the emigrationist logic was based on the avoidance of anticipated social upheavals and political crisis—that is, geared at the overseas resettlement of Germans in order to curb national social problems—the economic logic conceived of colonialism as the engine for industrial and commercial triumph.[206] Obviously, both ideologies were two sides of the same coin—while emigrationist doctrines which were born out of *Auswanderung*, ensured that Germans could resettle in Africa as an alternative to the greener pasture journeys to America—yet more effectively preserving the cultural heritage and contributing to the national economy—economic ideologies were the natural response to economic and political relevance vis-à-vis other European powers. While emigrationist proponents such as Robert Von Mohl justified the sanctity of the ideology as a solution to preserving German overpopulation and its cultural identity, economic colonialism proponents such as Friederich List and Lothar Bucher observed that economic dominance, especially through commerce, was the only way to attain grandeur—it had been the British way to greatness, and thus it was imperative that Germany replicate it.[207]

The main formulator of German colonial policy in *Kamerun* was Jesko Von Puttkamer who was the governor general of the protectorate from 1894 to 1906. A strong believer in the economic colonisation rationale, he placed much emphasis on plantation agriculture, principally in tropical cash crop. His administrative style consisted of forced labour and direct taxation to force Africans to labour conscriptions or to work for wages.[208] Germany initiated many plantation agricultural schemes throughout the protectorate, which required large intensive workforce. But as local populations were unwilling to work on these farms, colonial administrators became compelled to institute heavy taxes to force the population into wage labour.[209] Total German expenditure in Cameroon by 1905 stood at 1,400,000 German Marks.[210]

Notes

1 Cf. Alison Reppy, *19 Fordham Law Review* (1950) at 244; *See also*: John T. Parry, *35 University of Pennsylvania Journal of International Law* (2013) 299–487; *See*: Ruth Lapidoth, 6 *Journal of Maritime Law and Commerce* (1974–1975) at 263–264.

2 Charles de Secondat, Baron de Montesquieu, (Gallimard-Pleiade, 1951). Cf: Robert Howse, *31 Brooklyn Journal of International Law* (2006) at 694. In the words of Montesquieu: "the natural effect of commerce is to bring peace. Two nations that negotiate between themselves become reciprocally dependent, if one has an interest in buying and the other in selling. And all unions are based on mutual needs." (*See*: Howse, 'Montesquieu on Commerce, Conquest, War and Peace' at 693).

3 Stephen J. Rosow, *46 The Review of Politics* (1984) at 346–349.

4 Howse, 'Montesquieu on Commerce, Conquest, War and Peace' at 694.

5 Sanford H. Bederman, *21 The Journal of the Society for the History of Discoveries* (1989) at 64–66.

6 Stephen Gorove, *8 Journal of Public Law* (1959) at 128.

7 Voyslav M. Radovanovitch, *21 The American Journal of International Law* (1927) at 399–400; Gorove, 'Internationalization of the Danube' at 128.

8 Alexander D. Nzemeke, (Oxford University Press, 1988) at 67.

9 Ronald Robinson, (Oxford University Press, 1988) at 3.
10 Juhani Koponen, 2 *Nordic Journal of African Studies* (1993) at 130–131.
11 Koponen, 'The Partition of Africa: A Scramble for a Mirage' at 134.
12 Wolfgang Mommsen, "Bismarck, the Concert of Europe, and the Future of West Africa" in Forster, Mommsen & Robinson at 152.
13 John Mugambwa, *20 The Comparative and International Law Journal of Southern Africa* (1987) at 81.
14 Mommsen, "Bismarck, the Concert of Europe, and the Future of West Africa" in Forster, Mommsen & Robinson at 151.
15 Gustave Moynier, (Imprimerie Charles Schuchardt, 1883) at 23–24.
16 Émile Louis Victor de Laveleye, *15 Revue de Droit International et de Legislation Comparee* (1883) at 255, 261.
17 Abdulqawi Yusuf, (Hague Academy of International Law, 2014) at 68; Nzemeke, "Free Trade and Territorial Partition" at 66. It is also worth noting that when Portugal saw stumbling blocks all around its treaty with Britain, it suggested to Bismarck to rally European states for an international congress to once and for all resolve the conflicting claims over the Congo. However, except for this plea, it is not evident anywhere else that Portugal in addition played any other major role in the convening of the conference. (*See*: Daniel De Leon, 1 *Political Science Quarterly* (1886) at 127).
18 *Mémorial Diplomatique Française* at 249, 267–268; Jörg Fisch, "Africa as Terra Nullius" at 349.
19 *See*: Goeffrey de Courcel, 'The Berlin Act of 26 February 1885' in Forster, Mommsen & Robinson, *Bismarck, Europe and Africa* at 249; De Leon, "The Conference at Berlin" at 126.
20 Robinson, "The Conference in Berlin and the Future in Africa" at 8.
21 De Leon, "The Conference at Berlin" at 115.
22 Courcel, "The Berlin Act of 26 February 1885" at 251.
23 Elikia M'bokolo, (XIXème–XXème siècles, 2004) at 10.
24 Martti Koskenniemi, (Cambridge University Press, 2001) at 123.
25 Courcel, "The Berlin Act of 26 February 1885" at 249.
26 Jörg Fisch, "Africa as Terra Nullius" at 351.
27 Adam Watson, (Routledge, 1992) at 183, 186–187.
28 Watson, *The Evolution of International Society* at 183, 186–187.
29 Lewis H. Gann, 'The Berlin Conference and the Humanitarian Conscience' in Forster, Mommsen & Robinson at 322.
30 Mommsen, [*Preface*], *Bismarck, Europe and Africa* at viii.
31 Sir Edward Malet, the British ambassador to Germany at the time, was probably the only delegate who saw anything odd with the absence of Africans on the table. He made the following acknowledgement: "I cannot forget that the natives are not represented amongst us, and that the decisions of the conference would, nevertheless, have extreme importance for them."(*See*: Rosemarie Julie Gavin & J. A. Betley (eds.), (Ibadan University Press, 1973) at 222–223; Gann, "The Berlin Conference and the Humanitarian Conscience" at 321).

Moreover, although Zanzibar was acknowledged as a sovereign state, this did not trigger any need to invite it to the conference.
32 De Leon, "The Conference at Berlin" at 103.
33 Ibid at 103.
34 Gann, "The Berlin Conference and the Humanitarian Conscience" at 331; Ramage, 'The Partition of Africa.' at 227.
35 Forster, Mommsen & Robinson, *Bismarck, Europe and Africa* at vi.
36 Amadu Sesay, (Croom Helm Ltd, 1986) at 34–35; Luigi Nuzzo, "Colonial Law" in *European History Online (EGO), published by the Leibniz Institute of European History (IEG)*; (2012) 1–17 at 8.

37 Gann, "The Berlin Conference and the Humanitarian Conscience" at 322.
38 Prosser Gifford & Roger Louis, (Yale University Press, 1971) at 191–193; Jennifer Beard, (Routledge, 2007) at 138; Hannis Taylor, *41 American Law Review* (1907) 92–101; Beard, *The Political Economy of Desire* at 138–140.
39 Craven, 'The Invention of a Tradition' at 10.
40 Courcel, "The Berlin Act of 26 February 1885" at 247–261.
41 Martin Ewans, (Routledge Curzon, 2002) at 37–40, 101–103.
42 Mommsen, "Bismarck, the Concert of Europe, and the Future of West Africa" in Forster, Mommsen & Robinson at 164.
43 William Smith Culbertson, *9 The American Economic Review* (1919) at 326–328; Mommsen, "Bismarck, the Concert of Europe, and the Future of West Africa" in Forster, Mommsen & Robinson at 164.
44 Courcel, "The Berlin Act of 26 February 1885" at 250.
45 Robinson, 'The Conference in Berlin and the Future in Africa at 3.
46 De Leon, "The Conference at Berlin" at 128; Mommsen, "Bismarck, the Concert of Europe, and the Future of West Africa" in Forster, Mommsen & Robinson at 165.
47 Courcel, "The Berlin Act of 26 February 1885" at 251.
Over in the Indian Ocean, France was to facilitate the transit of international merchan dise over its territories, as well as the principle of free trade over any future territorial acquisitions. (Courcel, "The Berlin Act of 26 February 1885" at 251).
48 See: Articles 1–3 of the Berlin Act of 26 February 1885. [*Mild Emphasis Added*].
49 Courcel, "The Berlin Act of 26 February 1885" at 252.
50 Robinson, "The Conference in Berlin and the Future in Africa" at 7; Article 5 of the Berlin Act of 26 February 1885.
51 Courcel, "The Berlin Act of 26 February 1885" at 253.
52 Article 25 of the Berlin Act of 26 February 1885.
53 Articles 10, 11 and 12 of the Berlin Act of 26 February 1885.
54 Suzanne Miers, "Humanitarianism at Berlin: Myth or Reality?" in Forster, Mommsen & Robinson, *Bismarck, Europe and Africa* at 333.
55 Forster, Mommsen & Robinson, *Bismarck, Europe and Africa* at vi.
56 James Thuo Gathii, *37 Studies in Transnational Legal Policy* (2005) at 102; Peter Duignan & Lewis H. Gann, (Cambridge University Press, 1984) at 134.
57 Article 6 of the Berlin Act of 26 February 1885.
58 Westlake, *Chapters on the Principles of International Law* at 140.
59 While Kasson's sentiment strongly mirrored the tenor of the modern right of self-determination, this study recognises that while the doctrine was already expressed in the 1860s–70s, it was nevertheless not authoritatively affirmed as a rule of international law until after the Second World War.
60 Alexander Orakhelashvili, *17 European Journal of International Law* (2006) 315–347 at 326; Pasquale Fiore & Theodore Henckels, *6 Proceedings of the American Society of International Law at Its Annual Meeting* (1912) at 24.
61 Article 6 of the Berlin Act of 26 February 1885; Gavin & Betley (eds.), *The Scramble for Africa* at 242–243.
62 Gann, "The Berlin Conference and the Humanitarian Conscience" at 324.
63 Ibid at 325.
64 Article 9 of the Berlin Act of 26 February 1885.
65 Great Britain Foreign Office, (Forgotten Books, 2013) at 157–158.
66 Cf: Miers, Suzanne, S. Förster, Wolfgang J. Mommsen, and Ronald Robinson. (Oxford University Press, 1988) at 337.
67 Articles 6–9 of the Berlin Act of 26 February 1885.
68 Miers, 'Humanitarianism at Berlin: Myth or Reality?' at 336; Lauri Hannikainen, (Lakimiesliiton Kustannus, 1988) at 67–87.

69 Sybil Eyre Crowe, (Longmans, London: 1942) at 103.
70 Brussels Conference Act (*Convention Relative to the Slave Trade and Importation into Africa of Firearms, Ammunition, and Spiritous Liquors*) of 2 July 1890.
71 Gavin & Betley (eds.), *The Scramble for Africa* at 328.
72 Miers, 'Humanitarianism at Berlin: Myth or Reality?' at 344.
73 Gann, "The Berlin Conference and the Humanitarian Conscience" at 328.
74 Miers, 'Humanitarianism at Berlin: Myth or Reality?' at 338.
The society further contended that Africans were naturally more prone to drunkenness than Europeans, and alcohol could be of no good to them except to inspire boldness or encourage all kinds of social evils amongst them. (Miers, 'Humanitarianism at Berlin: Myth or Reality?' at 338).
75 Ibid at 340.
76 Jörg Fisch,*26 Franz Steiner Verlag Wiesbaden GmbH* (1984).
Cf: Jörg Fisch, "Africa as Terra Nullius" at 348.
77 *See*: Courcel, "The Berlin Act of 26 February 1885" at 255.
78 Hall, *A Treatise on International Law* at 87–89.
79 Articles 34 & 35 of the Berlin Act of 26 February 1885.
80 Fisch's depiction of Africa as *terra nullius*, is in effect at odds with the observation of Institut de Droit International and other international lawyers who conceived Africa rather as *territorium nullius*.
81 Jörg Fisch, "Africa as Terra Nullius" at 364.
82 Articles 34 & 35 of the Berlin Act of 26 February 1885.
83 It is worth pointing out that one scholar, Alexandrowicz has taken a dissenting position on the subject, contending that there was no uniform standard of annexation at Berlin, and the term occupation was "not used in the meaning of unilateral occupation but as occupation of territory acquired by any title in international law" (*See*: Charles Henry Alexandrowicz, (Sijthoff, 1973) at 4, 46.
However, there does not seem to be any credible evidential basis beside the claim. It is my contention that what ought to be of interest is the spirit of action and spirit of the law; and following the conference proceedings, the delegates were in one accord about transitioning from mere 'prise de possession' towards protectorates. In the end, all occupied territories were conspicuously conceived as protectorates, or variously dubbed as colonial protectorates—a clear indication of harmony around the concepts.
84 Jörg Fisch, "Africa as Terra Nullius" at 353.
85 Ibid at 358.
Normally, protectorates would have implied that fully functional governments were in place, with the colonial relationship not one of governance by the coloniser but protection rather. Europeans having dismissed African political institutions as failing to meet the test of government, African colonies were protectorates hence only in name and not in the classical meaning of the term as they did not share internal and external sovereignty with their European colonisers. They were instead directly administered and controlled by the latter—that is, engulfed into European administrative law. (*See*: Jörg Fisch, "Africa as Terra Nullius" at 364).
86 Jörg Fisch, "Africa as Terra Nullius" at 354.
87 Dakas C. J. Dakas, *7 African Yearbook of International Law/Annuaire Africain De Droit International* (1999) at 104, 117.
88 Nicholas Tarling, (Routledge: 2001) at 134.
89 Flint, "Chartered Companies and the Scramble for Africa" at 77; Courcel, "The Berlin Act of 26 February 1885" at 255.
90 Alexandrowicz, "The Role of Treaties in the European-African Confrontation" at 59.

91 Westlake, *Chapters on the Principles of International Law* at xiv. "The great human interest of that question would of itself have been sufficient motive for its introduction into this book, even had it not been required for the scientific purpose mentioned." (Westlake, *Chapters on the Principles of International Law* at xiv.).
92 Sir Travers Twiss for instance was a strong believer in "natives'" as original owners of private property rights, but which of course could be better managed by the civilised. (Twiss, *The Law of Nations Considered as Independent Political Communities* at 102–105).
93 These are the two most key aspects necessary to justify territorial sovereignty. While *dominium* denotes economic sovereignty over a territory (the right of ownership and control), *imperium* on the other hand signifies political sovereignty—the power to impose, regulate and making of rules.
94 Westlake, *Chapters on the Principles of International Law* at 133.
95 Ibid at 78–83.
96 Oppenheim, *The Collected Papers of John Westlake* at 142–145, 185.
97 Ibid at 145.
98 Hall, *A Treatise on International Law* at 170–173; Westlake, *The Collected Papers* at 144–145.
99 Westlake, *Chapters on the Principles of International Law* at 142.
100 Ibid at 139. [*Emphasis Added*]
101 Ibid at 105.
102 Gavin & Betley (eds.), *The Scramble for Africa* at 284.
103 John D. Hargreaves, (Macmillan, 1963) at 337; John D. Hargreaves, (Oxford University Press,) at 313; Matthew Craven, *3 London Review of International Law* (2015) 31–59 at 33–35.
104 Hargreaves, *Prelude to the Partition of West Africa* at 337.
105 Hertslet, *The Map of Africa by Treaty* at 668–670, 681–683.
106 Hargreaves, *Prelude to the Partition of West Africa at* 52–61.
107 Michael Mulligan, *11 Journal of the History of International Law* (2009) at 273.
108 Alexandrowicz, "The Role of Treaties in the European-African Confrontation" at 62.
109 Albert Sarraut, (Editions L'Harmattan, 2012) at 11–13.
110 David Kenneth Fieldhouse, *2 Economic History Review* (1961) at 195.
111 John Morris Roberts, *4 Tijdschrift voor de Studie van de Verlichting* (1976) 329–369.
112 See: Jack Ernest Shalom Hayward (Weidenfield & Nicolson, 1973) at 248. [*Emphasis mildly added*].
113 Suzanne Lafont, *32 Litteratures* (1995) at 105–118; Albert Sarraut, (Payot, 1923).
114 Gordon Cumming, *23 Journal of Contemporary African Studies* (2005) at 233.
115 Michael Crowder, (Oxford University Press, 1962) at 2.
116 Frantz Fanon, *Toward the African Revolution: Political Essays* (Grove Books, New York: 1964) at 38, 43.
117 H. Oludare Idowu, *9 Cahiers d'Études Africaines* (1969) 194–218 at 194.
118 Wallace G. Mills, 'French Approaches in Colonial Policy' (2011) at 1
119 Vincent B. Khapoya, (Prentice Hall, 1998) at 109.
120 Mamadou Diouf, *29 Development and Change* (1998) at 676.
121 Diouf, 'The French Colonial Policy of Assimilation and the Civility of the Four Communes' at 672.
122 Labouret, 'France's Colonial Policy in Africa' at 31.
123 Henri Lorin, (Étude d'Histoire et de Géographie, 1906) at 467–468. Translation: If we take a close look at [the French fortune abroad], we would realize that

the largest investments everywhere have been made in state funds ... However, very rarely have the issue of these loans been followed by orders to French industry or concessions to our trade.

124 Henri Labouret, *39 Journal of the Royal African Society* (1940) at 23–25.
125 Labouret, 'France's Colonial Policy in Africa' at 22, 27.
126 Michael Crowder, (Hutchinson, 1968) at 6.
127 Diouf, 'The French Colonial Policy of Assimilation and the Civility of the Four Communes' at 672.
128 Ibid at 673.
129 Ibid at 673.
130 Idowu, 'Assimilation in 19th Century Senegal' at 194.
131 Doudou Thiam, (Éditions Africaines, Paris: 1951) at 100; Idowu, 'Assimilation in 19th Century Senegal' at 194.
132 Idowu, 'Assimilation in 19th Century Senegal' at 195.
133 Ibid at 195.
134 Mills, 'French Approaches in Colonial Policy' at 4.
135 Ibid at 3.
136 Labouret, 'France's Colonial Policy in Africa' at 30.
137 Ibid at 30–31.
138 Ibid at 31.
139 Alain Clement, *123 Revue d'Économie Politique* (2013) at 51.
140 Albert Sarraut, *La Mise en Valeur des Colonies Françaises* at 7–11.
141 Ibid at 7–11.
142 Aisha Balarabe Bawa, (2013) at 1.
143 Colin W. Newbury & Alexander Sydney Kanya-Forstner, *10 The Journal of African History* (1969) at 254, 256.
144 Diouf, 'The French Colonial Policy of Assimilation and the Civility of the Four Communes' at 674.
145 Mills, 'French Approaches in Colonial Policy' at 4.
146 Khapoya, *The African Experience* at 117.
147 Anthony I. Nwabughuogu, *14 The International Journal of African Historical Studies* (1981) at 71.
148 Cherry Gertzel, *3 Journal of African History* (1962) 361–366 at 361.
149 Flora Shaw, 'Nigeria' *The Times* (1897) of 8 January 1897; See also: "Flora Shaw Gives the Name Nigeria": available online: www.nabss.org.uk/download/i/mark.../History%20of%20Nigeria.pdf Last Accessed: 2 April 2019.
150 Khapoya, *The African Experience* at 117.
151 Nwabughuogu, 'The Role of Propaganda in the Development of Indirect Rule' at 80.
152 Ibid at 69–70.
153 Nwabughuogu, 'The Role of Propaganda in the Development of Indirect Rule' at 66, 74.
154 Margery Perham, (Oxford University Press, 1937) at 21.
155 Arthur Berriedale Keith, (Clarendon Press, Oxford: 1919) at 49.
156 Chapters I, II and IV of the Berlin Act of 26 February 1885.
157 Andreas Exenberger, working paper: *University of Innsbruck: Department of Economic Theory, Policy and History and Vienna, Austria: Austrian Research Foundation for International Development* (2011) 1–29 at 7.
158 *See*: Martin Ewans, (Routledge, 2002) at 101; Thomas J. Watson, (Watson Institute for International Studies, 2007) at 12.
159 Catherine Coquery-Vidrovitch, (Éditions de l'École des Hautes Études en Sciences Sociales, 2013) at 26, 99–101.
160 Watson, *Colonialism in the Congo* at 12.

161 Alphonse Jules Wauters, *9 Journal of the Royal Institute of International Affairs* (1930) at 51; Reeves, 'The Origin of the Congo Free State' at 116.
162 Gustav Rolin-Jacquemyns, *21 Revue de Droit Internationale et de Législation Comparée* (1889) at 170.
163 Aldwin Roes, *62 South African Historical Journal* (2010) at 636.
164 Reeves, 'The Origin of the Congo Free State' at 118.
165 Roes, 'Towards a History of Mass Violence in the Etat Indépendant du Congo' at 638.
166 Watson, *Colonialism in the Congo* at 12.
167 Adam Hochschild, (Houghton Mifflin Co., 1998) at 120;

Watson, *Colonialism in the Congo* at 13; Asafa Jalata, *(ATINER). Athens, Greece* (2011) at 21, 29–30.
Victoria Brittain *236 New Left Review* (1999) 133–144 at 140.

168 Brittain, 'Colonialism and the Predatory State in the Congo' at 140.
169 Brittain, 'Colonialism and the Predatory State in the Congo' at 140.
170 "Rubber" Joel Mokyr, (Oxford University Press, 2003) at 407–412; Lewis H. Gann & Peter Duignan, (Princeton University Press, 1979) at 118.
171 Hochschild, *King Leopold's Ghost* at 159.
172 Ibid at xi-xvii, 6–8, 116–117.
173 Roes, 'Towards a History of Mass Violence in the Etat Indépendant du Congo' at 651.
174 Ibid at 639.
175 William J. Samarin, (Westview Press, 1989) at 47–48.
176 Martin Ewans, (Routledge Curzon, 2002) at 160–170, 228.
177 Gann & Duignan, *The Rulers of Belgian Africa* at 127.
178 Hochschild, *King Leopold's Ghost* at 120; Watson, *Colonialism in the Congo* at 13.
179 Stephen L. Harp, (Wiley, Blackwell, 2016) at 15–16; Kevin C. Dunn, (Palgrave Macmillan, 2003) at 21–59.
180 Dunn, 'Inventing the Congo' at 21–59.
181 Wauters, 'Belgian Policy in the Congo' at 54.
182 See for example, Robert Harms, *16 The Journal of African History* (1975) 73–88.
183 William Roger Louis & Jean Stengers, (Clarendon, 1968) at 252–258; Frederic Wertham, (Macmillan, 1966).
184 Watson, *Colonialism in the Congo* at 16.
185 Ibid at 17.
186 Ibid at 17.
187 Philippa Schuyler, *Jungle saints: Africa's Heroic Catholic Missionaries* (Herder: 1963) at 128.
188 Michel Dumoulin, Léopold II: Un Roi Génocidaire? (*Académie Royale de Belgique*, 2005) at 14–18.
189 Watson, *Colonialism in the Congo* at 19.
190 Edmund Dene Morel, (Clarendon Press, London/ Brussels: 1968) at 36.
191 Watson, *Colonialism in the Congo* at 19.
192 W. Roger Louis, *43 Revue Belge de Philologie et D'Histoire* (1965) at 572.
193 Joseph Conrad, (Brighthouse, 1923). Captivated by exploratory charm and moved by Eurocentric chauvinistic writings professing philanthropy, Joseph Conrad (1857–1924), who had longed wondered about the blank white spots on the African map at the age of 31, happily took a job as a steamer captain with a Belgian trading company for a mission to the Congo River. Filled with ecstasy to appreciate for himself the much heralded contribution of Europeans to the "dark continent," Conrad soon became highly disillusioned after arrival upon witnessing

the intensity of cruelty and inhumanity orchestrated on "natives" in the name of civilisation and was immediately provoked to re-enact his bitter voyage with fictional characters in the well-received novel *The Heart of Darkness*. He sarcastically described Europeans and advocates of the civilising mission project as the "conquerors of truth" not because of their rectitude in the portrayal of the reality of life in Africa, but rather for their infringing tendency to deceive with myths and their ability to articulate a narrow way of reading unknown landscapes.

194 Cf: Keith David Watenpaugh, (University of California Press, 2015) at 58.
195 Roes, 'Towards a History of Mass Violence' at 641; T. Jack Thompson, *26 International Bulletin of Missionary Research* (2002) 146–149
196 Driver Gondola, *The History of Congo* (Greenwood Press, 2002) at 67.
197 Sylvanus John Sodienye Cookey, (Longmans, London: 1968) at 4–6.
198 Reeves, 'The Origin of the Congo Free State' at 118.
199 Roes, 'Towards a History of Mass Violence' at 641.
200 Marie-Bénédicte Dembour, *26 Canadian Journal of African Studies/Revue Canadienne des Études Africaines* (1992) 205–225.
201 Ardener, *Eye-Witnesses to the Annexation of Cameroon* at 22–23.
202 Ibid at 22–23.
203 Woodruff D. Smith, (University of North Carolina Press, 1978) at 74; Frank R. Cana, *14 Journal of the Royal African Society* (1915) 355–365 at 361; Fuabeh Paul Fonge, (Africa World Press, 1997) at 32.
204 W. A. Crabtree, *14 Journal of the Royal African Society* (1914) at 9; Susan Diduk, *36 African Studies Review* (1993) at 1; Fonge, *Modernization Without Development in Africa* at 32.
205 C. T. Hagberg Wright, *1 Journal of the Royal African Society* (1901) at 23.
206 Woodruff D. Smith, *46 The Journal of Modern History* (1974) at 641.
207 Smith, 'The Ideology of German Colonialism' at 641–646.
208 Smith, *The German Colonial Empire* at 82.
209 Simon Constantine, *1268 Reviews in History* (2012) at 3.
210 A. Werner & R. Dilthey, *4 Journal of Royal African Study* (1905) at 238.

References

Alexandrowicz, Charles H.: *The European-African Confrontation: A Study in Treaty-Making* (Sijthoff, Leiden:1973).

———: 'The Role of Treaties in the European-African Confrontation in the Nineteenth Century' in A. Kodwo Mensah-Brown (ed.), *African International Legal History* (United Nations Institute for Training and Research-UNITAR, New York: 1975) 27–68.

Ardener, Shirley G.: *Eye-Witnesses to the Annexation of Cameroon 1883–1887* (Government Press, Buea: 1968).

Bawa, Aisha Balarabe: 'From Imperialism to Diplomacy: A Historical Analysis of French and Senegal Cultural Relationship' (2013) at 1. Available online: http://www.culturaldiplomacy.org/academy/content/pdf/participant-papers/2013-08-acd/Aisha_Bawa_-_From_Imperialism_To_Diplomacy-_An_Historical_Analysis_Of_French_And_Senegal_Cultural_Relationship.pdf. Last Accessed 31 March 2019.

Beard, Jennifer: *The Political Economy of Desire: International Law, Development and the Nation State* (Routledge, New York: 2007).

Bederman, Sanford H.: 'The 1876 Brussels Geographical Conference and the Charade of European Cooperation in African Exploration' *21 The Journal of the Society for the History of Discoveries* (1989) 63–73.

Brittain, Victoria: 'Colonialism and the Predatory State in the Congo' *236 New Left Review* (1999) 133–144 at 140.
Brussels Conference Act (*Convention Relative to the Slave Trade and Importation into Africa of Firearms, Ammunition, and Spiritous Liquors*) of 2 July 1890.
Cana, Frank R.: 'German Aims in Africa' *14 Journal of the Royal African Society* (1915) 355–365.
Charter of the United Nations and Statute of the International Court of Justice (United Nations Publications, San Francisco: 1945) at 1–2.
Clement, Alain: 'L' Analyse Économique de la Question Coloniale en France (1870–1914)' *123 Revue d'Économie Politique* (2013) 51–82.
Conrad, Joseph: *Heart of Darkness* (Brighthouse, London: 1923).
Cookey, Sylvanus John Sodienye: *Britain and the Congo Question, 1885–1913* (Longmans, London: 1968).
Coquery-Vidrovitch, Catherine: *Le Congo au Temps des Grandes Compagnies Concessionnaires 1898–1930, Tome 1* (Éditions de l'École des Hautes Études en Sciences Sociales, Paris: 2013).
Crabtree, W. A.: 'German Colonies in Africa' *14 Journal of the Royal African Society* (1914) 1–14.
Craven, Matthew: 'Between Law and History: The Berlin Conference of 1884–1885 and the Logic of Free Trade' *3 London Review of International Law* (2015) 31–59.
———: 'The Invention of a Tradition: Westlake, The Berlin Conference and the Historicisation of International Law' in M. Vec & L. Nuzzo (eds.), *Constructing International Law: The Birth of a Discipline* (Klosterman, Frankfurt: 2012) 363–403.
Crowder, Michael: *Senegal: A Study in French Assimilation Policy* (Oxford University Press, London/New York/Ibadan: 1962).
———: *West Africa under Colonial Rule* (Hutchinson, London: 1968).
Crowe, Sybil Eyre: *The Berlin West African Conference 1884–5* (Longmans, London: 1942).
Culbertson, William Smith: 'The "Open Door" and Colonial Policy' *9 The American Economic Review* (1919) 325–340.
Cumming, Gordon: 'Transposing the Republican Model? A Critical Appraisal of French Historic Mission in Africa' *23 Journal of Contemporary African Studies* (2005) 233–252.
Dakas, Dakas C. J.: 'The Role of International Law in the Colonisation of Africa: A Review in Light of Recent Calls for Re-colonization' *7 African Yearbook of International Law/Annuaire Africain De Droit International* (1999) 85–118.
De Courcel, Goeffrey: 'The Berlin Act of 26 February 1885' in S. Forster, W. J. Mommsen, & R. Robinson (eds.), *Bismarck, Europe and Africa: The Berlin Africa Conference 1884–1885 and the Onset of Partition* (Oxford University Press, Oxford: 1988) 252–260.
De Leon, Daniel: 'The Conference at Berlin on the West-African Question' *1 Political Science Quarterly* (1886) 103–139.
Dembour, Marie-Bénédicte: 'La Chicotte Comme Symbole du Colonialisme Belge?' *26 Canadian Journal of African Studies/Revue Canadienne des Études Africaines* (1992) 205–225.
Diduk, Susan: 'European Alcohol, History, and the State in Cameroon' *36 African Studies Review* (1993) 1–42.

Diouf, Mamadou: 'The French Colonial Policy of Assimilation and the Civility of the Four Communes (Senegal): A Nineteenth Century Globalization Project' *29 Development and Change* (1998) 671–696.

Duignan, Peter & Gann, Lewis H.: *The United States and Africa: A History* (Cambridge University Press, Cambridge: 1984).

Dumoulin, Michel: *Léopold II: Un Roi Génocidaire?* (*Académie Royale de Belgique*, Brussels: 2005).

Dunn, Kevin C.: 'Inventing the Congo: Henry Morton Stanley, Leopold II, and the "Red Rubber" Scandal' in Kevin C. Dunn (ed.), *Imagining the Congo: The International Relations of Identity* (Palgrave Macmillan New York/London: 2003) at 21–59.

Ewans, Martin: *European Atrocity, African Catastrophe: Leopold II, the Congo Free State and its Aftermath* (Routledge Curzon, New York/London: 2002).

Exenberger, Andreas: *Extractive Institutions in the Congo: A Long History Told in Brief* (Working Paper: University of Innsbruck: Department of Economic Theory, Policy and History and Vienna, Austria, Austrian Research Foundation for International Development: 2011) at 1–29.

Fanon, Frantz: *Toward the African Revolution: Political Essays* (Grove Books, New York: 1964).

Fieldhouse, David Kenneth: 'Imperialism: A Historical Revision' *2 Economic History Review* (1961) 187–209.

Fiore, Pasquale & Henckels, Theodore: 'Some Considerations on the Past, Present and Future of International Law' *6 Proceedings of the American Society of International Law at Its Annual Meeting* (1912a) 15–36.

———: 'Some Considerations on the Past, Present and Future of International Law' *6 Proceedings of the American Society of International Law at Its Annual Meeting* (1912b) 15–36.

Fisch, Jörg: 'Africa as *Terra Nullius*: The Berlin Conference and International Law' in Stig Forster, Wolfgang Mommsen & Ronald Robinson (eds.), *Bismark, Europe and Africa: The Berlin Africa Conference 1884–1885 and the Onset of the Partition* (Oxford University Press, Oxford: 1988) at 356.

———: 'Die europäische Expansion und das Völkerrecht.: Die Auseinandersetzungen um den Status der überseeischen Gebiete vom 15. Jahrhundert bis zur Gegenwart' *26 Franz Steiner Verlag Wiesbaden GmbH* (1984).

Flint, John: 'Chartered Companies and the Scramble for Africa' in Joseph C. Anene & Godfrey N. Brown (eds.), *Africa in the Nineteenth and Twentieth Centuries: A Handbook for Teachers and Students* (Humanities Press, London: 1972) 112–114.

———: *Sir George Goldie and the Making of Nigeria* (Oxford University Press, Oxford: 1960).

Fonge, Fuabeh Paul: *Modernization Without Development in Africa: Patterns of Change and Continuity in Post-Independence Cameroonian Public Service* (Africa World Press, Asmara-Eritrea: 1997).

Forster, Stig, Mommsen, Wolfgang & Robinson, Ronald (eds.), *Bismark, Europe and Africa: The Berlin Africa Conference 1884–1885 and the Onset of the Partition* (Oxford University Press, Oxford: 1988).

Gann, Lewis H.: 'The Berlin Conference and the Humanitarian Conscience' in S. Forster, W. J. Mommsen, & R. Robinson (eds.), *Bismarck, Europe and Africa: The Berlin Africa Conference 1884–1885 and the Onset of Partition* (Oxford University Press, Oxford: 1988) at 321–331.

Gann, Lewis H. & Duignan, Peter: *The Rulers of Belgian Africa: 1814–1914* (Princeton University Press, Princeton: 1979).

Gathii, James Thuo: 'How American Support for Freedom of Commerce Legitimized King Leopold's Territorial Ambitions in the Congo' *37 Studies in Transnational Legal Policy* (2005) 97–107.

Gavin, Rosemarie Julie & Betley, J. A.: *The Scramble for Africa: Documents on the Berlin West African Conference and Related Subjects, 1884–1885* (Ibadan University Press, Ibadan: 1973).

Gertzel, Cherry: 'Relations between African and European Traders in the Niger Delta 1880–1896' *3 Journal of African History* (1962) 361–366.

Gifford, Prosser & Louis, Roger: *France and Britain in Africa: Imperial Rivalry and Colonial Rule* (Yale University Press, New Haven: 1971).

Gondola, Driver: *The History of Congo* (Greenwood Press, Westport. 2002).

Gorove, Stephen: 'Internationalization of the Danube: A Lesson in History' *8 Journal of Public Law* (1959) 125–154.

Great Britain Foreign Office: *Correspondence Relating to Negotiations between the Governments of Great Britain and Portugal for Conclusion of the Congo Treaty London: 1884* (Forgotten Books, London: 2013).

Hall, Edward: *A Treatise on International Law*, A. Pearce Higgins (ed.), 8th revised edition Oxford University Press, Oxford: 1924).

Hannikainen, Lauri: *Peremptory Norms (Jus Cogens) in International Law: Historical Development, Criteria, Present Status* (Lakimiesliiton Kustannus, Helsinki: 1988).

Hargreaves, John D.: *Prelude to the Partition of West Africa* (Macmillan, London: 1963).

———: "The Berlin Conference, West African Boundaries and the Eventual Partition of Africa" in S. Forster, W. J. Mommsen, & R. Robinson (eds.), *Bismarck, Europe and Africa: The Berlin Africa Conference 1884–1885 and the Onset of Partition* (Oxford University Press, Oxford: 1988) at 313.

———: 'The Berlin West African Conference—A Timely Centenary?' *34 History Today* (1984) 1–8.

———: 'Towards a History of the Partition of Africa' *1 Journal of African History* (1960) 97–109.

Harms, Robert: 'The End of Red Rubber: A Reassessment' *16 The Journal of African History* (1975) 73–88.

Harp, Stephen L.: *A World History of Rubber: Empire, Industry, and the Everyday* (Wiley, Blackwell, West Sussex: 2016).

Hayward, Jack Ernest Shalom: 'National Independence and International Mission' in Jack Ernest Shalom Hayward (ed.), *The One and Indivisible French Republic* (Weidenfield & Nicolson, London: 1973) 241–258.

Hertslet, Edward: *The Map of Africa by Treaty*, 3 vols., 3rd edition Harrison and Sons, London: 1909).

Hochschild, Adam: *King Leopold's Ghost* (Houghton Mifflin Co., New York: 1998).

Howse, Robert: 'Montesquieu on Commerce, Conquest, War and Peace' *31 Brooklyn Journal of International Law* (2006) 693–708.

Idowu, H. Oludare: 'Assimilation in 19th Century Senegal' *9 Cahiers d'Études Africaines* (1969) 194–218.

Jalata, Asafa: 'European Colonial Terrorism and the Incorporation of Africa into the Capitalist World System' *Conference Proceedings Paper: Athens Institute for Education and Research (ATINER)*. Athens, Greece (2011) 1–37 at 21, 29–30. Available online: http://works.bepress.com/asafa_jalata/26 Last Accessed 18 September 2020).

Keith, Arthur Berriedale: *Belgian Congo and the Berlin Act* (Clarendon Press: Oxford, 1919).

Khapoya, Vincent: *The African Experience* (Prentice Hall, New Jersey: 1998).

Koponen, Juhani: 'The Partition of Africa: A Scramble for a Mirage' *2 Nordic Journal of African Studies* (1993) 117–135.

Koskenniemi, Martti: *The Gentle Civilizer of Nations: The Rise and Fall of International Law, 1870–1960* (Cambridge University Press, Cambridge: 2001).

Labouret, Henri: 'France's Colonial Policy in Africa' *39 Journal of the Royal African Society* (1940) 22–35.

Lafont, Suzanne: 'L'Afrique dans le Voyage au Bout de la Nuit' *32 Litteratures* (1995) 105–118.

Lapidoth, Ruth: 'Freedom of Navigation-Its Legal History and its Normative Basis' *6 Journal of Maritime Law and Commerce* (1974–1975) 259–272.

Laveleye, Émile Louis Victor de: 'La Neutralite du Congo' *15 Revue de Droit International et de Legislation Comparée* (1883) 254–262.

Louis, W. Roger: 'The Stokes Affair and the Origins of the Anti-Congo Campaign, 1895–1896' *43 Revue Belge de Philologie et D'Histoire* (1965) 572–584.

Louis, William Roger & Stengers, Jean: *E. D. Morel's History of the Congo Reform Movement* (Clarendon, London: 1968).

Mémorial Diplomatique Française, 2eme serie XII (Archives Diplomatiques, Paris: 1884).

M'Bokolo, Elikia: *Afrique Noire. Histoire et Civilisations*, Tome II (XIXème–XXème siècles, Paris: 2004).

Miers, Suzanne: 'Slavery and the Slave Trade as International Issues 1890–1939' *19 Slavery and Abolition* (1998) 16–37.

Miers, Suzanne, Förster, S., Mommsen, J. Wolfgang & Robinson, Ronald: "Humanitarianism at Berlin: Myth or Reality?" in *Bismarck, Europe and Africa: The Berlin Africa Conference 1884–1885 and the Onset of Partition* (Oxford University Press, Oxford: 1988) 333–345.

Mills, G. Wallace: 'French Approaches in Colonial Policy' (2011) at 1. Available Online: http://www.saylor.org/site/wp-content/uploads/2011/12/HIST252-French-Approaches-in-Colonia Last Accessed 31 March 2021.

Mokyr, Joel: *The Oxford Encyclopaedia of Economic History, Vol. IV* (Oxford University Press, Oxford: 2003).

Mommsen, Wolfgang J.: *Bismarck, Europe and Africa: The Berlin Africa Conference 1884–1885 and the Onset of Partition*, Stig Forster, Wolfgang Mommsen & Ronald Robinson (eds.) (Oxford University Press, Oxford: 1988).

Montesquieu, Charles de Secondat Baron de: *2eme Œuvres completes de l'Esprit des Lois* (Gallimard-Pleiade, Paris: 1951).

Morel, Edmund Dene: *E. D. Morel's History of the Congo Reform Movement*, Revised edition (Clarendon Press, London/Brussels: 1968).

Moynier, Gustave: *La Question du Congo devant l'Institut de Droit International* (Imprimerie Charles Schuchardt, Paris: 1883).

Mugambwa, John: 'Treaties or Scraps of Paper? A Second Look at the Legal Character of the Nineteenth Century British/African Colonial Agreements' *20 The Comparative and International Law Journal of Southern Africa* (1987) 79–93.

Mulligan, Michael: 'Nigeria, the British Presence in West Africa and International Law in the 19th Century' *11 Journal of the History of International Law* (2009) 273–301.

Newbury, Colin W. & Kanya-Forstner, Alexander Sydney: 'French Policy and the Origins of the Scramble for West Africa' *10 The Journal of African History* (1969) 253–276.

Nuzzo, Luigi: 'Colonial Law' in *European History Online (EGO), published by the Leibniz Institute of European History (IEG)* (2012) 1–17 at 8. Available online: http://ieg-ego.eu/en/threads/europe-and-the-world/european-overseas-rule/luigi-nuzzo-colonial-law Last accessed 28 January 2019.

Nwabughuogu, I. Anthony: 'The Role of Propaganda in the Development of Indirect Rule in Nigeria, 1890–1929' *14 The International Journal of African Historical Studies* (1981) 65–92.

Nzemeke, D. Alexander: 'Free Trade and Territorial Partition in the Nineteenth Century West Africa: Course and Outcome' in Stig Forster, Wolfgang Mommsen & Ronald Robinson (eds.), *Bismarck, Europe and Africa: The Berlin Africa Conference 1884–1885 and the Onset of Partition* (Oxford University Press, Oxford: 1988) 59–68.

Orakhelashvili, Alexander: 'The Idea of European International Law' *17 European Journal of International Law* (2006) 315–347.

Parry, T. John: 'What Is the Grotian Tradition in International Law?' *35 University of Pennsylvania Journal of International Law* (2013) 299–487.

Perham, F. Margery: *Native Administration in Nigeria* (Oxford University Press, London: 1937).

Radovanovitch, M. Voyslav: [Book Review] 'Le Danube et l'Application du Principe de la Liberte de la Navigation Fluviale' *21 The American Journal of International Law* (1927) 399–401.

Reppy, Alison: 'The Grotian Doctrine of the Freedom of the Seas Reappraised' *19 Fordham Law Review* (1950) 243–285.

Roberts, John Morris: 'Liberté, Egalité, Fraternité: sources and development of a slogan' *4 Tijdschrift voor de Studie van de Verlichting* (1976) 329–369.

Robinson, Ronald: 'The Conference in Berlin and the Future in Africa, 1884–1885' in Stig Forster, Wolfgang Mommsen & Ronald Robinson (eds.), *Bismarck, Europe and Africa: The Berlin Africa Conference 1884–1885 and the Onset of Partition* (Oxford University Press, Oxford: 1988) 1–32.

Roes, Aldwin: 'Towards a History of Mass Violence in the Etat Indépendant du Congo, 1885–1908' *62 South African Historical Journal* (2010) 634–670.

Rolin-Jacquemyns, Gustav: 'L'Année 1888 au Point de Vue de la Paix et du Droit International' *21 Revue de Droit Internationale et de Législation Comparée* (1889).

Rosow, Stephen J.: 'Commerce, Power and Justice: Montesquieu on International Politics' *46 The Review of Politics* (1984) 346–366.

Samarin, William J.: *The Black Man's Burden: African Colonial Labor on the Congo and Ubangi Rivers, 1880–1900* (Westview Press, Boulder: 1989).

Sarraut, Albert: *Grandeur et servitude coloniales* (Editions L'Harmattan, Paris: 2012).

———: *La Mise en Valeur des Colonies Françaises* (Payot, Paris: 1923).

Schuyler, Philippa: *Jungle Saints: Africa's Heroic Catholic Missionaries* (Herder: 1963).

Sesay, Amadu: *Africa and Europe: From Partition to Interdependence or Dependence?* (Croom Helm Ltd, London/Sydney/Dover/ New Hampshire: 1986).

Shaw, Flora: 'Nigeria' *The Times* (1897) of 8 January 1897; See also: "Flora Shaw Gives the Name Nigeria." Available online: www.nabss.org.uk/download/i/mark.../History%20of%20Nigeria.pdf Last Accessed 2 April 2019.
Smith, Woodruff D.: *The German Colonial Empire* (University of North Carolina Press, Chapel Hill: 1978).
———: 'The Ideology of German Colonialism, 1840–1906' *46 The Journal of Modern History* (1974) 641–662.
Tarling, Nicholas: *Imperialism in Southeast Asia: A Fleeting Passing Phase* (Routledge: New York: 2001).
Taylor, Hannis: 'Spheres of Influence and Protectorates' *41 American Law Review* (1907) 92–101.
The Berlin Act of 26 February 1885.
Thiam, Doudou: *La Portée de la Citoyenneté Française dans les Territoires d'Outre-Mer* (Éditions Africaines, Paris: 1951).
Thompson, T. Jack: 'Light on the Dark Continent: The Photographs of Alice Seely Harris and the Congo Atrocities of the Early Twentieth Century' *26 International Bulletin of Missionary Research* (2002) 146–149.
Twiss, Travers: *The Law of Nations Considered as Independent Political Communities: On the Rights and Duties of Nations in Times of Peace* (Clarendon Press, Oxford: 1884).
Watenpaugh, Keith David: *Bread from Stones: The Middle East and the Making of Modern Humanitarianism* (University of California Press, Oakland: 2015).
Watson, Adam: *The Evolution of International Society* (Routledge, London: 1992).
Watson, Thomas J.: *Colonialism in the Congo: Conquest, Conflict, and Commerce* (Watson Institute for International Studies, Providence: 2007).
Wauters, Alphonse Jules: 'Belgian Policy in the Congo' *9 Journal of the Royal Institute of International Affairs* (1930) 51–62.
Werner, A. & Dilthey, R.: 'German and British Colonisation in Africa' *4 Journal of Royal African Study* (1905) 238–241.
Wertham, Frederic: *A Sign for Cain: An Exploration of Human Violence* (Macmillan, New York: 1966).
Westlake, John: *Chapters in the Principles of International Law* (University of Michigan Press: Michigan, 1894).
———: *The Collected Papers on Public International Law*, Lassa Oppenheim (ed.) (Cambridge University Press, Cambridge: 1914).
Wright, C. T. Hagberg: 'German Methods of Development in Africa' *1 Journal of the Royal African Society* (1901) 23–38.
Yusuf, Abdulqawi: *Pan-Africanism and International Law* (Hague Academy of International Law, The Hague: 2014).

7 General Concluding Remarks

By and large, this study is a contribution to the nascent but growing critical accounts of international law historiography from non-western perspectives. The overriding focus of the examination is on Africa's historical encounters with the external since the 16th century, and the various set of resources from the continent that enabled the development and evolution of international law. Although the history of international law has traditionally been the least explored area of the discipline, there has nevertheless been an unprecedented upsurge during the past decade in scholarships dedicated to the study of the discipline's past. In spite of this groundbreaking drive, accounts about Africa have remained marginal at best and immensely unexplored at the very worst. As a remedy to this loophole, this study's starting point is rooted on the historical examination and explanation of the causes and structure of development and underdevelopment in the globe as founded, grounded, and legitimated on the same modes of production processes, and sub-Saharan Africa's role in the processes. It is observed that sub-Saharan Africa's immense contribution enabled European powers to realise primitive accumulation on a global scale and capitalism's maturity, thereby culminating to the world order as we know it today.

Emphasis is placed on various techniques through which European individuals, entities, and corporations habitually tied their endless quests for profit margins to the economic interests of their motherlands between the 16th and 19th centuries. The study finds that the actions and justifications of Europeans in non-European territories, including sub-Saharan Africa, became the main stimulant for the intellectual origins of political economy and international law. The said actions and justifications moreover legitimated the privatisation and commodification of capitalist accumulation schemes, by offering "authoritative vocabularies of private economic rights—namely private property rights, the right to trade, and the right to occupy," supposedly applicable to all nations.[1] Firmly bent on protecting and promoting acquired assets and the interests of their various nationals and corporations in distant lands, European powers simultaneously formulated new doctrines that justified the right to occupy and appropriate non-European lands, as well as project their professed

DOI: 10.4324/9781003265740-7

principles as universal norms. The doctrine of discovery that was front and centre of international legal discourse in the 16th century, and the doctrine of effective occupation (of Africa) that preoccupied 19th-century jurists and European powers' discourse, are just two such examples of recurrent hegemonic practices that stemmed from European projection of their particular visions as universal. The imbalance in power relations between Europeans and non-Europeans notwithstanding, these encounters and emanating legal regimes nevertheless continually led to the evolution of international law.

One key commonality amongst publicists of different epochs rests in their poised assumption of international law as the global natural regulatory regime in the face of international encounters or relations. The presumption is based on the rationale that international law is in place to solve world problems as well as address uncertainties including interstate crises and relations with non-state actors, thereby guaranteeing law and order in the global space.

Given that the set of resources from Africa emanating from the three epic defining capitalist schemes between the 16th and 19th centuries (plantation capitalism, industrial capitalism, and development capitalism, the third of which is mentioned but falls outside the scope of this study), weren't borne out of ordinary conditions, they could not also be addressed according to ordinary legal standards. During each of these critical epochs, international lawyers recurrently responded to emanating challenges by closely affiliating with specific Eurocentric normative orthodoxies, wherefrom they produced the badly needed answers by instituting dual legal systems in the international space. That is, in each of the encounters between Europeans and non-Europeans, Europeans habitually arrogated a privileged legal regime for themselves and their international relations (by virtue of being advanced or civilised nations), and quite another to deal with all the supposedly backward or non-civilised peoples of this world. Both legal streams at each instance were to rely on a cultural standard ascertained by the advanced/civilised. The standard—cemented on the idea of progress—morphed from evangelising mission as of the 16th century, to civilising mission at the dawn of the 19th century, and to development mission at the clock of the 20th century.

By and large, the set of resources from Africa throughout the three defining capitalist schemes respectively included slaves and slave labour during the first scheme (16th–18th centuries), and natural resources, industrial raw materials, cash crops, and human labour during the second scheme (19th century). The third scheme (20th century and beyond) was marred by the prolongation of the resources from the second scheme era together with poorly remunerated labour (especially by extraction industries/sectors and Foreign Direct Investors). To put it differently, Africa's attachment to the global order has historically been grounded on three benchmarks: the slave labour imperative, the territorial/natural resource imperative, and the current investment/underpriced labour imperative. In retrospect, these have all been very pertinent for the steady evolution of both political economy and international law making.

Concomitant with the overwhelming conception of international law by publicists as a function of power—that is, victors' justice—Hans Morgenthau, in *Politics Amongst Nations* (1948),[2] famously advanced a realist postulation to the effect that nation states habitually lock themselves within the international society, in a perpetual struggle to accumulate power. He further asserted that states typically entertain international relations firmly based around what he referred to as *relative power*. Reading Morgenthau's postulation in relation to the manifestation of the three defining epic schemes that have governed relations between Africa and the external since the 16th century, it seems to me that even more than political power, states tend to see their main duty within the international society as one of exploiting and accumulating wealth. This is notwithstanding the fact that states typically project their actions by variously invoking the paradigms universality and humanitarianism.

Demonstratively, legal ideas normally rely on human will for their realisation despite the fact that they typically express human aims.[3] Despite unanimity amongst publicists even today that humanity possesses a sacrosanct value, it is still imperative to dig into the structure and substance of what humanitarianism and universality entail when invoked, especially within the contexts that it was contextualised by academics and politicians between the 16th and 19th centuries. As the Austrian philosopher Ludwig Wittgenstein (1889–1951) pointed out in *Philosophical Investigations*, the only way to understand the meaning of words and concepts is to look at what the speaker or the one invoking the word does with it, and the context within which it is used.[4]

As this study has uncovered, the promise to emancipate and uplift Africa from backwardness towards progress was front and centre of all three historical defining capitalist schemes, frequently backed by international law. While the idea of humanity and claims of universality certainly provides the history of international law with a direction and purpose, they could just as well be a smokescreen to shield readers and observers from some untold stories. The French socialist Pierre-Joseph Proudhon reportedly famously remarked that "whoever says humanity [universality] wants to cheat."[5] While this assertion was certainly not a blanket indictment of every humanitarian missions, it certainly sought to caution readers to always interrogate and beware of the purposes and objectives of every purported universal undertaking. For instance, in the purported pursuit of political economy and international law's objectives, even the worst of European atrocities on "the other" during each of the defining global capitalist schemes were habitually vindicated as leading to a better future. Despite some genuine humanitarian concerns, international lawyers still articulated their discourse in terms of the logic of inclusion/exclusion.[6] This binary characterisation reveals the imperativeness to pay closer attention to the dichotomy between false and genuine universalism. Cosmopolitanism has often been cloaked with imperialist agendas. In the words of a reputed commentator, "love is often difficult to distinguish from a desire to dominate."[7] Evidently, during its early gestation, the emphasis of both political economy and *ius gentium* was geared at subordinating the universe to a particular world order rather than focusing on a just, equitable, and fair standard for all humankind.

Throughout the three defining capitalist schemes that form the basis of examination in this study, international lawyers habitually perceived the role of Europeans as one of civilising the behaviours of nations, especially in the colonies. Quoting the Belgian jurist Ernest Nys (1851–1920), one scholar has illustrated how three ideas dominated world history, to wit: progress, freedom, and the idea of humanity—each centred around a generous European contribution to humankind.[8] The premise of European relations with the "others" in fact evidences unequal encounters—a kind of paternalistic/child relationship that always ended up advancing the hegemonic interests of European powers to the detriment of the "others." The three defining capitalist schemes without doubt exemplified the apex of unequal encounters, especially outright disparity between sub-Saharan Africa and the external both during its initial incorporation and during the colonial era. All these relations were each predominantly triggered by a set of resources from Africa seen by outsiders as inevitable for progress in the international society.

The key commonality amongst the three big schemes underscored in this study certainly rests on the unfair techniques of exploitation of resources in the third world in general and sub-Saharan Africa in particular. Whenever we ponder of resources, it is typical to think of the most obvious categories such as the flora and the fauna, oil, mines, gas, diamonds, gold, and all related components under the soil. This study goes beyond this conventional categorisation, stipulating that at genesis, the disciplines of political economy and law of nations conceptualise human beings (and trade in humans) as morally and legally acceptable. Subjugated human beings were accordingly conceived to be legitimate private property—in other words, as acceptable factors of production.[9] The original human capital of the world system (as we know it today) were sub-Saharan Africans who were traded as slaves, legitimated and regulated by the Law of Nations by relying on edicts of natural law, to build the Americas for European settlers. Although the emphasis for Europeans during this era was on their own development in the so-called New World, I submit that African economy was proportionately affected by the same degree of the disruption, thereby laying down an enormous trajectory for underdevelopment.[10]

Despite the historical framing of the capitalist accumulation schemes around the idea of progress, the schemes in a practical sense archetypally had a stifling impact rather than liberating bearing on the economic, political, legal, and social well-being of colonised subjects in general and sub-Saharan Africa in particular. The usefulness of the three capitalist accumulation schemes certainly rests in their ability to succinctly elucidate the different techniques according to which different capitalist reproductions historically guided the nature of power, agency, and global order in general within the international society. The more sub-Saharan Africa complied and adapted to the politics of capitalism during each of the historical grand schemes, the more it was exploited by external forces and relegated to the periphery of world order, leading to its uneven development trajectory vis-à-vis Europe.

Notes

1 Fonseca, *Civilizing Nature* at 4–5.
2 Hans Morgenthau, (Knopf, 1985).
3 J. B. Bury, (Macmillan, 1932) at 1.
4 Ludwig Wittgenstein, (Wiley-Blackwell, 2010) at 163–167.
5 See Carl Schmitt, 'Völkerrechtliche Formen des modernen Imperialismus' at 162–180. Cf: Martti Koskenniemi, *16 European Journal of International Law* (2005) at 116. [*Emphasis mildly added*].
6 Martti Koskenniemi, (Cambridge University Press. Cambridge, 2001) at 128–130.
7 Martti Koskenniemi, 61 *University of Toronto Law Journal* (2011) at 11.
8 Martti Koskenniemi, (Oxford University Press, 2012) at 943–946. See generally, George Forji Amin, *16 Journal of the History of International Law* (2014) at 91.
9 Economists contend that there are four factors of production, namely: land, labour, capital, and entrepreneur. A state's development or underdevelopment is determinant on how it operates these factors of production. As the saying goes, countries eventually get what they deserved.
10 Walter Rodney, (Pambazuka Press, 2012); J. F. Ade Ajayi, 'The Continuity of African Institutions Under Colonialism'; James Thuo Gathii, *21 Leiden Journal of International Law* (2008) 317–349.

References

Ajayi, J. & Ade, F.: 'The Continuity of African Institutions under Colonialism' in T. O. Ranger & Chuo Kikuucha (eds.), *Emerging Themes of African History: Proceedings of the International Congress of African Historians held at Dar es Salaam* (East African Pub. House, Nairobi: 1965).

Bury, J. B.: *The Idea of Progress: An Inquiry into Its Growth and Origin* (Macmillan, London/New York: 1932).

Fonseca, Manuel Jiménez: *Civilizing Nature: Revisiting the Imperialist History of International Law (1511–1972)* (PhD Dissertation: Unigrafia, Helsinki: 2017).

Forji, Amin George: 'Book Review: The Oxford Handbook of the History of International Law, Bardo Fassbender, Anne Peters, Simone Peter & Daniel Högger (Editors)' *16 Journal of the History of International Law* (2014) 90–95.

Gathii, James Thuo: 'A Critical Appraisal of the International Legal Tradition of Taslim Olawale Elias' *21 Leiden Journal of International Law* (2008) 317–349.

Koskenniemi, Martti: *The Gentle Civilizer of Nations: The Rise and Fall of International Law, 1870–1960* (Cambridge University Press, Cambridge: 2001).

———: 'International Law in Europe: Between Tradition and Renewal' *16 European Journal of International Law* (2005) 113–124.

———: 'A History of International Law Histories' in Bardo Fassbender, Anne Peters & Daniel Högger (eds.), *The Oxford Handbook of The History of International Law* (Oxford University Press, Oxford: 2012) at 943–946.

Morgenthau, Hans: *Politics amongst Nations: The Struggle for Power and Peace*, 6th edition (Knopf, New York: 1985).

Rodney, Walter: *How Europe Underveloped Africa*, Revised edition (Pambazuka Press, Cape Town/Dakar/Nairobi/Oxford: 2012).

Schmitt, Carl: 'Völkerrechtliche Formen des modernen Imperialismus' in *Positionen und Begriffe im Kampf gegen Weimar-Genf-Versailles 1923–1939* (1988).

Wittgenstein, Ludwig: *Philosophical Investigations*, G. E. M. Anscombe, P. M. S. Hacker & Joachim Schulte (transl.), 4th edition (Wiley-Blackwell, New Jersey: 2010).

Index

Kolibri 360 GmbH
Ferdinand-Jühlke-Straße 7
99095 Erfurt, Deutschland
produktsicherheit@kolibri360.de